MERIT AND
RESPONSIBILITY

MERIT AND RESPONSIBILITY

A Study in Greek Values

BY

ARTHUR W. H. ADKINS

LECTURER IN GREEK
BEDFORD COLLEGE, LONDON

OXFORD
AT THE CLARENDON PRESS
1960

Oxford University Press, Amen House, London E.C.4

GLASGOW NEW YORK TORONTO MELBOURNE WELLINGTON
BOMBAY CALCUTTA MADRAS KARACHI KUALA LUMPUR
CAPE TOWN IBADAN NAIROBI ACCRA

PRINTED IN GREAT BRITAIN
AT THE UNIVERSITY PRESS, OXFORD
BY VIVIAN RIDLER
PRINTER TO THE UNIVERSITY

PREFACE

THE material here presented in book form was submitted as a doctoral thesis in the spring of 1957. It then bore the title 'The Development of the Concept of Moral Responsibility from Homer to Aristotle'. The argument and conclusions remain substantially those of the thesis; the intervening period, in which it has been prepared for publication, has been largely devoted to presenting the material in a form in which it may be available to readers with no knowledge of Greek. The subject is suited to such treatment, for it consists essentially of a discussion of a very limited range of Greek words. All these words have been transliterated, and all quotations translated. No Greek type now remains in the text; and I have retained the original Greek only in such footnotes as can be of no interest except to those readers with some knowledge of Greek. The other customary impediment to communication, the unnecessary technicalities and jargon with which the D.Phil. student is wont to cover his nakedness, I have attempted to eliminate by submitting the work to the judgement of non-specialists, and removing or explaining anything which was held to be needlessly obscure. Doubtless obscurities remain; but the Greekless reader is asked to believe that without the assistance I have received his plight would have been much worse.

The work, in its present form, is intended for three kinds of reader: for the professional Greek scholar; for the large and ever-increasing number of students of Greek philosophy and civilization who possess no Greek; and for any students of morals and society in general who may find this study of Greek values in relation to Greek society interesting. In an effort to be comprehensible to all three groups, I have attempted to keep the line of the argument as clear as the subject permits by excluding from the text what is not immediately relevant. Accordingly, I have relegated to the notes at the end of the chapters much collateral material, argument which, while necessary to a scholarly proof, is not essential to the main argument of the text, and some brief explanations of practices with which the non-specialist may be unfamiliar. I hope that many of the more detailed notes will, in fact, be of interest to others beside professional scholars; but, at least in intention, the argument is complete without them. The method adopted may occasionally give the impression that certain inconvenient questions are being quietly throttled in dark corners; but a trial of alternatives has convinced me that it is the best available in the circumstances.

Since Greek ethics and Greek values have been so frequently discussed by previous scholars, any novelty which this book may possess necessarily derives from the manner of treatment adopted; and it follows that reference to similar discussions of the same material could be almost continuous. As, however, the only fruitful method of examining such a topic as this is to set one complete discussion beside another, I have rarely given references to individual points treated in the works of other scholars, but have appended in the bibliography a list of similar studies which have influenced this one. It will be evident, however, that the manner of treatment owes much to Professor Snell's *Die Entdeckung des Geistes*, which has greatly affected my thought on the subject of *aretē*.

It gives me great pleasure to be able to thank here those who have helped in the production of either thesis or book. First, Professor E. R. Dodds, who has supervised and encouraged this work throughout its long period of incubation. To his views, both published and unpublished, and to his broad and humane scholarship in general, this book and I owe many debts, some immediately obvious, others of a kind which only the author himself can appreciate. Secondly, the Warden and Fellows of Merton College, Oxford, who, by electing me to a Harmsworth Senior Scholarship, enabled me to spend two post-graduate years in the uninterrupted pursuit of an idea which, at least in its early stages, was cloudy and vague in the extreme. I should like to express my thanks also to my examiners, Professor G. B. Kerferd and Mr. D. A. Russell, and to Mr. J. L. Ackrill and Professor P. T. Stevens, all of whom have read the whole or part of the typescript of either thesis or book, and have made suggestions which I have incorporated in the text.

My thanks are due also to my colleague Mr. P. T. Eden and to Mr. J. E. Garrod of the British Council, who have given me much assistance in reading the proofs, and to all at the Clarendon

Press who have borne with the vagaries of an author completely unused to the mechanics of book production; while both my Greekless readers and I have great reason to be grateful to my friend Dr. Ruth Roberts, who has read the whole typescript in their interest and pointed out numerous obscurities, some of which I have been able to remove.

A. W. H. A.

Bedford College, London
June 1959

NOTE ON
TRANSLATION AND TRANSLITERATION

A FEW words are needed to explain my transliterations. These are direct: each Greek letter is represented by its equivalent in the Roman alphabet, whether or no the English pronunciation of that letter coincides with that of the Greek. This has resulted in a few apparent anomalies: for example, the word normally spelt 'psyche' in English appears as *psūchē*, but as the Greek word has implications quite different from those of 'psyche', the distinction in spelling seems to me to be an advantage. The iota subscript forms ᾳ, ῃ, ῳ appear with the 'i' adscript, and the long vowel marked: *āi*, *ēi*, *ōi*. In general, I have marked long vowels on the first occasion of a word's appearance where the word occurs frequently; otherwise, on each occasion. Where the spelling of adjective and adverb differs only in the quantity of the final 'o'—e.g. *adikos* and *adikōs*—I have always marked the long 'o' of the adverb. For greater simplicity, nouns and adjectives are quoted in the nominative, singular or plural, verbs in the infinitive.

Pronunciation need present few difficulties, provided that it is remembered that there are no unpronounced vowels in Greek, i.e. that a word such as *dikē* is disyllabic. Apart from this, there is no agreed pronunciation of Greek among scholars in Britain; for example, different scholars pronounce 'ē' as in 'three', as in 'whey', or (roughly) as in 'bear'. (The 'i' of the iota subscript forms is not usually pronounced at all.) I have marked no accents—except on p. 310, to distinguish *káke*, 'badness', from *kaké*, 'bad'; the Greekless reader will be well advised to adopt a stress accent, and to place it on whatever syllable his knowledge of Latin or Italian leads him to believe plausible. This accent will be wrong, frequently in position, always in kind, for the Greeks of the classical period employed a pitch accent; but as the resulting pronunciation will bear a close resemblance to that of the majority of classical scholars educated in these islands, including the present writer, the non-professional may presumably be forgiven for using it.

CONTENTS

I say that a man's first duty is to learn to fight. If he can't do that, he can't set an example; he can't stand up for his own rights or his neighbours'; he can't keep himself in bodily health; and if he sees the weak ill-used by the strong, the most he can do is to sneak away and tell the nearest policeman, who most likely won't turn up until the worst of the mischief is done.

SHAW

—Τὸ δὲ μάθημά ἐστιν εὐβουλία περὶ τῶν οἰκείων, ὅπως ἂν ἄριστα τὴν αὐτοῦ οἰκίαν διοικοῖ, καὶ περὶ τῶν τῆς πόλεως, ὅπως τὰ τῆς πόλεως δυνατώτατος ἂν εἴη καὶ πράττειν καὶ λέγειν.
—Ἄρα, ἔφην ἐγώ, ἕπομαί σου τῷ λόγῳ; δοκεῖς γάρ μοι λέγειν τὴν πολιτικὴν τέχνην καὶ ὑπισχνεῖσθαι ποιεῖν ἄνδρας ἀγαθοὺς πολίτας.

PLATO

Chercher la science et la justice, disons d'un seul mouvement la Science de la Justice, cette alchimie sociale qui produira dans la Cité l'or d'une humanité heureuse.

HALÉVY

I

MORAL RESPONSIBILITY AND GREEK MORAL THOUGHT

A. INTRODUCTORY

THE research from which this book has developed was originally undertaken in the hope that it might make clear to me why I could not understand the moral philosophy of Plato and Aristotle; not, that is to say, the answers to individual questions, which frequently seemed clear enough; but the reason why Plato and Aristotle should have elected to answer these questions rather than others which seemed to me more interesting and more relevant. So far as I am concerned, it has fulfilled its purpose; and I hope it may perform a similar service for anyone else who, in beginning to study Greek ethics, finds himself equally puzzled. The result, however, is a book whose scope, content, and method all require explanation, and possibly some defence: for all three may apparently be charged with some degree of irrelevance or unimportance. The connecting thread of the discussion is the development of the concept of moral responsibility in Greek; a concept which, in the moral thought of the period discussed, undeniably held a minor position. The reader may well feel that it is merely perverse to endow it with an importance which the Greeks themselves would not have recognized. Secondly, though the discussion does return at intervals to the pleas accepted or rejected by the Greeks at different periods, even a casual reading will reveal that much of it is not a direct discussion of moral responsibility at all, but a more general survey of Greek terms of value, religious ideas, and social organization. Thirdly, though the moral philosophy of Plato and Aristotle provoked this research, the discussion ranges from Homer through the literary predecessors of these philosophers, who themselves receive a comparatively small share of the whole. Yet Plato and Aristotle undoubtedly had available to them all the material surveyed here, and much more besides; and they might well be held to have analysed, summed up, and improved upon their predecessors. Would it not be sufficient to consider the problem of moral responsibility as they found it, and the solutions which they offered? After all, this is by general consent a philosopher's topic; and the surviving predecessors of Plato and Aristotle are, on the whole, laymen. In answering these charges I shall endeavour to make clearer the purpose of this book.

B. THE FUNCTION OF THE PRESENT DISCUSSION

The first charge is readily answered. The importance of building this discussion round the Greek concept of moral responsibility lies precisely in the relative unimportance of that concept, as compared with the status which we should allot to it, for this radical difference of emphasis is a significant symptom of those basic differences in outlook which sometimes make Greek ethics so baffling to the modern reader; while to conduct the discussion in reference to a concept which he himself values so differently most readily enables the modern reader to see the extent of the divergences between the two moral systems. For any man brought up in a western democratic society the related concepts of duty and responsibility are the central concepts of ethics; and we are inclined to take it as an unquestionable truth, though there is abundant evidence to the contrary, that the same must be true of all societies. In this respect, at least, we are all Kantians now. Surely, we assume, in any society 'What is my duty in these circumstances?' is the basic question which the agent must ask himself in any matter which requires a moral decision; and since, as we all know, 'ought' implies 'can', anyone who has to pass judgement on any action must first inquire, in considering whether the agent did or did not do his duty, whether he could or could not have acted otherwise, and hence whether he may be held responsible for his actions or no. That there should exist a society so different from our own as to render it impossible to translate 'duty' in the Kantian sense into its ethical terminology at all—impossible, that is to say, to translate 'duty' by a word not only of equivalent connotation but also of equivalent status and emotive power—is, despite the evidence, a very difficult idea to accept. Even if we do accept it, we are only too inclined to interpret it merely as an indication of the moral deficiency of those who are so unfortunate as not to be Kantians; and we are most unlikely to see the full implications of the system of which this 'deficiency' is a symptom. That this symptom is present in Greek has long been recognized by classical scholars, but the full implications of this have, so far as I am aware, never been drawn out; nor, it seems to me, can they be brought out, and the true nature of the Greek moral scene thereby made clear to those with such different presuppositions as ourselves, except by some such discussion as the present one, which approaches the subject from what, from the Greek point of view, is the wrong angle altogether. If we can discover why the concept of moral responsibility is so unimportant to the Greek, we shall go far towards understanding the difference between our moral systems, and discovering the nature of each.

C. THE OBLIQUE APPROACH

Since the concept of moral responsibility is the connecting thread rather than the justification of the present discussion, the second charge falls to the ground at once. The general survey of Greek values has interest in its own right. But even were my purpose only to discuss this concept, a similar approach would still be necessary. This point illustrates even more clearly the manner in which the discussion of the concept of moral responsibility will be useful, and further, explains the method of approach I have adopted in subsequent chapters. It would indeed be possible to assemble all the instances in extant Greek literature of a man's being explicitly held responsible or not responsible for his actions; and an analysis of these would doubtless reveal the extent to which the Greek concept of moral responsibility resembles or differs from our own. But this would be a singularly barren exercise, for it could never supply any reasons for the differences which would immediately become apparent. Furthermore, it would be illogical, for the nature of the subject-matter demands an oblique approach. It is possible to elevate 'duty' to the most important position in a moral system; it is possible to ensure that 'Was the agent responsible for his actions or not?'

is the most important question which can be asked of any action to which reward and punishment may be relevant; but it is not possible to make this question logically primary, for it necessarily depends on the answers, implicit or explicit, given to a large number of others. Accordingly, the concept of moral responsibility cannot take logical priority in any moral system. That is to say, it cannot assume some form to which all other concepts must adapt themselves. Quite the contrary: it is in virtue of other beliefs, whether moral, of value in general, or (apparently) factual, that the concept of moral responsibility takes the form which, in any society, it does take. No one making a moral judgement on an action can decide from what he sees with his eyes alone whether the agent should be held responsible for that action or not. It is on his beliefs about that action, about action in general, about society in general, about the universe and its gods, or lack of them, that his judgement will depend, more or less logically according to the degree of logicality of the individual or his society. It is only in the light of these beliefs that the action takes the shape it does take, or indeed any shape at all; for it is only in the light of these beliefs that the person judging is able to abstract from the circumstances surrounding an action, otherwise only a collection of physical events among other physical events, those circumstances which are held by him, or by his society, to be relevant. The question of responsibility may still be the most important question which can be raised, but only if the answers given implicitly or explicitly to these other questions allow this.

It follows from this that no simple catalogue of examples illustrating this concept will throw light on anything. Any change in a society's view of this concept, any change, that is, in the group of actions or types of action held by that society to be responsible actions, will result from a change in other beliefs, from an increase in knowledge, or from an improvement— or change—in the circumstances or organization of that society. The change in the ascription of responsibility may not follow immediately; beliefs which involve reward and punishment are necessarily very difficult to adapt, for powerful emotions are involved; but this is the sequence in which the change must take place, and hence an oblique method of approach alone has any chance of success. Otherwise, one can only be irritated by what seem to be the absurdities of those whose beliefs differ from one's own; whereas, properly considered, such differences may well be readily explicable, together with any developments or changes which take place.

Evidently, then, cosmological, theological, and psychological beliefs (to go no further) must be discussed in any adequate treatment of moral responsibility. These will be found most helpful in considering the pleas of *force majeure*, or of inevitability, psychologically, mechanistically, or theistically determined, accepted by any society. Pleas of mistake or accident, however, even more evidently demand an oblique approach, particularly in a society far distant in space or time. It is the function of the category of mistake to distinguish from moral error those actions or types of action which fall under it. The manner in which it performs this function depends on the manner in which moral error and mistake are viewed by any given society; and this must be discovered not only by a general consideration of both types of action in the society, but also by an examination of the use in these and similar situations of the key terms of value, together with their implications. To make this point clearer, something must be said of the use of such terms in all languages.

In the first place, any word of general commendation will, in any society, be applied not at random but to persons or events possessing certain characteristics. Accordingly, any statement of the form 'X is (some general adjective of commendation)' may be glossed with a series of statements 'X possesses the characteristics a, b, c, &c.'; and, at all events when values are stable, any such commendation of X, or any other member of the class to which X belongs, will be employed in virtue of its possession of the characteristics a, b, c, &c. The word of general commendation cannot be translated into these other statements, for it possesses another element—whose nature it is unnecessary to discuss here—which is peculiar to itself; but the fact that the applicability of these other statements is a necessary condition of applying the word of more general commendation provides a means of estimating the peculiar flavour of that word and, in the present inquiry, of establishing how this affects ascriptions of moral responsibility. A word may remain the highest word of commendation while the circumstances to which it is applied change radically; and it is this type of change in Greek which provides the clue to this aspect of the investigation in hand. For it is inevitable that a word of general commendation which is applied to a number of different types of situation should be so applied as the result of a general world-view, whether consciously or unconsciously formulated. Accordingly, the range of application of such a term must be discovered, since it is on the general world-view, as has been said, that depends the form which the concept of moral responsibility takes.

Secondly, it is reasonable to inquire whether, in any given language, one particular term or complex of terms possesses a higher value than any other; that is to say, whether there exists some word or words which, if produced in ethical argument to characterize any person or action, ends the argument, if it is agreed by both parties that the characterization is correct, simply because there is no word of greater value in the language which might be brought against this one. If, for example, we value justice in our fellow men more highly than their success, it is pointless, if a man is unjust, to mention his success or any other attribute he possesses in an attempt to make his injustice seem unimportant; for though other qualities or services might be mentioned as mitigating circumstances, they cannot, if justice is most highly valued, override its claims altogether. In such an inquiry as this, it is essential to discover which is the most important term of value or complex of such terms, together with its implications; for terms of value have widely differing criteria of application, and the criteria of application of the most important term clearly both reflect and mould a society's view of life as a whole, and hence its ascriptions of moral responsibility.

Thirdly, it is necessary for the present purpose to distinguish two groups of values. In any society there are activities in which success is of paramount importance; in these, commendation or the reverse is reserved for those who *in fact* succeed or fail. In such activities, what a man intended to do is of little account in estimating his performance. On the other hand, in any society there are also those activities, such as contracts or partnerships, in which men co-operate with one another for a common end. Since the only basis for co-operation is fairness, however interpreted, it is in terms of fairness, or some similar word, that the relations of men who co-operate will be estimated. Fairness raises questions quite different from those of success or failure. It is perfectly reasonable to inquire whether any encroachment was deliberate or not, and to expect that different treatment will be given to the encroacher according to the answer; and further that this will be the most important question which can be asked about the encroachment.

Terms of value must of necessity be frequently applied to both groups of activities. Since the activities are so different in kind, it may well be found that they are commended by different terms, with the result that there may well exist two (or more) complexes of terms of value. Both complexes evaluate action, both are relevant to this work, and both have some claim to be termed 'moral', since competition requires such virtues as courage and endurance. To avoid confusion, the two will be distinguished hereafter as 'competitive' values or excellences and 'co-operative' or 'quiet' values or excellences.

The distinction between the two complexes of values is very much simplified here; but, taken with the second point above, it suffices to show the importance to a discussion of moral responsibility of the consideration of key terms of value. The very different attitude to intentions necessarily found in each of these groups makes it imperative to discover which is the more powerful; for this is bound to be the most important clue to the outlook on life as a whole of the men who use them, simply because the more powerful words *do* override the less powerful in any situation where both are relevant.

The discussion of the concept of moral responsibility, then, is of value in introducing Greek ethics to the modern reader not only because it supplies him with an approach to the subject from a direction with which he is familiar, but also because the discussion necessarily entails a survey of the whole Greek moral scene from this direction.

D. THE RELEVANCE OF WRITERS BEFORE PLATO

The third charge, however, seems more serious. There is an abundance of moral philosophy in the writings of Plato and Aristotle, and it might well appear that if it is necessary to survey Greek terms of value there is an abundance of them to

be found there, without going any further. Before answering
this charge, we may readily aggravate it. Not only are the
ethical works of Plato and Aristotle abundant: Aristotle, at all
events, furnishes an analysis of moral responsibility in the third
book of the *Nicomachean Ethics* which seems fully adequate:[a]

Since *aretē*[b] is concerned with passions and actions, and since
praise and blame are bestowed upon such as are voluntary, while to
such as are involuntary pardon is granted, and sometimes pity, it is
presumably necessary for those who are enquiring about *arete* to
distinguish the voluntary and the involuntary; and it is useful to
those who have to make laws, with a view to determining rewards
and punishments.

To any reader of the present day, this must seem admirably
sane, indeed the only reasonable attitude. Certainly anyone
who has to reward or punish ought to make clear to himself
the circumstances in which he is prepared to regard an act as
non-voluntary, and hence outside the realm of reward and
punishment: for by so doing he delimits the sphere in which he
intends to operate. The only problem, one might suppose, is the
interpretation of the terms 'voluntary' and 'involuntary'; that
is to say, the criteria which are allowed to be relevant: and in
fact Aristotle immediately goes on to consider such criteria.

Here, then, is a quotation which seems to make nonsense of
the defence offered to the two previous charges. We find here a
Greek moral philosopher offering what, in its full context, is an
extremely subtle analysis of moral responsibility, inhibited apparently neither by the alleged relative unimportance of that
concept, nor by his society's key terms of value.

This, however, is not enough. If we examine Aristotle's
moral position as a whole, we are not on such familiar ground as
might at first appear. Aristotle's concept of moral responsibility
is not identical with our own; for this to be so would require
not only a subtle analysis of voluntary and involuntary action,
but also a system of ethics which should enable the application
of this analysis in all cases in which we should consider this
relevant. Aristotle does not and cannot furnish such a system;
and the apparent familiarity of this analysis merely blinds us to
the dissimilarity of the whole. The reasons for this dissimilarity
lie in the presuppositions partly of Homeric, partly of later

---

[a] *E.N.* iii. 1109ᵇ30 ff.   [b] This term will be discussed below, pp. 30 ff.

Greek, social organization and habits of thought; presuppositions which, commended by the key terms of value, Plato and Aristotle never challenged and never analysed, since they were for them part of the data of ethics.

Since Plato and Aristotle were not fully conscious of the nature of these presuppositions, there is no reason why they should furnish better material for their study than do earlier writers. Indeed, the material is less readily studied in their works than elsewhere, for there the presuppositions are overlaid with philosophizing; and though the presuppositions naturally condition this philosophizing, they are less easy to discover than in less sophisticated writers. Further, some at least of these presuppositions are survivals, no longer relevant, from an earlier state of society to which they were strictly relevant; and it is not surprising that it should be more interesting and more fruitful to consider these in their proper context, for only in this way can they be fully understood. Thus, in order to determine as far as possible why Plato and Aristotle approached moral philosophy as they did, it is necessary to examine earlier situations, problems and solutions; for these throw considerable light which could not be derived from any other source.

II

HOMER: FREE WILL AND COMPULSION

A. INTRODUCTORY

In discussing moral responsibility it will be convenient to divide possible pleas, claims that one should not be held responsible, into two classes: that of mistake, 'I meant to do *A* and in fact did *B*', and that of compulsion or external interference, 'I was compelled to do *B* by some power or powers exterior to myself'. For the present purpose, mistake is to be taken as including madness, drunkenness, and all similar forms of 'not knowing'.

In this chapter I shall discuss the plea of compulsion as it appears in Homer, leaving that of mistake to Chapter III. This plea may become relevant at more than one level in the poems; for the Homeric world contains not only human beings interfering with one another's designs, but also active and quarrelsome gods, and *moira*,[a] which seems sometimes to co-operate with, and sometimes to thwart, those gods, and like them to interfere with human actions. The effect of all these forms of compulsion must be considered.

B. HUMAN COMPULSION

The compulsion of other human beings clearly gives rise to a valid defence. Even in the promiscuous slaughter in the Hall of Odysseus, Phemius the minstrel pleads, and says that Telemachus will confirm,[b] that he did not come of his own free will, *hekōn*, to sing at the suitors' feasts; the suitors were more numerous, and stronger than he, and they compelled him by force.[1] True, Phemius prefaces his plea with a reminder that good minstrels are hard to come by, and that Odysseus will regret it if he kills him, but it is as guiltless, *anaitios*, that Tele-

---

[a] See pp. 17 ff.   [b] *Odyssey* xxii. 351.

machus defends him: and Odysseus does not kill him. Again, in the *Iliad*,[a] at a critical moment in the battle, Poseidon threatens that any man who ceases from fighting *hekon* will become food for the dogs. *Hekon* is clearly significant. Uttered in a threat, it must exclude from the threat anyone who ceases from fighting *ākōn*: and in this context *akon* must mean 'as a result of forces beyond his control', presumably as a result of being wounded.

In the Homeric poems, then, it seems that a man is not held responsible for actions which he performs, or fails to perform, *akon* in the sense of 'under compulsion', at all events when that compulsion is exercised by other human beings. This is true in such cases as these: but, as will be shown below,[b] there are circumstances in which no defence is accepted.

C. THE GODS AS CAUSE

(i) *The Nature of the Homeric Gods*

We may now consider the status of actions controlled or influenced on the non-human level; and as preface to this it may be said that if any society believes that all human actions are controlled by the gods in such a manner that no man can affect the predetermined course of events in any way, it is to be expected that this belief will not affect ascriptions of moral responsibility in that society: for no society can accept as valid any plea which would exempt from punishment all wrong actions without exception. It is clearly impossible for a society not to punish any offences at all; and equally clearly such a belief cannot be used to distinguish one action from another, since all are affected. The adoption of a belief in psychological determinism might lead to a change in the *manner* of punishment, since the cause of action is 'within reach'; but this does not apply to theistic determinism.

At first sight it might appear that Homer held that all events in the world of men are supernaturally determined.[2] Both poems seem to assert this in their opening lines.[c] In the *Iliad* it is said that through the wrath of Achilles the plan of Zeus was fulfilled; and the return of Odysseus came about when the

---

[a] *Iliad* xiii. 234.   [b] p. 36.   [c] *Iliad* i. 5; *Odyssey* i. 17 and 60 ff.

gods granted to him that he should come home to Ithaca. Each
work, then, seems to be set by the poet in a framework of divine
planning. Further, within the poems, characters are able to
make forecasts of whole stretches of action: Zeus is able to
predict the action up to and including the death of Patroclus,
and Tiresias to prophesy the course of Odysseus' future trials,
for which purpose indeed he is called up from the dead.[a]

If Zeus, or any other non-human power, controls all human
actions, judgements of moral responsibility, as has been said,
are likely to remain unaffected. But no reading of the poems,
however casual, gives the impression that the Homeric Zeus,
however favoured his position, is omnipotent in the sense in
which a modern reader understands the word. To go no further
than the half line of the *Iliad* mentioned above: 'the plan of
Zeus was fulfilled' in that the wrath of Achilles caused great
woe to the Greeks; and Zeus hampered the Greeks with the
express purpose of causing this woe: but it is not presented by
Homer as a divine master-plan laid up in heaven *before* Agamemnon angered Achilles by taking his prize Briseis from him.
Zeus resolves to hamper the Greeks because Achilles' mother,
the sea-nymph Thetis, asks him to do so on Achilles' behalf;
and Achilles tells Thetis to reinforce her pleas by reminding
Zeus of the time when she helped him against the other gods,
who would have fettered him, had she not roused the hundred-
handed Briareus to help him.[b] In neither instance does Zeus
appear as an omnipotent governor of the universe.

The episode of Briareus is clearly a very primitive tale; but
the plainest statement of Zeus' powers, which occurs at the
beginning of *Iliad* viii, only serves to confirm that those powers
are limited. Zeus threatens that he will smite or cast into
Tartarus any god or goddess who assists either Trojans or
Greeks. Then that god will realize the extent to which Zeus is
the most powerful of the gods.[c] The proof is this: if Zeus were
to suspend a golden chain from the heavens, even if all the gods
and goddesses were to pull with all their might, they could not
pull Zeus from Heaven; whereas, if he wished, he could draw up
earth and sea as well. It may be said that the poet, with the
inadequate concepts at his disposal, is trying to assert the

---

[a] *Iliad* viii. 457 ff.; *Odyssey* xi. 90 ff.   [b] *Iliad* i. 396 ff.
[c] *Iliad* viii. 17.

omnipotence of Zeus; but we are concerned here with the
effects of the belief which he is able to form with these inadequate concepts: and these are far different from those of a
'philosophical' belief in omnipotence. The other gods are not
mere limbs or tools of Zeus, as they would be, were he fully
omnipotent; they want to go down to help the side they favour;
they could go down to help, in the sense that their wills are not
bound; they are simply afraid of Zeus, and were his attention
diverted, as Hera's deception of Zeus in *Iliad* xiv shows to be
possible, they would go down to help. Zeus has no perfections:
he merely possesses the qualities he does possess in a superlative
degree.

This point is expressed forcibly by Poseidon,[a] when Zeus
claims superiority both as first born and as stronger god:[3]
Zeus should remember that he is only one of Cronus' sons; that
Zeus, Poseidon, and Hades cast lots, each receiving a sphere—
earth, sea, and nether world—in which he was to rule: and that
in attempting to curb Poseidon he is overstepping the mark.
This is a serious limitation of Zeus' powers. In Homeric belief,
however, Poseidon and Hades have suffered from the encroach-
ments of Zeus: only Zeus can promote his plans from a distance, and only Zeus' plans, however his attention may be
distracted in the meantime, triumph in the end.

If the chief of the gods, being most powerful but not omnipotent, is limited, much more so are the lesser gods. They can
only affect the course of a battle if they are there in person;
and even when they are there, they may fail to notice vital
facts. The line 'and (some hero) would have perished, had not
(his protecting god) noticed' is frequent.[b] When not present,
these gods may readily be deceived:[4] the other gods decide to
bring Odysseus home at a time when Poseidon, being far away
among the Ethiopians, will not know anything about it.[5]

The Homeric gods, then, make isolated irruptions into human
affairs; not all human actions are caused, in whole or in part,
by them.

(ii) *The Effects of the Homeric Belief*

In these circumstances we should expect those cases in which
the Homeric gods are operative as external causes to be treated

[a] *Iliad* xv. 189.   [b] e.g. *Iliad* v. 311. Even of Zeus, *Iliad* viii. 131 f.

differently from cases in which they are not operative, particularly as the characters themselves believe that one may distinguish empirically between a state of affairs which is caused by some god, and an otherwise similar state of affairs which is not so caused. So Nestor suggests to Agamemnon[a] tactical arrangements by means of which he may discover whether his failure to take Troy is the consequence of a divine decree or of his men's cowardice and ignorance of war. Either may be the cause; but for the latter the gods are not responsible. Even when the gods are expressly said to 'put might (or fear) into' a man, he remains responsible for his actions.[b]

Presumably if, despite all efforts, he fails to attain his end, the Homeric hero assumes that the gods are not propitious: but no matter what may happen, he must not relax his efforts. In *Iliad* xiii,[c] Idomeneus attempts to excuse the present failure of the Greeks: no man can be the cause, *aitios*, since all are skilled warriors, and none has displayed fear or hesitation. No; it must be the will of Zeus that the Greeks should perish ingloriously far from home. To this Poseidon makes the reply already discussed:[d] that anyone who ceases to fight of his own accord will become food for the dogs. The tide is against them; but a man must keep swimming while he has the strength.[6]

Thus, the general influence of Zeus on a train of events is not treated as an excuse for failure. No fighting nation could allow such an excuse—in life; for it supplies nothing but a justification for cowardice.

Certain transactions between other gods and mortals, however, are differently treated. In Homeric belief, as has been said, only Zeus can promote his plans from a distance. The lesser gods must be present in person: and accordingly they go down from time to time into the battle to help their particular favourites and hamper their opponents. The combination of god and hero is formidable; and evidently anyone who is defeated by it may offer this fact as an excuse, or as an attempt to lessen the glory of his human antagonist. So, in *Iliad* xvi, Apollo comes down to help Hector, and knocks off Patroclus' helmet, dazing him to such an extent as to make him an easy prey.[e] Then, says the poet, Zeus granted Hector possession of

---

[a] *Iliad* ii. 367, cp. v. 103.   [b] Cp. p. 16 and Note 7.   [c] *Iliad* xiii. 222 ff.
[d] p. 11.   [e] *Iliad* xvi. 793 ff.

the helmet; and subsequently Euphorbus assisted Hector by striking Patroclus in the back with a spear. The dying Patroclus says

Well may you boast now, Hector; for Zeus and Apollo have given you victory, and have easily overcome me.

Left to himself, he could kill twenty men like Hector.

But baneful *moira* and Apollo have killed me, and of mortal men Euphorbus: you are merely the third who has a share in my death. But death and mighty *moira* are near you; you will perish at the hands of Achilles.

This passage shows the difference, from the point of view of responsibility, between Zeus' general influence on the battle, and Apollo's particular interference. Zeus granted possession of Patroclus' helmet to Hector, and Zeus, as well as Apollo, gave Hector victory. But when Patroclus calculates the number of his opponents, only Apollo is mentioned: the influence of Zeus is quietly forgotten. (That *moira* and Apollo, as is evident from the arithmetic, only count as one agent, is interesting; as the discussion of *moira* will show,[a] only Apollo's influence here affects the question of responsibility.) Evidently Apollo's presence lessens the disgrace of Patroclus' defeat; and to lessen this, as will appear,[b] is of the utmost importance.

When interfering in person, the lesser gods naturally cause the defeat, not the moral error, of those with whom they interfere;[c] and defeat so caused is evaluated quite differently from defeat resulting from the influence of Zeus. The reason for this difference seems clear. Patroclus' defence does not raise any problems for a fighting nation, for it is not drawn from life. In an actual battle a Patroclus could not know, even if he believed such a thing possible, that Apollo was opposing him in person, and hence could not offer such a defence. Only the omniscient epic poet can allow him to know that Apollo is present; whereas anyone in Idomeneus' position might always put forward Idomeneus' defence. Literature may admit what would be inadmissible in life.

We must not suppose that any distinction between 'Life' and 'Literature' was in Homer's mind: it is merely that in some passages, describing events which only a poet could claim to

know, he has more opportunity for free composition than when
he is describing events of a kind with which all men are familiar.
Accordingly, since the distinction is not consciously made, there
is always the danger that 'Literature' will infect 'Life': as seems
to have happened when Paris says to Helen in *Iliad* iii:[a]

Woman, do not taunt me. On this occasion Menelaus has defeated me with Athena's aid, but on another occasion I shall defeat
him; for we too have our gods.

This defence differs from that offered by Idomeneus and rejected by Poseidon, and resembles the defence of Patroclus,
inasmuch as the interference is not general but particular. In
one respect, however, it is entirely different: the poet is allowing
Paris to offer a defence which is not 'true' in the sense in which
Patroclus' defence is 'true'. Athena has in fact taken no direct
part in Paris' discomfiture; she did not interfere in his struggle
with Menelaus in any way whatsoever. Accordingly, Paris is
merely looking for an excuse, as a man might in real life.
'Life' has been contaminated by 'Literature'.

Gods may also interfere psychologically with individual
Homeric heroes, to inspire them with unusual valour or timidity.
This interference is never allowed to affect the hero's responsibility for his actions. A passage of *Iliad* xii[b] indicates the reason
for this. The Trojans would have suffered a reverse

Had not Zeus roused his son Sarpedon against the Greeks, like a
lion against cattle.

After a simile, the passage is restated thus:

So did his spirit, *thūmos*, urge Sarpedon to rush against the wall
and break through the battlements.

The causal chain, through a 'common-sense carelessness' of a
type frequent in Homer, is no longer pursued beyond Sarpedon's *thumos*; and actions to which a man is impelled by his
thumos are responsible actions.[7]

Thus, though its gods interfere only spasmodically in human
affairs, Homeric society does not normally allow a plea of
divine interference, unless the divine agent is present in a form
which, in Homeric eyes,[8] gives to his interference a difference
in degree, not in kind, from that of a human agent in the same

---

[a] *Iliad* iii. 438 ff.   [b] *Iliad* xii. 292 ff.

situation; and the passages in which this is found smell of
Literature, not Life, and are excuses for failure, not moral
error.

D. MOIRA

(i) The Nature of the Belief

In addition to their belief in the gods, Homer's characters
believe in a power referred to as 'moira' (and by a number of
other terms, aisa, moros, &c., which behave, for the present
purpose, in the same manner as moira) in which there seems to
be some measure of inevitability. The extent of this power and
its relation to gods and men evidently may affect the question
of moral responsibility.

The clearest assertion that 'Fate' in Homer is something
over against and superior to the gods[9] occurs at the beginning of
Iliad viii.[a] Zeus, having banished the other gods from the field
of battle, takes up his golden scales and places in them two
fates, kēre, of death, one for the Trojans and one for the Greeks;
and the 'fated day' of the Greeks sinks down. The scales are
something distinct from Zeus; the weight of the kēre is independent of Zeus, for otherwise there would be no point in
weighing them: and so there apparently exists a power over
which Zeus has no control, and to which he bows.[10] We need
not, however, assume more than is said. The 'fates' are 'fates of
death', not 'fates' in general: a point which is made clearer in
the Odyssey.[b] Athena, to hearten Telemachus, who has said that
he does not believe that Odysseus could now return home even
with the help of the gods, assures him that a god, if he wished to
do so, could bring home a man even from far away; but she
admits, with a side glance at the unhappy fate of Agamemnon,
that the gods themselves cannot keep death even from their
friends when the moira of death comes upon them.

Death, then, seems to be peculiar in being out of the control
of the gods. It is easy to see why such a working philosophy
should be adopted. While there is life there is hope, and even
the humblest may rise from his misery. Accordingly, while
there is life it is possible that the gods may help: there is
no reason to suppose that they cannot do so, for Homeric man

has not the requisite beliefs, whether about nature, mankind, or the gods, to produce any of the common forms of determinism. Death, however, is final; over death the gods can have no control, since even kings, whom the gods must love, since they prosper, die, and may die as miserably as Agamemnon died. Hence there must be something which can override the gods, something which cannot be propitiated.

This is quite natural: but though there is no reason to suppose from these passages that the sphere of *moira* extends further than death, other passages make it clear that such is the case. In the *Odyssey*,[a] when Polyphemus has been blinded by Odysseus, he prays in pain and rage to his father Poseidon that Odysseus may never reach home:

> But if it be *moira* for him to see his friends again and come to his home and his native land, may he come home late and in sorry plight.

This passage illustrates the nature of the belief in *moira*. If Polyphemus can pray in these terms, he must believe that even if it is *moira* for Odysseus to return, it need not be *moira* for him to return at a particular time or in a particular condition. Suppose on the other hand it is not the *moira* of Odysseus that he should return home safely: clearly, if Polyphemus is praying to Poseidon *at all*, he does not believe that it must therefore be the *moira* of Odysseus that something else definite should happen to him; that, for example, he should perish miserably in a shipwreck. If his homecoming is *not* guaranteed, then Poseidon has a free hand; but unless Poseidon uses his opportunity, Odysseus may reach home all the same.

In fact the situation is what Polyphemus fears: when Poseidon first notices Odysseus after the gods have commanded his homecoming, he is already near Phaeacia,[b]

> where it is *aisa* for him to escape the great doom of sorrow which is his. But still I think I shall persecute him until he has had his fill of woe.

If—or when—Odysseus reaches Phaeacia, it is *aisa* that he is safe. That is determined; but when Odysseus is to reach Phaeacia is not determined. So Poseidon, having a free hand in the

---

[a] *Odyssey* ix. 528 ff.; cp. v. 206 ff.   [b] *Odyssey* v. 288 ff.; cp. *Iliad* v. 674 ff.

matter, raises a storm and wrecks Odysseus' raft; and even though it is *aisa* that Odysseus is safe when he reaches Phaeacia, Leucothea[a] has to give him a lifebuoy to prevent his drowning on the way.

The world under the influence of *moira*, in fact, is not so much like a piece of clockwork as it is like a game of celestial snakes and ladders. Most moves are free; but should one alight at the foot of one's own particular ladder, or at the head of one's own personal snake, the next move is determined.

This seems clear-cut enough, but there is another group of passages which deserves notice. Hector, taking his leave of Andromache,[b] says that no one can kill him unless it be *aisa*:

But I tell you that no one, brave man or coward, escapes *moira* when once he is born.

This, for a man who believes in Destiny, is an impeccable statement. But in *Iliad* xxii[c] it is *aisa* that Hector should be killed; yet Zeus proposes among the gods that notwithstanding this Hector's life shall be saved. Athena replies

Father Zeus, what a thing to say! Will you snatch from death a mortal man, long subject to *aisa*? Do it, then; but we other gods will not approve.

So Zeus can, it seems, overset Fate, and save Hector, though Hector is doomed to death; but it is a shameful thing for him to do.[11] Similarly, men may overset Fate, or it may be feared that they will do so. When Zeus, in *Iliad* xx,[d] sends the lesser gods back into the battle to help whom they will, he does so in fear that Achilles may sack the Trojan wall though it is not *moros* for him to do so, *huper moron*; and later in the same book[e] Poseidon rescues Aeneas from danger lest Zeus should be angry if Achilles killed him, since it is Aeneas' destiny to escape.[f]

To these may be added a passage from *Odyssey* i.[g] Zeus complains of the accusations which men bring against the gods:

They say that woes, *kaka*, come from us; but they themselves suffer pain *huper moron* because of their own misdeeds.

Aegisthus, he continues, wooed Clytemnestra and slew Agamemnon *huper moron*. There was no need for him to do it: in

---

[a] *Odyssey* v. 333 ff.　　　[b] *Iliad* vi. 487 ff.　　　[c] *Iliad* xxii. 178 ff.
[d] *Iliad* xx. 30 ff.　　　　　　　　　　　　　　　　　[e] *Iliad* xx. 301 ff.
[f] μόριμόν δέ οἵ ἐστ' ἀλέασθαι.　　　　　　　　　　[g] *Odyssey* i. 32 ff.

fact Hermes was sent from heaven to tell him not to do so. Yet he did it—*huper moron*.

The last example is clearly a theodicy. Someone has said that evils come to men through the agency of the gods, intending thereby to avoid responsibility for his actions. It will be discussed below[a] whether this plea is allowed in Homer; here it may be noted that this solution to 'the problem of evil' may be offered without its appearing too illogical.

The other passages are best explained by the nature of the parts of the poem in which they occur. These lines are all spoken by gods: which is to say that they are drawn from the poet's imagination, not from life. In life, one does not know what one's fate may be, and so cannot reasonably claim to be acting in despite of it: it is only the poet who is privileged to see his world from more than one level, for he has created it. In life, a belief in *moira* serves no purpose at all unless what is *moira* must happen. This, then, is more 'Literature'.

This 'Literature', however, is helpful. If *in life* what is *moira* must happen, so far as individual events are concerned, the modern reader is tempted to lend to the word ideas drawn from centuries of philosophic reasoning on determinism. It is evident from what has already been said that such ideas are not relevant here; but it is not yet clear what ideas are relevant. The passages of 'Literature' quoted above help to make this clear, for they indicate the relationship of this apparently specialized use of *moira* to other uses.

A well-established use of *moira* is that in the sense of 'share', with no metaphysical overtones.[b] Even when personified, the *moirai* may be simply sharers, as in the line[c]

The *moirai* gave an enduring spirit to man.

They gave an enduring spirit to man as his 'share' or 'allotment'. We may consider too the frequently expressed commendation 'you have spoken *kata moiran*'. This we must translate 'you have spoken as is right', for 'you have spoken according to your share' means nothing: but 'as is right' cannot indicate the exact flavour of *moira*. 'You have spoken with due reference to the present situation and/or to your place in society'

---

[a] p. 22.   [b] e.g. *Iliad* x. 253.
[c] *Iliad* xxiv. 49; cp. Aeschylus, *Eumenides* 333 ff.

is implied; and here we have not a 'must' but an 'ought'. It has already been said that Homeric beliefs do not warrant any theory of determinism: Homeric man knows nothing of a 'clock-work' universe or an omnipotent god. Accordingly, the flavour of *moira* cannot be drawn from any such source. The only system which is forced upon the notice of Homeric man is the social system, in which he has an appointed place, an 'allotted share', according to which he *ought* to comport himself, and whose burdens he must bear. He has been allotted a station in life to which in a sense he must keep (for a beggar cannot become a king, particularly in Homeric society) though he may behave in a manner out of tune with it. Since this is the only system Homeric man knows, he cannot contrast it with any other, or draw concepts from any other. Accordingly, this is the nearest approach to inevitability which *moira* can possess for him, when viewed as a system. This is the manner in which Zeus may be presumed to see it. He knows what is *moira* for each man and what is not[a]—a statement which, of course, does not imply that everything which happens to a man is subject to *moira*—and hence what 'is to' happen to him: but since it only 'is to' happen to him in the sense that it is his share, Zeus, when treated as a character in an epic, need not let it happen. Just as in an earthly council one may or may not speak or act *kata moiran*, so in the Grand Council of Heaven.[12] In both cases it is shameful not to speak or act in such a manner: but in both cases it is clearly possible.

The human agent finds himself in a different position in life. It is clearly inevitable that he should die some day; if anything in fact happens to him, it was clearly his 'lot' that it 'was to' happen to him; and given this belief, any individual event envisaged beforehand may be his 'lot'. He is, however, only likely to regard as his 'lot' events which seem important to him; for there is nothing in these beliefs to encourage the human agent to construct a system to apply overtly to all actions and events; and such a system could not be a rigidly deterministic one, for Homeric man has not the concepts with which to construct such a system.

If, however, the human agent considers any individual event to be his *moira*, he must, as has been said, regard it as inevitable.

[a] *Odyssey* xx. 75 ff.

But this 'share' may involve very much or very little: it may be his death; his death at the hand of a particular person; the assurance that something will happen, with no guarantee how or when it will happen; the promise that if he performs some definite action, something else will happen; or any other individual snake or ladder. But these *are* individual: there is no feeling of a system.

(ii) *The Effects of the Belief*

Since *moira* is not concerned with all human actions, we might expect those with which *moira* is concerned to receive special treatment. This, however, is not normal Homeric practice. Death is the classic instance of an event which, in distinction from the generality of actions and events, is always subject to *moira*; but there is no feeling at all that, since *moira* is the external cause of every death, the responsibility of any human agent for that death is in any way diminished. Illogical as this may be in theory, it is precisely what is to be expected in practice: it seems inconceivable that any society should make no distinction between death from natural causes and homicide of every kind.[13] Again, when a general prophecy covering a long series of events, such as Zeus' prophecy of the crucial events up to the death of Patroclus,[a] is uttered, the experiences related must surely be the *moira* of the persons mentioned in the prophecy; but this in no way affects the treatment of these events on the human level as regards responsibility. The events are simply described on two levels which do not intersect.

To treat a series of events in this manner seems quite natural in practice; but when a single event is emphatically stated to be subject to *moira*, we might expect a different attitude. Homer's treatment of the adultery of Aegisthus and Clytemnestra proves the contrary. Agamemnon had left a minstrel behind to protect and watch his wife Clytemnestra; and Clytemnestra at first would not accept Aegisthus as a lover, for she was a virtuous woman.[b]

But when the *moira* of the gods[c] fettered her (him) so that she (he) was overcome, then Aegisthus took the minstrel to a deserted island and left him there to become the prey of birds. Whereupon

[a] *Iliad* viii. 477 ff.   [b] *Odyssey* iii. 269 ff.
[c] A curious phrase, but one which has no effects in practice.

Aegisthus of his own free will took Clytemnestra of her own free will[a] to his own house.

Unfortunately, the first line of this quotation contains a very vague pronoun.[b] This could in theory refer to any of the three; but the general run of the passage confines the choice to Clytemnestra or (less probably) Aegisthus.[14] In either case, *moira* is said to cause an action which a mere three lines later is said to be performed voluntarily by the agent.

This seems very odd indeed; and the passage indicates the reason for the other oddities which have been noticed already. Some of the earlier passages mentioned state merely that it is someone's *moira* that something should happen to him: a statement which might permit the (rather sophistic) argument that to have anything allotted to one as one's share does not cause its occurrence, and that Homer, unspoilt by philosophy, realized this. I have said that this is true from the point of view of Zeus. It is not, however, true for the human agent: and here it could not be stated more strongly that *moira* caused the event.[c] Yet the characters still act 'of their own free will', for the incompatibility of the two statements does not occur to the poet.[15] Common-sense carelessness again preserves individual responsibility.

E. POSSIBLE DANGERS OF THE HOMERIC POSITION

To rely on common-sense carelessness is dangerous. There is always the risk that someone may appear who is less careless than his fellows; and the implications of the language commonly used in Homer of gods and *moira* alike would, if drawn out, furnish a defence valid in practically any situation. One instance was noted above;[d] but the poems contain one passage which is much more significant.

When Helen feels ashamed on meeting Priam, to whom her presence in Troy has caused such woe, Priam excuses her for responsibility for the war, saying[e]

You are not the cause, *aitiē*; in my eyes the gods are *aitioi*, who have stirred up against me the woeful war with the Greeks.

---

[a] ἐθέλων ἐθέλουσαν.   [b] μιν.   [c] ἐπέδησε δαμῆναι.
[d] p. 16.   [e] *Iliad* iii. 164 f.

We are concerned here not with Helen's failure to achieve some end which she has set herself, but with her moral error; not with a god striking a blow in battle, but with divine influence on events from a distance; not with Literature, but with life, since this might readily be said in an actual situation. On the grounds of the general influence of the gods, Priam is willing to absolve Helen from responsibility for her actions.

Though this is an exception in Homer, it is an attitude quite natural to anyone who holds such beliefs about the gods, and one which has evidently occurred in the society known to the poet. It seems to have drawn a violent response. In the passage from *Odyssey* i quoted above,[a] Zeus complains that men blame the gods for the woes, *kaka*, which come to them.[16] He insists that they are wrong to do so, and says that men suffer pain beyond their allotted portion, *huper moron*, citing the case of Aegisthus. The gods warned him what would happen if he did what he did, and yet he did it; accordingly it is his own fault, and he has no case against heaven.

The point could have been made more clearly. Zeus is denying that woes, *kaka*, are sent to men from heaven. He evidently supposes that Aegisthus might make this charge when Orestes comes to avenge the murder of his father Agamemnon. Now *kaka* denotes things which are unpleasant, without any moral connotation;[17] and if Aegisthus is to complain of *kaka*, these must be things which are unpleasant for Aegisthus. The exact nature of these is doubtful. *Kaka* might refer simply to the return of Orestes and his vengeance: but in that case it seems rather odd that Zeus should be upset, for Aegisthus is then only accusing Zeus of having brought upon him a just vengeance, while the case of Odysseus which follows completely disproves Zeus' point, for the gods have undoubtedly caused Odysseus' *kaka*, his present unfortunate situation, in this sense. It seems much more likely that Zeus fears that Aegisthus may attempt to lay upon him, or upon superhuman influence in general, the blame for the whole complex of events in the House of Atreus beginning from the adultery of Aegisthus and Clytemnestra. This Aegisthus must have thought a good thing for himself, an *agathon*, at the time: but when revenge came, either Aegisthus or a spectator, given his opportunity by such phrases as 'but

[a] p. 19.

when the *moira* of the gods fettered her so that she was over-come' quoted above,[a] might say 'this is *moira*' or 'the gods have sent this' with reference to the whole sequence of events. Zeus denies that this is true: and his denial entails that a man may not blame the gods for his moral error when he is likely to be punished for it. That is to say, if he pursues a desirable end, an *agathon*, qua *agathon*, and this in the long run proves to be a *kakon* (which, as will be seen, is the manner in which Aegisthus would view these events) it is his fault and no one else's. Such an interpretation explains both the vehemence of Zeus' words and also the reason for their inclusion in *Odyssey* i. The passage has no dramatic relevance, and must have been added either as a comment by the poet himself on a contemporary belief, or as a reflection of some such comment. Further, the interpreta-tion gives a satisfactory contrast with the case of Odysseus; it is not his decisions which the gods have caused, but his external circumstances; and it is most unlikely that any early poet should have wished to deny that these are sent by the gods.[18]

This passage, then, seems to be a rejection of the type of attitude taken by Priam to Helen. Put as it is into the mouth of Zeus, it could have no higher authority. Such a defence is not to be tolerated; the god, as Plato was to maintain much later, is not responsible, *anaitios*.[b]

In Homeric society, then, the belief in non-human causation of human action has practically no effects on the ascription of responsibility. This discussion, however, will be of value in considering later writers; for many aspects of Homeric thought and expression which in Homer produce no untoward results cause considerable trouble to later generations, when the im-plications of such thoughts and expressions are realized.[c]

NOTES TO CHAPTER II

1. This is not the only possible plea. The herald Medon escapes because he was kind to Telemachus when Telemachus was a child. (The validity of the plea that one acted under compulsion *seems* to be most clearly shown in *Odyssey* iv. 646: Antinous asks Noemon, who has lent Tele-machus a boat, whether Telemachus took the boat from him by force, or whether Noemon gave it *hekon*. Antinous seems to be threatening Noemon; but though Noemon in fact says that he gave the boat of his

---

[a] p. 22. [b] Plato, *Republic* x. 617 E. [c] Cp. Chapter VI.

own free will to Telemachus, no reprisals are taken. Antinous may be simply anxious to discover the attitude of the inhabitants as exemplified by Noemon, or the lines may stand where they do for the sake of Noemon's highly moral reply, 649 ff. Noemon's name—'the intelligent one' —suggests the latter.)

2. On the gods in Homer, we may compare, e.g. Pierre Chantraine, 'Le Divin et les dieux chez Homère', *Fondation Hardt*, i. 47 ff. On the plan of Zeus, cp. W. C. Greene, *Moira*, pp. 13 ff.

3. Cf. M. I. Finley, *The World of Odysseus*, p. 148. This treatment of the Homeric social scene forms an essential background to the discussion of Chapters II and III.

4. G. M. A. Grube, *Studies Norwood*, p. 17, Note 9, maintains that all the gods know everything all the time in Homeric belief, but the poet, for dramatic reasons, sometimes allows them to overlook things (cp. also G. M. Calhoun, *Homer's Gods: Prolegomena*, TAPA 68, 19): and he cites a number of passages (*Odyssey* iv. 468, x. 305, 573, xiv. 443) in which gods are stated to be capable of knowing or doing everything. It seems unnecessary to adopt this theory. To allow a god (or an all-knowing seer) to overlook something is one thing: to *say* 'and (some hero) would have perished had not (his protecting god) noticed' is to draw violent and unnecessary attention to this discrepancy, if one really believes that the gods are all omniscient. Accordingly, it seems most unlikely that these incidents are conscious isolated curtailments of a fully formulated belief in the omniscience of all the gods: sooner are the examples cited by Grube isolated cases of an imperfectly formulated belief, whose implications Homer does not appreciate. After all, when Hermes says, *Odyssey* x. 305, 'It is difficult for men to pluck the herb moly; but the gods can do everything', he cannot mean that all the gods are omnipotent, since this is both logically impossible and also contrary to everything else we hear of the gods in Homer. The contrast I have quoted (p. 17), between the possibility of a god's bringing home Odysseus, if he is alive, *even from afar*, and the impossibility of even a god's saving a man from death, is relevant here too. Just as a god can pick moly, which is very difficult for a man, so can a god bring home Odysseus from the ends of the earth, which is very difficult for a man: but some things are not possible. So in saying that the gods can do anything, the poet has no more in mind than 'if you think of anything which is very difficult for a man, a god can do it easily'. I have already argued (p. 13) that even Zeus has no perfections, but merely possesses the qualities he does possess in a superlative degree: and the other gods fall in power between Zeus and men. And just as there exists at this time no 'philosophical' concept of omnipotence, so with omniscience: Proteus, *Odyssey* iv. 468, in reference to whom it is said that the gods know everything, knows everything in the sense that if he is asked any question he can supply the answer, however difficult: but he is not represented as actually, as opposed to potentially, knowing everything all the time. (Even the mortal Tiresias can claim to know everything in this sense.) Accordingly, the possibility of deceiving such gods (e.g. of

capturing Proteus while he is asleep) or the possibility of their failing to notice vital details, does not seem absurd. Here, as elsewhere in Homer, beliefs are not co-ordinated. We may compare the theory of 'mental parataxis', B. E. Perry, TAPA 68, 415 ff. Grube opposes this theory, but such lack of co-ordination is characteristic not only of the Homeric poems but also of much Attic drama, cp. pp. 116 ff. below.

5. In fact Poseidon only discovers the trick that has been played on him at *Odyssey* v. 281, when he happens to notice Odysseus on his raft.

6. A man must keep swimming when Zeus is on his side too, cp. *Iliad* xvii. 327 ff., where Apollo chides Aeneas for hanging back and failing to take advantage of the fact that Zeus is, for the moment, on the side of Troy. Neither fate nor the gods provide the hero with success without effort.

7. We may compare *Iliad* xiii. 59 ff. and ix. 109 ff., Nestor's rebuke to Agamemnon for yielding to his *thumos* when he slighted Achilles. Psychological functions are spoken of as acting independently with great frequency in Homer, but under no circumstances is the statement '(a certain psychological function) drove X to do Y' or 'X yielded to (a certain psychological function)' treated as in any way absolving the agent from responsibility. Cp. J. Böhme, *Die Seele und das Ich im homeri-schen Epos*, and E. R. Dodds, *The Greeks and the Irrational*, chap. i. Except for a brief period in the early sophistic movement, which will be discussed in Chapter VI, Greek common sense held instinctively to the view later formulated by Aristotle, *E.N.* 1110ª15, that one is responsible for actions whose originating cause, *archē*, lies within oneself. Cp. *Iliad* ix. 110, xiii. 224, *Odyssey* xiv. 246 and 262 for responsible actions so described.

8. That we can rationalize Apollo's dazing of Patroclus as sunstroke is irrelevant. In Homeric eyes, Apollo was present in the same manner as any mortal combatant.

9. Grube, op. cit., p. 4, argues that *moira* is always subject to the will of Zeus, even in the cases (*Iliad* viii. 70 ff., xxii. 209 ff.) where Zeus weighs the fates of heroes: 'In both cases the decisions are already taken, known both to Zeus and to us. The scales are but the concrete symbol of a decision and, like an oath, make it irrevocable, so that even Apollo abandons Hector after the weighing, and in the former instance [viii. 70] the gods are all on Olympus by order of Zeus, where they stay for a while at least. Consecrated by the scales, the decision must be accepted.' But why are scales used in this type of case only? Thetis, in *Iliad* i, asks merely for the 'nod' of Zeus in a different type of context, and (524 ff.) Zeus nods assent, adding, 'This is the surest pledge that I can give. Anything to which I nod assent is irrevocable, without deceit, and sure of fulfilment.' What more could anyone want? If Zeus' nod makes any of his decisions irrevocable, then the use of the balance must have some other motive: and the most reasonable motive seems to be the one suggested in the text (for which cp. e.g. C. M. Bowra, *Tradition and Design*, pp. 230 f., Andrew Lang, *The World of Homer*, pp. 120 ff.). That Zeus should also be depicted as having made up his mind beforehand does not affect

this conclusion. Homer is perfectly capable of looking at the same act in more than one light, cp. pp. 22 ff. and Note 15 of this chapter. The idea of Zeus weighing fates (which may possibly be Mycenean, cp. M. P. Nilsson, *Homer and Mycenae*, p. 268, fig. 56) is incorporated by the poet as *one* of his modes of viewing such an event as this; it does not exclude other modes: and it is unnecessary to attempt to make all fit into one mould. (For less constricting approaches to this problem, cp. Greene, op. cit., pp. 14 ff., Chantraine, op. cit., pp. 69 ff., H. Frisch, *Might and Right in Antiquity*, pp. 54 ff., quoting M. P. Nilsson, *Geschichte der griechischen Religion*, Handbuch der Altertumswissenschaft v. ii. 1, pp. 338 ff.; also R. B. Onians, *The Origins of European Thought*, III. viii.)

10. At *Iliad* xix. 223 f., 'When Zeus, who is the dispenser (ταμίης) of war for mortal men, inclines his balance', Zeus seems to be in control of the balance. There is no mention of 'fate', and we may have merely a shorthand expression of the belief discussed in the text. But we need not be surprised—in the light of the material discussed in this chapter—to find two attitudes even to this situation; and the very possibility of using such a shorthand expression makes the existence of two attitudes more likely.

11. On the ability of Zeus to go against *moira*, cp. H. J. Rose, *Fondation Hardt*, i. 41: '(Zeus) could, if he chose, take this unconstitutional step (of saving Sarpedon) as a human king might go against the traditional *themistes* (laws, or rather customs).' Cp. also Rose, p. 80, and G. Thomson, *Aeschylus and Athens*, pp. 37 ff., on the social aspects of *moira*; and generally, M. P. Nilsson, *Greek Piety*, p. 52, and R. B. Onians, op. cit. III. vii.

   One of the reasons adduced for the athetization of *Iliad* xv. 610 ff. (cp. e.g. Leaf and Bayfield ad loc.) is that there Athena is depicted as carrying out the behests of fate; which is contrary to normal Homeric theology. Now all that is said in that passage is that Athena 'was bringing his fatal day (μόρσιμον ἦμαρ) upon him'; a phrase which need mean no more than *moros*, i.e. death. That the commentators can be so sensitive to so mild an instance is a clear indication of the lack of any expressed relationship between the gods and fate in Homer generally.

12. In saying 'The Grand Council of Heaven', I do not wish to raise the question, discussed by Nilsson, *Homer and Mycenae*, pp. 266/7, and *The Minoan–Mycenean Religion and its Survival in Greek Religion*, p. 30, and by G. M. Calhoun, *Zeus the Father in Homer*, TAPA 66, pp. 1/17, of the *exact* earthly model on which Olympian society is based. It is sufficient for my purpose that it is a society in which discussions take place. (Cp. also G. Thomson, op. cit., p. 63 and references in footnote, for the relation between Olympus and earthly society.)

13. Nevertheless, cp. J. G. Frazer, *The Belief in Immortality*, i. 33 ff., for a remarkable collection of material: material which, however, is not relevant to the present discussion, since it shows the assimilation of natural death to homicide, not the reverse.

14. Clytemnestra seems the more probable for these reasons: she is the

more prominent throughout the whole passage; the poet is very interested in her (good) character, and hence is more likely to comment on her fall than that of Aegisthus; and she is mentioned at the very end of the line preceding the quotation, so that the pronoun most naturally refers to her. (Even were it the minstrel who was 'overcome', Aegisthus is implicated in the minstrel's death, and the situation remains essentially the same; though in that case the passage is merely an extreme instance of the manner in which Homeric society ignores the share of *moira* in every death.)

15. A similar passage occurs at *Odyssey* iv. 44 and 52, where Odysseus calls his companions 'foolish', *nēpioi*, despite the fact that he attributes their actions to the influence of 'the baneful *aisa* of Zeus'. This passage is evidently affected by the external valuation of action in Homer, discussed in Chapter III pp. 48 f. To be *nepios* is to produce the wrong result, without inquiry whether the agent could have helped it or not. Thus this use of *nepios* is explicable; but that the poet should insist so firmly that Clytemnestra and Aegisthus acted of their own free will remains surprising.

'Of their own free will' indicates that Homeric society distinguished between adultery and rape, but not necessarily that different treatment was accorded to each. Patroclus was *nepios* (in the sense of 'a child') and did not mean to kill the son of Amphidamas; but though this is said, *Iliad* xxiii. 85 ff., the punishment for such homicide is clearly the same as that for premeditated murder, cp. p. 53 below.

16. Cf. Greene, op. cit., p. 23, and Onians, op. cit., III. vii.

17. This point becomes much more important later, cp. Chapter XII, pp. 249 ff.

18. As so frequently in Homer (and later), this denial is probably to be taken as referring only to the type of situation explicitly mentioned, without thought of implications elsewhere. This development need not eliminate the type of thought represented by the Two Jars of Zeus, *Iliad* xxiv. 527, for this refers to things which are not dependent on a man's own decision (cp. Chapter IV, p. 64). We may compare Peleus' advice to Achilles, *Iliad* ix. 254: 'Hera and Athena will give you strength if they so choose; but do you restrain your great-hearted *thumos* in your breast.' Self-control is in one's own hands: but such things as seem evidently out of one's control—prosperity, disaster, personal qualities, &c.—are 'given by the gods' without any problems of responsibility arising for this society.

III

HOMER: MISTAKE AND MORAL ERROR

A. INTRODUCTORY

WHEN we turn to consider mistake and moral error, the need for an oblique approach, discussed in the first chapter, becomes more evident. To construct two lists, one of mistakes, the other of moral errors, can prove nothing. Only an examination of the terms used to decry mistake and moral error and commend the contrary states will reveal the extent to which Homeric society distinguished a category of mistake, and hence the nature of its concept of moral responsibility.

The noun *aretē*, with the adjective *agathos*, its synonyms *esthlos* and *chrēstos*, the comparative forms *ameinōn* and *beltīōn*, and the superlatives *aristos* and *beltistos*, are, as will be demonstrated below, the most powerful words of commendation used of a man both in Homer and in later Greek. The noun *kakotēs*, with the adjective *kakos*, its synonyms *deilos* and *ponēros*, the comparative form *kakīōn*, and the superlative *kakistos*,[a] are the corresponding words of denigration. The neuter adjective *aischron* (*aischīon*, *aischiston*) is the most powerful word used to denigrate a man's actions, together with the noun *aischos*; and *kalon* (*kallīon*, *kalliston*) is formally the contrary of *aischron*, though in Homer, as will be shown, it does not behave as such. In Homer the noun *elencheiē*, and some allied words, which possess the same emotive power as *aischron*, are also used in the denigration of actions.

Before discussing these words in detail, we may make some remarks about them which are relevant to this work as a whole. *Agathos*, *kakos*, and their synonyms are relevant to this discussion in the masculine and feminine forms, since, as they comment on the excellence of human beings, they may claim to be

---

[a] This list is not exhaustive. Other words will be added as the discussion demands them.

moral terms. The neuter forms *agathon* and *kakon* have no such claim: to say of an action 'it is *agathon* (*kakon*) to do *X*' is simply to say that it is beneficial (harmful) to do *X*, without passing any moral judgement on the rightness or wrongness of *X*. *Aischron* and *kalon*, on the other hand, are relevant only in the neuter forms, in which they are used, as has been said, to comment on actions in a manner which is, in some sense, moral. When used of people, they normally comment on physical beauty or ugliness: a sense which is also found in the neuter. The usage in all genders is, of course, related; the *agathos* is commended for his beneficial characteristics, like the action which is *agathon*; and the action which is *aischron* is denigrated for its general unseemliness, in the same manner as the man who is *aischros* to the eye. It is evident, however, that beneficial actions and ugly men are not immediately relevant to the present question; though actions which are *agathon* or *kakon* become very important later.[a]

Furthermore, we are concerned here only with the manner in which these words are used absolutely. The fact that, for example, *agathos philos* means 'good friend', does not prove that *agathos* in itself commends co-operative excellences, though the two words taken together undoubtedly do so. A friend is essentially a person who displays such excellences in his relations with oneself; and to term him *agathos* merely indicates that he is a good specimen of his class. *Philos* is not one of the most powerful words of commendation in Greek, and it must be *philos*, not *agathos*, which in such a phrase determines the emotive power of the whole. Accordingly, only if *agathos* in itself commends the co-operative excellences can they be commended in a manner which affects the present question.

B. THE MOST IMPORTANT QUALITIES

(i) *The* agathos *and his* arete

We may examine first *agathos*, *arete*, and related words. Being the most powerful words of commendation used of a man, they imply the possession by anyone to whom they are applied of all the qualities most highly valued at any time by Greek society.

[a] Cp. Chapter XII, pp. 249 ff.

In the *Iliad* and the *Odyssey* we see what is, so far as the use of these terms is concerned, the same society at war and at peace, and can thus evaluate the use of these terms in both.[1]

In the first place, *agathos* has in its normal use no 'quiet' moral connotation. In the *Odyssey*, Penelope's suitors chose out twenty *aristoi* for the ambush and attempted murder of their host Telemachus; and when the battle began in the Hall of Odysseus, Homer says that there were four men on the threshold, but within many *esthloi*. In neither case,[a] nor at any other time when the suitors are termed *agathoi* or *esthloi* in Homer, is Homer expressing 'moral' approval for their acts, for which indeed there should be strong social disapproval. There is a proper way to go wooing, and this is not it;[2] but the suitors remain *agathoi* none the less, for they have irrefutable claims to the title.

What is commended by these terms is firstly military prowess, and the skills which promote success in war, together with that success which, as will be seen, is indistinguishable in Homer from the skills which contribute to it. So Nestor tells Agamemnon[b] that if he reorganizes his troops from a conglomerate mass into their individual fighting units he will be able to discover, in the case both of leaders and of men, who is *kakos* and who *esthlos*, since the personal contribution of each to the fighting will then be apparent. Again, one Periphetes of Mycenae possesses 'all manner of *aretai*, both in fleetness of foot and in fighting'; while it is in ambush that 'the *arete* of men is most clearly seen':[c] a judgement which explains the selection of *aristoi* to ambush Telemachus.

But this is not all. More of the connotation of these words is shown by the claim of Odysseus, when disguised as a beggar,[d] that no one could match him at menial tasks, such as inferiors, *cherees*, perform for the *agathoi*. Here evidently *agathoi* and *cherees* characterize high and low social position respectively. This usage is not distinct from the former, but forms part of one world-view. *Agathos* commends the most admired type of man; and he is the man who possesses the skills and qualities of the warrior-chieftain in war and, as will be seen, in peace, together with the social advantages which such a chieftain possessed. To

---

[a] *Odyssey* iv. 778, xxii. 204.   [b] *Iliad* ii. 365, cp. *Odyssey* viii. 512.
[c] *Iliad* xv. 642, xiii. 277.   [d] *Odyssey* xv. 324, cp. *Iliad* i. 80.

be *agathos*, one must be brave, skilful, and successful in war and in peace; and one must possess the wealth and (in peace) the leisure which are at once the necessary conditions for the development of these skills and the natural reward of their successful employment.

We may now consider *aischron*, and the allied *elencheie*, the most powerful words available to denigrate actions. *Elencheie* is the state of mind, or the condition *vis-à-vis* his fellows, of the hero conscious of having done something *aischron*, or conscious that his fellows believe him to have done something of this nature: that is to say, it is the condition of the *agathos* who is conscious of having behaved like a *kakos*. The range of these terms is interesting. In *Iliad* ii Odysseus says to Agamemnon[a]

Now the Greeks are willing to make you most contemptible, *elenchistos*, in the eyes of all mortal men; and they will not fulfil the promise which they made when they were still on the way here from Greece, that they would return home only when they had sacked Troy.

He admits that long campaigns are hard, so that the Greeks are to be excused for wanting to go home; but nevertheless maintains that

It is *aischron* to remain for a long time and then return empty-handed.

Here both *elenchistos* and *aischron* decry failure in war: and this is the manner in which such failure is regularly treated. In peace, too, the same standards apply. Eumaeus the swineherd says[b] that he would have suffered *elencheie* had his watchdogs harmed the 'beggar' Odysseus when the latter blundered into his farmyard; while Penelope rebukes Telemachus by saying[c] that he would have suffered *aischos* and dishonour among men, had Odysseus received any hurt under their roof at the hands of the suitors.

This is the range of *aischron* and *elencheie*. As one would expect, *aischron* is used in the same class of situations as *agathos*, since the *agathos*, when values are stable, is the man who does not do *aischra*, whatever may be the connotation of the words at any period. It is *aischron* to fail, in war or in peace, and entails

---

[a] *Iliad* ii. 284 ff., cp. 119 ff. [b] *Odyssey* xiv. 37 f.
[c] *Odyssey* xviii. 223 ff.

elencheie, a feeling of shame combined with and resulting from the words and actions which a failure in Homeric society will have to suffer from his fellows, if he does fail, in war or in peace.

(ii) *The Justification of the* arete-*standard*

If we examine the culture revealed by these terms of value, we discover a society whose highest commendation is bestowed upon men who must successfully exhibit the qualities of a warrior, but must also be men of wealth and social position; men, too, who must display their valour both in war and in peace to protect their dependents: a function in which they must succeed, for the most powerful words in the language are used to denigrate those who fail. This is an aristocratic scale of values: but since not even Thersites, the only 'common man' whose voice is heard, denies the propriety of such values, it is reasonable to conclude that such a scale of values was generally acceptable, particularly as the state of society depicted in the Homeric poems furnishes good reasons for this.[3]

The following passage from the *Iliad* illustrates the point:[a] Sarpedon, to stir Glaucus to greater activity in the battle, asks him challengingly

Glaucus, why are we two honoured most highly in Lycia with a seat of honour, with choice meats, and with full cups?

Clearly the implication is that they are not earning this honour by their present inactivity; whereas if they fight bravely and do not shirk, the Lycians will say

Not ingloriously do our kings rule throughout Lycia, and eat fat sheep, and drink choice wine. No; they have excellent strength, for they fight in the foremost ranks of the Lycians.

The kings, here Sarpedon and Glaucus, are the *aristoi*: and this commendation from their followers is justified on the assumption that they will display outstanding prowess, and achieve outstanding success, in war and in peace.[4] The Homeric king does not gain his position on the grounds of strength and fighting ability. He belongs to a royal house,[5] and inherits wealth, derived from the favoured treatment given to his ancestors, which provides full armour, a chariot, and leisure. Thus equipped, he and his fellow *agathoi*, who are similarly endowed,

[a] *Iliad* xii. 310 ff.

form the most efficient force for attack and defence which Homeric society possesses. Should they be successful, their followers have every reason to commend them as *agathoi* and their way of life as *arete*; should they fail, their followers have every reason to regard this failure, voluntary or not, as *aischron*.

The same values are of the highest importance even in peace. War must always be in the minds of citizens of a small and insecure state; and in Homeric society we have not even a state, in the sense of a general organization to protect lives and property. The chieftains must protect their own families and followers, their *oikos*;[6] and if they, being away at the Trojan war, or for any other reason, are unable to do so, someone else may move in, as do the suitors. True, Telemachus hopes that the *dēmos* may be induced to do something about the suitors, for Odysseus, as Paramount Chief of Ithaca, has been a good king to them:[7] but the *demos* does nothing, and we hear nothing of the *demos* in either poem, whether booing or cheering its leaders or being cut down in swathes by some hero engaged upon an '*aristeia*',[a] to suggest that it was capable of much.[8] An assembly of families may be held to decide questions of justice, *dikē*, between them; but none is held in the twenty years between Odysseus' departure and Telemachus' summoning of one in *Odyssey* ii: so clearly individual heads of families were for the most part concerned with settling the affairs of their own family and followers, and being strong enough to protect their own guests and possessions.

Homeric values, then, are not the result of caprice. In war, the failure of one man may well contribute to the failure of his friends: a failure which, in the Homeric world, must result either in slavery or annihilation. Success is so imperative that only results have any value: intentions are unimportant. Similarly, and for similar reasons, it is *aischron* to fail in time of peace to protect one's family and guests, whatever one's intentions. If the head of the family cannot protect them, there is no one else to do so. In the palace of Odysseus, the responsibility falls to Telemachus alone; and since for this very reason the demand that he shall discharge it successfully is categoric, no excuses can be accepted. The host must, as the case of Eumaeus shows, protect his guest against unforeseen accidents too, for if he does

---

[a] i.e. Some part of the epic devoted to the exploits of one particular hero.

not *elencheie* results: and hence neither a plea of *force majeure* nor a plea of mistake can be accepted from anyone in this position. Thus, more exacting demands are made of the head of an Homeric household (for Eumaeus too, in relation to the 'beggar', occupies this position) than of his dependents: for the latter may successfully plead *force majeure*.[a] His actions must be judged by results; for it is by results that the household continues to exist or fails to do so: and unless it or some larger community exists, the quieter virtues cannot be practised.

Thus, Homeric society does value most highly the class it needs most: men who are well-armed, strong, fleet of foot and skilled in war, counsel, and strategy. Naturally, too, it values most highly in these men just those qualities which it recognizes as being essential to the security of society. In comparison with the competitive excellences, the quieter co-operative excellences must take an inferior position; for it is not evident at this time that the security of the group depends to any large extent upon these excellences. This is the justification of these values; but the justification must not be over-emphasized. *Agathos* and *arete* also denote a social class, and there is an inevitable tendency for such words to be used solely with reference to social position, irrespective of other qualities. So the suitors remain *agathoi* generally, though they are inferior to Odysseus in the valued fighting qualities; but Odysseus, disguised as a beggar, has no chance of marrying Penelope[b] even if, by succeeding in the Test of the Bow, he shows that he possesses these qualities, for he is of the wrong social position. Despite this, however, Homeric society clearly values the men and the qualities it needs most.

This account has a bearing on later usage; values which suit one society tend to persist unchanged, or insufficiently changed, from one society to another. To observe what is wrong later, it is useful to set out the original alignment of values.

(iii) *Women's* arete *in the Homeric Poems*

The *arete* of women, not surprisingly, differs from that of men. The qualities demanded are beauty, skill in weaving and housekeeping, chastity, and faithfulness: when Agamemnon says that Penelope, in opposition to Clytemnestra, has great *arete*, he is commending Penelope for not marrying one of the suitors

[a] p. 10.   [b] *Odyssey* xxi. 314 ff.

and murdering Odysseus.[a] For women, then, *arete* commends the quiet virtues; and *kakos* is naturally used to denigrate those women who are not quietly virtuous:[b] a usage which is impossible when male *arete* is in question.[9] The reason is twofold. Firstly, it is men who determine the nature of *arete* both for men and for women; and clearly it would be easier to live with a Penelope than with a woman manifesting the *aretai* of a Homeric hero. Secondly, a woman within a Homeric household, not being called upon to defend it herself, has not the same need of the competitive excellences; and thus *arete* may be used to commend the co-operative virtues. As a result, Homeric women may be effectively censured for actions which Homeric heroes have a strong claim to be allowed to perform.[c]

(iv) Arete *and the Co-operative Excellences*

It has already been shown that it is unnecessary for men to possess any of the quiet virtues in order to be *agathos*: the *agathos* need not be *pinutos, pepnūmenos, saophrōn,* or *dikaios*.[d] Thus far, however, it has merely been asserted that *agathos* is the most powerful term of value in Greek. That the assertion is true is easy to demonstrate. When Agamemnon, who is *agathos* par excellence, as the commander-in-chief of all the Greek troops, wishes to deprive Achilles of his prize, the slave girl Briseis, Nestor adjures him[e]

Do not, *agathos* though you be, take the girl from him.

That is to say, an *agathos* might well do this without ceasing to be an *agathos*, and indeed derives a claim to do it from the fact that he is an *agathos*; but in this case Nestor is begging Agamemnon not to do it. We may compare Nestor's parallel appeal to Achilles a few lines later:

Do not desire to strive with a king, Achilles; for a sceptre-bearing king, to whom Zeus has given glory, has no common share of honour.

This is the converse: *though* Agamemnon is *agathos*, let him refrain; *since* Agamemnon is a sceptre-bearing king, let Achilles refrain from opposing his desires. In *Iliad* i, again, Agamemnon[f]

---

[a] *Odyssey* xxiv. 193.   [b] *Odyssey* xi. 384.   [c] Cp. pp. 44 f.

[d] *Saophron* and *saophrosunē* are the Homeric forms of the words which will appear later as *sōphrōn* and *sōphrosunē*. The use of the words mentioned in the text is explained in Chapter IV, pp. 61 ff.

[e] *Iliad* i. 275 ff.   [f] *Iliad* i. 131 f.

complains of Achilles' claims *qua* warrior, and hence *agathos*. But he can only complain: he has no higher standards to which he can appeal.

The gods, not surprisingly, are believed to endorse this code of values. When Achilles drags Hector's body round the walls of Troy, Apollo says that Achilles should not act in this manner[a]

Lest, *agathos* though he be, we gods should be angry with him.

The gods do not approve of Achilles' action: but clearly the fact that he is *agathos* gives him a strong claim against gods and men to be allowed to do it.[10] Again, in the *Odyssey*,[b] Nestor, realizing that the stranger who accompanied Telemachus to his court was in fact the goddess Athena, says that he does not expect that Telemachus will prove *kakos* or *analkis* if, though he is still a young man, he already has gods for his companions. The gods too acknowledge the claims of the *agathos*, the man who is not *analkis*, without valour. This claim is not merely that of one class against another. To say that a man is *agathos* is not merely to call him a chieftain, but to apply to him the most powerful term of value, a term which, as has been seen, carries many overtones and implications. These passages show that neither *pinutos* nor any other 'quiet' term can successfully be opposed to *agathos*. Nestor wants to restrain Agamemnon from behaving as he does; Apollo and the other gods would like to pass effective censure upon Achilles. Were there any word of censure strong enough to override the claims of the *agathos* to do as he pleases, they would surely have used it. But there is no such word: society's need of the *agathos* is too strong.

(v) *Persuasive Definitions in Homer*

What has been said so far is generally true of Homeric values. The Homeric poems, however, contain a wide variety of material and portray a wide variety of characters, frequently in conditions of great stress. It would be very strange if none of these characters at any time ventured on a 'persuasive definition'[c] and attempted to alter the normal usage of Homeric terms of value in his own interest.

Three passages are worth considering here. When, in *Odyssey*

---

[a] *Iliad* xxiv. 53.   [b] *Odyssey* iii. 375 f.
[c] Cp. for this phrase C. L. Stevenson in *Mind*, 1938, pp. 331 ff., where its usage is explained at length.

xxi, Eurymachus expresses the shame which all the suitors feel at being unable to draw Odysseus' bow, Penelope immediately replies[a]

Eurymachus, it is impossible for men to be well spoken of, *euklees*, who dishonour the house of a chieftain and devour his possessions. Why regard your failures as *elenchea*?

Evidently Penelope wishes by implication to term the suitors' breach of the quiet virtues *elenchos*, and indeed more of an *elenchos* than to fail in drawing the bow: a use of words which I have said to be impossible. In fact, neither *euklees* nor *elenchos* is so used anywhere else in the Homeric poems; and the situation explains their use here. Penelope is at the end of her tether; and in these circumstances she (or rather the poet) attempts a new use of language, a 'persuasive definition', which, if accepted, would effectively restrain the suitors. The definition cannot succeed. Eurymachus could well reply, relying both on 'ordinary language' and on the facts of Homeric life, 'Certainly it is possible for us to enjoy a fair reputation if we behave in this manner and *succeed*; and we call our failures *elenchea* because they are *elenchea*'. No matter what his character, estimated in terms of the quieter virtues, any Homeric hero would answer in these terms. Hence any such persuasive definition must fail, as it fails here, to affect the action of an *agathos*: for in performing an action in which he remains *agathos* he cannot incur *elencheie*.

Earlier, Penelope had tried a different approach,[b] saying to Antinous, one of the foremost suitors, that though he is reputed to be *aristos* in counsel, he has shown by his actions that he is not so. The situation here is more complicated. The rebuke is addressed solely to Antinous, whose family is under a hereditary obligation to the house of Odysseus; and at all times it is held that a man should reciprocate favours received.[11] Such a rebuke is nowhere addressed to the other suitors; and the implication is that in their case such a rebuke is impossible. Even here, Penelope can only term the ignoring of this obligation 'impious':[c] she cannot term it *aischron*, which would be stronger. It is for the gods to punish the impious: and even the gods, as has been shown,[d] may be puzzled by the claim of the *agathos* to do

[a] *Odyssey* xxi. 331 ff.   [b] *Odyssey* xvi. 418 ff.
[c] οὐδ' ὁσίη.   [d] p. 38.

as he pleases. Penelope, however, claims that Antinous is failing to show himself to be *aristos*: not *aristos tout court*, however, but *aristos* in counsel. This too is clearly a persuasive definition: to be *aristos* in counsel is normally to be most capable of planning one's own success and that of one's friends in peace or war. It is, however, a more promising persuasive definition than the former one: as later chapters will show, to demonstrate that action in accordance with the quiet virtues is the mark of the truly intelligent man is the best way of inserting these into traditional *arete*. Unfortunately, such a demonstration is far beyond the abilities of Homeric society; and unless Antinous manifestly *fails*, he will not regard himself as lacking in intelligence. This persuasive definition, too, must be unsuccessful in the circumstances.

Another persuasive definition occurs in *Iliad* ix.[a] Achilles, reflecting on the enormity of Agamemnon's depriving him of Briseis, maintains that any man who is *agathos* and prudent[b] loves and cherishes his own wife and does not lust after other women. This claim bears no relation to Homeric (or later Greek) male *arete*, which is not concerned with chastity at all. Achilles, or anyone else in his position, has clearly an interest in changing the normal use of language; but no successful *agathos* is likely to agree. Homeric society is unable to coerce a man in Agamemnon's position, and there are no religious scruples in favour of chastity; accordingly, neither in this case nor generally has this definition any more chance of success than the others. In fact, in considering the effect of Homeric values on ascriptions of moral responsibility, we need discuss only the normal pattern of those values.

C. OTHER TERMS OF VALUE

The competitive system of values, then, must always in the last resort override the co-operative in Homer, for very good reasons. The results of this situation will be discussed below. Other terms of value, however, seem to offer more hope to the concept of moral responsibility; and though such passages as have already been discussed make it clear that this hope must be illusory, the other terms deserve consideration.

[a] *Iliad* ix. 341 f.　　　　　　　　　　　　[b] ἐχέφρων.

The noun *aischos*, the adjective *aeikelios*, the adverb *aeikeliōs* and similar words are used occasionally in contexts where a modern reader expects some word to decry breaches of the co-operative virtues. Two passages of the *Odyssey* in particular illustrate these usages. Telemachus says[a] that it would be better for him to die than

Ever see deeds which are *aeikea*, strangers being maltreated and men dragging the serving-women *aeikeliōs* through the palace.

Again, in *Odyssey* i[b] the disguised Athena complains of the behaviour of the suitors, and says that any man who was prudent, *pinutos*, would be angry at seeing many *aischea*.

Here, we might suppose, *aeikea*, *aeikeliōs*, and *aischea* are instances of words related apparently (from their kinship with *aischron* and similar words) to the most powerful system of values, but nevertheless used in 'quiet' contexts. The use of these words, however, requires further examination; for the fact that it seems possible to replace them here by 'wrongful', 'wrong-fully', and 'wrongs' proves nothing. The exact flavour is only indicated when the full range of these terms is considered.

Aeikeliōs evidently does not correspond to 'wrongfully': that is to say, since the term is used to bring discredit upon someone, it is not the suitors who are discredited here. Neither *aeikelios* nor *aeikeliōs* is used on any occasion to decry breaches of the co-operative virtues. When Odysseus says that he fears that the Phaeacian youth may defeat him at running,[c] since he has been weakened *aeikeliōs* by his privations at sea, he is using the word as it is normally used.[d] To find oneself in a condition which can be characterized as *aeikelios*, or to undergo experiences which are *aeikelia*, is to be situated as an *agathos* may not be situated and remain fully *agathos*. That is to say, it is to have one's military or social success, one's reputation for that success, or one's physical prowess, impaired in some manner; and the discussion of *arete* has made it clear that to be in such a condition in Homeric society is a reproach to oneself alone, save when one is the dependent of another. In these circumstances, the master of the house should not allow his dependent to come into such a condition. Accordingly, the condition of his serving-maids is

---

[a] *Odyssey* xvi. 108 ff. [b] *Odyssey* i. 228 f. [c] *Odyssey* viii. 231.
[d] Cp. *Odyssey* iv. 244, vi. 242, ix. 503, xiv. 32, xvii. 357, &c.

a reproach to Telemachus too: for though they could not, *qua* serving-maids, be *agathai*, they need not be thus mishandled. The effect of *aeikeliōs*, then, is to draw attention to the pitiable condition of the serving-maids, a condition into which, however, it is not *aischron* for the suitors to bring them. Similarly, when Penelope chides Telemachus[a] for allowing the 'beggar' to be thus maltreated, *aeikisthēmenai*, both the situation and the rebuke are the same. The 'beggar' and Telemachus are each discredited, for each has in his own way fallen short of *arete*. The suitors are not reproached at all: to do *kaka*, to do harm, is not to be *kakos*; to be *kakos* is to be the sort of person to whom *kaka* may be done with impunity, since he cannot defend himself: and it is this condition which is *aischron*.

Aischos and *aischea* behave in a similar manner. Both may normally be rendered 'insults', provided that it is remembered that it is only *aischron* to receive insults, not to deliver them.[12] Accordingly, in the passage from *Odyssey* i quoted above, Telemachus, not the suitors, should feel ashamed, for it is he whose condition is *aischron*. Any feeling of quiet values derives from the fact that, as is said, a *pinutos*, a prudent man, should feel anger, *nemesis*, at the sight: just as when Menelaus in the *Iliad*,[b] referring to Paris' abduction of Helen, says that the Trojans have no lack of insult and *aischos* to heap upon him, the feeling of quiet values is derived from Menelaus' threat in the following lines that Zeus Xeinios will avenge the *aischos*. In itself the *aischos* is shameful to Menelaus alone. The *nemesis* of the *pinutos* will be discussed below; here it suffices to show that *aischea* are in no sense 'wrongs'.

Other terms, however, are less clear than those already discussed. The word *aeikēs*, for example, is certainly used on many occasions to decry military and social failure. Anyone defeated and killed in Homer may be said to have met an end which is *aeikes*;[c] and here naturally it is the vanquished, not the victor, who is discredited.[d] No judgement in terms of quiet values is thereby passed upon anyone. Similarly, Andromache laments that her son Astyanax will fall into slavery and be forced to perform actions, *erga*, which are *aeikea*: menial tasks

---

[a] *Odyssey* xviii. 222.   [b] *Iliad* xiii. 623.
[c] ἀεικέα πότμον ἔπεσπον.
[d] Cp. *Odyssey* ii. 250, iv. 339 f., *Iliad* iv. 396, &c.

such as the *agathos*, in virtue of his social position, need never perform. Thus far *aeikes* conforms to the usage of *arete* and *agathos*; and that Clytemnestra's adultery, and her murder of Agamemnon, should also be spoken of as an *ergon aeikes* is not surprising, since it has already been shown that such actions detract from a woman's *arete*. We have no reason to suppose that men's actions will be similarly treated. Yet it is said of Aegisthus that he plotted *aeikea* against Agamemnon;[a] Penelope, complaining of the behaviour of the suitors in the palace of Odysseus, refers to their *aeikea erga*;[b] and Achilles intended *aeikea erga* to the corpse of Hector, when he proposed to drag it about the walls of Troy.[c] It is difficult to interpret these passages on the analogy of *aeikeliōs* and *aischea*, to maintain, that is, that these *aeikea erga* are discreditable to the person who suffers them and to him alone. In all cases where *ergon aeikes* refers to a defeat, military or social, it is the person who 'performed' the *ergon aeikes* who is discredited;[d] and it is unreasonable to expect a different idiom in these passages.

Here then, it seems, we have a term of value which, unlike those so far considered, spans both co-operative and competitive excellences. There are other terms whose behaviour is similar, notably the group of words related to *aidōs*, shame. When Hera shouts to the Greeks[e]

Aidos, for shame! base *elenchea*!

the *aidos* is closely related to defeat and *elenchos*. But it may be said of the suitors that they have no share of *aidos*;[f] Agamemnon in his relations with Achilles displays shamelessness, *anaideiē*,[g] and the suitors in their dealings with the household of Odysseus are regularly said to be shameless, *anaideis*;[h] while Diomedes[i] and Telemachus,[j] as a result of the *aidos* which they feel before their elders and betters, may well fail to act as is best to secure perfectly justified ends: and here *aidos* evidently approximates to 'bashfulness'.

Kalon, too, deserves consideration. On two occasions we find[k]

---

[a] *Odyssey* iv. 533.   [b] *Odyssey* iv. 694 f.   [c] *Iliad* xxii. 395, xxiii. 24.
[d] *Iliad* xiv. 13, xix. 132 f., xxiv. 733, and cp. *Odyssey* xxii. 432 and xx. 394, which do not refer to defeat.
[e] *Iliad* v. 787.   [f] *Odyssey* xx. 171.   [g] *Iliad* i. 149.
[h] *Odyssey* i. 254, xiii. 376, &c.   [i] *Iliad* x. 238.
[j] *Odyssey* iii. 24.   [k] *Odyssey* xx. 294 f., xxi. 312 f.

It is not *kalon* or just, *dikaion*, to maltreat any of Telemachus' guests.

Further, when Antinous is discourteous to Odysseus the 'beggar', Eumaeus says[a]

Antinous, *esthlos* though you are, your words are not *kala*.

Again, Odysseus in Phaeacia, replying to Euryalus who has taunted him, says[b]

Stranger, what you say is not *kalon*: you seem to be a presumptuous man.

He contrasts Euryalus with the man who has gentle *aidos*. In the *Iliad* Achilles says to Phoenix, his companion,[c]

It is *kalon* to join me in troubling anyone who troubles me.

Agamemnon, in the Assembly of *Iliad* xix, says, appealing for fair treatment,[d]

It is *kalon* to listen to a man who is standing up to speak, and unseemly to interrupt him.

Such usages seem very hopeful. Strictly, *kalon* is the contrary of *aischron*, and hence should be very powerful: and if the period discussed in the present work is considered as a whole, the coupling of *kalon* and *dikaion* must seem very 'advanced', for it is precisely this coupling which is found, centuries later, in the 'moralizers' of fifth-century Athens. Unfortunately, closer examination belies this hope. *Kalon* does not behave as the contrary of *aischron* in Homer: it is not used to glorify victory as *aischron* is used to decry defeat. Such functions are discharged by other words;[e] and accordingly *kalon* has *in Homer* no real link with the competitive excellences, from which alone it could draw real power.[13] Its real weakness is seen in the speech of Eumaeus, quoted above. Eumaeus can maintain that Antinous has said words which are not seemly, *ou kala*, but he cannot say that Antinous becomes *kakos* or not *esthlos* as a result: for being *agathos* or *esthlos*, as has been shown, is not affected by such considerations. Antinous remains *agathos*: his *arete* is unsmirched by his ill-mannered behaviour. Had it been possible successfully to use *ou kalon* to oppose the claims of the *agathos* to do as he pleases, Nestor would have said that Agamemnon's robbing Achilles of Briseis was *ou kalon*, and Apollo would have claimed

a *Odyssey* xvii. 381.   b *Odyssey* viii. 166.   c *Iliad* ix. 615.
d *Iliad* xix. 79.   e κλέος, κῦδος, &c.

the same of Achilles' maltreatment of Hector. Evidently it is not possible. *Ou kalon*, then, in Homer, since it is not used to decry failure, is not an equivalent of *aischron* either in usage or in emotive power. *Ou kalon* is opposed to *agathos* in 'quiet' contexts, but is not strong enough to override it: *aischron* would be strong enough to override it, but is not so used. In order to restrain the claims of the *agathos* to do as he pleases, it would be necessary to say[a]

This is *aischron* even for future generations to hear of

with reference to breaches of the quiet virtues: and this cannot be said. The demands of success are too strong in the case of men. It can be said of Clytemnestra that she[b]

Brought *aischos* upon women even of future generations,[c] even those who are virtuous.

It can be said, for, as a result of the nature of women's *arete*, Clytemnestra has shown herself to be *kakē* by her actions. Similar condemnation of Agamemnon and the suitors is not found, and, persuasive definitions apart, cannot be expected; for no matter what their breaches of the quiet virtues, men remain *agathoi*; and to be *agathos* cannot be *aischron*, nor involve a man in *aischos*.

This use of *kalon*, then, can have little effect in the last resort. There remain *aidos* and *aeikes*: but the effect of these upon the concept of moral responsibility must be small. True, they span both competitive and co-operative excellences: but this is only one condition of usefulness. They must also be key terms of value: and this they are not. *Aischron, agathos, arete, kakos,* and *elencheie* are, for excellent reasons, the key terms of value; and though a word which spans both groups of excellences will have the emotive power of the key terms of value when it is associated with them, it must have a very much reduced emotive power when it is associated with terms which commend the co-operative excellences. The *aidos* which the Greeks should feel at defeat[d] is powerful, for it is associated with a condition of *elencheie*: but the *aidos* which might have restrained the suitors would have been a much weaker emotion, for should they be *anaideis*, in the sense of 'not *pinutoi*', and successful, they run no

---

[a] *Iliad* ii. 119.
[c] Reading ἐσσομένῃσι.
[b] *Odyssey* xi. 433.
[d] p. 43.

risk of *elencheie*. The distaste felt by a man for *aeikea erga*, too, must vary according to the applicability of the key terms. Naturally, to say that this distaste, this *aidos*, is weaker when the quiet virtues are in question is not to say that it does not exist; and it must be such *aidos* which holds Homeric society together, in so far as it is held together, for a society of *agathoi* with no quiet virtues at all would simply destroy itself. But, as will be evident when Agamemnon's 'apology' is considered below, as soon as a crisis forces the essential framework of values into view, the competitive values are so much more powerful than the co-operative that the situation is not treated in terms of the quiet values at all; and as it is precisely with such crises that the concept of moral responsibility is concerned, it is evident that such terms as *aidos* and *aeikes*, however useful to society in general, cannot affect the development of the concept of moral responsibility, for they are ineffective at the crucial moment. Accordingly, in future chapters it will be unnecessary to discuss these terms, for their value in commending quiet moral excellences is precisely that of the words which specifically commend those excellences. It will be sufficient to discuss the history of the specific terms, *dikaios*, *saophron*, &c., in relation to the key terms of value.

D. THE RESULTS

(i) *The Claims of Society*

The nature of the Homeric system of values is now clear. It is a system based on the competitive standard of *arete*, a standard which, while not involving the co-operative excellences at all, gives society a strong claim against the *agathos*, but the *agathos* an equally strong claim against society. Both of these claims affect the concept of moral responsibility, as does the sanction which maintains the system. These topics may conveniently be discussed separately.

The effects of society's claim against the *agathos* require little illustration. We have already seen[a] that *arete* is used to commend skills, physical gifts, or inherited social advantages. None of these can be attained merely by good intentions; indeed,

---

[a] pp. 31 ff.

intentions are almost irrelevant. To a modern reader courage might appear to differ from the other qualities commended in being more dependent upon the will; but it is *aischron* to fail, in war or in peace, whatever one's intentions.

Two examples in which moral error is contrasted with mistake or incapacity will serve to illustrate this. In *Iliad* vi Hector rebukes Paris on finding that he is not on the field of battle:[a]

No right-thinking man would pour scorn upon your deeds of war, for you are *alkimos*. But you shirk *hekon*, of your own accord, and are unwilling to fight: and my heart is grieved when I hear *aischea*, insults, against you in the mouths of the Trojans.

Paris is *alkimos*; a word which naturally spans both courage and the physical endowments necessary to a Homeric warrior, since this system of values allows no distinction between the two: so when Hector points out that it is *aischron* (or that he has been hearing *aischea* about it) for Paris to shirk fighting in a war of which he is the occasion, the rebuke stirs him on. But if Paris were not *alkimos*, then anyone might 'pour scorn upon his deeds of war': it would still be *aischron* for him not to be a successful warrior, even if physical disability prevented him from fighting. However good his intentions, he would be *kakos*, *analkis*, no use for protecting society.

We may compare two similar speeches uttered by Hector. When Andromache urges him to remain in safety within the walls of Troy, he replies:[b]

I feel shame, *aideomai*, before the Trojans, both men and women, if like a *kakos* I skulk away from the war.

Later, when Hector discovers that by leading the Trojan army into the field he has exposed it to needless danger, he says:[c]

But now, since I have ruined the people by my folly, I feel shame, *aideomai*, before the Trojans, both men and women, lest some day some base fellow (someone more *kakos* than I) may say 'Hector by trusting in his might has ruined the people'.

He concludes that as a result of this,

Polydamas will be the first to bring *elencheie* upon me.

In the first of these passages, Hector rejects the suggestion that he should behave in a cowardly manner; in the second, he

---

[a] *Iliad* vi. 521 ff.   [b] *Iliad* vi. 442 ff.   [c] *Iliad* xxii. 104 ff.

has made a mistake, perhaps as a result of overconfidence, but a mistake for all that, not a moral error. So we should distinguish; yet these situations are treated in precisely the same manner. In both cases, Hector feels *aidos* before the Trojans; *aidos* in the highest degree, since it is associated with defeat:[a] from which it is apparent that when *arete* is in question, results are so important that intentions are not considered at all.

(ii) *The* Agathos *and the Sanction of Homeric Society*

We may now turn to consider the sanction employed by Homeric society to ensure that its *agathoi* display *arete*, and its effects on the ascription of responsibility; for though success is *per se* desirable for the *agathos*, it is inconceivable that any society should take no steps to ensure that its highest standards of behaviour are maintained.

This sanction is overtly 'what people will say', as is made quite clear when the suitors protest that the disguised Odysseus must not be allowed to attempt to draw the bow which they have failed to draw. Eurymachus does not fear that, even should the 'beggar' succeed, Penelope will marry him:[b]

No; we feel shame at what men and women will say—lest at some time some base fellow from among the Greeks should say: 'Surely very inferior men are wooing the wife of an excellent man, for they cannot draw the bow; and yet some wandering beggar has come and drawn the bow with ease and shot through the line of axes.' So they will say: and these things would become *elenchea* for us.

What people will say, the *dēmou phatis*, is recognized to be the most important standard. Public opinion will mock the suitors' failure in itself, but it will also mock them if, *agathoi*, rich and powerful warriors, as they are, they are worsted by a beggar, a *kakos* or *deilos*. The standard is the same for women, though naturally different actions are expected and different actions reprehended.[c] For both men and women it is not what has been done that matters, but what people say has been done. So when Zeus terrifies Diomedes' horses with a flash of lightning,[d] Nestor, who is acting as his charioteer, immediately counsels retreat. Diomedes replies that if he retreats Hector will be able to say that Diomedes once gave ground before him. Nestor reassures

---

a Cp. p. 45.   b *Odyssey* xxi. 323 ff.
c Cp. Nausicaa, *Odyssey* vi. 255 ff.   d *Iliad* viii. 147 ff.

him: 'What a thing to say. Even if Hector does call you *kakos* and *analkis*, the Trojans and their wives whose husbands you have slain will never believe it.' Nestor cannot say, 'Don't worry. It isn't true.' If the Trojans did believe it, Diomedes would incur *elencheie*, and there is nothing more important than this: he would feel terrible *aidos* were such a thing to happen.

Here too it is evident that facts are of much less importance than appearances, and hence that intentions are of much less importance than results. The Homeric hero cannot fall back upon his own opinion of himself, for his self only has the value which other people put upon it. Diomedes' bravery is worth nothing unless his fellows believe him to be brave; and what other people believe about his actions is quite independent of his own intentions, and may be quite at variance with them.

Thus the neglect of intentions which is necessitated in certain important circumstances by the state of Homeric society is reinforced by that society's standard of values. It is not necessary to suppose, however, that the state of society created that scheme of values which constitutes a shame-culture.[14] A feeling of pain and anger is the natural response to failure, whether or no anything of importance hangs on that failure. So *elencheie* results from failure in the games not because the games are a training for war, but because the hero feels shame at failure *per se*, and other people will mock it *per se*. Even in a society which is able to distinguish clearly in theory between moral error and failure, the feeling of shame plays its part in confusing the distinction in practice, when emotions are sufficiently aroused. There is no reason to explain the existence of this system of values, for it springs from what is primitive and primary: it would be better to say that society is not yet sufficiently well organized to allow the reflection (or coercion) which might produce a different system.

(iii) *The Claims of the* Agathos

Society's claims against the *agathos*, then, and the sanction employed to enforce them, both entail that intentions are widely ignored, with the result that moral error and mistake cannot be distinguished. The *agathos*, however, has himself the strongest of claims against society;[15] and this too affects ascriptions of responsibility. To complete this chapter, we may consider a number of situations in which the claims of the *agathos* and the nature of his society produce results which to the modern reader must appear highly unusual.

If the *agathos* chooses to make use of his advantage, his fellows may grow angry with him, and attempt to restrain him by force; but if for any reason they are unable to do this, his claim to act as he pleases in respect of the co-operative excellences is stronger than any claim they can bring against him;[16] and if he feels that any thwarting of his desires would be failure, the *aidos* which he feels at not being *agathos* must be stronger than the *aidos* which he feels at not being *pinutos*.

Agamemnon chooses to push his claim to the hilt against Achilles. He fails, and is finally convinced that he was in some sense 'wrong' to deprive Achilles of Briseis. The passage must be considered in some detail, since it shows the manner in which responsibility is felt in the most powerful group of values. Agamemnon says:[a]

Often indeed did the Greeks tell me this, and abused me.[17] But I am not the cause, *aitios*, of this. No; Zeus and *moira* and the Fury who walks in darkness are the cause; for they put fierce blindness, *átē*, into my mind in the assembly on that day when I deprived Achilles of his prize. But what could I do? The god brings all things to pass.

He goes on to say that *Ate* (personified) can blind anyone; that once she even blinded Zeus, and was cast out of heaven for it. After a long digression on this subject, he continues:

So I too, since mighty Hector has been killing Greeks by the sterns of the ships, am unable to forget the blindness by which I was first blinded. But since I was blinded and Zeus took away my wits, I am willing to make amends, and give abundant recompense.

The sense in which Agamemnon believes he was 'wrong' appears from the second passage. *Since* Hector is now killing Greeks by the Greek ships, Agamemnon cannot forget the blindness (or the goddess) by which he was first blinded. That is to say, it is blindness, *ate*, to dishonour the man who is *aristos*, because one will probably feel the lack of him if he sulks in his tent; and only if one does feel the lack will one consider it to be *ate*. Agamemnon, under the influence of anger, has made a mistake; he is

---

[a] *Iliad* xix. 85 ff. and 134 ff., cp. viii. 237.

'wrong' in the sense that he has miscalculated the effect of the loss of Achilles. We have only to compare the parallel which he draws with Zeus to realize that this is the light in which Agamemnon sees it. Zeus too was blinded by *ate*; but it was not a moral blindness. *Ate* simply saw to it that Hera's deception of Zeus was successful: the function is that of Sleep in *Iliad* xiv. Zeus promised Hera that the man born of his blood that day should rule—meaning Heracles. Hera saw to it that the birth of Heracles was delayed, and that of Eurystheus, a child equally of Zeus' blood, advanced; and the promise was fulfilled in the person of Eurystheus. Zeus made a mistake: if there was a moral error, it was Hera's.

Thus *ate* too spans mistake and moral error: like Hector above,[a] Agamemnon does not distinguish the two. The reason is clear. Both in his relations with Achilles and as leader of the Greeks against the Trojans, Agamemnon is regarded by himself and his followers as *agathos*. *Qua* more powerful chieftain (and hence *ameinon* in a sense, though Achilles attempts to use *agathos* differently[b]) he has a claim to take Briseis if he will; *qua* leader of the Greeks, he must maintain himself as an *agathos*, and not fall into *elencheie*, as would be the case should the Greeks fail to take Troy. The one is permitted, the other demanded, by this competitive system of values. Agamemnon believed these two purposes to be compatible: having discovered this to be false, he relinquishes the minor purpose in order to achieve the major, and *acknowledges that he has made a mistake*. The fact that Agamemnon has incurred social disapproval for his failure gives the transaction an appearance of 'quiet' morality which it does not possess. The only aspect of *arete* in which Agamemnon has fallen short is success in war: the quieter virtues are so much less important that Agamemnon does not see the transaction in this light at all. In these circumstances, to plead *ate* cannot be an attempt to evade responsibility for one's actions,[18] even if one says roundly 'I am not *aitios*', and maintains that no fewer than three gods were the cause: an assertion which may imply that the mistake is a curious one,[19] and one which the agent feels he would not 'normally' have made, but which does not make

---

[a] p. 47.
[b] *Iliad* i. 244. Achilles claims to be *aristos* of the Greeks on the basis of his prowess as a warrior.

the mistake anything other than a mistake. The reason is twofold. Firstly, it has been shown that only in special cases, of
which this is not one, may responsibility be laid upon a god.
These cases are 'literary'; and here we have not 'Literature',
but 'Life', for Zeus, *moira*, and the Fury were not represented as
deceiving Agamemnon in *Iliad* i. Agamemnon is thus speaking
as men in Homeric society must have spoken in life, not making a
statement which only the poet, from his position of omniscience,
can know to be true. Secondly, since Agamemnon regards his
action as a mistake, the sense of 'responsibility' is peculiar: in this
sense responsibility is not moral, but cannot be avoided. No man
can expect to evade the consequences of his mistakes: a man
is very fortunate if he is able to rectify them. Thus Agamemnon
'must' recompense Achilles to rectify his mistake and bring
Achilles once again into the fighting: he has no alternative.

Such are the implications of the competitive scheme of values.
Moral responsibility has no place in them; and the quieter
virtues, in which such responsibility has its place, neither have
sufficient attraction to gain a hearing nor are backed by sufficient force to compel one. In some cases the gods guarantee the
quieter values; but this aspect of Homeric belief must be left
till the next chapter. On the human level, chieftains can settle
disputes among their own followers, their position being strong
enough to enable them to do it; but disputes between chieftains
of equal power, if they are sufficiently angry to refuse arbitra-
tion, as, given their competitive scheme of values, they are only
too likely to do, cannot be settled easily.[20] The organization to
coerce them does not exist: and since any concession might be
regarded by public opinion as a sign of failure or weakness, and
failure is *aischron*, than which nothing is worse, there is always
the danger that such a situation as arose between Agamemnon
and Achilles will occur again.

This point will become clearer if the manner in which this
society treated homicide is considered. The Homeric poems
provide a full and varied selection of cases of homicide, of which
those of Theoclymenus, Patroclus, the attempted murder of
Telemachus, and Odysseus' killing of Antinous are the most
interesting.

Theoclymenus introduces himself to Telemachus thus:[a]

a *Odyssey* xv. 272 ff.

I too have fled from my native land, for I have killed a man of
my own tribe.[a] There are many kinsmen of the dead man[b] in
Argos, and they hold sway over the Greeks. I am running away,
fleeing from black death at their hands, since it is now my lot to
wander among men.

We may presume that the homicide was intentional: at all
events, Theoclymenus does not deny it. Patroclus' ghost, however, recalls a different kind of homicide. He reminds Achilles of
the day[c] when Menoetius brought him from his home

When I killed the son of Amphidamas—child as I was, and not
intending to kill—in anger over a game of dice.

Patroclus was a child, he did not mean to kill, he acted in
anger: any punishment which fell to him would *a fortiori* fall to
an adult who killed in anger. Again, when Odysseus shoots down
Antinous, the suitors, until he discloses his identity, are under
the impression that the supposed beggar has killed accidentally;[d]
and yet they threaten him with instant death.

Theoclymenus was probably a wilful murderer. Patroclus was
a child, and acted without premeditation, in anger, with some
provocation. Odysseus is believed to have killed by accident.
Yet clearly the penalty for each is the same: unless the killer
takes himself, or is taken, out of reach of the offended parties,
whether relatives or, as seems to be the case in the last example,
some other body of people with whom the dead man is associated, he will be killed in his turn.

With this may be compared the advice of Antinous to the
suitors when Telemachus evades their ambush. They should kill
him before he reaches the city, lest he call an assembly;[e] for, if
Telemachus is not prevented from speaking, the suitors may be
driven from their homes. Presumably if they did not go, they
would suffer the same fate as a murderer. This is an extreme
case of *nemesis*, social disapproval, which would naturally manifest itself in hostile action, not merely in words. Hence as
regards punishment no distinction is drawn between deliberate
homicide, homicide with provocation or without premeditation, accidental homicide, and (possibly) attempted homicide.[21]

The reason is clear. The society of the Homeric poems,

---

[a] ἄνδρα κατακτὰς ἔμφυλον.   [b] κασίγνητοί τε ἔται τε.
[c] *Iliad* xxiii. 85 ff.   [d] *Odyssey* xxii. 27 ff.   [e] *Odyssey* xvi. 380 ff.

however much the author may imply that the manner of living of the Cyclopes is old-fashioned, inasmuch as each administers justice to his own children and dependents and has nothing to do with his neighbours, is in feeling and in its terms of value, which help to maintain the *status quo*, still much more an agglomeration of individual 'Cyclopean' households than an integrated society.[22] The assembly, when it is summoned, may decide ordinary matters of justice, *dike*, between households. Homicide, however, is too great a strain: society, as we see it in the poems generally, is not strong enough to control the emotional stresses of such an act. Accordingly, punishment is left to the individual families, who slay the slayer, if he is not quick enough to escape, or ensure that he is driven from his patrimony. It is not a question of war between the two families: his own household gives no help to the murderer. Given anger uncontrolled by a court of law, combined with the fact that it is *aischron* that a member of one's family should be killed without requital and that intentions are generally irrelevant, it is difficult to see how a graduated system of punishments could have been devised; and the Homeric practice does at least prevent the outbreak of vendetta between the families.

'Pollution', so important later, plays no active part in the beliefs of Homeric man. Theoclymenus has killed a man of his own tribe; yet Telemachus, in sharp contrast to fifth-century Greek practice, takes him on board ship without a qualm; and it is the custom that exiled murderers should take refuge at another king's court, where they are welcomed.[23] There is no supernatural danger in consorting with a murderer.

Odysseus' treatment of the suitors betrays a similar attitude. Having slain Antinous, he reveals himself and says:[a]

Dogs, you did not think that I would return home from Troy; for you have consumed my possessions, lain with my maidservants by force, and wooed my wife while I was yet alive, fearing neither the gods who inhabit broad heaven, nor yet that there would be any retribution from men hereafter: but now the doom of death is upon you all.

The chief crime of the suitors is that they have disregarded Telemachus and ravaged Odysseus' possessions.[24] This they have done deliberately, and the act constitutes a declaration of

---

[a] *Odyssey* xxii. 35 ff.

war on the house of Odysseus. Homer says of them that they have staked their heads on the success of the venture: a phrase which he uses elsewhere of pirates.[a] The suitors can make no attempt to justify themselves on this count. Eurymachus[b] attempts to lay all the blame on the dead Antinous; but that there is blame cannot be denied. Odysseus, however, also charged the suitors with having wooed Penelope while he was still alive; but, though none of them supposed that he was still alive, none of the suitors attempts to say 'We didn't know.' They have wooed a woman whose husband is in fact alive; and unless they can buy him off, as Eurymachus tries to do, or are strong enough to prevent it, he will kill them.[c]

The reasons are clear: anger, the shame of letting such an insult go unavenged (for unless Odysseus does something heroic, the situation is comic: and where the standard of a man's worth is public opinion, no man can afford to be mocked), and the fact that one must protect one's own property or perish oneself. This is a hard society: it can rarely spare a thought for intentions.

Homeric values, however, suit Homeric society, inasmuch as they commend those qualities which most evidently secure its existence. Life is a matter of skill and courage; hence skill and courage are most highly commended. Wrong-doing is not admired by those who suffer from it; but right-doing, 'quiet' virtue, is less highly admired by society as a whole than skill and courage, for the latter are more evidently needed. That the organization of society, its values, and the sanction by which those values are sustained all lead to the ignoring of intention is unfortunate, but of less importance than the possible inability of the basic social unit, the household, to hold its own against other such units; and accordingly the problems are not keenly felt. Systems of values, however, persist while societies develop; and the Homeric system conflicts violently with any form of society which attempts to allot reward or punishment to an action simply on the basis of the characteristics of that action, irrespective of any other claims to consideration the agent may possess. The persistence of the one system is certain to confuse any attempt to introduce the other.

---

[a] *Odyssey* ii. 237, iii. 74.
[b] *Odyssey* xxii. 48 ff. In ii. 182, Eurymachus clearly believed Odysseus to be dead.
[c] Cp. Menelaus' comment, *Odyssey* iv. 333 ff.

Signs of such confusion existing already in Homer may be seen in the chariot race of *Iliad* xxiii. We regard a race as a trial of prowess on a particular day. Whether or no the best man wins, the winner deserves the first prize, the second the second prize, and so on; but when Eumelus comes in last, Diomedes, who won, is given the first prize, but Achilles proposes to give the second prize to Eumelus, since[a]

The man who is *aristos* has finished last.

Everyone approves of Achilles' decision except Antilochus, who finished second. His protest is successful, but he does not say 'This is unreasonable. I never heard of such a thing', but 'Eumelus should have prayed to the gods, and anyway you can easily give him another prize.' That is to say, he does not regard it as unreasonable that, even in a race, a man's *arete* should be held to be more important, for the purpose of distributing prizes, than his actual performance. On the other hand, though Menelaus *is* 'mightier in *arete* and in strength',[b] he insists that this must not be the reason why he should be placed second rather than Antilochus; the reason is that Antilochus has broken the rules by crowding and crossing. And yet he also says to Antilochus 'You have brought shame upon my *arete*';[c] and nothing is more important than this.

This is a hopeless tangle of values. Unless the allotment of prizes bears some relation to the result of the race, there is no point in running at all, since the prizes could be distributed before the race starts. Accordingly, some attention must be paid to the result; and yet clearly in this society some attention must be paid to the *arete* of the respective competitors as well. Such a situation can only lead to doubt, confusion, and argument. In a chariot race, this may be unimportant; but we have here in microcosm the tangle of values which prevailed in the Athenian law-courts and assembly, with such disastrous results.[d] The problem is a serious one; and since it is closely related to the problem of moral responsibility, the successive attempts at its solution must be considered in subsequent chapters.[25]

Indeed, the fact that, when the protection of oneself and

---

[a] *Iliad* xxiii. 536. Clearly it would be unreasonable for the winner not to receive the first prize.

[b] *Iliad* xxiii. 578.

[c] *Iliad* xxiii. 571.

[d] Chapter X *passim*.

one's associates is in question, moral error and mistake are not and cannot be distinguished in many cases, while competitive excellences completely override the quieter moral virtues in cases where they can, sets the most serious problem for moral responsibility in the centuries after Homer. The problem on the practical level is clear; and on the theoretical level too there are serious difficulties. Since the attainment of success and fame, both desirable in themselves, and the avoidance of failure and disgrace, both undesirable, are the chief aims of Homeric man,[26] aims whose fulfilment is unconditionally demanded of him, and since this, as has been seen, results in the complete unimportance of intentions, it follows that all action taken to these ends must be seen in terms of successful and unsuccessful calculation, of hitting or missing the mark. The psychological 'picture' must be one of calculation; and though common sense may succeed in using this picture, philosophical analysis may well feel the effects. In Homer, however, and for centuries thereafter, it is the practical difficulties which are the most pressing. In the attempted solution of these difficulties certain beliefs about the gods which are found already in Homer have their part to play. These beliefs will be considered in the next chapter.

NOTES TO CHAPTER III

1. The *Odyssey* seems more developed in that the quieter values are more evidently supported by the threat of divine sanctions than in the *Iliad*. The terms under discussion here, however, undergo little change other than what would be expected in passing from a poem of war to one of (comparative) peace.
2. Cp. Finley, op. cit., p. 138.
3. In the society for which 'Homer' was composing, on the other hand, these values may well have become anachronistic, cp. Finley, op. cit., p. 35, on democracy in Chios.
4. On this topic cp. Frisch, op. cit., pp. 78 ff., and Finley, op. cit., p. 106.
5. For the exact sense in which this statement must be understood, cp. Finley, op. cit., pp. 93 ff.
6. Ibid., pp. 62 ff., 116 ff.
7. Ibid., pp. 100 ff.
8. Ibid., pp. 102 ff.
9. *Kakotes* is not used *of men* to decry breaches of the quiet virtues. At *Iliad* iii. 366, Menelaus says 'I thought I should punish Paris for *kakotes*'. Liddell and Scott, ed. 9, render *kakotes* as 'wickedness'. But there is

nothing to indicate that Homer is speaking of *Paris' kakotes*, which would entail such a translation. *Kakos* and *kakotes* in Homer normally decry failure (*Iliad* x. 71, *Odyssey* v. 290, 379, xvii. 517, &c.); so it is clear that the poet is speaking of *Menelaus' kakotes*, his evil plight resulting from the *elencheie* to which Paris' act has brought him. (This is the view of Ebeling, *Lexicon Homericum*, s.v.) Since Homer knows only one sense of *kakotes*, there can be no ambiguity here. (*Odyssey* iv. 167 is another passage in which, though the actual sense is quite clear, the translation 'wickedness' would make sense.)

10. Accordingly, when Finley says (op. cit., p. 130) that Achilles' refusal of penal gifts (and later his treatment of Hector's body) 'placed him temporarily beyond the pale' and 'marked him as a man of unacceptable excesses', this statement must be read with the claims of the *agathos* in mind. Achilles, in his relations with Agamemnon and with Hector's corpse, is doubtless *anaides*, cp. p. 43; but what he is doing is not *aischron*, and he remains *agathos*, 'within the pale'.

11. Cp. Finley, op. cit., pp. 68 ff., 119 ff.

12. When, *Iliad* iii. 38, &c., one hero addresses another with words which are *aischra*, i.e. insults, the meaning is certainly not that these words are shameful to the speaker. There is nothing in the society depicted in the poems to suggest such a conclusion. It is the man insulted who should feel ashamed.

13. Nevertheless, the linking of *kalon* and *dikaion* might appear hopeful for the future: when *kalon* became the true contrary of *aischron*, it might have drawn *dikaion* with it. This is over-optimistic: the occurrence of a link between *kalon* and *dikaion* in these instances indicates the difficulties facing any extension of the usage. It is not *kalon* or *dikaion* for one guest to insult another precisely because in this situation all competition should be abandoned, since the safety of both is guaranteed by their host: a situation which does not exist between household and household in this society. In fifth-century Athens, the city should have stood in this relationship to all its citizens; but as will be seen in Chapter XI, traditional habits of thought, combined with certain practical needs, kept the relation between households competitive; with the result that *kalon*, in so far as it became the true contrary of *aischron*, could not readily be linked with *dikaion*.

14. For this cp. Dodds, op. cit., pp. 17 f., with n. 106.

15. We may compare *Iliad* ix. 496 ff., for the claims of *arete*: The gods have more *arete* than men; *and yet* they may be swayed by prayer. Cp. also *Iliad* xv. 185.

16. Finley, op. cit., p. 72, says: 'Even in the distribution of booty . . . the head of the *oikos* (household) or . . . king or commander-in-chief . . . was obviously bound by what was generally deemed to be equitable. The circumstance that no one could punish him for flouting custom, as in the conflict between Agamemnon and Achilles, is irrelevant to the issue. For the very fact that just such a situation gave the theme for the *Iliad* illustrates how dangerous the violation could be. In this world custom was as binding upon the individual as the most rigid statutory

law of later days.' This reflects the general situation: *agathoi* must be *pinutoi* most of the time, if only from lack of opportunity to be anything else. It must be emphasized, however, that to say that Agamemnon 'was (normally) bound by what was agreed to be equitable' is not to say that Agamemnon was either legally or morally bound to act equitably. Since 'no one could punish him for flouting custom' (and since there are no laws to enjoin this), he cannot be legally bound; and since Homeric society cannot even censure Agamemnon effectively provided that his flouting of custom does not entail, as it does in the *Iliad*, failure to perform those functions which society demands of him, he cannot be morally bound either.

17. The word I have translated 'abuse' (νεικείειν) covers the senses 'chide', 'rail at', 'upbraid' (Liddell and Scott, s.v.). 'Upbraid' or 'chide' might seem more in point here: I have selected 'abuse' to emphasize that in a society which does not distinguish between moral error and mistake, it is impossible to distinguish mockery, abuse, and rebuke. There is only one situation: unpleasant words directed at a man who has *in fact* fallen short of the expectations of society.

18. Accordingly, when Greene, op. cit., p. 21, says that 'Agamemnon is merely trying to excuse himself', he is concealing the true facts of the situation. Similarly, Chantraine, op. cit., pp. 48–49, says that Agamemnon is not 'coupable' for his errors. I have argued against this in the text. Chantraine's other example is no more satisfactory. At *Odyssey* xxiii. 11 ff., Eurycleia is certainly not excused because, as Penelope thinks, the gods have made her mad. At line 21, Penelope expressly says that if any of the other servants had behaved as Eurycleia has done she would have been punished: Eurycleia escapes because she is an old family retainer. Again, Helen is not trying to avoid responsibility, *Odyssey* iv. 261, when she says that Aphrodite sent *ate* upon her, nor is it for this reason that Menelaus has not killed her. By Homeric standards a wife, particularly a Helen, is a valuable possession; it would be foolish to destroy it, once recovered. (The claims of the story, too—*Odyssey* iv makes a very pleasing narrative—doubtless have their part to play in keeping Helen alive for Homer.)

19. Cp. Dodds, op. cit., chap. i *passim*.

20. Cp. Achilles' language of himself, *Iliad* i. 293. Agamemnon would have felt the same if he had withdrawn from his position, though he was in the wrong; cp. E. *Phoen.* 510 ff. for the general attitude. Note, too, how this scale of values makes it incumbent on a man to die fighting; which may be admirable in war, but will lead to less desirable results in peace, cp. *Odyssey* xxiv. 433 ff.

21. Patroclus' statement that he was a child and did not mean to kill *may* have made some difference to the attitude of non-interested parties to him, though such people evidently gave a ready welcome even to wilful murderers; but clearly it made no difference at all to the attitude of the avengers; and this alone is relevant here, since they alone control the punishment he would receive. On the other side, there might be some difference in treatment if the kinsmen were particularly enraged by the

enormity of the crime. The case of Melanthius, *Odyssey* xxii. 126 ff., suggests that Homeric society was used to torture.

22. True, the suitors fear that Telemachus may be able to raise the whole people against them; but this is unusual (cp. Finley, op. cit., pp. 100 ff.). He *should, Odyssey* xxiv. 455 ff., have been able to raise the people against the suitors when they forced their way into his house; there *should, Odyssey* i. 228 f., have been a general feeling of *nemesis*, social indignation, against the suitors; and this *nemesis should* be translated into action, and *could* be, if the people as a whole felt it. But everything depends on feeling, not organization; normally each household must look after itself, and the suitors can rely on being undisturbed.

23. The *thambos*, awe, which is said to seize those who look on when the murderer arrives at the house of some wealthy man in the late book *Iliad* xxiv may be a hint of the belief in pollution (cp. Chapter V, Note 13); and the peculiar treatment of the minstrel, *Odyssey* iii. 270 f., suggests the treatment of Antigone, S. *Ant.* 775 ff. and 1042, which *is* adopted to avoid pollution. Since the belief in pollution is Indo-European, mention of it must have been deliberately suppressed by Homer and the society for which he was writing. Evidently the society had not the *language* of pollution as we know it in fifth-century Athens: the use of the phrase *katharos thanatos, Odyssey* xxii. 462, to mean (apparently) a 'quick, easy, death' indicates this, for where there is a belief in pollution no death is *katharos*. On this topic, and on homicide in Homer generally, cp. G. M. Calhoun, *The Growth of Criminal Law in Ancient Greece*, chap. ii, and Frisch, op. cit., pp. 110 ff.

24. To protect one's own possessions (and if possible acquire more) is, given the structure of Homeric society, an ever-pressing necessity. Hence the importance laid on the suitors' wasting of Odysseus' possessions throughout the *Odyssey* (xviii. 144, &c.). In addition to security, possessions bring honour, *tīmē*: one becomes more worthy of respect (*aidoioteros*) and friendship (*philteros*), *Odyssey* xi. 360.

25. 'The community could only grow by taming the hero'; Finley, op. cit., p. 129.

26. The Choice of Achilles (*Iliad* ix. 410 ff., a *late* book) shows that the quiet life, at least in the later strata of the *Iliad*, is considered as a possible alternative to the life of glory; but Achilles chooses glory, and the whole system of values is opposed to the quiet life.

IV

'JUSTICE': HOMER TO THE FIFTH CENTURY

A. THE PROBLEM

In Chapter III the importance of the group of values based on *agathos* and *arete* was stressed, and it was insisted that, for readily comprehensible reasons, the 'quieter' values, expressed by *pinutos*, *saophron*, *dikaios*, and similar words, were less valued. They cannot, however, be completely unvalued in any society. To say that they are less valued is to say that an observer, in considering his fellows in Homeric society, more readily sees the need for their *arete* than for their moderation, *saophrosune*: it is not to say that, if he is himself wronged, he does not resent it and set a high value on the quieter virtues in others.

In most cases, of course, the claim of *arete* remains a claim, for his fellows will give the individual *agathos* no opportunity for overstepping the mark. His inferiors can readily do this in some conditions of society. If a ruler merely leads his men in war and decides disputes in peace, without being much more wealthy and powerful than his followers, he may well be coerced if his followers refuse to perform services for him, or deny him his special privileges. Sarpedon's speech to Glaucus seems to reflect such a society.[a] If the Lycians came to wonder why they honoured Sarpedon and Glaucus above all, they might cease to do so: and though here *arete* is in question, justice, *dikaiosune*, might be similarly assured.[1] But given a strong centralized monarchy with inherited wealth and power, or any other situation in which an *agathos* is insufficiently restrained by his fellows, such sanctions could not be applied. In such circumstances, though an ideal hero like Telemachus might wish to be both *agathos* and 'prudent', *pepnumenos* or *pinutos*,[2] it is inevitable, given the Homeric alignment of values and the natural inclinations of mankind, that many an *agathos*, strong,

[a] Above, pp. 34 f.

brave, and skilful in war, should pursue his own interest at the expense of others, particularly since he can do so without forfeiting his claim to the highest term of approbation which Homeric and later society possessed. In this chapter I shall discuss the various answers offered by the Greeks to this serious problem between Homer and the fifth century.

B. JUSTICE AND THE GODS

(i) *Non-moral Gods*

In the circumstances described above, there is no earthly sanction to aid the weaker against the stronger, to ensure either just decisions in legal matters, or equitable treatment in general. Yet such aid must be found; and if earthly aid is denied, it is natural to look to the gods. At all events, it is natural to look to the gods if the gods are themselves just; for otherwise there can be no help in Olympus either. This help is doubtful in Homer. Chapter III showed that the gods are believed to endorse the *agathos*-standard;[a] and the gods as portrayed generally in the Homeric poems are far from just. Though right triumphs in the main plots of both *Iliad* and *Odyssey*, it does not do so *because* it is right.[3] Achilles obtains divine aid because he has, through Thetis his mother, the ear of Zeus himself; and Odysseus is assisted by Athena because she is, for reasons never made clear by Homer, his patron-goddess.

The relations between such gods and mankind are clearly not founded on justice, as may be seen from the reprisals they take against men in the poems. Oeneus sacrificed hecatombs to all the other gods and goddesses, but not to Artemis: he either forgot, says Homer, or he did not think of it.[b] There was nothing deliberate in this slight; yet Artemis sent a wild boar to ravage the land: an act which harmed not merely Oeneus but the people as a whole. Again, the plague which ravaged the Greek army in *Iliad* i was at first believed to be a punishment for a forgotten hecatomb.[c]

Further, when Odysseus and his remaining comrades were weatherbound on the Thrinacian isle,[d] while the food given them by Circe remained they were content with that. But at

---

[a] Above, p. 38.   [b] *Iliad* ix. 536 f.   [c] *Iliad* i. 65.
[d] *Odyssey* xii. 340 ff.

last, famished, they slaughtered the Oxen of the Sun, knowing that the Sun would be angry, but preferring any death to starvation, and hoping that if they promised to make offerings to the Sun when they returned to Ithaca he would be appeased. The Sun was not appeased, but demanded immediate vengeance from Zeus. This was granted, and Odysseus' last ship was wrecked.

Yet again, Odysseus had to blind the Cyclops to survive;[a] the Cyclops had behaved in a manner shocking to Greek ideas of hospitality: and yet he had only to pray to his father Poseidon for the latter to take vengeance on Odysseus and his crew. The gods accept neither the plea of mistake, nor that of compulsion, nor that of self-defence, where their own interests are at stake.

The reason for this belief is clear. Plagues, earthquakes, shipwrecks happen, wild boars ravage the countryside; and it is in such events, which are beyond human control, that the influence of the gods is most clearly seen. The gods must be angry; and since it is by prayer and sacrifice that the gods are appeased, some such thing, if no positive offence can be discovered, must have been omitted. The motives for divine anger are readily comprehensible. The gods have more *arete* and *timē* than men.[b] Like men, they may be presumed to be very touchy with regard to that *time*, which stands at the opposite pole to *elencheie* and covers both one's rightful position and the glory attaching thereto, together with the attentions which others must pay in order to acknowledge and maintain it. The maintenance of his *time* is the chief aim of Homeric man and Homeric god; and god, like man, ever fears that it may be diminished:[4] for it depends on others, and on their acts, not their intentions.[c] Accordingly, it is acts, not intentions, of which gods take account, spurred on by the shame and anger always encouraged by a scale of values in which one's position is so precarious. In a sense, the gods must be even more touchy than men. That they have more *arete* and *time* than men is, apart from their immortality, the only clear distinction between the lesser Homeric gods and mankind. Indeed, it is by an excess of *arete* that men become gods;[d] an excellent reason why the gods

[a] *Odyssey* ix. 251 ff.   [b] *Iliad* ix. 498.
[c] Cp. Arist. *E.N.* 1095^{b}23 ff.
[d] Arist. *E.N.* 1145^{a}22. (The case of Heracles is the most obvious.)

should not only resent slights upon their *time*, but should also be jealous of human success, which constitutes so large a part of *arete*.[5]

True, if one does offer sacrifice to these gods, they are expected to take a personal interest in one's prosperity.[6] So at the beginning of the *Odyssey* Athena asks Zeus[a]

Was not Odysseus wont to gratify you with sacrifices by the Greek ships in the wide land of Troy? Why then were you so angry with him, Zeus?

Odysseus has offered abundant sacrifice; so how could Zeus have a reason for anger? Apart from caring for those who have made them debtors by sacrificing to them, however, and seeing to it that their *time* is properly respected, these gods concern themselves on earth only with their part-human offspring, their possessions, and their priests;[7] and to judge from the prayer of Chryses,[b] even a priest must remind a god of services rendered.

When viewed in this light, the gods are no more likely to be just than men are, for they use the same 'non-moral' code of values; and yet the weaker must have some protection against the stronger, or some hope that his misdeeds may be punished.

There is one solution to this problem which occasionally appears in the Homeric poems, and which presupposes no qualities in the gods save malice or caprice. The picture is that of the Jars at the Threshold of Zeus, whose contents, good or ill, he scatters among mankind not according to merit, but as he will.[c] When the disguised Odysseus, having beaten Irus the beggar at wrestling, warns Amphinomus, he shows the manner in which such a belief may be of use to morals. He says[d]

No man, while the gods furnish him with *arete* and his limbs are nimble, supposes that he will suffer woes in the time to come; but when the gods bring hardships upon him, he bears these too, against his will, with an enduring heart.

From this empirical observation he concludes

Therefore let no man be utterly lawless; let him rather quietly possess such gifts as the gods give him.

Odysseus has been treated as no Homeric beggar should be treated, but he does not reply 'The gods will punish you for

---

[a] *Odyssey* i. 60 ff., cp. *Iliad* xx. 297 ff.   [b] *Iliad* i. 37 ff.
[c] *Iliad* xxiv. 527 ff., cp. *Odyssey* vi. 187 ff.   [d] *Odyssey* xviii. 130 ff.

this.' Instead, he merely says 'Life has its ups and downs. You should be cautious. One day you may be in my position, if the gods choose to deprive you of your *arete*, and you will then need just treatment from others.'

Since this attitude is founded on empirical observation, and makes only minimal demands from the gods, such a solution may be successful, not indeed in making the practice of the quiet virtues essential in some sense to *arete*, which, as will be seen, is the most desirable solution, but at all events in making the *agathos* cautious, provided always that the *agathos* sees the facts in this light. If on the other hand life seems less contingent; if his lands or his flocks are big enough to survive one or even a series of bad years; if later, with the invention of coined money, much of his property is independent of bad harvests: then the *agathos* may feel himself able to snap his fingers at such 'acts of God'.

(ii) *Moral Gods*

In these circumstances, more will be asked of the gods than caprice; and, at least in the later sections of the Homeric poems,[8] the gods are already held to guarantee some moral relationships. For example, it is clear from the repeated question of the traveller in the *Odyssey*[a]

What sort of men live here? Are they violent, wild and unjust, or are they well-disposed to strangers and of a god-fearing, *theoudēs*, mind?

that to be just is to be *theoudēs*, however 'just' is to be defined.[9] Again, all beggars are under the protection of Zeus; and when Odysseus comes as a suppliant before Alcinous, Alcinous is reminded that suppliants are similarly protected.[b] In all these cases, the weaker are protected against the stronger by the threat of divine sanctions.[10] Beggars and suppliants are defenceless against any man, or they would not be beggars and suppliants; and the traveller, far from his country in a time when news travelled slowly and a man's disappearance would readily

---

[a] *Odyssey* vi. 120, viii. 576, ix. 176:

ἦ ῥ' οἵ γ' ὑβρισταί τε καὶ ἄγριοι οὐδὲ δίκαιοι
ἦε φιλόξεινοι, καί σφιν νόος ἐστὶ θεουδής;

[b] *Odyssey* xiv. 56 ff., vii. 159 ff., cp. ix. 267 ff.

be believed to be the result of an accident, was in great need of protection against those whom he met.

It is the king above all who is in a position to do wrong with impunity. Hence we should expect to find him above all threatened with divinely caused disaster if he is unjust, and promised great prosperity if he is just. This we find in an important passage in the *Odyssey*.[a] Odysseus, still disguised, says to Penelope, who has treated him well,

Your fame reaches the wide heaven, like the fame of some blameless[11] king, a man *theoudes* in his rule over many mighty men and an upholder of justice; in whose land the black earth bears wheat and barley, while the trees are heavy with fruit, the flocks bring forth without fail, and the sea provides fish, as a result of his good leadership, and the people prosper, *aretān*, under him.[b]

The importance of this passage lies in the fact that in it *dikaiosune* is explicitly linked to the most important value, as means to an end;[12] for *aretan* is to have *arete*, to be in a flourishing condition as a fully functioning human being in one's society:[13] and the king, as described here, is in this condition even more evidently than his subjects. Since this end is desired, *dikaiosune* must be desired too; and *dikaiosune* thus gains a firm place in the scheme of values.

To consider the gods as moral, however, while clearly an advance in thought, has its dangers unless it is accompanied by other advances. Expecting from the gods the sanctions against powerful wrongdoers which he would himself employ if he were stronger, the wronged man will be content provided that some harm in fact comes to the person who has wronged him. If the latter continues to flourish, a crisis of values results.

The more naïve thinkers might believe that such a situation could not arise. So Agamemnon, when Pandarus treacherously shoots Menelaus,[c] threatens the Trojans with divine vengeance for breaking their oaths. He will not be worried if vengeance does not come at once:

For even if Zeus does not bring it to pass at once, he does so later, and the oath-breakers pay dearly, with their own heads, their wives, and their children.

Though he includes the destruction of the family, Agamemnon

---

[a] *Odyssey* xix. 108 ff.   [b] ἀρετῶσι δὲ λαοὶ ὑπ' αὐτοῦ.   [c] *Iliad* iv. 160 ff.

clearly believes that vengeance will come in the oath-breaker's lifetime. The belief that injustice does not pay is necessary if *dikaiosune* is to be upheld; for otherwise a Hesiod may well say[a]

Now may neither I nor my son be *dikaios* any more among men; for it is a bad thing, *kakon*, to be just if the unjust man is to come off better.

The Greeks in general were too hard-headed to be just if it were not visibly advantageous to do so. Hesiod himself believed that the gods invariably punish the wrongdoer in this life. Others were certain to be more clear-headed. No people oppressed by cruel and prosperous rulers could be convinced by Hesiod; and the tyrannies, some at least of which fulfilled these conditions, were soon to come.

When a theory, moral or otherwise, fails to cover observable facts, it must be amended: if a man can be unjust and prosper in this life, then the simple theory of earthly punishment must clearly be adapted to cover this fact. Since the Greeks already in Homer believe in some kind of life after death, it might seem natural to believe that the misdeeds of this life are punished in Hades. It is, however, not merely not natural but impossible to suppose this. The shades, *psūchai*, of *Odyssey* xi merely gibber; except for the admirable Tiresias, they carry on as pale shadows of their earthly existence. So Minos continues to be a judge even among the dead.[b] He does not, however, assign everlasting punishment for wrongs committed upon earth; he merely decides disputes among the dead, as he did among the living, just as the wraith of Orion, set next to him in the narrative, continues to hunt. True, Tityus, Sisyphus, and Tantalus are punished; but no general moral rule is drawn from them. Nor can there by any such moral; these are not men who have committed 'human' offences, but men who have offended the gods on their own level.[14] Ordinary men and women cannot hope to do wrong on this scale, and may be left to gibber. A Clytemnestra merely suffers *aischos* in the next world:[c] a highly unpleasant fate, but hardly divinely inflicted retribution. Nor does the glimpse of Hades in *Odyssey* xxiv add anything; the heroes simply reminisce and prolong interminably the memories of earthly triumphs and failures.

[a] *W. and D.* 270 ff., cp. *Odyssey* v. 7.   [b] *Odyssey* xi. 568 ff.
[c] *Odyssey* xi. 432 f.

If the next life is ruled out, punishment for wrongdoing must, if *dikaiosune* is to be valued, be meted out in this. It is evident that the wrongdoer frequently escapes himself: accordingly, his descendants must suffer. That the kinship-group was originally more important than the individual, and indeed existed in a sense in which the individual did not, has been argued in detail in reference to Greek society by Glotz.[15] Hence the injustice of punishing the children for the sins of the fathers was originally less felt; and if the children may be punished for the sins of the fathers, the theory once again covers the facts, for five generations, or more,[a] may elapse before punishment is exacted. This point of view is stated quite unemotionally, as fact, by Theognis.[b] He insists that the gods always punish wrongdoing in the end, but men do not realize this, for the gods do not always exact the penalty when the offence is committed.

No; one man pays the grievous debt in his own person, and does not leave disaster, *ate*, hanging over his dear children, while another man is not overtaken by justice, for death sits upon his eyelids beforehand, bringing his end.

Evidently the second man does leave disaster hanging over his children; and here Theognis does not complain.[c] Other writers are equally willing to accept the situation; and so long as the situation is accepted, the theory is admirable: if a man is unjust and prospers, his descendants are sure to suffer; if he does not prosper, it is only what he deserved; if he is just and prospers, he deserves to prosper; and if he is just and does not prosper, he is merely suffering for the misdeeds of some ancestor. Formally this theory is flawless: and the first three possibilities given above are conducive to good behaviour, on the grounds both of ordinary affection and of that Greek belief about the next life which holds more or less confusedly that the dead are still sentient and powerful in their graves, not in Hades, and still require rites and nourishment if they are to survive and be happy. If one threatens a man that, if he does wrong in certain ways, his family will be blotted out, one is threatening him with a miserable existence after death, since there will be no one to perform the rites. Hence in threatening his descendants one is

---

[a] Cp. Gyges, Hdt. i. 91.
[b] Theogn. 205 ff. Solon 13. 25 ff. (Bergk) is equally unemotional.
[c] Contrast 735 ff.

threatening the man himself: a sufficient guarantee of good behaviour, provided that the theory is believed.[16]

The fourth possibility of this theory, however, that one should be just but nevertheless suffer for the sins of one's fathers, is much less useful, regarded as part of a theory which is to encourage good behaviour. Even if the individual holds himself to be of much less importance than the family, it presses hard; and the more the individual grows in importance, the more the manifest injustice of this 'justice' must be felt. It has been felt by Theognis, or by one of the writers of the Theognid corpus. He addresses Zeus, and claims that the gods should see to it that the sinner[a]

should straightway pay for the harm, *kaka*, he has done, that the wrongdoing of the father should not be harmful, *kakon*, to his children and that children of an unjust father who are themselves just—fearing your anger, O Zeus—and love justice among their fellow-citizens from the very beginning should not pay for the transgression of their father.

In fact, the writer complains, the reverse is true:

As it is, the man who does wrong escapes, and another man comes to harm, *kakon*, hereafter.

The writer is in full revolt against this belief; and with reason. Given the Homeric system of values, it is even more necessary than in most societies that *ouk aretāi kaka erga*,[b] that one cannot be unjust and prosper, and conversely that if one is just one shall prosper. But it now appears that the gods, who are supposed to be just in these relationships, frequently allow the unjust man to prosper, and bring ruin upon his sons, whether they are just or not. Thus, so far as the individual is concerned, there is no supernatural link between being *dikaios* and being successful: one may be doomed to ruin anyway for the crimes of one's ancestors. The link between the less-valued *dikaios* and the highly valued *agathos/arete* being thus broken, there must be a strong temptation to pursue *arete*, which includes material prosperity, through the medium of injustice, if need be, and chance the vagaries of divine retribution. One can only be certain that reprisals will be attempted by men; so one must be careful to be only so unjust as one's power will allow. This is the period in which coined money appears, and the rich gain greater stability; this is also the period of tyrannies. A man's power might well allow injustice on a very large scale. The tyrant flourishes, is *agathos*, and may think nothing of justice; yet the heavens remain placid. Therefore let everyone pursue success as far as he may, and let justice go by the board; any ruin that comes might have come anyway, had one been poor but honest.

Thus this attempt to link the quieter values with *arete* fails in its purpose; and this being so, the alignment of values encourages the pursuit of success, *arete*, at the expense of all other claims. Inevitably, action viewed in these terms, as was seen in the first chapter, does not even raise the right moral questions; and until the right questions are asked, there can be no hope of a development of the concept of moral responsibility.

C. JUSTICE AND *ARETE*

(i) *Homer and Hesiod*

There are, however, other means by which the quieter virtues might become linked with *arete*. *Dikaiosune* might become part (or even the whole) of *arete*, could it be realized that the quieter virtues are essential to the stability and prosperity of society. Such a realization must result from a change in the conditions of life, for the Homeric *arete* or *aretai* suited the Homeric situation. The type of man most needed was most admired; and problems of values were settled within the framework of this *arete*, despite implicit incoherences. Homeric society was even calm enough to realize that other peoples in different circumstances might be suited by different *aretai*, without valuing its own *aretai* any the less on that account. Alcinous says to Odysseus: It is quite reasonable that you should want to display your *arete*, for you have been insulted;[a] but let me tell you of our *arete*:[b]

We are not boxers or wrestlers. We run swiftly, and we are *aristoi* with ships; and fencing, stringed instruments and dancing, changes of clothing, warm baths, and the pleasures of love are ever dear to us.

---

[a] Odysseus has been taunted with being a merchant, and no athlete, and wishes to show by his prowess that this is untrue.

[b] *Odyssey* viii. 236 ff.

They are not fighters but sailors, sailors who, when at home, live in luxury. They have no need of warlike pursuits, for they live far from other men. Their lives are quite different from those of the battered warriors and storm-tossed travellers of the *Odyssey* and *Iliad* in general; and yet Homer shows no desire to prove that one set of *aretai* is intrinsically superior to the other. Each set is suited to the people which possesses it.

This is the clearest of signs that the society for which the Homeric poems were composed[17] found that its values suited its way of life and contributed to stability and prosperity: troubles and privations quickly produce a less tolerant attitude to others' standards of value, and a re-examination of one's own. However, the very success of these values may have its own drawbacks. Of the qualities commended by *arete* in Homer, some are fundamental, while others are, whether the priority of the former group is temporal or merely logical, accretions. But though this is true, it need not be realized to be true: it is not necessary that the justification of such a system of values should be always before the mind. Indeed, the more stable society becomes, the less likely it is that the true justification will be remembered, and the more likely that non-essentials will come to the fore. The Homeric hero is *agathos* because his skills and qualities make him most able to defend his society; and yet we find men who fall short in these respects termed *agathoi* purely in virtue of their wealth and social position.[a] In Hesiod it becomes even more evident that the original justification of the *agathos*-standard has been forgotten. The *Works and Days* reveals to us a level of society which, though not the highest[18] (being clearly inferior to that of the sceptre-bearing kings who dispense justice), is at least articulate, and has a definite standard of *arete*, whose nature is evident from the address to Perses.[b] The gods, says Hesiod, have set much toil and sweat in the way of the acquisition of *arete*; but it is easy once the summit has been reached. The 'best' man, *panaristos*, is the man who foresees everything for himself; he is a 'good' man, *esthlos*, who takes advice: but the man who neither foresees nor takes advice is useless, *achreios*. The subject of the advice is clear from what follows. It is the subject of the *Works and Days*: how to be a successful farmer, to avoid famine, and be prosperous. To

[a] Cp. p. 36 above.   [b] *W. and D.* 286 ff.

achieve this a corpus of knowledge and skills different from those of the fighting man are needed; but it is with knowledge and skills that we are still concerned. There is no necessary link between this *arete* and justice,[19] as the use of *esthlos* in an earlier passage shows:[a]

Insolence, *hubris*, is a bad thing, *kake*, for a poor man, *deilos*: even an *esthlos* cannot readily bear it but is weighed down by it and meets with *ate*.[b] The better road is to make for justice; justice has the better of insolence in the end. . . .

Even the successful man, *esthlos*, should avoid injustice, since he will almost certainly suffer for it in the end. These lines are merely prudential.

Here, then, the link between *dikaios* and *agathos* remains tenuous. There are better elements in Hesiodic morality:[20] but these lines are the most important for the present question. The *arete* of Hesiod is something new. Even in Homer some of the heroes have particular skills highly developed: one man is *agathos* at the war-cry, another has skill in counsel, a third is a good runner. Yet on the whole all the chieftains before Troy satisfy, more or less, the claims of general *arete*. In Hesiod, however, we find an articulate section of society pursuing a specialized activity with the intention of attaining material success and the good repute which goes with it under the unqualified title of *arete*. Two deductions may be drawn from this. Firstly, for Hesiod's society *arete* can denote and commend material success, however arrived at, without demanding military prowess: these *agathoi* have no real justification for their title. Secondly, since, as Hesiod's lines show, the good farmer claims to be *agathos tout court*, a title which the sceptre-bearing kings have certainly not relinquished, there now exist at least two kinds of activity, which need have nothing in common,[21] contending for the most powerful term of value. Hesiod feels no conflict, for he considers only his own class; but should it become necessary to decide between the contenders, the decision must be based on first principles. The quality or qualities most essential to society

---

[a] *W. and D.* 214 ff.

[b] *Ate* means both 'blindness' and 'disaster' resulting from such (mental) blindness, just as *arete* spans both skill and the success resulting from it. A shame-culture cannot draw distinctions between results and the mental states which produce them, cp. p. 47 above.

must be determined; and Hesiod's use of *arete* makes it clear that the answer would not be easy to find.

(ii) *Tyrtaeus*

The outstanding success of one farmer in a community of farmers does not evidently contribute to the stability of society as a whole; but provided there are no unusual stresses, the claim of such a farmer to be *agathos* may not be challenged. Stress, however, will force a decision between claimants: a stress which may be of different kinds, and produce different results, as the contestants draw attention to the advantages of the skill or quality favoured. Tyrtaeus in the seventh century,[22] under the stress of the Messenian War,[a] finds it necessary, faced with the complex Homeric *arete*, to emphasize one aspect of it at the expense of the rest. He begins

I would not reckon a man as being of any account because of the *arete* of his feet or for his wrestling. . . .

Speed and wrestling ability *are aretai*, in the thought of the day, as are the other qualities which the poet goes on to enumerate; but, says Tyrtaeus, not even if a man has all these qualities, not even

if he had every ground for fame but fierce valour; for a man does not become *agathos* in war if he should not hold firm when he sees bloody carnage and thrust at the enemy from close at hand. This is *arete*.[b]

Sparta is in a critical situation. Only courageous fighting can save her: hence the *arete* of the stable Homeric society must be shorn of its irrelevances. *Agathos* must be *agathos* in war: this is *arete*.

The results of Tyrtaeus' 'Eunomia',[23] with its insistence on this *arete*, may be seen in fifth-century Sparta.[24] His insistence reflects the insecurity of Sparta; and since no Greek city-state ever was, or felt itself, fully secure, *arete* tends to have this predominant flavour even in fifth-century Athens. This insecurity exerts its influence continually against such speculations as will be considered below.

---

[a] Tyrtaeus 12 Bergk.   [b] ἥδ' ἀρετή.

(iii) *Xenophanes and Solon*

Once this fragmentation of values has begun, anyone may offer his views. A Mimnermus may say 'Rejoice your heart while you can', sitting in the sun and harming no one;[a] but the Greeks were rarely disposed to take advice of this nature. Xenophanes, faced with a type of stress different from that of Tyrtaeus, adopts similar exhortation in the interests of *his* favoured *arete*. To this end he pours scorn on a number of activities, from whose nature one might deduce that Colophon was suffering from athletic mania, saying that for an athletic victory a man would be awarded a front seat at the games, meals at the public expense, and a prize in kind,[b]

though he is not worth it, as I am. For better than the strength of men and horses is my wisdom, *sophiā*.

The athlete is not so worthy of such a reward as is Xenophanes: for not even if a man excelled in all sports

would his city be any the more in a state of sound government, *eunomiā*.

Like Tyrtaeus, Xenophanes is saying 'This is the type of man and the type of behaviour the city needs.'[c] Yet he does not say 'This is *arete*' as Tyrtaeus does; and this may be significant. Tyrtaeus can plausibly claim to be merely stripping *arete* of irrelevances: Xenophanes would be innovating, in a manner unlikely to be successful. Like Tyrtaeus, he attacks the *aretai* of the athlete as irrelevant; and since his *sophia* is more important than these *aretai*, he must be claiming implicitly that it is an *arete*. But a citizen of a city-state could no more claim than could Homeric man that the *arete* of the soldier was not of the utmost importance;[25] and this doubtless prevents Xenophanes from maintaining that his political skill is *arete* without qualification. If this is so, we have here the first hint of a problem which was to beset the Greeks throughout the whole period covered by this book.[d]

It is noteworthy that Xenophanes, like Tyrtaeus, seems concerned with *eunomia*; but unlike Tyrtaeus he is not concerned

---

[a] Mimnermus 7 Bergk.   [b] Xenophanes 2 Bergk.
[c] For Tyrtaeus, cp. also poem 10 Bergk, discussed below, p. 163 f.
[d] Cp. esp. Chapter XVI.

here with an external threat. It seems clear that there is civil strife in Colophon, or at least that the affairs of the city are not running as smoothly as was once the case. Xenophanes professes to be able to cure the state's ills, to be the man society needs, and claims that the system of values should be realigned in his favour.

The poems of Solon depict a similar situation: Athens will never be destroyed by the gods, for Athena prevents it;[a] but her own citizens are ruining her by their folly. The mind of the people's leaders is unjust, they are swollen with pride, *hubris*, and they grow wealthy from unjust deeds. Solon lists the ills of the city, and says that his heart bids him tell the Athenians

that *dusnomiā* brings very many woes, *kaka*, upon the city, whereas *eunomia* makes everything orderly and as it should be, and often fetters the unjust.

Eunomia will restore civic calm, prevent unjust judgements, and subdue *hubris*. All will then be well.

In these writers, and in the title of Tyrtaeus' work, there is a heavy emphasis on *eunomia*, with the implication, expressed in Solon, that what actually exists is *dusnomia*, that all is not well in the state.[26] The reasons for this, and its bearing on moral responsibility, must now be considered.

(iv) *Theognis*

Xenophanes and Solon wish to improve the organization of their respective states. They wish to achieve this by legislation: and from the surviving references to Solon's legislation it can be seen that the problems which he detected were serious ones.[b] Some of them must have been solved; but they do not touch the root of the trouble. The basic need is not for a new kind of legislator with a new kind of skill, *arete*, but for a new kind of citizen with a new kind of civic *arete*. That there is a need for new values should be evident. In essentials the current values are still those of Homeric society; and as was said above, these values, though suited to that society, are unlikely to suit any other. Homeric values are suited to a community organized primarily on a basis of scattered individual households. Its values stress the prowess of the individual, and justify in the

---

[a] Solon 4 Bergk, esp. 11 and 32 f.   [b] Cp. Arist. *Ath. Pol.* 5 ff.

individual at the least a considerable panache; and accordingly the Homeric hero requires free space in which to manœuvre.

In a city, more co-operation is required from heads of households than the implications of *arete* are likely to produce; and the theological difficulties experienced in guaranteeing *dikaio-sune* by divine sanction aggravate the problem. Even had there been no other change in society than its greater concentration, difficulties would have resulted. There had, however, occurred one other change of the greatest importance: the invention of coined money. Coined money differs from other kinds of wealth in several significant respects, some of which have been mentioned above. Most important here is the fact that it may be earned in many ways, including means such as commerce which the old *agathoi* may be unable or unwilling to employ. Hence many people who, under the old system, were *kakoi* in the sense which has been made clear in Chapter III, become prosperous and successful. This strains the system of values. The qualities commended by the word *agathos* in Homer, there always found together, are now spread over society in a different manner. Men of low birth acquire great wealth, and men of high birth are, either relatively or absolutely, less prosperous. Society must now decide which of these men are *agathoi* and which *kakoi*. The question is important, in view of the great claims which the *agathos* has against his fellows; and it forces the society, as does external danger, to decide which quality is fundamental to the idea of *agathos*, fundamental, that is, to a man's being of the greatest value to society.

Inth is moral, social, and economic confusion so emotive a question can hardly be decided without conflict: and the *dus-nomia* of Xenophanes and Solon doubtless reflects not only the difficulty of fitting *agathoi* into cities, but also the problem of the nature of *agathoi*. It is from such stresses, not from the relative calm of Homeric values, that new insights spring; and we are fortunate in possessing in the Theognid corpus a group of short poems which seems to illustrate the development of such an insight from such a conflict. Whether or no the passages quoted here are from the hand of one author is irrelevant. It is sufficient that they should be of the same general period and provoked by similar situations: which seems to be the case.[27]

The decision is a difficult one; and it is not surprising that the Theognid corpus preserves more than one solution—or un-reflective attitude. One may lay emphasis on birth, and say of the situation[a]

They honour wealth. The *agathos* has married from the house of the *kakos*, the *kakos* from the household of the *agathos*. Wealth has thrown lineage into confusion.

Alternatively, one may ignore birth, and acknowledge the success of the new class and the failure of the old. So, the writer says, the men who used to wander in goatskins outside the city walls[b]

now are *agathoi*; and those who were *esthloi* before are now *deiloi*.

Both good birth and success are implied by Homeric *arete*: either of these attitudes could claim precedents. In Theognis' Megara, however, either attitude has its difficulties: though the writer of the second passage seems quite resigned to the change, it is natural for the old *agathoi* to be just as anxious to retain the right to the term *agathos* as the new successful class is to gain that right. This may show itself in many ways. The old *agathos* may snarl[c]

For the majority of men there is only one *arete*: to be wealthy.

Or he may try self-consolation:[d]

To many useless men the god gives good, *esthlos*, prosperity, which is of no benefit to the man himself or his friends;[e] but the great fame of *arete* shall never die, for a spearman preserves his native land and his city.

Here too the writer separates wealth from the idea of *agathos/ arete*, and in these lines falls back on the basic justification for applying the terms. It is not here stated explicitly that one may be *agathos* and poor, though one can be *kakos* and rich: but another quatrain in fact maintains this:[f]

Many *kakoi* are rich and many *agathoi* are poor, but we will not take wealth in exchange for our *arete*; for the one remains with a man always, but possessions pass from one man to another.

  [a] Theogn. 189 f.
  [b] Theogn. 57 f., cp. 1109 f., and Alcaeus frag. 49 Bergk.
  [c] Theogn. 699 f.   [d] Theogn. 865 ff.
  [e] The lines are corrupt. The sense may be 'to a man who is of no use to himself or his friends'. The effect of the whole, however, remains much the same.
  [f] Theogn. 315 ff. The lines are also attributed to Solon, frag. 15 Bergk, cp. Sappho, frag. 80 Bergk.

These are violently partisan poems, not philosophical reflec-
tions; but, however selfish may be the writer's own motives, the
concept of *arete* is 'loosened up' and trimmed of irrelevances by
these means. It is possible to hold that wealth is unnecessary to
arete; and that *arete* must be something permanent inhering in
its possessor, not some transient possession like money: it must
hold out, unlike the *arete* of Eumaeus and Penelope in Homer,[28]
against the vicissitudes of life.

This inherent *arete* is most likely to be skill in warfare or high
birth. Nothing has been found in Greek values so far to suggest
anything else. Suddenly, however, we find in the Theognid
corpus the amazing couplet[a]

The whole of *arete* is summed up in *dikaiosune*; every man, Cyrnus,
is *agathos* if he is *dikaios*.

Aristotle cites this couplet as a proverb.[b] At the time of its
composition, however, far from being a proverb, it was not even
a proposition to which the majority of Greeks would give
assent if it were put to them. This is no tame equation of *arete*
and *dikaiosune*:[29] in view of the connotation of *arete*, the writer is
saying something as startling as did the Stoics when, in a
similarly disintegrating society, they claimed that the wise man
was the only true king. The writer is not merely claiming that
one may only be termed *agathos* if (whatever other conditions
may be necessary in addition) one is *dikaios*, which, though far
from Homeric, could be fitted into Homeric values. He is claiming that *anyone* who is *dikaios* is *agathos*; and this smashes the
whole framework of Homeric values. The writer, faced with a
society in which none of the important terms of value could be
confidently applied and the civic turmoil which (the poems
make clear) accompanied this, has realized under the pressure
of events that it is the quiet excellences which are above all
essential to the stability of the city; and finding *agathos* 'loosened
up', is able, by annexing it to the *dikaios*, to give him the highest
commendation. Splendour, position, success: all these are part
of the flavour of *agathos*. The man who is *dikaios*, claims this

---

[a] Theogn. 147 f. The first line of the couplet also appears as Phocylides frag. 10.
Theognis' words are

ἐν δὲ δικαιοσύνῃ συλλήβδην πᾶσ' ἀρετή 'στι·
πᾶς δέ τ' ἀνὴρ ἀγαθός, Κύρνε, δίκαιος ἐών.

[b] Arist. *E.N.* 1129ᵇ29, παροιμιαζόμενοι.

writer, possesses all these in the true sense, as no one else does.

This couplet is the result of much more thought than the snarls and self-consolations quoted above. Though not the most influential, it is for the purpose in hand the most significant of all the judgements of value which survive from this period. Its immediate results, if accepted, are twofold. In the first place, if *dikaiosune* and *arete* are identical, there is no need any longer to justify *dikaiosune*; for to pursue it is to pursue *arete*, and this is a desirable end. Secondly, if *dikaiosune* is *arete*, then the acts of the *agathos* will be judged in accordance with their *dikaiosune*: which is to say that, when questions of responsibility are raised, there is no higher system of values to which appeal may be made, and which may prevent decision being given in terms of such awkward questions.

Had this equation of *dikaios* and *agathos* been generally accepted, the development of the concept of moral responsibility in particular applications from this time onwards should have been rapid. Such elegiac utterances, however, had not the status of dogma. There was no tradition of Greek sacred books into which they could be inserted; and at this period there was no formal philosophy to consolidate the insight. Aristotle calls this couplet a proverb. This might suggest that it sank into the popular consciousness; but if it did so, it sank without trace. It is only after much further thought that any change comes over the general sense of *agathos*. Ordinary usage in the fifth century before the period of the sophists is unaffected; and it seems likely that the couplet only appeared as a proverb to Aristotle as a result of the intensive moral speculation of the late fifth and fourth centuries.

Thus, the practical result of the thought of these years is small. Theognis' enlightenment, produced by a crisis, may well have lasted no longer than the crisis. After all, in normal circumstances the *arete* of Tyrtaeus is much more evidently necessary to a Greek city-state than is the *arete* of Theognis. Yet Theognis has reached essentials; and while in Homer the problems of the fifth century may be seen in microcosm, Theognis provides in microcosm some of the answers.

NOTES TO CHAPTER IV

1. We may compare the manner in which Telemachus should be treated in virtue of his position as a judge, δικασπόλον ἄνδρα, *Odyssey* xi. 184 f. This may also hold good between people living far apart, cp. Odysseus' words to Polyphemus, *Odyssey* ix. 350 ff., which are hardly relevant when addressed to the Cyclops, but would be so if used of the relations between traders from different lands.

2. *Pinutos, pepnumenos*, and *saophron* basically mean 'prudent in one's own interests', but such words readily commend moderation in a man's behaviour, simply because the average man cannot exercise his *arete* all the time. Cp. below, Chapter XII, pp. 246 ff.

3. Cp. Dodds, *The Greeks and the Irrational*, p. 32: 'I find no indication in the narrative of the *Iliad* that Zeus is concerned with justice as such' (quoted by Chantraine, *Fondation Hardt*, i. 75, where see his discussion). Kitto, however, ibid., p. 86, suggests that the *Odyssey* is a poem about divine justice, and contrasts it with the probable shape of a 'romantic' *Odyssey* written as such. This judgement depends on the fact that the beginning of the *Odyssey* 'gives away' the end, as a poem whose interest was primarily narrative would not do. Even if this view is accepted, however, the generally inadequate idea of the gods as just which prevails throughout the poems entails taking Kitto's words in a very restricted sense.

4. We may compare the attitude of Poseidon to the Greek Wall, built without hecatombs, *Iliad* vii. 446 ff. If the Greeks are allowed to act in this manner, no one will ever again make offerings to the gods; which is loss of *time*, and the material loss which accompanies it. Cp. also *Odyssey* xiii. 128, Poseidon and the Phaeacians.

5. Cp. generally Thomson, *Aeschylus and Athens*, p. 63.

6. Cp. Frisch, *Might and Right in Antiquity*, pp. 51 ff.

7. At *Iliad* xxi. 462 ff. (also *Iliad* i. 573 ff.) it is recognized that it is odd that the gods should trouble themselves about mortals: it is not seemly that one god should do violence to another in such a cause.

8. I am not concerned here to discuss the 'strata' to which the different beliefs about the gods should be assigned: for which cp. e.g. Leitzke, *Moira und Gottheit* and Ehnmark, *The Idea of God in Homer*. It seems most likely that the more moral strata are the later ones, but all these beliefs could exist at once, as they did in Attic tragedy, and I am here concerned only with the effects of these beliefs.

9. *Theoudes* is subject to the confusions which will be discussed in Chapter VII, pp. 131 ff. It refers in *Odyssey* xix. 364 ff. to the offering of hecatombs.

10. This is clearly the function of 'the suppliants' Zeus', *Zeus Hiketēsios*. The gods uphold moral standards more generally at *Odyssey* i. 262 f., where it is said that they disapprove of arrow-poison. On the whole, they seem to dislike atrocities: cp. the attitude of the gods to the maltreatment of Hector's body, *Iliad* xxiv. 53, though as was said in Chapter III, p. 38, they are confused there by Achilles' undoubted claims *qua agathos*.

11. *Amūmōn*, which literally means 'blameless', belongs to the *agathos*-group of terms. It does not commend the king's justice here. (Even Aegisthus is *amumon* in the social sense in *Odyssey* i. 29; and presumably in the sense of 'courageous' too, for Homer does not represent him as a coward, though he disapproves of his staying at home, iii. 263 ff., and he was certainly not so great a warrior as Agamemnon, 250.)

12. Cp. the very similar passage in *Iliad* xvi. 384 ff., which has been argued to be of late date on quite different grounds.

13. *Aretan* is presumably an *ad hoc* coinage for this purpose. It only occurs twice before the late prose writers, here and in *Odyssey* viii. 329 (*ouk aretāi kaka erga*), on each occasion not merely in moral contexts, but to convey this particular moral point.

14. Tityus had attempted to rape Artemis (or Leto), Apollod. 1. 4. 1, &c. Of Tantalus there are several accounts: he had either divulged the secrets entrusted to him by Zeus, offered the gods a 'Thyestean' banquet, or offended them in some similar 'person to person' manner, Diod. 4. 74, Hyg. *Fab.* 82, Hor. *Sat.* 1. 1. 68, Ov. *Met.* 4. 457, &c. Sisyphus too had divulged the secrets of the gods, by one account, Servius on *Aeneid* 6. 16, or had committed crimes on a similar scale, Apollod. 1. 9. 3, 3. 12. 6, Theognis 703. (Cp. *Dictt. Ant.*) These crimes are not viewed as instances of immorality: they are insults to the *time* of the gods on an unparalleled scale, and provoke an unparalleled revenge.

On this topic, cp. Glotz, *Histoire grecque*, i. 498, and Note 91. Frisch, op. cit., p. 171, opposes Glotz: 'For instance, Glotz says (loc. cit.) that there is in this case no allusion to a righteous punishment in the lower world; there are here only gods who avenge their personal injuries (it is not easy to see any great difference!).' Surely the difference is in fact easy to see: if these notable men were merely taken as *examples* of a post-mortem punishment which awaits every sinner, Homer must either have indicated that hosts of other shades were being punished in different ways or (unhomerically) drawn some moral. But in fact, as stated in the text, these 'sinners' seem to be no more like examples than Minos is like a judge of sins committed on earth. Admittedly, *Iliad* iii. 278, perjurers are said, in the invocation of an oath, to be punished below the earth; here by two gods (dual τίνυσθον, 279), presumably Zeus of the lower world and Persephone, mentioned in *Iliad* ix. 457; but we see no sign of this either in the Nekyia of *Odyssey* xi or in that of *Odyssey* xxiv. Accordingly, it seems not to have been assimilated by the Homeric Hades, but to have existed illogically, though serving a very definite function, as do so many Homeric beliefs about the supernatural.

15. Glotz, *La Solidarité de la famille*, passim. On the belief, and its concomitants, cp. Rohde, *Psyche*, Eng. trans., xii. 7. 65, xiv. ii. 96.

16. We may compare Hesiod, *W. and D.*, 284 f. If anyone wilfully forswears himself, 'His family is less illustrious thereafter; but the family of a man who keeps his oaths is "better" in future years.' True, it is not stated explicitly that the family will be completely wiped out; but for an added inducement not to harm one's descendants cp. *Odyssey* xi. 495 ff. One of Achilles' chief desires in the next world is to know whether

or no his son Neoptolemus enjoys fair fame. If one's family did become 'less illustrious', it would of course be *aischron* for the whole family, including the dead in so far as they are conscious of the situation. This continues to be important, cp. Aristotle's difficulties in *E.N.* 1101ᵃ22 ff.

17. This statement requires explanation, since 'Homer' is the final product of a repeated working of traditional material. It is intended as a short way of saying that this material was worked over during a period in which the normal Homeric *aretai* succeeded in maintaining a stable society without social problems; for though epic is not elegy, and its purpose is not to comment on life, comments may well be reflected in it, cp. *Odyssey* i. 32 ff., discussed above, pp. 24 f. Not even Thersites, *Iliad* ii. 225 ff., objects to Homeric values: his claim is not that he is as good as Agamemnon, but that Achilles is manifestly better, 239.

18. On the 'middle-class' status of Hesiod, cp. Verdenius, *Fondation Hardt*, i. 42.

19. On *arete* in Hesiod, &c., cp. Wilamowitz, *Sappho und Simonides*, pp. 169 ff.

20. e.g. *W. and D.* 311, 'Work is no disgrace: it is idleness which is a disgrace': a good attitude for a working farmer, but one which might well be excluded by some interpretations of *arete*. (The Homeric *agathos*, however, was expected to be a skilled farmer; cp. Odysseus' challenge to Eurymachus, *Odyssey* xviii. 365 ff. Odysseus is disguised as a beggar; but the 'beggar's' claim that he is a better reaper and ploughman than the princeling is pointless unless the princeling is expected to be a good reaper and ploughman.) *Kakotes* appears to mean 'wickedness' in *W. and D.* 740, but the line is evidently spurious, since its style is completely unlike that of Hesiod. It was in fact athetized by Aristarchus, cp. Mazon, *Comment. d'Hésiode*, p. 146.

21. It is, however, unlikely that they should have had nothing in common. A Boeotian farmer must have played some part in his country's defence: but if *arete* characterizes the whole way of life of the sceptre-bearing kings (as it must) such a farmer has no chance of being termed *agathos* on the grounds of his fighting ability alone. Hesiod, however, calls the good farmer *panaristos* and *esthlos*, not in such terms as to suggest that he means 'the good farmer is the man who does this'; he evidently means 'the man who does this is the best type of man'. For the reasons given in the text, there is, despite this, no conflict of values in Hesiod: but that *arete* so clearly commends success *per se* in his eyes is significant, in view of the conflicting claims found in Theognis.

22. Cp. Frisch, op. cit., p. 147. Wilamowitz, *Sappho und Simonides*, p. 257, regarded this fragment as belonging to 'die Sophistenzeit' on the grounds of its form, which is highly schematic. But cp. Xenophanes, frag. 2 Bergk, discussed on pp. 74 f., which, though later, is certainly not of the sophistic period. And since the poet of the *Odyssey*, viii. 236 ff., cp. p. 70 above, is already capable of distinguishing between two sets of *aretai*, even if he does not prefer one to the other, it is quite conceivable that a poet of the period of Tyrtaeus should be able both to distinguish the elements of *arete* as popularly conceived and to state

firmly which he regards as essential. Form by itself, accordingly, gives insufficient grounds for such a radical redating of this poem.

23. One of Tyrtaeus' poems seems to have borne this title, cp. Arist. *Pol.* 5. 6. 2, Strabo 8. 362.

24. On *eunomia*, cp. e.g. Sinclair, *A History of Greek Political Thought*, pp. 21 ff., with footnote and references, pp. 31 f.

25. Though in frag. 1. 20 and 23 *arete* seems to be used in a very 'civic' and 'advanced' manner. It is there, however, allowed to take its meaning from its context: a very different matter from saying baldly 'This is *arete*', to the exclusion of all other claimants.

26. *Eunomia* is used to commend a condition of good order in the state, *dusnomia* to decry civic disorder: the terms do not imply that the laws themselves are good or bad.

27. For a survey of the views relating to the date of Theognis, cp. Frisch, op. cit., pp. 210 ff. While I incline to Frisch's conclusion, it suffices for the point I am making that the poems should fall anywhere between Tyrtaeus and Aeschylus, or that they should be an assemblage of poems written by different people—faced with similar circumstances—throughout this period. Cp. also Carrière, *Revue des études grecques*, 1954, 39 ff.

28. Both Penelope, *Odyssey* xviii. 251 and xix. 124, and Eumaeus, *Odyssey* xvii. 322 f., lament the loss of their *arete* (in different ways) as a result of external circumstances. In so far as it is beauty, success, or prosperity, *arete* cannot be inherent.

The lines referring to Eumaeus' loss of *arete*, or rather to that of slaves in general, are very odd. Eumaeus ascribes the poor condition of Odysseus' dog to the carelessness of the female slaves, says that slaves never behave properly when their masters are absent, and concludes: 'For Zeus takes away half a man's *arete* when slavery comes upon him.' Both the use of *arete*, and the construction of the passage, are odd. Eumaeus is talking of women, then refers to male slaves (320 f.), and finishes with a general reference to 'a man' in the couplet quoted. In view of the very different qualities expected from men and women in Homer, the loss of *arete* has very different implications in men and in women, and the transitions in thought are thus difficult. Considering the general flavour of *arete* in men, one can only be surprised that the occasion of Eumaeus' reflecting upon its loss should be failure to take care of a dog. This passage certainly is not sufficient in itself to show that *arete* commends a sense of duty (so Merry, ad loc.). There is no sign of this elsewhere in the use of *arete*: and the confusion of arrangement in this passage, coupled with the fact that the couplet is *in a different context* a simple statement of fact about traditional Greek values (cp. Simonides, poem 5 Bergk, below, p. 165) suggests that this passage either did not originally stand here, or that the poet, with the aid of the link-lines 320 f., has inserted a favourite but inapposite reflection. Plato, *Laws* 777 A, quotes the lines as

ἥμισυ γάρ τε νόου ἀπαμείρεται εὐρύοπα Ζεύς
ἀνδρῶν, οὗς ἂν δὴ κατὰ δούλιον ἦμαρ ἕλῃσι,

replacing *arete* by *noos*: 'For Zeus takes away half a man's wits . . . '. This would make excellent sense: and though there seems no possibility that all our manuscripts of Homer are corrupt here (particularly as Plato's version in other respects suggests that here, as often, he is quoting from memory) it is interesting to note the direction in which Plato's memory leads him in going astray. (On this topic, cp. J. Labarbe, *L'Homère de Platon*, pp. 249 ff. While I agree with Labarbe that *arete* must be read in Homer, I cannot agree—for reasons made clear in Chapter III—that *arete* here makes any real sense, or that *noos* is nonsense. Labarbe insists that *noos* is always used of intellectual qualities in Homer; but since philosophy is not a Homeric pursuit, such qualities must always be displayed *in action*; and since right action is viewed as intelligent action (*saophron, pepnumenos,* &c.) *noos* may readily be used in such a context as this, cp. e.g. *Iliad* x. 122.)

29. Other passages of Theognis approach the insight of this passage, e.g. at 393 the man who is *ameinon*, 'better', is just even when he is poor, whereas the *deilos*, the inferior man, is not; but here too the poet seems to be contrasting the standards of the aristocrat with those of the common people: unlike the couplet quoted in the text, which virtually makes the just man into an aristocrat. Similarly at 322 there occurs what seems to be a 'moral' use of *kakiā*, and what may be a 'moral' use of *aischea* at 388 (and cp. 546). Other examples could be cited: but even these, considered in their context, will be seen to possess in all probability, given the previous history of the words, a strong social and political colouring. Lack of a sufficiently extensive context normally prevents a decision on the exact sense of such passages in Theognis: for passages where we may have the language of morals, or merely that of party politics, cp. e.g. 43 ff. (almost certainly political), 289 ff., 305 ff., &c. In the last example, note how readily *sophrosune* in the sense of 'having the right views in politics' may join the *agathos/arete* group of terms. (For the doubtful position of *sophrosune* in Greek generally, cp. pp. 246 ff.) In so far as these are a development on previous usage, they seem to have had little effect on the usage of the earlier fifth century: except that Aeschylus would presumably agree that deceitful gain is *aischron*, 607 ff., since, *P.V.* 658, he holds it to be *aischron* to tell lies even with kindly intent; and the writers of the period might well have agreed with Theognis as to what kinds of behaviour at drinking parties are *aischra*, 502 and 607. Of course, the extent to which success justifies deceit raises a problem: deceit may well be an *arete*, cp. 699 ff., where it is bracketed with the prudence of Rhadamanthus and the speed of the winds in running; for in this passage all the qualities mentioned are clearly held by Theognis to be *aretai*. In short, in this time of turmoil the Theognid poems adopt practically every conceivable attitude, while the earlier fifth century in Athens, not having the same political confusion, was not tempted even to Theognis' occasional insights.

In view of the couplet quoted in the text (147 f.) Sinclair, op. cit., pp. 24 f., seems to me rather to underestimate Theognis as a political thinker.

Both Pittacus, 1. 2 Bergk, and Chilo, 1. 4 Bergk, have uses of *kakos* (and Chilo also of *agathos*) which might refer to 'quiet' virtues but which, like the passages of Theognis cited above, can just as easily be read as 'social' sneers.

V

'POLLUTION'

A. THE NATURE OF THE BELIEF

(i) *'Pollution' in Homer and Hesiod*

Thus far, the most important obstacle to the development of a more sensitive attitude to moral responsibility has been the nature of Greek values. This remains true; and the subsequent development of those values will be considered below. First, however, the ground must be cleared by an examination of some other beliefs of the period which in different ways obscure the issue; for in some of its less attractive aspects the fifth century in Athens, the only city for which any detailed evidence survives, seems much more remote from us than does the world of Homer. The most prominent of these aspects is the phenomenon of 'pollution', now for the first time forced upon our notice.[1]

Here some definition is necessary. In the form in which we find it in the fifth century, 'pollution' can hardly be said to exist in Homer and Hesiod: and yet some discussion of these authors is necessary both to indicate their differences from the fifth century and also to point out certain resemblances. Accordingly, we will take here as a general definition of 'pollution' the presence (or supposed presence) of any substance, of whatever kind, which is believed to hamper men's relations with the supernatural. A belief in pollution so defined is, as Moulinier shows, present in Homer and Hesiod. Indeed, it would be surprising were it not present, since a belief in 'pollution' in one form or another seems to be common to the whole Indo-European stock.[2] But there seems to be nothing metaphysical about this 'pollution'. It is dirt, real, physical dirt, which must be removed before a man may pray to the gods with any expectation that they will listen to him; and this is the only 'pollution' which Homer knows.[a] As Moulinier says,[3] 'La seule vraie souillure, la seule dont on se purifie dans l'*Iliade* et dans l'*Odyssée*, la seule qui exclut des rapports avec les dieux, c'est

---

[a] But cp. Note 13.

la saleté.' And the same is true of Hesiod:[4] for example, a man is 'polluted' after sexual intercourse[a]—in any circumstances, not merely those deemed immoral—and might 'pollute' the (divine) fire on the hearth; but merely to wash himself suffices to cleanse him. The only metaphysical aspect of such a relationship must be derived from the distaste which the gods are believed to feel for this completely physical dirt.

In comparison with the 'pollution' of the fifth century this phenomenon may seem trivial. Two points, however, are worth notice. Firstly, though we are concerned here with the removal of physical dirt, and though the Homeric heroes cleanse themselves in a very matter-of-fact way, the very fact that the gods seem unlikely to accept the prayers of a man who prays with dirty hands may well endow such dirt with some metaphysical significance; and this might have far from trivial results in a society less self-confident than that of Homer. Secondly, though Homer has not the 'pollution' of the fifth century, he has, to characterize *his* 'pollution', many of the key words used by the fifth century: for example, *katharos*, pure, *miainein*, to pollute, and *miaros*, polluted. These words are naturally used here to signify the presence or absence of physical dirt. Naturally, too, they do not raise questions of moral responsibility: another trivial point which proves to be of importance later.

These authors illustrate another important point. In Homer, as we have already seen,[b] the murderer is not 'polluted' in what will be shown to be the fifth-century sense. If his hands are physically covered with blood, he would be well advised to wash before praying to the gods; but his disabilities extend no further. For other cogent reasons, as has been shown, he must flee from home; but 'pollution' has no part in this. On the other hand, as we have just seen, a belief in 'pollution' in some sense exists in Homer; but it naturally does not result in exile, since the 'polluted' man is not dangerous, and in any case can cleanse himself with cold water. Exile and 'pollution', then, need not be related phenomena.

(ii) *'Pollution' in later writers*

When we turn to the 'pollution' of the post-Homeric period, all is changed. Even the most casual reader could not suppose

---

[a] *W. and D.* 732 f.   [b] Above, pp. 54 ff., and cp. Hesiod, *Scutum, ad init.*

this 'pollution' to be a trivial phenomenon. Such a reader, however, might mistake its true character; for superficially 'pollution' might appear to represent in the thought of this period—in a somewhat materialistic way, it is true—a sense of guilt. But if 'guilt' is taken in a moral sense, that is to say if we expect the word to be used in situations which the society of the period holds to be immoral, and for which the 'polluted' person is in some sense morally responsible, *and in no other situations*, then 'pollution', *miasma*, is, as was shown with great eloquence by Rohde,[5] far from being guilt. Yet this non-moral phenomenon is powerful, and its influence is felt strongly in certain moral contexts. Accordingly, it is relevant to the purpose in hand to investigate its effects; but though its effects alone are strictly relevant, it will be necessary briefly to consider theories which relate to the origin of the belief in 'pollution', since only in this manner can its nature and strength be appreciated, and the measures taken by reformers to circumvent it be fully understood.

In fifth- and fourth-century writers, homicide is the most important occasion of 'pollution': this will be discussed in detail below. One is also 'polluted' by having a bad dream;[a] by contact with death,[b] a contact from which the Olympian gods are completely debarred; by childbirth;[c] and by diseases of a certain—repellent and unnatural—kind.[d] Further examples could be quoted;[6] but these are sufficient to show the range of 'pollution'. 'Pollution' is still a taint, a stain; but it is no longer merely a physical stain. For example, the murderer, as will be seen, can no longer remove the 'pollution' as readily as he washes the blood from his hands; and an Athenian mother, wash as she will, remains 'polluted' for ten days after giving birth;[e] while the 'taint' of a bad dream is hardly physical. Furthermore, 'pollution' is now dangerous, both to its possessor and to those associated with him. The group is 'polluted' by the presence of a 'polluted' individual; and this 'pollution' may have disastrous consequences. It is the disasters of the Theban people as a whole which induce Oedipus to send Creon to Delphi to ask for a remedy; and these disasters prove to have

---

[a] Aesch. *Pers.* 176 ff., esp. 201 ff.　　　　[b] E. *Alc. ad init., Hipp. ad fin.*
[c] Cp. Moulinier, *Le Pur et l'impur*, p. 68.　　　　[d] S. *Phil.* 1032.
[e] E. *Elec.* 654, 1124 ff., discussed by Moulinier, p. 68.

been caused by the 'polluted' Oedipus, the incestuous parricide. But this is not a belief restricted to tragedy or to legend;
belief in 'pollution' and its consequences is an everyday feature
of life even in Athens in the fifth and fourth centuries: a belief
which does not belong merely to some hypersensitive priestly
class, but is part of the outlook of the 'ordinary Athenian'.
Given suitable circumstances, the belief may even affect public
policy, as may be seen from Thucydides' account of the pro-
gressive purification of Delos.[a] The first step was taken by
Pisistratus, who purified as much of the island as could be seen
from the temple. Later, in the sixth year of the Peloponnesian
War, all the corpses were disinterred, and it was decreed that in
future no birth or death—both events which 'pollute'—should
take place on the island, and that in all cases in which this
seemed imminent the affected person should be ferried across
to Rheneia. Lastly, in the tenth year of the war, the Delians
themselves were expelled from their island, since the Athenians
thought[b]

that there was some reason from former days why the Delians were
not pure, *katharoi*, and also that they had omitted this one aspect of
purification, *katharsis*.

Both examples show that 'pollution' is felt to be dangerous;
for it is clear that the Athenian solicitude for the purity of
Delos originated from their lack of decisive success in the
Peloponnesian War.[7] The second shows that no distinction *in
kind* is drawn between 'pollution' caused by the simple presence
of a corpse and that occasioned by a wrongful act of the type
which results in 'pollution', whether the act be of the present or
of an earlier generation. The first type cannot be moral: it is
not immoral to be dead. Accordingly, neither is moral.

But whether 'pollution' is moral or no, the 'polluted' man is
dangerous, and must be treated as such. A 'polluted' man should
be expelled from the country; even if he is not to be harmed, no
one must have anything to do with him;[c] a 'polluted' man must
come indoors, lest he 'pollute' the sun;[d] Antigone is given food
in her cave, to keep up the fiction of voluntary starvation, in

---

[a] Thuc. iii. 104. For the dangers, cp. Thuc. ii. 102, Hdt. vi. 91.
[b] Thuc. v. 1.
[c] S. *O.T.* 229, &c.; cp. *O.C.* 941, *E.H.F.* 1281.
[d] S. *O.T.* 1422 ff.

order that the whole city may escape 'pollution';[a] though Creon denies that an unburied body can 'pollute the gods', events prove him to be wrong;[b] if a murderer touches an altar, he 'pollutes' it;[c] Heracles, having killed his own children in a fit of madness, is afraid that 'the pollution of a child-slayer' may come upon Theseus if he stays with Theseus;[d] and though one should welcome a guest-friend even if he is 'polluted', one should keep him in quarantine.[e]

'Pollution' is dangerous; accordingly, its removal is important. 'Pollution' is non-moral; accordingly, its removal, where removal is possible, is non-moral too. If one has a bad dream, one will wash in a pure spring;[f] if a murderer touches the altar and image of a god, one will wash what is movable in the sea, and purge the temple with fire; one will also wash the murderer, whereupon he becomes an acceptable sacrifice;[g] if one has killed a man, one should purify oneself with fire: but if one intends to kill someone else soon, one may as well wait till one has killed the second man, to reduce the effort and expense of purification-rites.[h]

Clearly there is nothing more moral in this than in washing ink from one's hands. There may also be legal sanctions against such of these actions as are reprehended by society, but the moral aspect is confused or submerged by this non-moral belief. There is, however, a sub-class of 'pollution' which cannot be washed off. It is quite in order for Thebans to meet Argives in battle, for such blood may be cleansed away,[i] but if Eteocles fights and kills his brother Polynices,[j]

This type of *miasma* does not grow old.

The 'pollution' here is of a special indelible kind, such as that which the Erinyes claim adheres to Orestes when he has killed his mother,[k] or that of the *Ion*, where it is suggested that Creusa shall sit as a suppliant at the altar, so that anyone who kills her shall incur the 'pollution' of 'blood which cries out to the gods

---

[a] S. *Ant.* 775 ff.   [b] S. *Ant.* 1042.
[c] Aesch. *Eum.* 40, 167, E. *I.T.* 1032 ff.   [d] E.*H.F.* 1153 ff.
[e] E. *I.T.* 947 ff.   [f] Aesch. *Pers.* 201 ff.   [g] E. *I.T.* 1191 ff.
[h] E. *H.F.* 935 ff. The passage may well be a covert criticism of the formal nature of such rites.
[i] αἷμα γὰρ καθάρσιον.
[j] Aesch. *Septem* 680 ff.   [k] Aesch. *Eum.* 652 ff.

for vengeance'.[a] The indelibility of this type of 'pollution' does not entail that it should be equated with moral guilt. It is simply a stain which cannot be washed out. There can be no question of justification. The Erinyes claim that Orestes has *in fact* killed his mother, and it is their function to haunt matricides; and even had Creusa poisoned Ion as she intended, to kill her at the altar would be to incur indelible 'pollution' as surely as would an unprovoked attack on an innocent person in the same circumstances.

Neither the ordinary nor the indelible forms of 'pollution', then, behave in accordance with the categories of morals. The general deficiencies are these: those not even causally responsible may suffer, it is believed, as much as the cause of the 'pollution'; *miasma*, spanning as it does both those actions which we should regard as immoral and those in which we should suppose that the question does not arise, entails that both classes of actions are viewed in the same manner; and the examples quoted above make it clear that this manner is not a moral one.

B. THE ORIGINS OF THE BELIEF

What has been said so far makes it clear what the belief in 'pollution' which we find in post-Homeric writers is not; it does not, however, make it clear what such 'pollution' is, nor what power it has over the mind. To accomplish this, it is necessary to consider theories to explain the state of affairs which we find at this period. 'State of affairs'; for it is difficult to be more precise than this. On the basis of the evidence quoted, it would be tempting to say 'reasons for changes and developments in the belief in "pollution" after Homer' or even (defining 'pollution' in such a manner as to exclude the Homeric phenomena) 'reasons for the appearance of the belief in "pollution" in post-Homeric society'. Homer, however, seems to suppress what he finds offensive,[8] while Hesiod's *Works and Days* is a short poem, which makes no attempt to be comprehensive; and since a belief in 'pollution' in some form, as has been said, seems to be Indo-European, it is safest to define the present search as one for reasons for the intensification of the belief in 'pollution' in

---

[a] E. *Ion*. 1260, προστρόπαιον αἷμα.

the post-Homeric period. Intensification certainly: the Homeric poems imply the existence of a class which had not the 'later' belief in 'pollution', or at all events did not take it seriously; but there is no such class in fifth-century Athens.

We might conduct this search in two ways, considering either the reasons why the individual became more prone to consider himself 'polluted' or the reasons why society became more prone to believe this of the individual. 'Pollution' is a highly complex, non-rational phenomenon, and it is most unlikely that it should be possible to explain it in terms of one cause; and it seems probable that among the causes of the belief in 'pollution' are both the (irrational) guilt-feelings of the individual and the attitudes of society to some (not necessarily the same) actions.[9] Here I have confined the discussion to the attitude of society, since in the case of homicide, which is the most important for my purpose, it is evidently the more relevant.

Rohde[10] argues persuasively for connecting homicidal 'pollution' with the revival or persistence of the cult of souls believed to be not, as in Homer, at all events in those levels of society with which Homer is concerned, far away in Hades and completely separated from this world, but lurking in their graves, needing rites and nourishment, and taking an interest in events in the world of the living. Then the man who has been killed, whether deliberately, accidentally, or in self-defence, is still present to resent the continued sight of his killer enjoying the pleasures of life; and since the resentment might be dangerous both to the killer and others, the homicide must be treated as 'polluted', and exiled.

This relation of 'pollution' in the case of violent death to the wrath of the *psūchē*, shade, of the dead man is supported by ancient writers. Plato, in the *Laws*,[a] decrees that the man who kills by accident must employ 'means of purification greater and more numerous than those employed by persons who kill a man at games' and in addition 'let him not disregard one of the old myths'. This 'myth' states that a free man with a free man's passions[11] is angry when he is still newly dead, and resents his killer's enjoying the things of which he is deprived. From this myth Plato derives the penalty for accidental homicide, a year's exile.

[a] *Laws* 865 D 3 ff.

Further support for this theory might be derived from the insistence of the writers of this period, in dealing with violent death, on the seeping of blood into the ground. Such phrases as 'the earth drank the blood' or 'when once blood has fallen on to the ground, there is no cure' are frequent. If the blood from 'deeds of blood of old' has seeped into the ground, the earth may breed strange monsters, and a seer-physician, a relative of Apollo, may be needed to handle the situation.[a] The earth, immediately below its surface, is clearly of importance in contemporary belief.

Rohde, in fact, proves his case that 'pollution' in cases of homicide is related to the idea of the dead as near and malignant; which is his purpose. He is not discussing 'pollution' in general, however: for this purpose it seems necessary to insist that 'pollution' is a much more complex phenomenon. For were we simply concerned with the anger of the dead man against his killer, and against his own relatives if they should fail to avenge him, we should expect to find, if the only cause of belief in 'pollution' were that other men are afraid of what the dead man may do, that both the murderer and the relatives are equally 'polluted' until vengeance is taken;[12] and also that the mere removal of the murderer, without any other rites, should end the 'pollution'; for there is no reason why the dead man should remain angry once his victim has departed.

For the present purpose, the full range of situations which entail 'pollution' must be considered. They must be believed to possess some characteristic in common; and it is evident that this characteristic lies not in the situations themselves, but in the attitude adopted towards them by society or by the individual. There seems, in fact, to be something 'queer' about all of them: society regards them with awe and fear. Dead bodies are 'queer'; birth is 'queer'; bad dreams are 'queer', and excite a feeling of unease in the dreamer; being a murderer is 'queer'[13] and being a parricide 'queerer' still: and being married to one's mother is very 'queer' indeed.

We may say, provisionally, then, that the homicide is 'queer': society regards him with awe and fear. The anger of the dead man might produce this result; there may, however, be an

[a] Cp. Aesch. *Septem* 806, *Choeph.* 48, 66, *Eum.* 976 ff., *Supp.* 262 ff., and Scholiast on E. *Phoenissae* 937.

additional reason. This derives from the practice, found in the
Shield of Achilles[a]—which seems to belong to the latest strata of
the Homeric poems—by which the relatives of the dead man
accepted a sum of money from the homicide as indemnity;
whereupon the homicide was presumably allowed to go on
living in the community. The economic loss sustained by the
family in having lost a producer is deemed to have been made
up: possibly more than made up, in an attempt to appease the
family as well.

This practice may well have appeared to have social advantages. In Homer no distinction was drawn between premeditated and accidental or justifiable homicide, so far as concerns
the fate of the killer: the purest accident might deprive the
community of a member it could not spare. The payment of an
indemnity in lieu of flight or of a killing in retaliation would
solve this aspect of the problem; but it is very doubtful whether,
given a state with as yet no strong central system for the enforcement of its will against the wills of individual families,
such a system could ever fully succeed. A man is not merely an
economic unit; and when he is killed, his loss is not felt merely
in economic terms. Even if an indemnity is paid, rancour remains; a rancour which, while the families remain scattered
throughout the countryside, may find few occasions for expression, but which, as civic life gradually develops, may well be
aggravated every day by the sight of the killer walking about
unharmed. Justice may have been done; but the connotation of
agathos does not suggest that the claims of *arete* have been fulfilled.[14] Should an opportunity arise, a blow will be struck in the
name of *arete*; and even if the opportunity does not arise, there
must always be a feeling of uneasy expectancy on both sides.
A society containing such elements will be for ever looking over
its shoulder. It must realize that the killer is a potential source
of trouble; but it cannot rid itself of him, for his indemnity has
been paid. It can only look askance at him, be afraid of him: he
is 'queer'. Now Athenian law[b] expressly forbade the payment
or acceptance of indemnity in case of murder.[15] Rohde claims
that the fear of the anger of the dead man accounts for this;
but the proven social disadvantages of the method might
equally be the (first) cause. The fact that the dying man could,

---

[a] *Iliad* xviii. 497 ff.   [b] Quoted by Demosthenes, *In Aristocratem* 28.

by forgiving his slayer, free him from 'pollution', is not decisive for either theory. If the dying man forgave, his spirit would not be angry; but the remainder of the family would have little claim to vengeance either.

But whatever may be the relation to 'pollution' of the anger of either the dead man or his relatives, it should be evident that neither of them *is* 'pollution'. The anger of the family, even frustrated, does not explain the transferability of 'pollution', nor the necessity for cumbrous rites of purification. Nor yet is the *normal* feeling of 'queerness' before the range of experiences given above sufficient in itself to explain the phenomenon. Homeric society must have experienced the whole range; and yet Homeric society had no such belief in 'pollution'. These, taken together, may be the soil which the idea needs if it is to grow; but a seed, too, is necessary.

The seed is the seed of despair; despair before situations which society can neither explain nor cure, as should be clear from actual cases to be found both in legend and in history. The people of Thebes are suffering from all manner of calamities. There must be some cause; and in such matters it is best to consult Delphi. Delphi pronounces that the king's murderer, still within the city's lands, is the cause: from his 'polluted' presence are derived all the woes of the city. Again, the final purification of Delos took place at the end of the Archidamian War; a war which had not merely not resulted in the expected easy victory, but had exposed the Athenians to privation and pestilence in a manner to which the inhabitants of that fortunate city had become unaccustomed. There must be something— something supernatural—wrong: what more likely than that there is some stain on the Sacred Island?[16]

These two individual examples show an argument from an effect (disaster) to a presumed cause ('pollution') in a society in which the belief in 'pollution' is fully developed. But a similar argument, or a similar irrational jump, will produce such a belief in the first case, if the disaster occurs. One might, however, wonder why the blame should be laid on a 'polluted' person, rather than on an angry god. The latter would have been the natural reaction of a Homeric Greek: it may seem curious that his descendants should change their habits.

If the practice of paying indemnity for murder left the killer in the awkward position that has been suggested above, there is no problem. Never was a man better qualified for the role of Jonah than the killer of whom society would like, but is unable, to rid itself; against whom, in addition, it is probably believed that the dead man is angry too; and who has had, physically, blood on his hands. Even if life is generally prosperous, his fellow citizens will look askance at such a man; and given defeat, civil strife, famine or pestilence, their anger, despair, and bewilderment will discharge upon him with such force as to endow him, in their eyes, with a new quality, that of being 'polluted': a quality which, if the emotions be strong enough, will seem almost visible and tangible and which, since the city, being in general distress, is clearly generally 'polluted', will be rubbed off readily upon any person or thing which he touches.

The dark centuries between Homer and the fifth century provided no lack of war and civic change, and doubtless famine and pestilence were present too. We have seen[a] that the Homeric/ Hesiodic belief that the gods do not listen to the prayers of a man who is physically unclean might readily become metaphysical in character. If this is added to what was said in the previous paragraph, it is not surprising that, as life became harder and narrower, a belief in 'pollution' as we find it in post-Homeric writers should develop, and attach itself both to homicide and to any other situation which, particularly to sensibilities heightened by privation and despair, appeared 'queer', whether to the agent himself or to society. I have said, however,[b] that exile and the Homeric 'pollution' need not be related phenomena. This is true also of the later belief; and accordingly, since only in the case of homicide (and possibly one or two other cases[17]) was society anxious to be rid of the person 'polluted', only there was exile a necessary consequence of 'pollution'. In other cases suitable rites and (sometimes) the lapse of a limited period of time[c] sufficed to render the 'polluted' clean again.

The extent to which 'pollution' 'exists' on the person 'polluted' (it requires considerable mental effort in reading Greek tragedy to remember that, for example, Orestes *looks* normal) is a sure sign of the dark and powerful emotions that were present

[a] Above, p. 87.   [b] Above, p. 87.   [c] Cp. p. 88.

at its birth. With that birth Delphi seems to have been concerned. This at first sight appears rather surprising. The *Oresteia*
leads us to regard Delphi and its god Apollo as civilizing and
rational forces, both generally and in the particular field of
'pollution'. It seems odd, then, that Delphi should associate
itself with such a phenomenon as 'pollution' which, especially
from the point of view of morals, seems an irrational superstition.

If 'associate itself' is understood as 'invent', the situation
is odd. If, however, the analysis of the situation given above is
correct, 'invent' is the wrong word: one cannot invent such a
belief, or transplant it into a society which does not furnish
a suitable soil. No priestly clique could have foisted it upon
Homeric man, perfectly at home in his world. 'Pollution' must
have 'existed', in the presence of emotions born of despair in the
face of disaster and discharged upon suitable Jonahs, before
Delphi could act. All that Delphi, if Delphi it was, need do or
could do was to give a name to the phenomenon, and prescribe
a means for its cure. So, in the case of homicide: 'This man is . . .
queer? . . . "polluted"? . . . is causing the city harm by his
presence? He must be expelled, and the city cleansed by . . .
the following rites.' To say this is not to invent a superstition:
it is to acknowledge an existing situation which, deriving as
it does from non-rational causes, is not susceptible to rational
argument, and to prescribe a cure for it. The cure is completely unrelated to the facts of the situation; but so is the
alleged cause; and the existence of a prescribed form of cure—
any prescribed form—is psychologically valuable. The removal
of the Jonah will relieve the irrational fears of those who remain.

Possibly the mysterious men of Delphi lacked the information
to argue precisely in this manner; but their actions must have
had this effect, and some such effect must have been intended.
Accordingly, like other attempted solutions of problems treated
in Chapter IV, these actions were not obscurantist in character,
but, despite the difficulties which they caused to later thinkers,
an honest attempt to improve an intractable situation.

C. THE PROBLEMS FOR MORALS

In so complex a situation, however, good intentions are not
enough: any future moralist must find his difficulties acute.
Though a cure has been found for this psychological ailment,

it is naturally a non-moral cure, and one which ensures that a considerable number of situations will be considered primarily in non-moral terms. This, though inevitable, is undesirable; and the labelling of the phenomenon makes matters worse in yet another manner. In the first instance, presumably the disaster came first, and the search for a scapegoat afterwards; but once the cause of 'pollution' and the means of its cure become codified, it must be held that certain acts *per se* engender 'pollution', and the emotions originally engendered by despair and disaster will be transferred to the act of killing in its own right. There will thus be a horror of the killer, but not a moral horror which will conform to moral categories: a superstitious horror, a violent non-moral *frisson*, deriving from a fear that the 'pollution' which attaches to a man who has *in fact* killed may cause general disaster if the man be not expelled and the objects he has 'polluted' cleansed. Identity of fear will guarantee that no distinction is drawn between different classes of homicide. True, no distinction was drawn in Homeric society; but the free play of anger which we find there offers the future moral reformer much more opportunity for persuasion than does blind superstitious fear.

The situation is clearly shown by the plots of tragedy, notably that of the *Oedipus Tyrannus*. Oedipus has, despite all his efforts to avoid it, killed his father and married his mother; accordingly, he is a parricide and incestuous, and there can be no extenuating circumstances. 'The pollution of blood shed within the family' adheres to him;[18] that is a fact, and the only relevant fact. True, he says[a] that Apollo has caused his woes[19]—a strange way in itself of looking at oracles—but he draws no conclusion from this. He curses those who preserved his life when he was a child.[b] He should have been left to perish; for then

> I should not have come as my father's murderer, nor yet have been called by men the bridegroom of her from whom I was born. But as it is, I am unholy, *atheos*, and the child of unhallowed parents, *anosioi*.

He did not come with criminal intentions, but nothing can alter the fact that he is, as he has now discovered, *atheos* and the child of *anosioi*.[20] Soon afterwards,[c] he says that he does not know how he will be able to look upon his parents in Hades,[21]

---

[a] S. *O.T.* 1329 ff.   [b] *O.T.* 1349 ff.   *O.T.* 1373 f.

to whom I have done deeds which merit a worse death than hanging.

What he has done, not his intentions, is all that is taken into account. He is 'polluted' and must be driven out.

This, and the many other passages which could be cited from the tragedians, might suggest that 'pollution' incurred by homicide is a thing so terrible that anyone so 'polluted' will be cast forthwith over the city's borders, never to return. Yet the earliest relevant Athenian document which we possess, the Homicide Law of Draco,[22] draws a clear distinction in punishment for various types of homicide; namely wilful, accidental, and justifiable. This distinction remains unchanged in Athenian law throughout the whole period covered by the present work. The penalty for wilful homicide is death, or alternatively perpetual exile, if the accused chooses to fly the country, and confiscation of property. For accidental homicide the penalty is exile until agreement is reached with the family of the dead man. 'Pollution' being what I have argued it to be, one would expect that this was the limit of leniency which any law could allow; and yet there was in Athenian law a category of *phonos dikaios*, homicide for which the law prescribed no penalty, and allowed the injured family no recompense. The fragment which we possess does not contain all these provisions; but it may be supplemented from literary sources, since it seems never to have been altered, and to have been known at all times as 'The Law of Draco'. It is justifiable homicide to kill a murderer who does not fly the country;[a] to kill while defending oneself against attack on one's life, or against kidnappers;[b] to kill an adulterer caught in the act, 'whether with one's wife, one's sister, or one's daughter, or with a concubine, if one is maintaining her with a view to begetting freeborn children': and death caused accidentally either in the games or in war is not held to be culpable.[c]

In view of the nature of 'pollution', some of these provisions seem difficult to understand. True, the murderer who fails to leave the country is *atimos*, deprived of his citizen rights; and if one may not kill a man condemned to death without incurring 'pollution' and exile oneself, the situation is impossible.[23] True,

---

[a] CIA i. 61. 30, cp. Dem. *In Arist.* 37.
[b] CIA i. 61. 37, cp. Dem. *In Arist.* 60.
[c] Dem. *In Arist.* 53.

the adulterer was regarded as an enemy who had declared war on one's property; and accordingly if one killed him only the most formal purification was necessary, since it was long since the killing of enemies in war had been felt to entail any but the most formal 'pollution'.[a] The state, while curbing private enmity in general and subordinating it to the claims of law so far as possible, persisted in allowing a man to take the law into his own hands in such cases, just as in Homer. Again, some similar justification might be adduced for killing in self-defence,[b] but there seems to be nothing in 'pollution' as a concept which would exempt from 'pollution' the man who causes, however unintentionally, the death of a man who is neither *atimos* nor an enemy. Hence the exemption from 'pollution'—pollution, that is, which entails exile—of the man who commits accidental homicide in the games or in war seems odd.

Whatever the reason for this, it is not that the power of the belief in 'pollution' over men's minds has diminished, even in cases of accidental homicide, in situations which Draco's law does not pronounce to be *phonos dikaios*. This may be seen clearly in the speech *On the Chorister*, attributed to Antiphon. This speech is the defence of a man accused of causing the death of a boy chorister by the administration of a draught, intended to improve the voice, which in fact resulted in the boy's death. The prosecution admits that death was not caused intentionally;[c] from the point of view of 'pollution', however, this makes no difference. The speaker is able to turn this to his advantage by pointing out that[d] 'on the day of the boy's death, and on the following day, not even the prosecution themselves thought of accusing me of having played any criminal part in the accident. On the contrary, they neither avoided meeting me nor speaking to me'. Later[e] he tells how Philocrates, the dead boy's brother, joined him on the tribune and conversed with him, his hand on his arm. No Athenian of the period would have so behaved to another whom he believed to be responsible for the homicide of one of his close relatives; and accordingly the speaker is able to dwell upon the astonishment of the authorities when the same Philocrates proceeded to indict him for homicide.

---

[a] E. *H.F.* 935 ff., cp. Aesch. *Septem* 679 f.   [b] But see below, p. 104.
[c] *Chor.* 19.   [d] *Chor.* 34.   [e] *Chor.* 40.

This prosecution seems in fact to have been a piece of opportunism on the part of the dead boy's relatives, who wished
to keep the accused out of the agora, from which as an accused
murderer he would be debarred,[a] in order that he should be
unable to prosecute them for peculation, as he had intended.
But though the belief in 'pollution' was used here as a legal
device, the belief was far from being a legal fiction. The intending prosecutor had to give public notice of the identity of the
accused, and by this means banish him from the agora and the
sacred places;[b] but as the case of the chorister shows, this action
did not *create* the 'pollution', which was incurred from the
moment the man was killed, but simply drew the attention of
the state to the matter. Philocrates should have regarded the
alleged killer of his brother with equal horror before giving
public notice, whether the death was accidental or not.

'Pollution', then, is still regarded with awe, as transferable
and dangerous to others, towards the end of the fifth century in
Athens, in cases of accidental homicide which are not declared
to be *phonos dikaios* by Draco.[24] In these circumstances it seems
curious that Draco should have found himself able to except any
cases of accidental homicide, however useful to the state such
an exception might be. The reason is doubtless that Draco was
a nomothete.[c] Nomothetes do not argue, they issue fiats; and
a fiat may well be the best way of handling a non-rational
phenomenon such as 'pollution'.[25] Whatever the means, however, the results are clear: Draco was able to set limits on this
non-moral phenomenon and restrict the field in which moral
judgements did not apply. But though Draco might speak *ex
cathedra* and be believed by the people of his own day, the
problem appeared in a new form at the end of the fifth century.
The intellectual *francs-tireurs* of this period were not the men to
believe something merely because it had been said by a nomothete. They needed intellectual justification for what they
believed, if it was not to be changed; and if they wanted to
change anything, they needed intellectual justification for that
too. Such men, on taking a general view of 'pollution', found a

---

[a] [Antiphon] *Tetral.* Aa 3, Aa 10, Ba 2, *Murder of Herodes* 10/11, Lysias 13, 81.
[b] Dem. *In Macart.* 57, *In Pantaen.* 59.
[c] A legislator; but the word implies much more autocratic power than its
English equivalent, and is applied to men entrusted with a thorough revision of a
legal code.

belief in a metaphysical stain which attached itself to the person as a result of homicide *qua* homicide (save in a few specified cases) and to certain other acts as acts, motive, or the general rightness or otherwise of those acts, not being taken into account. One causes a certain state of affairs, and 'pollution' automatically adheres to one *qua* cause: accordingly, one might logically expect to be 'polluted' in a manner entailing exile in certain circumstances in which law and custom maintain that one is, in Athens, not so 'polluted'. The conclusion of a valid argument must be accepted; and yet the claims of morals and of practical politics—if there are to be games, or training for war, the participants must have some such safeguard—demand that in these cases one should not be so 'polluted'. There is no possibility of carrying the position by assault, for the thinkers of this period are not the men either to accept or to issue fiats without logical justification; guile, in the form of a more subtle argument, is needed.

D. SOLUTIONS

That the guile was not lacking may be seen in the *Tetralogies* ascribed to Antiphon. These I take to have been composed in Athens, by Antiphon or another, in the last quarter of the fifth century.[26] They purport to be law-court speeches, but are clearly not so. There are no witnesses, no laws, and no psephismata;[a] and speeches are composed for both sides, which no speech-writer would do in an actual case. If they are not intended for delivery, it might appear that these speeches are specimens composed by a sophist; and the *Antilogiae* of Protagoras comes to mind as a possible parallel. The object of these speeches, however, is different if, as seems likely, Protagoras' work furnished for each argument a contradictory one, equally valid in appearance; for in the *Tetralogies*, on the basis of the arguments presented, the last speech in each tetralogy clinches the matter, and the speaker should win his case. The writer has a point to make. One's view of the nature of that point depends on the general view taken of the *Tetralogies*.

The author's use of language is significant. On two occasions[b]

[a] Decrees passed by the assembly, which might well be quoted in a genuine forensic speech.

[b] Bb 9, Bc 7.

one of the speakers says that 'the law . . . forbids a man to kill,
whether unjustly, *adikōs*, or justly, *dikaiōs*'. This could not be the
law of any state in the world: no law could forbid a man to do
anything which it recognized in the same breath as just. Accordingly, this must be a rather misleading condensed expression, in which two standards are hurled at one another's heads.
The tetralogies make it clear[a] that the demands of 'the law' are
those of the belief in 'pollution' in its most unrestricted form;
hence *dikaiosune* here represents human standards of justice, and
'the law' the claims of superstition.

The writer is clearly on the side of human justice; and so
superstition must be circumvented by argument: an argument
which in the second and third tetralogies is essentially the same.
It is necessitated by, and depends on, the following fact: whereas
in modern thought there can be a violent death without anyone
being guilty of culpable homicide, in Greek there can be no
phonos (violent death) without someone being *aitios phonou*. This
is a simple causal law in the first instance; but it is to the *aitios
phonou* that 'pollution' adheres. Hence lack of intention is not
enough, for one is none the less *aitios*, cause, of the death. Even
the defence has to admit in the second tetralogy that had the
boy prosecuted shot accidentally into the crowd of spectators at
the games, 'We should have had no argument to prove that we
were not homicides, *phoneis*'.[b] Given this situation, one can
only try to plead that one is not *aitios phonou*, in the strict sense of
'cause', or submit to the penalty. That defence is here put
forward. The situation is this: at javelin practice, while the
others were throwing, one boy ran across the line of fire and was
killed. The defence maintains that the dead boy died as a result
of his own mistake[c] and so caused his own death. (It is admitted
that this is an unusually closely reasoned defence.) The boy
with the javelin shot straight for the mark; so the dead boy was
'not struck, but of his own accord, *hekousiōs*,[27] ran into the flight
of the javelin'; and 'those who do anything of their own accord
are the cause, *aitioi*, of their own misfortunes'. In the second
defence speech it is maintained[d] that if the trainer called the
boy across at the fatal moment, he is the *aitios* of the boy's
death; and hence *he* is 'polluted'. The throwing cannot be the
cause; or all the other throwers are equally guilty. The speaker

concludes[a] that the dead boy 'perished as a result of his own
mistakes, and in one and the same moment made his mistake
and was punished by himself'. A few lines later he claims[b] that
since the dead boy did cause his own death, he will leave no
supernatural contagion upon anyone; and the speech ends with
these significant words: 'Acquit us: we are not *aitioi phonou.*'

The third tetralogy concerns the killing of an older man by
a younger whom he had insulted and assaulted. The essentials of
the first speech are that the man did not die at once, but some
days later, under the hands of a doctor. The doctor was a poor
one: and hence, according to the defence, was responsible for
the death of the wounded man. The prosecution very reasonably rejects this view, saying that the doctor is protected by law,
and in any case was not responsible:[c]

We entrusted the dead man to the care of the doctor as a result of
the blows he suffered from the accused. How could anyone else be
the homicide, *phoneus*, rather than the man who compelled us to
employ this doctor?

A reasonable point, but a dangerous one: the defence at once
retorts[d]

If the man who struck the blow, inasmuch as he compelled you to
resort to a doctor as a result of the blow, is more the *phoneus* than the
man who actually killed him, then the man who struck the first
blow is the *phoneus*; for he compelled the man who was defending
himself to strike a blow in reply, and the man who was struck as a
result to visit the doctor.

As the circumstances are presumably fictitious, it seems most
likely that the doctor is only introduced so that the defence may
make this point. At all events, this is the burden of the defence:
the man who struck first was *aitios* of his own death, while the
other defended himself and 'did not "do" anything'.[e] 'Pollution' adheres to the man who initiated the causal sequence;
hence, it is argued, in neither case is there any religious bar to
acquittal, for in neither tetralogy did the accused *cause* the
death of the dead man. Indeed, the third tetralogy, by denying
that the man who defended himself 'did' anything, stresses the
continuity of the causal sequence to such a point that he ceases
to be an agent at all.

---

[a] Bd 8.   [b] Bd 9.   [c] Cc 5.   [d] Cd 3.
[e] Cd 6, ἠμύνετο καὶ οὐκ ἔδρα.

These defences are not couched in 'ordinary Greek'. Considerable strain of language is involved; and hence any other
passage which betrays the same mode of thought should be
easily detected. Such a passage occurs in the *Oedipus at Colonus*.
We left Oedipus in the *Oedipus Tyrannus* incestuous and a
parricide, condemned by his acts. Even had Sophocles the will,
he had no means of acquitting Oedipus of his unintentional
crimes. Nor did Oedipus expect it. But a far different Oedipus
appears in the *Oedipus at Colonus*, written in or just before 406
B.C. As soon as he appears on the stage he rebukes the Chorus:
they must be terrified by the mere name of Oedipus, for there is
nothing to fear in Oedipus himself:[a] 'For as to my deeds—I
suffered them rather than "did" them.' Later[b] the point is put
succinctly, and forced home to the audience, in an exchange
between Oedipus and the Chorus:[28]

Cho: You have suffered. Oed: I have suffered things not to be
forgotten.
Cho: You have 'done'. Oed: I have not 'done'.

This he explains by saying 'I received a gift . . . '. True, this
refers to his incestuous marriage with Iocasta, not to the killing
of Laius in self-defence; but 'I have not "done"' is the same
plea, couched in similar strained language, as 'He defended
himself and did not "do" anything'. Such a coincidence of
oddities must spring from a common source.

With this passage may be compared one from Euripides'
Orestes.[c] Helen denies that she can be 'polluted' by speaking to
Orestes:

I am not 'polluted' by speaking to you, for I ascribe your error to
Phoebus.

Orestes is not 'polluted' at all. Phoebus caused the sequence of
events which led up to the death of Cleopatra; hence Phoebus is
'polluted', not Orestes. This subtle argument, here presented in
two lines, reflects a much wider discussion. Otherwise Euripides

---

[a] S. *O.C.* 266 f.　　　　　　ἐπεὶ τά γ' ἔργα μου
　　　　　　　πεπονθότ' ἐστὶ μᾶλλον ἢ δεδρακότα.
[b] *O.C.* 538 f.　　　Cho: ἔπαθες. Oed: ἔπαθον ἄλαστ' ἔχειν.
　　　　　　　　Cho: ἔρεξας. Oed: οὐκ ἔρεξα.
For the language, cp. also *Tetr.* Bb 7, Bc 3.
[c] E. *Orest.* 75 f.

would have had to explain: and the argument is similar to that of the third tetralogy.

The tetralogies attributed to Antiphon, then, are closely linked in thought to other Athenian documents which can be dated; and as there is nothing to prevent us from believing them to be Athenian, it seems reasonable to regard them as an important document from that type of thought which is reflected in the *Oedipus at Colonus* and the *Orestes*; a type of thought which presumably took its rise between the production of the *Oedipus Tyrannus* and that of the *Orestes*. It is possible, though not necessary, that the *Tetralogies* themselves initiated this type of argument. At all events, some more detailed discussion than that which appears in these two plays must have preceded their production. This thought was doubtless necessary. The intellectual excitement of the period led men to push to their apparent logical conclusions the implications of ordinary language and traditional belief: a tendency which will be seen also in the next chapter.[a] The idea of 'pollution', as it appears in Athenian homicide law, contained evident illogicalities. It was too powerful a phenomenon to leave any hope that it could be eliminated together with its illogicalities;[29] and accordingly these illogical leniencies must, as the tetralogies set out to do, be shown to be logical. The justification of existing law at such a time is of great importance; but, as is evident from the *Oedipus at Colonus* in particular, this thought also made it possible to eliminate certain applications of traditional belief which had become repugnant, and to emphasize individual intention and moral responsibility over a wider field.

It only remains to show that the fourth century still felt the need of this intellectual justification for the exemptions of the homicide law. This is clearly the case. Demosthenes, glossing the provision that no penalty is to be exacted for accidental death caused in the games, says[b]

But if the dead man was too weak to bear the strain involved in contending for victory (the nomothete) held that he was *aitios* of his own misfortune, and so allocated no punishment for his death.

The circumstances differ from those of the second tetralogy, but the explanation is the same: the man caused his own death.

---

[a] Below, pp. 124 ff.   [b] Dem. *In Arist.* 53.

The explanation must be given: the 'pollution' must go somewhere.[30]

In Plato, too, though there is no explicit mention of the fine-drawn theories of the *Tetralogies*, there are indications of their presence. No reason is given in the *Laws*[a] why

If death is caused in the games, or ensues from injuries there received; or if a man kills a friend accidentally in war or in practice for war, when he has been purified as is laid down by the Delphic law, he is to be considered pure, *katharos*.

If formal rites of pollution are performed, all will be well. This is not explained;[31] but when Plato turns to accidental homicide, he says[b]

But if a man kills with his own hand, *autocheir*, but unintentionally, whether with his own body or with a tool or weapon or by the administration of food or drink or by the application of heat or cold or by the deprivation of breath, whether he does this with his own body or through the agency of the bodies of others, he is by all means to be treated as one who has killed with his own hand, and is to pay the following penalties. . . .

The great insistence on causality here is very reminiscent of the *Tetralogies*.[32] The most significant words, however, are 'with his own hand'. They imply that, in turning from the above-mentioned cases which carry no penalty we have now come to a new category in which the killer *is* considered to have killed with his own hand; evidently the killer in the former cases is not considered to have so killed, and is for this reason able to go scot free. This irresistibly recalls the *Tetralogies*.

The homicide laws of Plato, then, composed at the end of his life, show no significant difference from the current Athenian laws. Accidental homicide must still be punished by exile, restricted to a year: no more lenient penalty is possible in a state which, as do both Athens and the state sketched by Plato in the *Laws*, still maintains a court to sit upon animals and inanimate objects which cause death[c] and cast them, when proved to be the cause, beyond the borders. In suitable cases, however, the thought of the sophists was able, not to argue the Athenians out of this non-rational belief altogether, but to justify intellectually the assertion that in some cases the belief

---

[a] *Laws* 865 A.   [b] *Laws* 865 B.   [c] *Laws* 873 E, Dem. *In Arist.* 76.

was not applicable. The sophists could not, perhaps would not have wished to, remove the belief altogether; but they penned this non-moral belief, which affects ascriptions of moral responsibility, into as small a corner as possible, and allowed the ordinary concepts of value to operate over the rest of the field.

NOTES TO CHAPTER V

1. The indebtedness of the present discussion to Rohde, *Psyche*, esp. chap. v, to Dodds, *The Greeks and the Irrational*, and to Moulinier, *Le Pur et l'impur dans la pensée des Grecs* is evident throughout: and is so prevalent that to acknowledge it on each occasion would be to multiply endlessly footnotes in a chapter already overburdened with them.

2. Moulinier, pp. 15 ff., shows how slender is the evidence for the existence of the belief in prehistoric Greece; but for evidence from a wider field, cp. Rohde, op. cit., chap. ix, n. 98; Keith, *Religion and Philosophy of Veda and Upanishads*, 382 ff., 419 f.; Rose, *Primitive Culture in Italy*, 96 ff., 111 ff.; and Wagenvoort, *Roman Dynamism*, chap. v (all cited by Dodds, op. cit., p. 62, n. 109). There are significant differences between the views of the various peoples discussed by these authors; but in view of the wide definition of 'pollution' which I am using here, they will serve as evidence.

3. Moulinier, op. cit., p. 33.

4. Ibid., p. 34.

5. Cp. Rohde, op. cit. (Eng. trans.), especially p. 294; also Latte, *Schuld und Sünde in der griechischen Religion*, Archiv für Religionswissenschaft, xx. 254 ff.

6. For further examples, largely evidence drawn from outside the period under discussion, see Rohde, op. cit., app. v.

7. The purification of Delos shows that the demand and counter-demand by Athens and Sparta at the beginning of the Peloponnesian War, that the accursed be cast out, was not a pointless one. Nothing resulted from the demands; and naturally there is a difference between turning out a few Delians and depriving the nation of a Pericles: but there are signs (cp. Thuc. vii. 18. 2) that after ten years of a war in which neither side had won any striking success, feeling both in Athens and in Sparta was more sensitive in these matters than it had been at the outset.

8. Cp. Dodds, op. cit. 43 f.; Moulinier, op. cit., 58 ff.

9. For the guilt-feelings of the individual, cp. Dodds, op. cit., pp. 45 ff.

10. The argument is persuasive: but Rohde's point (op. cit. v. 3) that vengeance for murder as we find it in Homer *must* depend on an earlier view, now faded, that the dead man is crying out for vengeance, and is not in Hades but near by, seems an overstatement; grief and anger being basic human emotions, only a consciousness of relationship or friendship is needed to ensure that the dead will be avenged, even if it is

believed that death entails complete extinction, particularly in a society which lives by the Homeric standard of *arete*. But the nature of the funeral rites for Patroclus seems to justify Rohde's contention (ibid. i. 1. 5) that the cult of souls is pre-Homeric, and merely submerged in Homeric society, at all events in those levels of society which we meet in the poems.

11. The connotation of *agathos* is clearly relevant here.

12. In Athens, the intending prosecutor had to give public notice of the identity of the accused, thereby banishing him from the agora and the sacred places, Dem. *In Macart.* 57: but the prosecutor was not banished in this way. True, if he failed to prosecute where the situation demanded, the 'pollution' would be transferred to him, *Euthyphro* 4 c; but this is a different matter.

13. As seems to be felt already in the late passage *Iliad* xxiv. 480 ff. The murderer comes to the house of a powerful man in another land, and awe, *thambos*, falls upon the onlookers. This awe is not the normal Homeric attitude to a killer, and may mark the beginnings of an attitude which contributed to the belief in 'pollution'. Frisch, op. cit., p. 111, explicitly contrasts this *thambos* with religious awe. Certainly it is not religious awe, or anything like it; but it seems to me to be one of the seeds from which, given the other conditions suggested in the text, a belief in 'pollution' in this sense might spring, or rather be brought into the foreground. For other indications in Homer, cp. *Iliad* i. 314, *Odyssey* xxii. 480 f., discussed by Nilsson, *Geschichte der griechischen Religion*, i. 82 f. The Greeks cleansed themselves and threw the scourings into the sea in *Iliad* i, after the divinely sent plague had ended; and Odysseus in *Odyssey* xxii, having already cleansed his bloodstained palace with water, also purified it with sulphur. These passages show the difficulty of separating the physical from the metaphysical with any certainty in such contexts. It is impossible to be certain whether these precautions are religious or hygienic or both; the fact that Odysseus cleanses his palace twice proves nothing—it must, after all, have been very dirty after the massacre and the cavalier treatment it had received from the suitors—and the fact that he says that sulphur 'cures *kaka*' is equally indecisive: for the presence of dirt is itself *kakon*, harmful and unpleasant. Odysseus may be afraid of 'pollution' in the later sense; but his matter-of-fact attitude, typical of Homeric cleansing of any kind, is very different from that of the fifth century. The statement of the position in the text, p. 86, conveys the essentials of the Homeric belief.

14. Cp. (Antiphon) *Tetralogies* Aa 8. The accused had been much harassed in the courts by the man he was alleged to have killed, and was soon to have been prosecuted again for embezzling sacred monies. So, the speaker alleges, he murdered his enemy, hoping that he would not be detected, and that none of the relatives of the dead man would pursue the charge of embezzlement: 'And even supposing that he should be convicted (of embezzlement) he thought it more *kalon*, noble, to suffer the penalty when he had taken his revenge than to be destroyed by the indictment in a manner unbefitting to a man, *anandrōs*, i.e. without

retaliating.' Here, at the end of the fifth century, the pressures of the *arete*-standard within a civic community are clearly seen.

15. On this point see Rohde, op. cit., v, n. 154, where the opposing view is discussed and rejected.

16. True (Thuc. v. 32. 1) the Athenians shortly afterwards restored the Delians, 'since they were concerned at their misfortunes in the war, and the god of Delphi had told them in an oracle to do so'. This, however, does not prove that the original purification was not the result of anxiety over the success of the war, but rather encourages this supposition: the Athenians' aims had not changed, but Apollo told them that the means were the wrong ones.

17. The possible cases are sacrilege and incest. Incest seems very doubtful. It is indeed difficult to define, since Attic law in certain cases enjoined matrimony upon close relatives, for economic reasons (cp. *Dictt. Ant.*, s.v. *epiklēros*). If we restrict the term to mean sexual relations with one's mother, sister, or daughter, the position remains unclear. Plato, *Laws* 838 A ff., expresses the utmost horror of incest: he calls it 'the most *aischron* of all *aischra*', 838 C 1, but, 838 B 1, relies on an 'unwritten law' to prevent its occurrence. There is no mention of 'pollution' or exile. Cimon, indeed, who married his sister Elpinice, had to go into exile (Plut. *Cim.* 4. 14. 15): but his exile was the result of ostracism, and he was not ostracized for this reason. Nor do the orators (cp. Lysias, *In Alc.* 1. 41; Isaeus, *De Dicaeog. hered.* v. 39) mention such a penalty: while Socrates, Xen. *Mem.* 4. 4. 19 ff., only maintains that the children of incestuous unions will be inferior. Lastly, when Oedipus says that he will never be able to return to Thebes, S. *O.C.* 600 f., it is as his father's murderer, not as incestuous, that he is excluded.

Sacrilege seems at first sight more likely. In Plato's *Laws*, 854 D ff., any slave or alien who commits sacrilege is to be flogged and flung naked over the state's boundaries, while any citizen who commits the offence is to be executed, and to have his body flung beyond the borders; and Xenophon, *Hell.* 1. 7. 22, shows that the latter provision is part of Athenian law. This suggests 'pollution', but 'pollution' is not explicitly mentioned. (*Akathartos*, *Laws* 854 B 3, is insufficient to suggest this, for the reference is general.) Athenian law, too, treats traitors and the sacrilegious alike (Xen., loc. cit.); but traitors are certainly not formally 'polluted', and it seems unnecessary to explain differently two cases which fall under the same law. The traitor and the man who commits sacrilege have in different ways offended against the gods of the state; for treachery too is a crime against them. This is surely enough to ensure that such men are cast out and denied burial. (The case of Cylon, discussed by Moulinier, op. cit., pp. 46 ff., is different. This crime, which rendered the Alcmaeonids 'polluted' and accursed in future generations, was not merely sacrilege but sacrilege aggravated by murder. Murder committed in a sacred place naturally results in—indelible—'pollution', cp. E. *Ion* 1260, p. 90 above.)

18. The indelibility of blood shed within the family needs explanation. It might be explained on the grounds that, under early methods of

property-tenure, no member of the family, save its head, possessed any individual property, and that hence in such cases no indemnity could be paid—as would be possible where property was to be transferred from one family to another—so that only perpetual exile could serve as a punishment. But if, as I have argued, the practice of paying indemnity in lieu of execution or flight contributed largely to the growth of a belief in 'pollution', such a solution is impossible. In any case, in itself it explains neither the horror attaching to such a crime nor the transferability of pollution. The peculiar heinousness of this crime is surely attributable (a) to the violation of natural family ties, (b) to the strong temptation, particularly where land is short and is the basic standard of wealth (to say nothing of Freudian motives), to kill a father or an elder brother, either to inherit at once or to increase one's own share. Natural horror, and a necessity to set a strong curb on a strong temptation (otherwise difficult to curb, as Rohde, op. cit., p. 179, points out: since it was the relatives who had to avenge, the murderer and the natural avenger might well be the same person), would guarantee the special place of murder within the family. The peculiar horror guarantees the indelibility: an inference strengthened by the fact that other heinous murders entailed indelible pollution, cp. Creusa, *Ion* 1260 ff., p. 90 above.

19. He uses the word *pathea*, sufferings. The word is without philosophical implications in the *O.T.* Contrast *O.C.*, p. 105.

20. This passage shows how the idea of 'pollution' can affect the meaning of such words as *atheos* and *anosios*. Cp. Chapter VII, pp. 135 ff.

21. This passage indicates that, whatever its origins may have been, the belief in 'pollution' in the fifth century no longer depends on the belief that the dead are at this very moment actively angry, roaming the land or lurking in their holes just beneath the earth. Oedipus believes that his parents are in Hades, and that he will meet them only when he is dead; and he does not know how he will *then* address them. His parents are in the Homeric Hades far away; and yet he is 'polluted'. The century wavers regularly between the idea of the dead as in Hades and as lurking in their graves, even in the course of a few lines. In the *Choephori*, 138 ff., Electra and, 479, Orestes pray to their father as to a powerful free-lance spirit lurking in his tomb; and the whole of the latter passage down to 509 generally regards him as such. But, 354 ff., we find an account of the splendid life Agamemnon would have led in the next world had he died an honourable death before the walls of Troy; and this passage undoubtedly postulates a Hades of the type depicted in *Odyssey* xxiv. Perhaps it may appear a little more attractive than it does there, but this doubtless results from the element of 'what might have been' in the *Choephori*. Such a confusion about the next life is common in any society; but its occurrence in passages such as this, where 'pollution' is important, suggests yet again that this society was not quite so hag-ridden by the idea of the dead as powerful, malevolent, and present as the attempt to deduce the phenomenon of 'pollution' from their anger alone would suggest.

22. The extant portions of the law of Draco do not in fact mention 'pollution', but its existence is clearly implied, and it may have been mentioned explicitly in the lost sections. The Attic orators at all events are in no doubt as to the reason for the provisions of the law.

23. Since from Homer onwards it is felt that the injured family has the right to kill the murderer without retribution, the executioner should not be regarded as 'polluted' on any theory of 'pollution' which derives it from the anger of the living; but on Rohde's theory it seems difficult to see why the *murderer's* spirit should not be angry when he is executed, however justly. Cp. Clytemnestra's ghost, *Eum.* 94 ff.

24. As is shown by the frequently quoted plea in Antiphon, *Murder of Herodes* 82, that though many men who were not pure, *katharoi*, in respect of their hands, or had some other 'pollution', have been known to cause the destruction not only of themselves but of those who were pure, *hosioi*, as regards the gods, yet the accused did not prove to be a Jonah on the sea-crossing to Athens. (The exact evaluation of the passage is difficult. Though the presence of 'pollution' is still in part an experimental issue as it was for Orestes, *Eum.* 284 f., this is by no means the only plea which is advanced by the defence. One cannot offer to undergo ordeal by salt water to prove one's innocence.) An ingenious counter, still accepting the fact of 'pollution' and its dangers, is put forward by Lysias *In Andoc.* 19 ff.: 'Have the gods spared the 'polluted' Andocides, though he is a ship-owner and goes voyaging on the sea? The deity was enticing him on, so that he might return to the scene of his iniquities and pay the penalty at my insistence.'

25. It is possible that Draco was merely codifying current practice in regarding accidental homicide in games and in war as not entailing 'pollution' in any sense which necessitated exile. It might be urged that such acts had never entailed 'pollution' in this manner; but this, though the contrary cannot be proved, seems unlikely. It seems much more likely, on the theory of the origin of the belief suggested here, that all types of homicide originally entailed 'pollution' and exile, but that this was later modified (by Draco or another, or by gradual change) in the light of experience. That this was so, at all events in the case of involuntary homicide, is strongly suggested by *Laws* 865 B ff., where the penalties for such homicide are given. If a metic accidentally kills another man, he must be exiled for a year, as must a citizen. But if a foreigner accidentally kills another man, be the man killed a foreigner, a metic, or a citizen, he must, in addition to the purification imposed, be banished for life. Now this is against the whole trend of Platonic legislation. In other cases, the foreigner is punished more mildly than the citizen, for he has not had the benefit of the moral training prescribed by Plato (cp. *Laws* 854 D ff.). Why then this difference in the case of murder? There can only be one reason. This is an element of earlier legislation (presumably surviving in some state known to Plato) which Plato found himself unwilling to discard. From this it may be deduced that all men were originally in the condition in which the foreigner now finds himself; but the state has need of the metic and still more of the

citizen, and hence custom and superstition have been modified in their favour. This suggests that the acts allowed to be justifiable homicide may have been later developments too.

The passage shows that the reason for perpetual exile is 'pollution', and hence that this is the reason for all such exiles, not simply the rational one that the temper of the dead man's relatives will require time to cool. The prescriptions against the exile's return show this. If he return willingly, the law-wardens are to execute him and hand over any property he may possess to the next-of-kin of his victim; if he return unwillingly, if for example he is driven there by bad weather while travelling by sea, he shall camp with his feet in the sea, and watch for a ship to take him off; or if he be brought back forcibly by land, the first magistrate who meets him shall loose him and send him back over the border unharmed. These provisions show quite clearly that the killer was not exiled for his own security, or to ensure the stability of the state *in a rational manner* by discouraging private vengeance. After all, even if he dabbles his toes in the sea, the avenger could readily reach him. The state, in fact, is afraid of him; it insists that he keep himself at all costs beyond the boundary of the sacred unity formed by its territory: and the only possible reason for this is that, despite the formal purification already demanded of him, he is still dangerously 'polluted'. The manner in which such a person would disrupt the state is not natural, but supernatural.

26. It is alleged that these speeches can have nothing to do with Attic law, since though the three tetralogies are concerned with deliberate homicide, accidental homicide, and justifiable homicide respectively (or rather are said to be: in fact both the second and the third tetralogies would fall under the Athenian category of *phonos dikaios*), they do not cite the Athenian law under which accidental homicide in the games and homicide committed in self-defence were specifically exempt from penalty, but instead resort to argument to prove that no penalty may be exacted in this case (K. J. Maidment, *Minor Attic Orators*, Introd.). It is true that the *Tetralogies* do not *use* Athenian law; but there are other possible relationships. (On the view of Maidment, presumably the writer is trying by sophistry to slip round the provisions of the law on behalf of his client; or perhaps one might say, since the circumstances are hypothetical, that he is trying to persuade some state to change its law.) Maidment produces one other positive argument against the Attic origin of the *Tetralogies*: he asserts that death is stated to be the penalty for accidental homicide in Bb 10. Two things may be said in reply to this. Firstly, the prosecution only asks that the jury should 'exclude the homicide from those things from which the law excludes him', and not allow the whole city to be 'polluted' by him (Ba 2, cp. Bc 11); and this phrase is not a euphemism for execution but the normal expression for exclusion from the sacred places or banishment; so that it seems that 'destruction' (διαφθορά) and 'childlessness' (ἀπαιδία) in Bb 10 refer to the speaker's loss of his son by banishment rather than by death. Secondly, even were death the penalty for accidental homicide,

this would not exclude the relationship of the *Tetralogies* to Attic law which I have posited in the text. There is in fact no solid reason against the supposition that these speeches were composed, albeit not by Antiphon, in a context of Attic law. For stylistic evidence against ascribing them to Antiphon himself, see Maidment, op. cit., pp. 36 f.; and for evidence that the problem of responsibility in such matters was discussed in Athens, see Plut. *Pericles* 36 (Pericles and Protagoras).

For a variety of other possible motives for the composition of the *Tetralogies*, motives which seem to me to be less plausible in view of the evidence from the tragedians, cp. Kells, *Antiphon and Homicide Law*, Proc. Lond. Class. Soc. i.

For a similar approach to a similar problem, cp. Keith, op. cit., p. 478.

27. Maidment, ad loc., translates *hekousiōs* by 'deliberately'. This is an overtranslation. The use of *hekousiōs* here is evidently related to that of Aristotle, *E.N.* 1109ᵇ30 ff., where *hekousia* are defined (with qualifications) as actions of which the first cause, *archē*, lies in the agent himself. Clearly the boy did not run into danger deliberately; but he was not compelled to do so, and the *arche* was thus certainly in himself.

28. For a further instance of Sophocles' (new) sensitivity to intention and its absence, cp. S. frag. 604 Nauck, ἄκων δ' ἁμαρτὼν οὔτις ἀνθρώπων κακός, 'No man who commits an error unintentionally is *kakos*'. The fragment is from the *Tyro* which, from Aristophanes' references to it in the *Lysistrata*, 138 (and cp. schol. ad loc.), seems to have been composed in or about 411 B.C. (This attitude is of course in complete contrast to traditional values, cp. for example Simonides 5 Bergk, below, Chapter VIII, pp. 165 f. and Appendix, pp. 355 ff.)

29. Though a theory which would have entailed this seems to have been tried. In Euripides' *Hippolytus* (428 B.C.) the Nurse asks Phaedra, 316 f., ἁγνὰς μέν, ὦ παῖ, χεῖρας αἵματος φορεῖς; 'Are your hands pure of the "pollution" of blood?' Phaedra replies χεῖρες μὲν ἁγναί, φρὴν δ' ἔχει μίασμά τι, 'My hands are pure, but my mind, *phrēn*, has some *miasma*'. Again, in the *Orestes* (408 B.C.) Menelaus, 1604, says to Orestes ἁγνὸς γάρ εἰμι χεῖρας, 'I am pure in respect of my hands', and Orestes replies ἀλλ' οὐ τὰς φρένας, 'But not in respect of your mind, *phrenes*'. Phaedra is referring to her guilty desires, while Orestes is complaining that Menelaus has not helped him. In neither case has the person whose *phren* has been 'polluted' *done* anything to incur 'pollution'; and Euripides seems to be attempting to extend (or transfer) 'pollution'-terms to cover moral guilt. The attempt evidently met with no success, as might indeed have been expected: the change in usage is too violent.

30. Demosthenes also assigns as the reason of the lawgiver that he did not consider the result but the intention of the agent, which was to defeat the man, not to kill him. This clearly reflects legal discussion on contexts which do not entail 'pollution'; but by itself it can have no effect, for in cases of ordinary accidental homicide, where no other recipient of the 'pollution' can be found, the fourth century can no more acquit the homicide than could earlier centuries.

31. Earlier, civic interest is assigned as the reason for the existence of no penalty for accidental homicide in military training, *Laws* 831 A; and for self-defence, and the killing of burglars and adulterers, a man is to be considered *katharos* as if he had killed an enemy in war. Yet the use of *autocheir* is significant.

32. Some at least of the provisions are designed to forestall or counter arguments of the type 'It was the bullet that killed him. I only pulled the trigger', a trend of thought which both the *Tetralogies* and Gorgias' *Helen* might well suggest. (See Chapter VI, pp. 124 ff.)

VI

EXTERNAL INTERFERENCE

A. 'COMMON SENSE'

IT was shown in Chapter II that Homeric man, despite his belief in gods who interfered spasmodically, and frequently with great malevolence, in his affairs, was, except in certain isolated instances with a pronounced flavour of 'Literature', disinclined to believe that these gods furnished him with an excuse for his misdeeds or his failures. The analysis of Homeric society and Homeric standards of value suggested reasons for this. However, as was seen in the last chapter,[a] at least towards the end of the fifth century in Athens thought and argument on the subject of causation had become very subtle indeed; and this new sensitivity might be expected to have its effect on cases such as these.

First, however, the gap between Homer and the sophists must be filled. When nothing else is involved but a simple relation between gods and men, common sense continues to prevail. The typical attitude is that expressed by Neoptolemus in his rebuke to Philoctetes:[b]

Men needs must bear the fortunes sent to them by the gods; but men who wilfully wallow in misfortunes have no right to compassion or pity.

Philoctetes' disease was sent by the gods and must be borne. But if he now refuses to leave the island on which he has been marooned, when he has the chance, this is sheer wilfulness, and the gods have nothing to do with it.

This typical example shows how little effect such a belief need have on ascriptions of moral responsibility. Its whole basis is the distinction between things which happen to a man, and over which he can have no control, and his own actions and decisions, for which he is fully responsible.[1]

[a] Above, pp. 102 ff.　　　　　　　　　　　　　　[b] S. *Phil.* 1316 ff.

Such a belief could only seriously affect moral responsibility if it were interpreted with sophistic refinement. Generally, however, such is not the case. 'Divinely caused events' are as strictly limited and as empirically judged as are 'acts of God' in our law, and actions are left as free as common sense would have them.

The beliefs of this period, however, are no more unified than were those of Homer. Different phenomena evoke different beliefs, and no attempt is made to co-ordinate them; hence it is only to be expected that any attempt to make one system out of them will reveal contradictions. To attempt to remove these contradictions is to misrepresent the nature of the evidence; the different trends, with their different implications, must be evaluated separately.

If the belief in interfering gods is combined with historical narrative or prophecy, a different situation is produced, for such a narrative by its very nature involves the gods much more generally in the events related, and hence, it might be supposed, raises more serious problems of responsibility. In history, a decision and a plague are both events; and there is much more temptation in such circumstances to ascribe both to the gods. Such temptation was resisted in Homer; and in the fifth century this is generally still the case. The typical manner in which this situation is treated is shown by the historical narrative of the *Persae*.[a] We are first informed that the past success of the Persians has been caused by *moira*:

For through the favour of the gods *moira* prevailed in former years and laid upon the Persians tower-destroying wars, the mêlée of cavalry fights, and the sacking of cities.

Later remarks make it clear that the Chorus is afraid that the gods may now (without motive, as was their original grant of success) be about to cast the Persians down again. In the middle of these remarks, however, there occurs a stanza in which events are described as under the control of the human performers:[b]

They learned to look upon the plain of the broad-wayed sea as it grows white with foam before the boisterous wind, trusting in slender cables and in devices for carrying men.

No causal or other relationship is asserted between this stanza

[a] Aesch. *Pers.* 93 ff., and cp. 108 ff.   [b] Ibid. 100 ff.

and the last. They are simply placed side by side, and no more
incongruity is felt than was felt in Homer.[2] The two levels on
which the events are described still do not intersect. The reason
is not that, if all events are theistically determined, the fact that
they are so determined ceases to be of relevance in ascribing
responsibility; for there is no evidence that any writer of this
period consciously held that all events are so determined. In
fact, 'free will' and 'determinism', as applied to philosophical
views of life, have no relevance to this period, which has neither
the desire nor the philosophy to sustain them. The reason is still
to be sought in a mere failure to see the implications of the
language used, implications that are only likely to be fully realized by those whose concern is more with theory than with
practice.[a]

Nor has the practice of consulting oracles any greater effect
on personal responsibility. A consideration of the motives for
consulting an oracle shows clearly why this is so. One consults
an oracle in order to discover what is going to happen, or to
discover what one ought to do. In the first case, one's desire for
information about the future is prompted by the belief that one
can do something about it; and in the second case, there is no
sense in asking what one ought to do in order to attain a desired
end if it is determined beforehand that one will or will not do it
anyway. Anxiety to know the future produces the oracle as an
institution; an anxiety which may be expressed in words as a
belief that the future may be unpleasant but that, if known, it
can be altered. The anxiety is the important element in the
situation, one sufficiently powerful normally to prevent the
reflection that for the future to be known it must be fixed in
some sense. Here again we have a belief which, though curious
in theory, is perfectly comprehensible in practice.

We may take as an example the oracle which, Herodotus
reports, was given to the inhabitants of Siphnus:[b]

> But when in Siphnus the town hall is white, and white-browed the
> market-place, then indeed is there need of a shrewd man, to beware
> of a wooden ambush and a ruddy herald.

This is interpreted by Herodotus as referring to the assault on
Siphnus by the Samian exiles, which caused great loss of pros-

---

perity to the island. The implications are the usual ones: One day the Samians[3] will come to Siphnus. This will be a time of great peril, and the Siphnians must deliberate very carefully whether to do X or Y. That is to say, at the moment of the 'fixed' event deliberation is not pointless but especially necessary, for affairs are 'on the razor's edge'.[4] The outlook of the man who believes in oracles is this: the gods, while leaving most events free, are given to strewing calthrops in men's paths. These calthrops, if due care is exercised, and warning obtained from oracles, can usually be avoided. Such calthrops are moments of crisis: moments at which one's present decision will influence the rest of one's life for good or ill.[5]

Some calthrops are not to be avoided. The gods have made their decision, and it is not to be overridden by men. Such is Philoctetes' disease, which prolongs the siege of Troy to its allotted span, and such is the normal manner of thinking of death. It was believed[a] that in the legendary past men had been able to foresee the time of their own deaths; and even though they had lost this power, there remains a strong temptation to suppose that the time of so important an event must be fixed. In the face of death, man's precautions are futile; accordingly, it must be in the hands of the gods. A fatalistic attitude to the whole of life, however, does not result from this. Death is, as in Homer, still expressly contrasted with events which *are* controllable. As Callinus says,[b]

You will die when the *moirai* spin death for you; but a man should march straight forward brandishing his spear.

There may be a bullet with your name on it, but until you meet it your actions are in your hands, and it is shameful to succumb. More generally, one only assumes that there is no escape when events have made this clear beyond doubt. Seers occasionally grow fatalistic, for they know what is to happen;[6] but the ordinary man's faith in oracles is the reverse of fatalistic. It is not a normal Greek reaction, on being told by an oracle that one will kill one's father and marry one's mother, to reply 'Ah, well, what must be must be.' The Greek gets up in a hurry and puts as great a distance as possible between his supposed parents and himself.

[a] Aesch. *P.V.* 248, Plat. *Gorg.* 523 D.   [b] Callinus 1. 8 Bergk, cp. E. *H.F.* 309 ff.

B. ABNORMAL SITUATIONS

The ordinary man of the fifth century, then, feels little temptation to thrust responsibility upon the gods. There are, however, in the myths of the period, situations which are far from ordinary. Of these, the most important for the present purpose is the belief in the inherited curse, treated by Aeschylus in the chronicles of the houses of Laius and Atreus. The curse is working, in the house, in the blood, in the mind, as the successive generations appear, driving them—irresistibly?—on to evil and destruction. The accursed, it seems, are no longer free agents; and a sensitive thinker may see the implications.

Aeschylus was undoubtedly a sensitive thinker; but in the *Seven against Thebes* it is doubtful whether he does see this point. The crux of the play is Eteocles' last speech:[a]

When the gods send evils, *kaka*, one cannot escape them.

So Eteocles expresses his belief that the family curse is driving him on to fight his brother Polyneices in order that the house of Laius may perish. He does fight him, with disastrous results. The audience know, even as Eteocles utters the line, what must happen; and as the line is an accurate prediction, and furthermore ends an argument, there is a strong temptation to suppose that this is Aeschylus' 'message' in the *Seven against Thebes*. For, from the moment when Eteocles realizes[b] that he has stationed himself where he 'must' fight Polynices in single combat, he begins to speak of the curse of Oedipus:

Alas, now are the curses of my father coming to fruition.

He continues to be convinced of the inevitability of the single combat throughout the argument with the Chorus which ensues, though the Chorus tries all manner of counter-persuasion, and assumes Eteocles' freedom of action, supposing, in the normal Greek manner, that even if the Erinys is serving as a calthrop, an offering to the gods may well put matters right.[c] Eteocles, however, closes the argument with the line quoted, and rushes out; and immediately[d] a mood of foreboding comes over the Chorus, who sing of the Erinys who is about to fulfil the angry

---

[a] Aesch. *Septem* 719.   [b] *Septem* 653 ff., esp. 655.
[c] Ibid. 698 ff.   [d] Ibid. 720 ff.

curses of Oedipus. They seem convinced by Eteocles' actions
that the curse is responsible for what they have seen; and it
seems impossible that, given the arrangement just described,
any audience could deduce that Aeschylus' intention was to
show that the Chorus was right in the first place, and Eteocles
wrong, about the situation. Thus, as the curse is responsible,
we might suppose that Eteocles is not responsible, and hence
should be absolved from blame on these grounds.

Such a supposition, however, would be dangerous. Aeschylus
is not ascertainably preaching in the *Seven against Thebes*: there
is no 'message'. Were this a *pièce à thèse*, Eteocles' lack of
responsibility for his actions would surely be more heavily
emphasized. In the play as we have it[7] there is an excellent
opportunity for this. Eteocles and Polynices were equally under
the influence of the curse. Accordingly, when Antigone says
defiantly that she will bury the traitor Polynices, she could
have justified her action (perhaps in a manner not very suited
to her character; but *pièces à thèse* have other criteria) by saying
that neither brother should be held responsible for his actions,
since those actions were in both cases controlled by the curse.[a]
Since neither Antigone nor anyone else in fact says this, it is
safe to conclude that Aeschylus, in writing this play, had no
thought of the issues of responsibility involved.[8] Eteocles' use of
the word 'evils', *kaka*, to characterize the situation emphasizes
events rather than decisions, though decisions are involved; and
this doubtless confuses the matter.[9]

When his thoughts are turned on such issues, Aeschylus
leaves no doubt of his attitude to the responsibility of the
accursed. At the end of the *Agamemnon*, the question of responsibility is brought to the fore when the Chorus says[b]

Daemon, you who fall upon the house and the two descendants of
Tantalus . . . .

The daemon falls upon the house . . .: Clytemnestra, profiting
from Aeschylus' new sensitivity, a sensitivity which seems to be
not entirely his own, but one which contemporary thought has
brought into a new prominence, immediately seizes on this
ascription of responsibility to a power beyond herself, thereby
hoping to disclaim her own responsibility:

Now you have directed rightly the judgement of your mouth, in naming the thrice-gorged daemon of this race.

This is indeed a new sensitivity for Aeschylus. The Chorus for some time remain in the same frame of mind, talking in terms of the curse; but then change their tone, and apostrophize Agamemnon, saying that he was

Smitten in a treacherous death by a two-edged weapon wielded by the hand of a wife.

Clytemnestra immediately realizes that the implications of this are different:[a]

You say this is my deed.

Denying the imputation, she says,

No; taking the form of the wife of that dead man, the old bitter spirit that takes vengeance for the crime of Atreus has offered him as payment, having sacrificed a full-grown man on top of young ones.

It was really the Alastor, the avenging spirit, who killed Agamemnon; and by her words Clytemnestra carries the minds of the audience back to the first crime of the accursed house. The implication is clearly that the sequence of events since then is beyond human control. The Chorus, again quickly seeing the point, rejects this plea:

Who will bear witness that you are guiltless, *anaitios*, of this murder? Yet the avenging spirit sprung from a father's crime might be a sharer in the deed.

Clytemnestra may not shift the blame. Aeschylus—for it is certainly Aeschylus speaking here—allows that the Alastor may have helped: for Aeschylus, fully conscious of the complexity both of life and of the stories on which he had to work, finds it impossible to cut the Gordian knot by denying the efficacy of curses, a denial which his audience would certainly have refused to accept. But the Alastor is only partly responsible: Clytemnestra could have helped doing what she did; and she must be punished to the limit.[10]

This, from any point of view, is a remarkable scene. It must seem to us psychologically subtle:[11] Clytemnestra, in her shock

---

[a] Aesch. *Agam.* 1497 ff.

at the act she has committed, feels that it is not her act, that she is caught up in a stream of events over which she has no control. For the present inquiry, however, the scene has a different significance. The manner of speaking is not new: it is the linguistic usage of ordinary Greek. The passages from the *Persae* discussed above differ from it in only one way: there the implications of such a manner of speaking are not drawn out. It is unlikely that Aeschylus should have set up such a position as this merely for the pleasure of knocking it down: surely this new sensitivity must be a more general phenomenon whose implications Aeschylus finds it desirable to oppose. This seems in fact to be the case: in two instances Herodotus records that Delphi furnished excuses for favoured persons, on the grounds that the misdeeds they had committed were part of a divine plan. Timo, the priestess of Paros who had behaved treacherously with Miltiades, was excused in these terms:[a]

Timo was not the cause, *aitiā*, of these events. It was decreed that Miltiades should come to a bad end, and so Timo was sent to tempt him on to his ruin.

Again, both Delphi and Dodona held that Evenius, who had allowed some sacred sheep that were in his charge to be eaten by wolves, should not have been punished:[b]

The Apolloniats had acted unjustly in depriving Evenius of his eyesight, for they (the gods) themselves had sent the wolves.

Both of these judgements occurred before the production of the *Oresteia* in 458 B.C.: Miltiades attacked Paros soon after the battle of Marathon, while Evenius was the father of the man who was seer to the Greeks at the battle of Mycale, and Herodotus tells the story[c] in such a manner as to imply that Evenius' misfortune had occurred before that battle. Once the implications of these judgements, and of the general current of opinion whose presence they indicate, had come to his notice, Aeschylus might well feel impelled to declare his opposition; for while the gods' willingness to furnish Evenius with an excuse for his mistake may be a moral advance,[d] the same cannot be said for their claim to have caused Timo's immoral decision. Aeschylus asserts that even in the extreme case of the accursed family,

---

[a] Hdt. vi. 135.　　　[b] Hdt. ix. 93.　　　[c] Cp. ix. 94 *ad fin.* and 95.
[d] Contrast the earlier belief, above, pp. 62 ff.

though some may be predisposed towards evil by supernatural agency, none are so predestined. Though the choice may be harder for some than for others, there is always a choice; and hence no one may escape responsibility for his actions on these grounds.

C. SOPHISTIC INFLUENCES

It is particularly in that Greek literature which draws upon myth and legend that such problems as this are likely to occur; for in such myths and legends the functions and particular acts of the gods are specified. Accordingly the later tragedians too may be expected to be concerned with the problem, particularly when, as has been seen, the thought of the end of the fifth century rendered much more sensitive the theorizing on cause and effect. Here divine interference may be considered together with other alleged restraints, since these are found together in the relevant writers.

It is in the *Troades* of Euripides, produced in 415 B.C., that the problem is most evident.[12] The play contains a full-dress debate, almost a trial scene, on the subject of Helen's guilt or innocence.[a] Speeches are delivered by the defence and by the prosecution. Some of the pleas relate to circumstantial evidence, but many are directly relevant to the question of responsibility. Helen, speaking in her own defence, pleads first that the fault was not hers but Hecuba's, inasmuch as Hecuba bore Paris, and Priam's, inasmuch as Priam did not kill the child.[b] The relation of the thought in this plea to the pleas in homicide cases considered in the last chapter[c] is evident. Later, Helen pleads that Paris had Aphrodite with him, a goddess so powerful that even Zeus cannot resist her;[d] and argues that her action in leaving her comfortable home with Menelaus to go sailing on the high seas proves that she was not in her right senses at the time.[e] She ends her speech[f]

If you wish to overrule the gods, your desire is foolish.

This is the chief burden of her defence:[13] no one can resist the gods; and Hecuba, as prosecuting counsel, seems to accept the

---

[a] E. *Tro.* 914/1059.   [b] Ibid. 919/922.
[c] pp. 102 ff.   [d] E. *Tro.* 950.   [e] Ibid. 945 ff.
[f] Ibid. 964 f.

contention that *if* Aphrodite herself had taken a hand in the matter, then Helen's defence would stand. But she insists[a]

My son was of outstanding beauty, and your mind, in seeing him, was transformed into Aphrodite. It is man's own folly which is Aphrodite, and it is with justice that the name of the goddess begins the word *aphrosunē*, folly.

It was not Aphrodite's fault. You saw the beauty of Paris, and your mind was swayed: that is all. Anyway, your story of Aphrodite coming in person with Paris is a stupid lie; could she not have accomplished everything while remaining quietly in heaven?

Greek tragedies, and those of Euripides in particular, seem sometimes to reflect contemporary discussions; discussions which are usually lost. In the case of the Trial of Helen, however, we possess, in the *Helen* of Gorgias, a contemporary treatment of the same topic with which Euripides may well have been familiar. Gorgias' work is in the form of a defence of Helen: he makes no attempt to compose for the prosecution. The defence is very systematic. Gorgias lists four possible reasons or causes of Helen's flight to Troy.[b] She was either (*a*) influenced by the purposes of chance and the plans of the gods and the decrees of necessity or (*b*) snatched away by force or (*c*) persuaded by arguments or (*d*) captivated by love.[14] We might grant that this was a full analysis of the possible reasons or causes, and then expect Gorgias to show that Helen was influenced by (*b*) or possibly (*a*), since (*b*) is certainly, and (*a*) possibly, a good defence. Gorgias in fact argues that, no matter which of these was in fact the reason, Helen should be acquitted.

His argument runs as follows: If a god caused Helen to do this, and a god is greater than a man in might and wisdom and other respects, then Helen must clearly be acquitted. And if Paris carried her off by force, Paris did wrong, while Helen was unfortunate; for he did terrible things, but she suffered them. It is right then to pity her, but to hate him. And if it was speech, *logos*, that caused Helen's downfall, speech is a mighty master and has great powers over men. Gorgias lists some of its powers in causing fear, grief, and other emotions, and concludes that speech, in persuading her mind, compelled it to believe what was said and consent to what was done; the

[a] Ibid. 987 ff.   [b] Gorgias, *Helen* 6 ff.

persuader, then, inasmuch as he compelled has done wrong, while she who was persuaded, inasmuch as she was compelled, is wrongly blamed. And so on this supposition too Helen did not do wrong but was unfortunate, and should be acquitted. Lastly, Gorgias takes the supposition that Helen acted under the influence of love: not of a god, but of a passion. Saying that love is produced by what we see, he cites instances to show that many people have been terrified out of their wits by what they have seen; and he uses words which emphasize the suggestion that something is done to the observer *from without*.[a] We might suppose, then, that Gorgias would attempt to assimilate to compulsion the effects upon the emotions of things seen; which would furnish him, if his argument were accepted, with a valid defence. Instead he says, supposing Helen's passion not to be due to the influence of a god, but to be merely a human 'disease' and ignorance in the soul, that even so it ought not to be blamed as an error but regarded as a misfortune. The sight of Paris came upon Helen by accident, and hence she acted as a result of the 'snares of chance', not the plans of the mind, and as a result of the necessities of love, not the schemes of design.

Certain things are clear at once. As might have been expected, this encomium of Helen strongly resembles in thought and language the arguments relating to 'pollution' and causation which were discussed in the last chapter. There is the same acute sensitivity to the idea of cause, the same insistence on the distinction between acting and suffering, and on misfortune as opposed to wrongdoing.[15] Clearly speculation on cause and effect is one of the chief topics of the sophist of the period: a speculation which may or may not prove beneficial in practice.

Here, however, the distinction between the trial of the *Troades* and the encomium of Gorgias should be noted. Gorgias, as an encomiast should, undertakes to prove Helen innocent no matter what caused her to leave with Paris. Reduced to its simplest terms, his thesis is: 'If Helen can say "I did *X because Y*", no matter whether *Y* is a record of external compulsion, a motive, or a denial of intention, Helen may disclaim responsibility.' Euripides, however, makes it clear through the mouth of Hecuba that, so far as he is concerned, the hypothetical 'If the gods cause a person to do *X*, then that person is not responsible for *X*' is

a παρέσχετο, ἐνεργάζεται, Gorgias, *Helen* 18.

valid, but that if Aphrodite is merely the lust which the sight
of Paris caused in Helen, this is far from being a defence, but
rather an admission of full responsibility: a view, both of causation and of the actual situation, with which the Aeschylus of
the *Oresteia* would readily have agreed.

Euripides will not accept the extreme view, though he must
surely have known of it; and the reason is clear. A drama is a
practical work; it involves action. People appear on the stage
and behave as they do in real life; and hence, however much
Euripides may be fascinated by the theoretical disputes of the
sophists, when a decision is made in a drama it is made with
both feet on the ground. True, in conducting a defence, Euripides is apt to throw all manner of intellectual litter into the
scale: we have seen Helen try to throw responsibility for her
adultery on Priam and Hecuba. The lines, however, must be
seen in their wider context: they are ignored by Hecuba, and
have no effect on any judgement of responsibility passed by
anyone in the play. They would serve to titillate the audience;
and this is their sole function. When it comes to the point,
Euripides, like the Greeks in general, at all events during the
period covered by this work, takes a commonsense view of
causation and responsibility, particularly in relation to the
individual act.[16]

Gorgias, however, is differently situated. He has merely to
spin his words, and split his hairs, at leisure. He has no need to
show his characters in action. His work is a work of theory, like
the *Tetralogies*. The *Tetralogies*, however, left their mark on later
Greek thought, even if, being designed to provide a theory to
support what was already general practice in Athens, they could
not affect action. But the *Helen* of Gorgias, had its recommenda-
tions been put into practice, would have affected action very
decisively: the closing of the law courts would have been the
least of its results. Of course such a danger was never real: the
surviving documents of the fifth century indicate that it is not
the general practice of that century, any more than that of the
Homeric world, to attempt to evade personal responsibility by
ascribing the original cause of actions either to its gods or to
chains of events in the natural order, whatever the apparent
encouragements of 'ordinary Greek'. Individual attempts are
made; but they are either vigorously opposed or ignored.

NOTES TO CHAPTER VI

1. Cp. the harsh words of Solon, frag. 4 Bergk. Athens might have been put in jeopardy by divine action (meaning presumably famine, plague, drought, earthquake, &c.); but this is not the reason for the present troubles, but rather the unjust minds of her rulers. For this contrast cp. also Hesiod *W. and D.* 320; Pindar *Nem.* 8. 17; Theogn. 833 ff.; Eur. *Phoen.* 18, and especially 999 ff.

2. I select this example because the juxtaposition is so close; but the dual attitude occurs even more clearly elsewhere in the play, e.g. at 345 ff. The messenger says that some daemon has been destroying the army, that fortune was not balanced evenly for the Persians, and that the gods have saved the city of Pallas. We may deduce from this that the messenger believes that the gods normally balance fortune equally; and for the idea that the gods are responsible we may compare 454 f., 514, 532, 911. Yet despite this, at 1025 ff. credit for the victory is given (not surprisingly, before a Greek audience) to the qualities of the Greek fighting man. Similarly, despite the ascription of the rise of the Persians to *moira* at 93 ff., in the résumé of Persian history at 759 ff., especially 765 ff. and 782 ff., the whole sequence is treated in terms of the good and bad qualities of the various kings. The attitudes stand quite happily side by side; which, though illogical, is perfectly natural as a belief to live by. Cp. Dodds, op. cit., 7, 16, 30 f., 51 (10).

3. The Samians are not mentioned by name, but the event is 'fixed' by being given a fairly full oracular description. It might be thought that the oracle is merely saying, 'If ever you become wealthy, and can afford to face your public buildings with marble, expect trouble'; but comparison with such oracles as those given to Croesus, Hdt. i. 55 and i. 85, shows that this was not the manner in which such advice was regarded. These both refer to definite future events (the accession of Cyrus and the end of the dumbness of Croesus' son) as fixed, and give advice to be followed when these events occur. On 'conditional prophecy', cp. e.g. Greene, op. cit. 23 f., 121, 348, 376, with app. 6.

4. The phrase and the thought it implies are both common from Homer onwards, cp. *Iliad* x. 173; Hdt. vi. 11; Theogn. 557; S. *Ant.* 996; E. *H.F.* 630.

5. Cp. the common story of the man who is warned by a seer not to have a son, as the son will kill him. The unborn son will be harmful: that is fixed, but it is possible to take precautions now by not having a son.

6. The case of seers is significant. Since they know the inevitable before it happens, they must be inclined to take a fatalistic attitude to any approaching calthrop of an unavoidable nature. Cp. *Septem* 615 ff. (Amphiaraus), *Agamemnon* 1301 (Cassandra), *P.V.* 101 ff. (Prometheus). The attitude of Prometheus is only one of a number of inconsistent attitudes which he is forced to adopt as a result of the peculiar nature of the folk-tale plot, whose attitude to causal relationships and determinism is even more primitive than that of the early fifth century.

7. Admittedly the end of the *Septem* (1005 ff.) has been held with great

probability by Bergk and others not to be by Aeschylus; but unless we
suppose that the lines which we have replace an ending in which Antigone *did* claim that neither brother should be held responsible for his
actions—which seems, to say the least, highly unlikely—the argument
in the text will stand.

8. In view of the 'carelessness' in such matters of the *Persae* and *Septem*,
we should surely not assume that Aeschylus means to raise questions of
responsibility unless the text makes this abundantly clear. The first
chorus of the *Agamemnon* is relevant here. Page, in the introduction to
the Denniston/Page *Agamemnon*, xxiv, n. 4, maintains that 'the whole
course of Aeschylus' exposition shows the clear intention of absolving
Agamemnon from responsibility (for having sacrificed his daughter
Iphigeneia)'. Later, Page asks whether this point could not have been
made more clearly, and replies for Aeschylus '*No: it is definitely stated
that he put on the harness of Necessity (218): a man who acts under Necessity
does not act voluntarily. It is further stated in unambiguous terms (223) that his
mind was deranged (παρακοπά) before the trouble could be begun (πρωτοπή-
μων)*'. In a further reply, Aeschylus is made to say '*It is clearly stated that
Artemis compelled Agamemnon to commit the crime, and that she did so for
no fault on his part: it remains nevertheless an abominable crime, and he committed it, and he must pay for it. The plea of compulsion will not avail him, any
more than the plea of total unawareness availed Oedipus*'. In view of the last
statement, I should prefer to say that Aeschylus does not absolve Agamemnon from responsibility in the sense in which 'responsibility' is
used in this book, since he remains fully liable to punishment. More
generally, it would surely be safer to say that Aeschylus does not raise
the question of Agamemnon's responsibility here at all. True, he makes
statements which in our eyes inevitably raise this question: if we suppose a man to have committed a crime when out of his mind and under
duress, we inevitably suppose him not responsible for his actions. But
Agamemnon in the *Iliad* (cp. Chapter III, pp. 49 ff.) claimed to have
been out of his mind when he wronged Achilles, and this did not affect
his responsibility at all. We have no reason to suppose that the position
has changed; and we have seen in the text how little effect the representa-
tion of an event or action as inevitable need have. And if Aeschylus
does not raise the question, it is clear that it would not occur to the
audience here any more than in the *Septem*, or indeed in the *Oedipus
Tyrannus*. Had the *Agamemnon* been written in 408 B.C. instead of 458
B.C., Aeschylus would have had to make his position clear, to draw a
conclusion rather than merely to state the facts as he saw them. Possibly he is fortunate in not being forced to do so; though this of course
does not diminish the stature of the *Agamemnon* as a tragedy.

9. Though a similar expression had not confused the matter for the poet
in *Odyssey* i. 32 ff., cp. Chapter II, pp. 23 ff.

10. When face to face with Orestes, Clytemnestra goes no further than to
claim, *Cho.* 910, that *moira* was a contributory cause, *paraitiā*. She seems
to hold that this should be an extenuating circumstance; but there is
no sign that this is Aeschylus' own view. Orestes replies with a mere tit

for tat, *Cho.* 911: if Fate or the curse helped to kill Agamemnon, then the same Fate or curse is urging Orestes on now. But in the *Eumenides* Orestes makes no attempt to defend himself in these terms, and Apollo does not advance the plea on his behalf: Orestes' will was not forced.

11. This effect may be accidental. The manner in which the scene is written shows that its chief point is the one discussed in the text; but it is certainly impossible to read the scene now without giving it also this perhaps unintended effect.

12. The effect on Sophocles of this type of thought has already been described in Chapter V, p. 105.

13. Helen, as her last plea, 1042 f., attributes her actions to a disease sent by the gods; but Menelaus, as his ensuing conversation with Hecuba, 1046 ff., shows, does not accept it.

14. The (*d*) is supplied by Diels–Kranz, ad loc. Whether it is read here or not, it is one of the possibilities which Gorgias considers.

15. Indeed, δρᾶν becomes almost a technical term of this type of thought, cp. Gorgias, *Helen* 7 with Chapter V, pp. 105 f.

16. Even Plato, who in the *Republic* found so much evil to say of vulgar Greek belief in the gods, did not assert that fatalism was a fruit of these beliefs.

VII

THE WAYS OF GOD TO MAN

A. A POSSIBLE SOLUTION?

THE fourth chapter made it clear that the function of the gods in underwriting morality, and hence in linking *dikaiosune* to *arete*, was an essential one, even if it led to problems; for there was not enough systematic thought to sustain, or suitable conditions of life to encourage, Theognis' equation of *dikaiosune* and *arete*. The problems, however, were serious, and it is natural to inquire whether some approach can be found which avoids them. *Dikaiosune*, after all, refers explicitly to relationships between man and man, drawing in the gods only as an afterthought. Possibly some word or words used to denote and commend relationships between man and god might prove more useful to the moralist; for since the gods now seem to require from man some 'quiet' moral behaviour, such words must surely be applied in virtue of this behaviour.

The facts are not so simple. True, the underwriting of morals was, in the scanty surviving literature of the period between Homer and the fifth century, the most prominent divine function; true, belief in the gods as upholders of the quieter moral virtues persisted into the fifth century; yet this belief in no way destroyed or inhibited belief in other, non-moral forms of divine behaviour. It could not: the myths and legends which portrayed the Greek gods as non-moral and frequently malevolent beings were part of general Greek culture and belief, while the situations which had evoked those legends in the first place still existed. A Xenophanes might complain:[a] the whole weight of tradition was against him, confusing the moral function of the gods and preventing the relevant questions from being asked.

These myths are the framework on which Greek tragedy is built; and the non-moral extremes which they sometimes reach

[a] Xenophanes frags. 11 and 12 D/K.

are shown by the plots of, for example, the *Prometheus Vinctus*, the *Ajax*, the *Hippolytus*, and the *Heracles*. Aeschylus may attempt to solve the problems posed by these myths, Euripides may be using them for his own purposes: here all that matters is that the myths exist as part of popular belief.

In this light, the words which denote relationships between man and god seem much less likely to be of use to morals, and they might almost be dismissed out of hand. If, however, we are to demonstrate why such words play only an inconspicuous part in the ethical writings of Plato and Aristotle, some examination is necessary. This examination may be confined to a survey of the range of instances in which the words are used: it is unnecessary for my purpose to attempt to assign an original or nuclear meaning to them, since such a survey will indicate clearly enough the reason for their uselessness in solving the present problem.[1]

B. *HOSIOS* AND *EUSEBES*

(i) *Quiet Moral Usages*

The relevant words of praise are *hosios* and *eusebēs*,[a] their contraries being *anosios*, *asebēs*, and *dussebēs*.[2] *Hosios* and *eusebes* frequently commend those who honour the relationships which the gods are believed to uphold, firstly relationships within the family and between the family and its guest-friends, and between the state and those who are bound to it by either birth or treaty. So one may show oneself *eusebes* in receiving suppliants; one should perform the rites for the dead with a mind that is *eusebes*; Polynices in attacking his native Thebes has a mind that is *asebes*; and we find the *eusebes* contrasted with men who are hostile to strangers and unmindful of the gods.[b] To steal Helen is to do deeds that are *anosia*; to be killed by one's nearest kin is to die by a death which is most *anosios*; the Phoenicians may refuse to sail against Carthage since, if they did so, they would be doing things which are not *hosia* inasmuch as they would be fighting against their own descendants; and it is the

---

[a] The nearest equivalents for these words are 'pious', 'devout', 'religious'; but of course the present discussion indicates that none of these is adequate.

[b] Aesch. *Supp.* 419; Pind. *Ol.* 3. 41; Aesch. *Septem* 831, 602 ff.

mark of *hosioi* to succour suppliants, whereupon Zeus protects
their houses.[a] The words are also used in more general moral
situations. Atrocities, in particular, are *anosia*: they were de-
precated by the gods even in Homer.[b] Such are the suggestion
of Lampon that Pausanias should impale the body of Mar-
donius after the battle of Plataea; the trade in eunuchs; and
Menelaus' sacrifice of children in order to obtain a fair wind.[c]
These general examples are drawn from Herodotus; but already
in the *Seven against Thebes* we find[d]

> Alas for the fate which unites a just man, *dikaios*, with men who are
> *dussebeis*.

Eteocles is referring to the practice of the gods in punishing the
dikaios together with the *adikos* in a general disaster. The linking
of *dussebes* with these words seems to guarantee its general moral
use; and there is no lack of parallels.[3]

Eusebes and *hosios*, then, have in the fifth century a well-
established moral use, to characterize and commend certain
relationships between man and man. Indeed, since the gods
rarely appear overtly in these relationships, it might be felt that
in such uses *eusebes* and *hosios* are as purely moral as (say)
dikaios. If, however, these words are also used explicitly to
commend certain relationships between man and god, and if
(as has been seen to be the case) the gods are believed to uphold
all these quiet moral relationships, it seems difficult to deny that
the fifth-century Greek, in using the words, had this aspect of
the gods in mind.

Since *hosios* and *eusebes* commend the man who upholds these
quiet moral relationships, they might appear, like *dikaios*, to
raise the correct questions for the present inquiry and, like
dikaios, only to require suitable divine sanctions; sanctions
which, from the nature of the words, can hardly be withheld.
This is not the case. To discover the exact flavour of such words,
it is always necessary to consider the full range of uses in comparable instances.[4] It was said above that the belief in the gods
as capricious and malevolent was not dead in the fifth century. Such gods must be appeased or if possible won over to a
non-moral favouring of one's purposes; and since they are

[a] Hdt. ii. 114. 2, ii. 121 ε. 2, iii. 65. 5, iii. 19. 2; Aesch. *Supp.* 27.
[b] Cp. Chapter IV, n. 10.
[c] Hdt. ix. 78. 1, viii. 105. 1, ii. 119. 2.   [d] Aesch. *Septem* 598.

non-moral, they must be won over in a non-moral way. Sacrifices must be performed, temples made beautiful or wealthy by the gift of costly articles; and there must be words to commend those who please the gods in this manner too.

(ii) *The Barter-relationship*

It may be unnecessary *a priori* that the same words should be used as in the moral relationships; but it soon becomes evident that in Greek such is the case. When Bacchylides addresses the tyrant Hiero

Do *hosia* and cheer your heart; for this is the greatest of benefits,

it is inadvisable to translate hastily: 'Cheer then thy heart with righteous deeds.'[a] The context shows the real meaning: Bacchylides has been singing of Croesus, who sent many gifts to Pytho, and yet was overcome by the Persians. Having ascended a funeral pyre with his family, he gave orders that the pyre should be kindled. But Zeus sent a shower of rain and extinguished the flames; and Apollo carried off Croesus and his daughters to the land of the Hyperboreans

On account of his *eusebeia*, in that he had, more than any other mortal, sent gifts to goodly Pytho.

Croesus' *eusebeia* is his sending of gifts to Apollo's oracle; and for this he expects great recompense. The greater the gifts, the greater the favours which may be expected in return; for Bacchylides goes on

Yet, illustrious Hiero, no man of those who (now) hold Greece in sway will claim that he has sent more gold to Apollo than you have.

The line of argument is clear: 'You may not be as rich as Croesus; yet you have given more gold to Apollo than any other Greek; and so, being more *eusebes*, you may expect more in return.' Accordingly, when Bacchylides adjures Hiero 'Do *hosia* and cheer your heart', it is quite clear that he means: 'Continue to give gifts to Apollo; and you may then have many more years of wealthy life.'[b]

The standards of a people are revealed in and formed by its

---

a Bacchylides 31 (3), 83. This is the rendering of the Loeb translator.
b ζώαν βαθύπλουτον, mentioned in the line above.

favourite stories. The story of Croesus was clearly a favourite in fifth-century Greece. It varies in some details,[5] but the essentials remain: the richest of all mortals has given abundantly to the gods; yet he falls, and cries 'Where is the gratitude of heaven?'; and heaven in one form or another shows gratitude for Croesus' *eusebeia* in giving the gods expensive presents.[6] That one's *eusebeia* should thus depend on the extent of one's possessions is a doctrine which suits the wealthy tyrant; but it is not one invented to enable the tyrant to salve his conscience. It is a basic belief of primitive Greek religion;[7] and in the fifth century it is by no means confined to tyrannies. Euripides finds it necessary to oppose it:[a]

Be assured that when any man who is *eusebes* sacrifices to the gods, he secures his safety even if the sacrifice is a small one.

True, Euripides uses *eusebes* here with a sense quite different from that in which it is used of Croesus; but the position is evidently worth attacking, and it is evidently that of Croesus, which has a real claim to be called *eusebeia*. Indeed, any belief in propitiatory or expiatory sacrifices entails the view that one's *eusebeia* is proportional to one's pocket-book. If a sacrifice will avert or forestall the anger of a god, clearly the more expensive the sacrifice (or the gift), the more certainly the anger will be averted.

This practice, and the use of *hosios* and *eusebes* which depends on it, derives not from a desire for ostentation but from a genuine anxiety about the future; but this anxiety is not related to a feeling of moral guilt, and is not felt before the gods as moral agents, but as powerful and probably malevolent beings; and accordingly this use of *hosios* and *eusebes* does not raise questions of moral responsibility. To be unable, or to forget, to give gifts to the gods must be as heinous as wilfully to refuse them.[b]

(iii) 'Pollution'

In situations which involve 'pollution', man is again face to face with the supernatural; but in view of the nature of 'pollution', there is again no reason to suppose *a priori* that *hosios* and *eusebes* will be used in such contexts. Yet such is the case; both

[a] Eur., frag. 946 Nauck, cp. frag. 327.   [b] Cp. Chapter IV, p. 62.

hosios and *eusebes* appear in contexts which relate to 'pollution'. Clearly it will be in most cases impossible to discover the exact flavour of such words in these contexts, since frequently 'holy', 'righteous', or their contraries are perfectly apposite in the situation. A crucial example is needed; and when in Euripides' *Suppliants* the Chorus sings

I have come to the fire-receiving altars of the gods, falling before them in supplication, not *hosiōs*, but from necessity; and yet we have justice on our side . . .[a]

we have such an example.[b] The chorus of suppliant women are not *hosiai*, for their children lie unburied outside the walls of Thebes. The women are 'polluted' by this fact; and this is simply a matter of 'pollution', not of right and wrong, for they can also maintain that they have justice on their side. Responsibility and morality have no place in such a use of *hosios*.

It is more difficult to discover a certain example of *eusebes* so used; but in the *Oedipus at Colonus*, when Oedipus says[c]

And when you look upon my head, which is hard to look upon, do not esteem it lightly; for I come as a man hallowed and *eusebes*, and I bring with me a benefit for the men of this city,

the prevailing sense of *eusebes* seems to be 'ritually clean', and the connection of thought is: 'Not merely shall I cause no harm to the citizens (for I am clean) but I shall actually bring them a benefit.' This interpretation is encouraged by a similar passage from the *Electra* of Euripides. Orestes laments[d]

To what other city am I to go? What guest-friend, what *eusebes* will look upon my head, now that I have killed my mother?

This is the other side of the picture: the two passages taken together give the whole. When Oedipus speaks of his head as being hard to look upon, he is not referring merely to the terrible blind ruin of his eyes, or to his tattered condition, but to the 'pollution' for which he was once driven out of Thebes, and which he now denies that he possesses or ever possessed. The expression is condensed; but it is clear that the Chorus believes him to be still hard to look upon in this sense, and that they are

---

[a] ἔχομεν δ' ἔνδικα.

[b] E. *Supp.* 63 ff., cp. *I.T.* 1037 ff., esp. 1161 and 1194. Also Antiphon, *Murder of Herodes* 82, and S. *O.T.* 1357 ff.

[c] S. *O.C.* 285 ff.   [d] E. *Elec.* 1195 ff.

not convinced by his words that he is *eusebes*; just as Orestes says that if he goes to another city, no *eusebes* will wish to look on him, the matricide, for by so doing he would cease to be *eusebes*, and might be implicated in the ruin of Orestes. *Eusebes* in these passages carries the idea of 'pollution' more strongly than any other.

(iv) *Conclusions*

Hosios and *eusebes*, then, are used in the Greek of the fifth century to span what we should consider to be a heterogeneous collection of situations and standards; and the effect of this on the value of these words to the moralist must now be considered.

In the first place, two of these standards may clash: one may feel impelled to term the same action *hosios* and *anosios*, *eusebes* and *asebes*. This problem occurs in the Atreus-cycle and in the *Antigone*. Orestes in Euripides' *Orestes* says[a]

I know it: I am *anosios* in that I have killed my mother, but *hosios* in another sense in that I have avenged my father:

while Antigone says in the *Antigone*[b]

Through behaving as a *eusebes* I have incurred a charge of *dussebeia*.

Orestes is caught between two irreconcilable supernatural claims. He cannot fulfil both, and in either case he is *anosios*, and will be punished. In Antigone's case, only one of the claims is supernatural, since *dussebeia* denotes her failure to show the reverence which she should have shown to Creon. In neither case is there any misuse of language. All of the actions or states may legitimately be termed *hosios* or *anosios*, *asebes* or *eusebes*; and herein lies a problem.

It is not, however, the most important problem, simply because it appears as a problem; for to see the existence of a problem such as this is to be half-way to finding an answer.[8] The difficulties for moral responsibility arise from the fact that normally no difference is felt between these highly heterogeneous cases. The words must be applied to all these cases in virtue of some characteristic which they are felt to have in

[a] E. *Or.* 546 f. ἐγῷδ', ἀνόσιός εἰμι μητέρα κτανών,
    ὅσιος δέ γ' ἕτερον ὄνομα, τιμωρῶν πατρί.
[b] S. *Ant.* 924. τὴν δυσσέβειαν εὐσεβοῦσ' ἐκτησάμην.

common, or some attitude which they evoke, not in virtue of the different characteristics which we feel impelled to emphasize in these different cases. For those who used these words had no other language into which to translate them; and it is only reasonable to assume that they viewed in the same light all these situations in which they used the same words. The distinctions drawn here, in fact, are of use only for the purpose of exposition: they answer to nothing real in the material.

It is now clear why *hosios*, *eusebes*, and related words could be of little use to Plato and Aristotle as moralists. In addition to their usage in quiet moral contexts, they readily denote the relation of barter between man and god, and the state of 'pollution' and its absence. The *eusebeia* of barter lays emphasis on the size of the gift, irrespective of the ability to give of the donor. The *asebeia* of 'pollution' depends on the supposed presence of this non-moral phenomenon, whether incurred by one's own actions or not. Neither necessarily involves either morality or responsibility, and yet *hosios* and *eusebes* may legitimately be applied to both cases. Evidently these words are by no means as suitable as *dikaios* for commending the quieter virtues for, faithfully reflecting, as they do, the theological difficulties of the Greeks, their use can only lead to confusion in the field of morals.[9]

The idea of responsibility cannot be focused clearly in these words. As will appear below, the intellectual climate of the late fifth and early fourth centuries would have rendered them practically useless to Plato, even had they raised no difficulties; but as it is, it is unreasonable to hope that words so confused and so confusing could be of any great assistance in solving a critical problem of values.

C. *DIKAIOSUNE* AGAIN

(i) *Divine Sanctions in Life*

If *hosios* and *eusebes* are useless, *dikaios* and allied terms must be relied upon; and here the problem of the sanction to sustain these values remains. The dominant strain of thought of the fifth century, like that of earlier centuries, assumes that this life is all, and the next a mere shadow, in which there can be no question of reward and punishment. Those who hold this view must believe that, in so far as the gods are moral and uphold *dikaiosune*, reward and punishment must be allotted in this life. That this belief continues to be the normal one may be illustrated by two examples drawn from the end of the century. In the *Oedipus at Colonus* which, as has been shown, is in many ways an 'advanced' play,[a] Oedipus piously maintains that the gods reward the *eusebes* and punish the *dussebes*, but when Ismene, expressing the hope that Oedipus may now cease his wanderings, says[b]

In time past the gods destroyed you: now they are raising you up again,

Oedipus replies

It is an empty thing to raise up an old man who fell when he was young.

It is useless for the gods to rehabilitate Oedipus now, for this life is all, and he has little of it left.[10] Oedipus, unknown to himself, is to become a Hero, which is a recompense, for his tomb will be honoured with regular rites, and his shade will be a powerful earth-bound spirit; but the general application of his words holds good.[11] Again, in the *Electra* of Euripides, Electra says that she is sure that Orestes will be successful in avenging his father:[c]

For if injustice is to get the better of justice, we must no longer believe that the gods exist.

Wrongdoers must still be punished here, visibly, in this life: that some reward or punishment might await men beyond the grave is not even considered. If Orestes later goes mad,[d] then Orestes is hated by the gods; and while Oedipus is prospering in Thebes, the gods are held to be honouring him, even in a context[e] in which the whole curse-cycle is recapitulated and the end is known. To be mad is to be hated by the gods, and to be wealthy is to be beloved of the gods: that is all, even when the gods are moral. The dangers of the belief that the just must prosper here and now have been discussed above.[f] It need only

[a] Cp. Chapter V, p. 105.
[b] S. *O.C.* 394 f. Written in or a little before 406 B.C.
[c] E. *Elec.* 583 f.   [d] E. *Orest.* 531 ff.   [e] Aesch. *Septem* 775 ff.
[f] Chapter IV, pp. 66 ff.

be said here that, with the rise of the sophists, the dangers of a tenet so empirically falsifiable are many times multiplied.

(ii) *Sanctions after Death*

But though this belief, and the system of values, emphasizing fame and prosperity, which naturally accompanies it, continues to be dominant, the literature of the fifth century also provides evidence of a belief which, though it has evidently existed for a considerable period,[a] has hitherto been hardly attested. To call it *a* belief is in fact misleading, for the doctrine of a 'real' future life with alternative treatment after death for different classes of people appears as 'Orphic', 'Pythagorean', &c. For the present purpose, however, the exact provenance of the beliefs is unimportant: it is only necessary to distinguish the beliefs firstly as more or less moral, secondly as depending more or less closely on 'mystery-cults'. This too has its relevance, for where men may be classified as initiated and uninitiated, even if they are classified as moral and immoral as well, the first classification may prove morally confusing. But since the principal literary sources of our information are Aeschylus, Pindar, Aristophanes, and Plato, to attempt to allot more accurate labels than these to the beliefs is useless; for no such label would readily fit any of these writers.

We may then confine ourselves to discussing the effect on ideas of reward and punishment which resulted from these beliefs, only discussing their provenance where it throws light on this question. Belief in a pleasant life after death is prominent, as one would expect, given that such a belief exists at all, in the *Threnoi* (*Laments for the Dead*) of Pindar. Here the belief seems certainly to depend on some mystery-cult;[b] for one of the fragments may be translated: 'Blessed is he who has seen these things before descending beneath the earth: he knows the end of life, and its principle, given by Zeus.' Clearly 'he who has seen these things' is the initiate, the type of man before whom are spread in the other fragments the sights, sounds, scents, and pleasures of the world to come. The initiated are to have their own sun perpetually, and flowery meadows, shady trees, and golden fruits; they are to ride, wrestle, play dice, and in general live as gentlemen of leisure.

[a] Cp. (Homer), *Hymn to Demeter*, 480/2.   [b] Pind. *Threnoi* frag. 137 (102).

In these fragments of the *Threnoi* nothing is said of the manner in which these delights are to be obtained, save that 'Blessed is he who has seen these things'. Certainly they are fragments, quite small fragments: the lack of reference to any moral requirements might be due to the accidents of survival. There is no need, however, to assume this: these passages strongly resemble the 'Orphic' fragments which have been preserved in the form of gold tablets buried with the 'Orphic' dead.[12] The reason for their existence is significant: they contain factual information and forms of words to be used by the shade, *psuche*, at suitable occasions on its journey to Bliss below.[a] The *psuche* will find a spring on the left of the palace of Hades, and by it a white cypress; it must not, however, drink from this spring, but seek another cool spring which flows from the Lake of Memory. There it is to address the guardians of the spring: 'I am the child of earth and starry heaven, but my birth is heavenly. This you know yourselves. I am parched and perishing with thirst. Give me straightway water from the Lake of Memory.' The guardians will thereupon give water to the soul, which will then 'reign among the other Heroes'. Other tablets seem to refer to formalities to be gone through between drinking from the spring and reigning among the Heroes. The *psuche* appears before Persephone and the other infernal gods, and is to address them: 'I come pure from pure, *ek katharōn katharā*.[b] I claim to be of your blessed race, having paid the penalty for unjust acts committed when *moira* and other immortal gods overcame me. . . . But now I have come as a suppliant before the Lady Persephone, that she may graciously send me to the abodes of the pure.' Persephone is then to reply: 'Blessed and fortunate being, you shall be a god instead of a mortal. You have fallen as a kid into milk'; and the soul presumably receives its reward.

The dogma behind these tablets seems clear. The reason for the presence of man upon earth is that he has committed misdeeds in some other existence, and has been condemned as a result to serve a term upon earth as a punishment. But if, when he returns to Hades, he is able to declare that he comes 'pure from pure' and, having drunk from the Lake of Memory, still

[a] Orpheus frag. 17 D/K, cp. 17a.
[b] Orpheus frags. 18, 19, 19a, 20 D/K. The version given in the text is a conflation.

retains his wits, he may pass into a state of blessedness, and
become a god or a Hero. This is clear; but the implications for
morals are not. The tablets do not tell us enough, if there is
more to be told. A tablet from Thurii adjures the newly dead
soul to be cautious and wary:[a] doubtless it must be careful not
to drink from the wrong spring, and not to forget the form of
words with which to address first the guardians of the spring,
and then Persephone, lest it fail to receive its deserts. There is
nothing moral here; for the declaration that one is *katharos* can
hardly be treated as such without further evidence. It is certain
that ritual abstentions were practised; and the word need mean
no more than 'ritually clean'.[13] On the other hand, there is
equally nothing in these tablets to prove that moral standards
were not demanded. Just as Pindar, in lamenting the dead,
might well dwell on promised rewards to hearten the living
relatives, so these tablets might well dwell on rewards for a life
of virtue, at a time when these are to be received; and the
emphasis on directions to be followed is quite comprehensible,
in view of the anxieties which naturally surround the idea of
death, even were the emphasis *in life* on adherence to a moral
code. But, though it would be quite possible for moral ideas to
exist in such a framework, it remains unnecessary to assume
that this was always the case. In any movement such as this
there will always be different levels of enlightenment; and the
basic theological ideas behind the belief reflected in these
tablets seem not to demand the moral life as a condition of
becoming again a god or a Hero. One sins in some other existence, and one's *psuche* is condemned to be imprisoned on earth
for a term of years. In view of the emphasis on proving oneself
katharos, the soul is presumably considered to be unclean as a
result of this prenatal sin. The uncleanness is different in kind
from the usual Greek *miasma*;[b] but as ordinary 'pollution' is
removed by non-moral means, there is nothing in the ideas
associated with the word which would encourage anyone to
assume prima facie that any other than non-moral means, such
as abstention from eating flesh, were needed to remove such a
'pollution': the soul's sojourn on earth in itself might be judged
sufficient to expiate the prenatal sin, provided that these abstentions were also observed.[14]

[a] Orpheus frag. 20 D/K.   [b] Cp. Chapter V, pp. 87 ff.

There is, however, more evidence. Empedocles in the *Purifications* shows himself to owe something to this type of belief, for he too believes that life on earth is a punishment for sins committed in another existence;[a] and in another fragment he produces the remarkable phrase 'to fast from *kakotes*'.[b] This is clearly not ordinary Greek; but, though Plutarch only quotes this phrase, the meaning seems clear. It is pointless to command anyone to fast from anything, unless it is in his power to do so or not at will. Accordingly, Empedocles cannot be using *kakotes* in the sense of 'faring badly'—the normal sense in early Greek writers—and must be using it in the sense of 'behaving badly' (in a quiet moral sense), since the latter does depend on the agent's will: a supposition encouraged by Empedocles' usage in two other fragments.[c] 'To fast from *kakotes*' presumably ranks for Empedocles as a purification; and hence this is first-hand evidence that for one writer at least 'Orphic' or Pythagorean[15] doctrines contained moral requirements.[16] The extent to which Empedocles was typical will be discussed below; it may be said at once, however, that the *form* of the phrase, the assimilation of right-doing to abstinence, suggests that abstinence was the most prominent element of such belief in the eyes of those who held it as well as in the eyes of those who did not.

Before any conclusions are drawn, the remainder of the evidence concerning punishment after death, whether overtly connected with the mystery-cults or not, must be considered. In Aeschylus and Pindar, neither of whom can convincingly be labelled as an adherent of any particular mystery-cult,[17] this belief is made to serve a moral end. Except in the *Threnoi*, Pindar usually adopts the normal view that this life is all; but in the *Second Olympian*, written for Theron of Acragas, he suddenly says[d]

All men who have had the courage three times . . . to keep their *psuche* utterly free from injustice, have accomplished the road of Zeus to the tower of Cronos: in the islands of the blest sea breezes waft about them and golden flowers blaze.

Rewards and punishments are meted out after death according

---

[a] Empedocles, frag. 115 D/K.
[b] Id., frag. 144 D/K: νηστεῦσαι κακότητος.
[c] Empedocles, frags. 112. 3 and 145 D/K. [d] Pind. *Ol.* 2. 55 ff.

to one's (moral) deserts; and hence the *psuche* must be kept from injustice. There is 'someone' who will punish after we have left the realm of Zeus. Similar passages occur in Aeschylus, and presumably express the poet's own belief.[18] Danaus in the *Suppliants* maintains that no man who forced marriage on his daughters would be pure, *hagnos*,[a] but that even when dead he would have to pay a penalty:

In the next world, it is said, another Zeus pronounces final judgement among the dead for wrongdoing.

Again, in the *Eumenides*,[b] the Furies threaten that they will wither Orestes and carry him off below to pay the penalty for his matricide. Then, as amplification of this, they add

There you will see all other mortals who have impiously wronged a god, some guest-friend or their dear parents, each receiving his deserved punishment. For Hades is a mighty judge of mortals beneath the earth, and he watches everything with faithfully recording mind.

Clearly Hades, the 'other Zeus', is believed in these two passages to punish crimes against all the basic relationships recognized by Greek morals, those which a man has with his family, his guest-friends, and the gods. In other words, Hades punishes in the next life all those transgressions which the Olympian gods—whose jurisdiction of course does not extend beyond the grave—are expected to punish in this.

This belief seems not to be shared by the other tragedians, but Aristophanes, in the *Frogs*,[c] tells the audience that certain classes of people are plunged in Everlasting Mud, namely

Anyone who has ever wronged a guest-friend . . ., or thrashed his mother, or struck his father on the jaw, or sworn an oath forsworn.

These again are the basic immoralities recognized by the Greeks.

In all these passages, the belief in a different treatment after death for different classes of men is made to serve a moral end, and to uphold the claims of *dikaiosune* in quite a general sense; but it is unclear what relation these beliefs have to the 'Orphics' or to any other mystery-cult. Another passage from the *Frogs*, however, might appear to provide a link. Aristophanes

---

[a] Aesch. *Supp.* 228 ff., cp. also *P. Oxy.* 2256. 9(a) 21.
[b] Aesch. *Eum.* 269 ff.   [c] Ar. *Frogs* 145 ff.

brings on to the stage the Initiated in Hades; and these banish from their dances[a]

Whoever is ignorant of these words, or is not pure in mind, or has not seen the rites of the noble Muses nor danced their dances . . . or takes pleasure in ribald words when the time is not fit, or does not put an end to civic strife, and is not on friendly terms with the citizens,

and further anyone who betrays or defrauds the city in her time of trouble. The speakers are the Initiated in Hades; therefore, one might assume, when they banish from their number the unjust and the politically undesirable, they are speaking in the name of the Mysteries. But unfortunately they are not merely the Initiated; they are also a comic chorus: and it is the business of a comic chorus to castigate precisely these misdeeds. One of comedy's weapons is to deny to those of whom it disapproves the delights which it gives to its favourites;[19] and being in Hades, the Initiated can hardly do better than to deny to those whom they dislike the pleasures which they themselves are enjoying there. This passage proves nothing either way.

This constitutes the primary literary evidence for the period under discussion. That is to say, if the 'Orphic' tablets are taken as representative of earlier practice, this is the available evidence in writing for the beliefs which Plato attacks in *Republic* ii; and it is clear that there is considerable confusion here. The passages (Aeschylus, and Pindar in *Olympian* ii) which mention a *judgement* after death make no mention of initiated and uninitiated, whereas those which refer to initiation have no mention of a *judgement* after death, even where, as in Empedocles, some moral standards seem to be demanded. In Empedocles and Aristophanes, the method of separating just from unjust seems not to be considered; and while one of these certainly derived his beliefs from 'Orphic' or Pythagorean doctrines, there can be no certainty in the other case, particularly in view of the non-literary evidence which will be discussed below. If the idea of a 'real' future life is treated as belonging to one tradition, it is evidently a very confused tradition.

For the present purpose, however, even evidence of confusion is helpful; and here archaeological evidence (or rather a literary record of such evidence) is of great value. Pausanias' account of

[a] Ibid. 354 ff.

Polygnotus' painting in the Hall of the Cnidians at Delphi shows what must have been the common view of the furnishings of Hades at this period, for the painting evidently reflects general belief (or tradition), not that of any mystery-cult or cults, for it was painted under the auspices of a whole state.[20] The Homeric Heroes are present, enjoying themselves at dice and similar pastimes;[a] Tantalus and Sisyphus are visible, undergoing punishment for their insults to divine *time*;[b] and the unhomeric Ocnus fruitlessly plaits his rope, apparently as an allegory.[c] Together with these, however, a man who had not been just to his father in life is being throttled by him;[21] while elsewhere in the picture, in contrast, a young and an older woman are shown carrying water in broken potsherds—and these are 'some of the women who were not initiated'; and elsewhere again a family is depicted pouring water into a (presumably) perforated jar—and these are supposed by Pausanias to be representative of those who made light of the rites performed at Eleusis.[d] Here in one picture we find all the attitudes and beliefs about the next world (save that of Aeschylus and *Olympian* ii) which had existed up to the time of Polygnotus, juxtaposed with no thought of consistency. The Homeric view of a Hades neutral for all but superhuman sinners, the belief in punishment after death for certain misdeeds, and the belief that simple failure to be initiated may be eternally punished cannot logically coexist. Yet clearly neither Polygnotus nor his employers were worried by this: which once again indicates contemporary confusion.

In such circumstances, to distinguish any given belief as the property of one particular body of people is impossible. *Knowledge* of all these beliefs was evidently spread throughout society, even if the beliefs were not generally held with any fervour: the crossing and confusion of one belief with another was almost inevitable. The criticism expressed by Plato in the *Republic* serves to illustrate this.[e] Adeimantus, complaining of the manner in which other people praise justice, says of 'Musaeus and his son' that they 'offer to the just still more extravagant benefits from the gods. Taking them in word to Hades, and making them recline on couches and arranging a drinking-party of the

---

[a] Pausanias 10. 31. 1.
[c] Ibid. 10. 29. 1.
[e] Plato, *Rep*. 363 c 3 ff.

[b] Ibid. 10. 31. 10 and 12.
[d] Ibid. 10. 28. 4, 31. 9, 31. 11.

holy, they make them pass all their time drunk, regarding everlasting drunkenness as the fairest reward for virtue'. This is moral in a sense, however much Plato may disapprove of it; and yet a few lines later[a] Adeimantus complains that other men 'bring out a host of books of Musaeus and Orpheus with which they persuade both individuals and cities that they have means of purification for wrongs done[b] by means of sacrifice and pleasures of play, some for the living, others for the dead, which they call initiation-ceremonies, which free us from the terrors of the next world; *whereas if we do not sacrifice terrors await us*'.[c]

From the manner in which these passages[22] are introduced, it is evident that Plato regards them as belonging to the same tradition; for there is no hope of distinguishing 'Musaeus and his son' from 'a host of books of Musaeus and Orpheus'. This tradition, then, embraces all levels of moral sensitivity and sophistication; and, since it is probable that Plato is castigating all such beliefs under these heads (for his attack must be meant to include *all* others who have praised justice or held beliefs which rendered it unnecessary, and the other mystery-cults appear nowhere else) it is likely that all such beliefs in a 'real' existence after death were found in varying degrees of moral sensitivity: a fate which is likely to overtake any religion which contains a considerable formal element. [23]

The effect on moral responsibility, for those who held them, of the two extremes of such belief can readily be seen. The belief of which Adeimantus complains first, whereby it is the just and the unjust *tout court* to whom Bliss and Mud are assigned, is gross, certainly; but in so far as this belief is held, it does perform the necessary function of linking *dikaiosune* to the desired prosperity, *olbos* or *arete*, after death: as Plato acknowledges, in effect, by including it among the ways in which *dikaiosune* is praised. Though the rewards are gross, the right questions are asked; and such beliefs are, from this point of view, the most satisfactory ones which had any popular currency before Plato.[24]

The crude belief in formal initiation as a ticket to Bliss, non-initiation as a ticket to Mud, is of course not moral at all,

[a] Plato, *Rep.* 364 E 3 ff.
[b] λύσεις τε καὶ καθαρμοί.
[c] And compare the earliest source, (Homer), *Hymn to Demeter*, 480 ff.

and could have only a negative effect on morals; for thereby the four classes of whose fate we should be informed, the initiated and just, the uninitiated and just, the initiated and unjust, and the uninitiated and unjust, are simply reduced to two, the initiated and uninitiated. The second passage, from 'the books of Musaeus and Orpheus', makes it clear that Plato knew of such a belief; in the closing words of the quotation above, not merely do those who are initiated and unjust escape retribution, but those who are just but not initiated must expect the worst.

The mingling of such disparate beliefs in the same tradition must cause great confusion: not everyone can be an Aeschylus. Accordingly, it is quite natural that Plato should wish to sweep the whole tradition away, particularly as even the best elements are, as Plato depicts them, gross in the extreme. The Platonic myths naturally attempt to replace these with nobler beliefs; with gods who infallibly discern justice and injustice in the soul, and allot just recompense for each.[25] These myths are of the utmost importance to Plato's own world-view; but as solutions to the problem with which Plato was faced they are merely peripheral. The inadequacies of Greek belief in the gods, sophistic scepticism, and (doubtless) the morally unjustifiable material success of Athens combined to render belief in the gods practically non-existent in Plato's opponents.[26] Out of the confused tradition of punishment after death Plato might derive a belief intellectually more satisfying than any earlier belief of this kind; but if the initial belief in the gods is lacking, this can be of little general influence. Plato had to use other means; and these, together with their effect on the concept of moral responsibility, will be considered in the following chapters.

NOTES TO CHAPTER VII

1. For discussions of the nuclear meaning of these words, cp. J. C. Bolkestein, *Hosios en Eusebes*, and van der Valk, *Mnemosyne* 1942.
2. ἁγνός is not even prima facie relevant. To term anything ἁγνός is merely to express one's awe of it *qua* supernatural, without, as is the case with the terms discussed in the text, even the appearance of anything more. The awe may be felt before some pure *thing*: hence sacred groves, springs, the oracle of Loxias, a shrine, an altar, sacrifices, may all be characterized as ἁγνός (Pind. *Ol.* 5. 10; *Pyth.* 4. 204; E. *Ion* 243; *I.T.* 1155; *Androm.* 427; S. *Trach.* 287). But it is naturally the use of ἁγνός to

refer to human beings which is the most interesting here. Here to be ἁγνός is simply not to be 'polluted', cp. Aesch. *Eum.* 287 (linked with καθαρμοῖς), *Supp.* 364 (opposed to ποτιτρόπαιον), *Eum.* 685 f. In S. *Trach.* 258 ἀλλ' ὅθ' ἁγνὸς ἦν means 'when Heracles had removed the "pollution" incurred by killing Iphitus', cp. *Ajax* 654; E. *Her.* 1009; S. *Ant.* 889. Apart from this, its chief use seems to relate to virginity; it is used regularly of Artemis (e.g. Aesch. *Supp.* 144 f., 1030 f.; *Agam.* 133); and Iphigeneia is described as ἁγνᾷ δ' ἀταύρωτος αὐδᾷ *Agam.* 245, where the collocation of words seems to show what is meant. Similarly when Hippolytus says of his relations with Aphrodite (E. *Hipp.* 102, cp. 1003) πρόσωθεν αὐτὴν ἁγνὸς ὢν ἀσπάζομαι, the reference is clearly to his own chastity, which he, unusually among Greek males, prized so highly. If it is recollected that sexual intercourse was held to be a source of (easily removed) 'pollution', at least in the Homeric/Hesiodic sense (cp. p. 86), it is clear that the flavour is the same in both sets of examples. A word with such a flavour is of no use in moral contexts, since (cp. Chapter V *passim*) its 'logic' is not that of moral words. This should be borne in mind even in passages where ἁγνός seems strongly moral, as in Aesch. *Supp.* 221 ff., quoted on p. 144. With the best will in the world, Aeschylus could not make such a word understood as purely moral by his contemporaries, even if he could have so used it himself. The disadvantages of ἱερός are similar.

3. We may compare S. *Phil.* 1050, where *dikaios* is linked with *eusebes*; E. *Ion* 1092, where *eusebeia* is contrasted with being *adikos*; *Helen* 900 ff., where *eusebeia* is contrasted with being *ekdikos*, lawless; *Helen* 1632, where *kakistē* is contrasted with *eusebestatē*; and *Phoen.* 525, where *adikein*, to be *adikos*, is contrasted with *eusebein*.

4. That is to say, in instances where it is used of persons or their actions. It is pointless for my purpose to argue from the fact that (say) both holy men and holy water are termed 'holy', unless it can be shown that those who use the word in such disparate cases are incapable of distinguishing between the uses. If, however, as here, a word such as *eusebes* can be shown to have confusing uses when confined in use to persons and actions, clearly there is a confusion, from the point of view of this question, in the minds of those who use the words.

5. For example, Herodotus, i. 91, gives the excuse of Delphi for the fall and subsequent captivity of Croesus—he was expiating the sins of his ancestor Gyges—while Bacchylides employs the miraculous intervention of Apollo to ensure that Croesus really benefited in the end.

6. In Herodotus (i. 87) when Cyrus is ineffectually trying to quench the fire, Croesus calls upon Apollo to help him, if ever the god has received any pleasing gift from him: and Apollo promptly helps him.

7. To go no further, we find it in *Iliad* i. 39 ff., where Chryses the priest of Apollo prays: 'Apollo, if ever I burned in your honour the fat thighs of bulls or goats, grant me this prayer.' Such behaviour is not characterized as *eusebeia* in this passage; but in *Odyssey* xix. 364 ff., the new word *theoudes*, god-fearing, cited (with reason) as a word which shows a new attitude to the gods in other passages (cp. Chapter IV, p. 65), is used of

a man's offering hecatombs. Given these confusing beliefs about the gods, any word must be affected as soon as it is coined.

8. So, in his version of the Atreus-cycle, Aeschylus attempts to solve the problem of Orestes' situation by asserting the moral overlordship of Zeus over the whole universe, even the powers below, *Eum.* 614 ff. In other cases there is really no answer. Artemis says, E. *Hipp.* 1328 ff., that the reason for what has occurred is that no god likes to thwart another (an explanation which is already doing service in Homer, cp. *Odyssey* vi. 328 ff., xiii. 341); and hence, since she was afraid of Zeus, who would have been angry had she thwarted Aphrodite, she let her have her way. Since to be *hosios* is to do what is pleasing to the gods, simply to admit that the gods have different wishes is no solution (cp. following note). Antigone is morally victorious over Creon; but the fact that both the relationship to the dead and the gods and that to Creon have to be expressed in the same terms reduces the relationships to the same level. Hence Antigone's argument (74 ff.) that she should seek to *please* the dead, since she will have longer to dwell with them than with the living. She cannot appeal to any set of value-terms to prove Creon to be *wrong* to which Creon cannot equally appeal to justify his own actions.

9. Euthyphro, in Plato, *Euth.* 6 E 10 ff., defines the *hosion* as 'being on good terms with the gods'. Given a supernatural so irresponsible, malevolent, and amoral as that of common Greek belief in the fifth century, no such term could hope to be either moral or unconfused. True, when pressed, Euthyphro alters his definition of the *hosion* to 'what all the gods approve of'; but it would be very difficult to fill out this definition with any detailed series of actions or states.

10. The *dramatic* purpose of these lines is doubtless to contrast Oedipus' expectations with the glory which is in fact to come to him when he is heroized. This, however, merely emphasizes the position of the ordinary man: Heroes are rare.

11. For heroization as a recompense for suffering, cp. E. *Hipp.* 1423 ff.

12. Though these tablets fall in date after the end of the present inquiry, they must surely reflect earlier belief and practice. (I do not discuss whether these tablets are in fact 'Orphic', 'Pythagorean', or related to some other mystery-cult, for the reasons given in the text. Only their moral or non-moral nature is relevant here.)

13. For Orphic vegetarianism cp. Ar. *Frogs* 1032 f.; E. *Hipp.* 952 ff. For Pythagorean abstentions, cp. the fragments of comedy quoted in Athenaeus iv, pp. 160 F ff. For abstention from beans, Empedocles, frag. 141 D/K.

14. It may seem impossible that anyone could hold that a man's presence on earth is due to some prenatal sin, and yet that no specific moral behaviour is required to attain to a life of Bliss in the next world. It is illogical, certainly; but it is precisely the kind of illogicality which we should expect. Life is hard, and some explanation of our presence here is necessary: we must have done (some unspecified) wrong in some other existence to deserve it. Death is terrifying, and some means of alleviating its terrors is desirable: initiation, and a vegetarian regimen

(in some cases), may still suffice to ensure a pleasant existence beyond the tomb. We have seen many times already that explanations which involve the supernatural are rarely co-ordinated in early Greek thought; and here the explanations are designed to fulfil quite different functions.

15. Tradition makes Empedocles a Pythagorean: cp. Diog. Laert. 8. 54, Athenaeus 1. 5 E.

16. The use of *kakotes*, though still not quite clear, gains added probability when added to that in frags. 112 and 145. If the fragments of Empedocles stood alone, it might be supposed that Empedocles had redefined *kakotes*, and that 'behaving badly' was simply failing to abstain where ritual demanded. But compare the general references to such beliefs in Plato, discussed on pp. 146 ff.

17. Though Aeschylus seems to have been an initiate, Arist. *E.N.* 1111ª10, of some (presumably the Eleusinian) mysteries.

18. Aeschylus himself presumably believed in a post-mortem moral judgement since, unlike the court-poet Pindar, he had no incentive to profess beliefs which were not his own. But he was unable to use this belief to produce a general, coherent solution to his theological and ethical problems. For example, *Choephori* 306 ff. express the values in terms of which Orestes and Electra see their own and Agamemnon's situation, and the view of life and death on which these values depend. The view, and the values, are essentially Homeric: this at a crucial point in the *Oresteia*, where the introduction of the belief in post-mortem reward and punishment would have helped to provide Aeschylus with a solution to a very difficult problem. In fact, there is just as much emphasis on the idea of fame, success, and prosperity in Aeschylus as in Sophocles and Euripides: and Eteocles' speech, *Septem* 683 ff., expresses the belief which sustains these values, cp. Chapter VIII, p. 155.

19. So Dicaeopolis is left banqueting, Lamachus nursing a broken head, at the end of the *Acharnians*.

20. Cp. the south Italian vases illustrated and discussed, e.g. by Guthrie, *Orpheus and Greek Religion*, pp. 187 ff., and Nilsson, *Gesch. d. gr. Rel.* i. 651 ff. and 767 ff.

21. Fear of the attitude of one's relatives in the next life is not, of course, dependent on the idea of a moral Last Judgement; cp. S. *O.T.* 1371 ff.

22. I do not cite *Gorgias* 493 A as evidence, since the interpretation there may be Plato's own. The *Republic* by itself provides adequate illustration.

23. The power which such beliefs had over men's minds must, as one would indeed expect, have varied from individual to individual. Cephalus, in *Republic* i. 330 D 3 ff., represents it as a fear which only assailed men in old age, whereas Democritus, frags. 199 and 297, attacks it as a belief which made the whole of life a misery. Certainly in the class whose beliefs are represented in literature it has little currency; but this class is only a small part of the whole, and the extent of these beliefs in the remainder of society cannot be estimated.

24. The relation of this belief to that of Aeschylus and Theron (for the belief is surely Theron's, not Pindar's) is unclear. There is no mention of

initiation here either; but the belief of Aeschylus in particular seems
much more austere than that reprehended by Plato; and, since it seems
unlikely that any aspect of the 'Orphic' tradition could have dispensed
with initiation entirely, Plato may well have left out this aspect of the
most moral 'Orphic' views, judging that this aspect was sufficiently
castigated in the attack on the non-moral ones. (Unless *anosioi*, 363 D 6,
is a misleading—but perfectly possible, cp. p. 136 and pp. 141 ff. above
—way of saying 'uninitiated'.) Further, there is no mention of a
judgement in Plato. On the other hand, Pindar, *Ol.* 2. 55 ff., knows of a
cycle of lives, a belief also known to the 'Orphics'. In fact, such questions as these cannot be answered. Our difficulties lie not only in the
scanty evidence, but in the nature of the phenomenon itself. The
existence of such men as Pindar, representing in the *Threnoi* and in
Olympian ii two quite different facets of the same tradition, and probably holding neither himself, adequately explains the confusion; for
since the beliefs were evidently known to all, more or less confusedly,
even if held by comparatively few, 'crossing' was almost inevitable.

25. So, *Gorgias* 523 C ff., the misdeeds of this life were formerly judged by
men on this earth, and men who had handsome bodies or ancient
families or wealth, or could furnish false witnesses, succeeded in obtaining wrongly favourable judgements. Accordingly Zeus appointed Minos,
Rhadamanthus, and Aeacus to judge the souls naked after death.
These judges judge 'the soul in itself' with their 'soul in itself', and only
justice is taken into account. For the peculiar relevance of these words
to Greek courts of law, cp. Chapter X below. (The mention of these
judges might seem to indicate that where these judges are depicted in
art, as on the south Italian vases, a Last Judgement of this nature is
envisaged. This is not necessarily true: Minos is in Hades already in
Homer, but his functions are there quite different, cp. Chapter IV,
p. 67: and where the vase portrays also the traditional trappings of the
Homeric Hades—Sisyphus, Heracles, &c.—there is no reason to suppose that anything so austere as Plato envisages is in the mind of the
artist or his public.)

26. Cp. especially Critias, *Sisyphus* (Critias, frag. 25 Diels–Kranz), which
shows the sort of things that were being said. Materialism played its
part: cp. Plato, *Laws* 891 B.

VIII

THE PERSISTENCE OF TRADITIONAL VALUES

A. A LESS CONTROVERSIAL APPROACH

In Chapter IV it was shown that from Homer onwards the chief problem of Greek values was the need to discover a means of relating *dikaios* to *agathos*, *arete* and associated words in such a way as to make *dikaiosune* either the whole or a part of *arete*, and hence render it an essential element of the most attractive group of values; or alternatively, as a second best, to demonstrate or assert that to be *dikaios* is a necessary, if troublesome, means to becoming or remaining *agathos*, to the desired state of existence in this world, or to happiness in the next. The last chapter illustrated one belief which tended towards this alternative goal; but since this solution is a second best, and since it depends on a belief in the gods not on the whole held by the articulate classes in the centuries under consideration, the system of values of the fifth century must be examined as a whole, in an effort to discover any development towards the more desirable and less controversial solution. Now that the extraneous influences considered in Chapters V and VI have been dealt with, the problems of this system of values, leading as they do almost inevitably to Athenian difficulties and Platonic solutions, are left as the most important question for discussion.

It has been seen that Theognis, or one of the writers of the Theognid corpus, in fact asserted the identity of *dikaiosune* and *arete*. Since this is the desired goal, the problem might appear to be solved: once *dikaiosune* has thus become identified with the highest standard, one might suppose that it only remains to refine the concept of *dikaiosune* where this proves necessary. Unfortunately, however, to assert an identity is not the same as to have it accepted. What is said in Megara at a time of stress need not be accepted in Athens, or even in Megara under different conditions; and in fact the values of the Homeric world persist throughout the fifth century. They do not persist unchallenged: already in Aeschylus, and even in Pindar, there are signs of a stirring of new values. Since these values, which will be discussed in subsequent chapters, conflict violently with the Homeric system, it will be useful to show in some detail here the extent to which traditional values continue to exist, as a background and frame of reference.

B. GENERAL STANDARDS

(i) 'Shame'

The persistence of Homeric standards becomes evident as soon as the end of life aimed at by post-Homeric Greeks is considered. In Homer the end is undoubted: the chief good is to be well spoken of, the chief ill to be badly spoken of, by one's society, as a result of the successes and failures which that society values most highly. In other words, Homeric society is a 'shame-culture'. But the Homeric poems seem to constitute a world to themselves, and it is tempting to assume that with Hesiod all was changed. A few examples will show that such is not the case. When Theognis writes[a]

One man finds fault with the *agathoi*, another man praises them; but of the *kakoi* no mention is made at all,

it is clear that if no one thinks to mention you, your fate is even worse than if you are unpopular with some people. Pindar, too, makes this clear when he writes[b]

Aretai which involve no danger win no honour either on land or in hollow ships; but many men remember it, if something *kalon* is achieved with much labour.

Agathos and *arete*, as we have seen, commend the highest standard; but it is clear that if, *per impossibile*, the reputation which normally attaches to the actions which they commend were withdrawn, *agathos* and *arete* would cease to be valued.[1] The standard remains *overtly* 'what people say'. In Attic tragedy this attitude, together with the belief that helps to sustain it, is clearly shown by Eteocles' speech in the *Seven against Thebes*:[c]

---

[a] Theogn. 797 f., cp. Heraclitus, frags. 29 and 135 D/K; and Theogn. 665 f.
[b] Pind. *Ol.* 6. 9, cp. *Ol.* 10. 91.   [c] Aesch. *Septem* 683 ff.

If some power should be bringing disaster, *kakon*, upon me, may it be one without disgrace, *aischūnē*; for this is the only thing which profits among the dead. But you cannot mention any good reputation, *eukleia*, to be won from events which are both disasters, *kaka*, and shameful, *aischra*.

Eteocles aims at *eukleia*, since a good reputation in this world is the only thing which matters to a dead man. This life is all: the next remains, in general belief, a pale unreality. Accordingly, in this life one must attempt to secure for oneself the most durable element in a world of change: a position of fame and respect for oneself and one's family, a good reputation which will persist after one's death. Nothing else can matter so much.

This is the normal attitude of the period. In tragedy, the Chorus consoles the doomed, where consolation is possible, with thoughts of reputation.[a] Consciousness of virtue, divorced from this, is not a consolation at all: even Antigone insists that the Chorus is really on her side, and has to be assured by them as she goes to her death that her fame is secure.[b]

The corollary is obvious. If to have a good reputation is more important than anything else, 'loss of face' must be as terrible as it was in Homer. Examples abound: Theognis apostrophizes his heart, *thumos*, urging it not to give in, for surrender would delight his enemies; Hesiod, earlier, recommends that one should not marry a wife who will make one the laughing-stock of the neighbours; Ajax, on coming to himself, refers to the mockery and insult he has suffered; Electra, apostrophizing the absent Orestes, says that he is dead and gone, and their enemies are laughing; and Megara says significantly that death is a terrible thing, but that to die in a manner which would give her enemies the opportunity to mock would be a greater evil than death.[c]

Expressions of this nature are, in fact, a fixed feature of the Greek moral landscape, common to all men (and women). Until Socrates,[d] no one takes a firm stand and says 'let them mock'. It cannot be done: if others' opinion is overtly the

---

[a] Cp. e.g. E. *Or.* 1140 ff. In this case it is Pylades who offers consolation.
[b] S. *Ant.* 508 ff., 817 ff.
[c] Theogn. 1033; Hes. *W. and D.* 701; S. *Ajax* 367; S. *Elec.* 1152 f.; E. *H.F.* 281 ff.; cp. also S. *Ant.* 647; S. *Phil.* 1023; S. *O.C.* 902, 1339; E. *Bacch.* 842, 1080.
[d] Cp. Plat. *Euthyph.* 3 c.

standard, and if one's beliefs about the nature of life support that standard, it is both logically and psychologically impossible to set one's own views against it. Socrates had his *daimonion*; and needed it.[a]

(ii) *The* Agathos-*standard*

In Homer the most powerful terms of value were *agathos* (*arete*) and *kakos*, used of men, and *elencheie* and *aischron*, used of their actions. These words, commending the values of the warrior chieftain as fighting leader in war and governor of a largely self-sufficient unit in peace, took precedence over such words as *pepnumenos* and *dikaios*, which commended the quiet values: though it was desirable for a chieftain to be *pepnumenos*, he did not cease to be *agathos* if he were not. That this situation still exists is clear. When the two sets of values clash, as they do, for example, at the time of Agamemnon's murder, the precedence is evident. In Sophocles' *Electra*,[b] Electra retorts to her mother

You say you killed my father. What admission could be more *aischron* than this, whether you killed him justly, *dikaiōs*, or no?

Here, and in two similar passages in Euripides, there can be no doubt of the precedence.[c] To say that an action is *aischron* is to play the ace of trumps: to justify performing it, one cannot press the claim that it is *dikaion*, for this is of less importance, but must maintain that it is in fact not *aischron* after all.[d] It will be shown below[e] that this and similar passages have greater significance than is suggested here; but the point made here holds good.

The alignment of values, then, remains as it was in Homer. We have yet to show, however, what is commended in the fifth century (and, as will be seen, in the fourth century too) by *agathos*, *arete*, and related words, and decried by *kakos*, *aischron*, and related words, in usages which will in future be referred to as 'traditional' to distinguish them from those discussed in Chapter IX.

Since Homer used *agathos* above all to commend the fighting qualities of the warrior, it will be convenient to begin here. To be *agathos* in respect of one's *psuche*[f] is still to be brave, while to

a Below, Chapter XIII, pp. 260 f.   b S. *Elec.* 558 ff.
c Cp. E. *Elec.* 1051; E. *Orest.* 194.   d Cp. E. *Supp.* 767 ff.; S. *Ant.* 511.
e Chapter IX, pp. 185 ff.   f Aesch. *Pers.* 442.

be *kakos* in respect of one's 'inward parts' is still to be cowardly.[a]
Significantly, one may still speak of a man as being *agathos* at
fighting:[b] *agathos* retains strongly the sense of 'good at' in all
contexts; and *agathos* and *arete* continue to commend courage in
Sophocles, Euripides, Herodotus, Thucydides, and later writers.[2]
It was seen in Chapter III[c] that *agathos* and *arete* were reckoned
by results rather than intentions, and reasons were given for this.
The attitude, together with the reasons, still holds.[3] In Euripides' *Suppliants*[d] Theseus replies as follows to the demand of
Creon that he shall not assist Adrastus to bury the Argives lying
dead before Thebes: You have no reason to prevent the burial,

> For supposing you have suffered something at the hands of the
> Argives, they are dead. You have resisted the enemy *kalōs*, but in a
> manner shameful, *aischrōs*, for them; and justice has been done.

Here and elsewhere[e] it is clear that *kalon* and *aischron* neither
evaluate the situation in terms of quiet morals, nor pay any
attention to the efforts of either side. It is *kalon* for the victors
to have won, *aischron* for the vanquished to have been defeated,
whatever the circumstances of victory or defeat, and whatever
the rights of the case. It happens in the *Suppliants* that justice has
been done *in addition*, but this is a different question. Even if one
is in the wrong, it is still *aischron* to get the worst of it; which
already shows the difference between the 'logic' of *aischron* and
that of (say) 'wrong'.

In addition to waging war with success, the Homeric *agathos*
had successfully to defend those who threw themselves upon his
protection. Here too to fail incurred *elencheie*, was *aischron*. In
the fifth century we find the Greek city or its rulers in the position of the Homeric warrior chief as protector of suppliants;
and here too it is clear that good intentions are not enough. To
fail shames, *aischūnei*,[4] as Demophon says in the *Heraclidae*:[f]

> You had no chance of taking (these suppliants) from me by force,
> and so shaming, *aischūnein*, me; for it is not a city subject to Argos that
> I govern, but a free city.

Relations between individual households in fifth-century Athens

---

[a] Aesch. *Septem* 237, κακόσπλαγχνος.   [b] Hdt. i. 136, cp. *Septem* 568 f.
[c] pp. 46 ff.   [d] E. *Supp.* 528 ff.
[e] Cp. Hdt. i. 128, vi. 45, and (in the light of this passage) Thuc. v. 9. 9.
[f] E. *Heracl.* 285 ff.

will be discussed below.[a] Here it suffices to say that, if the city is taken as a unit *vis-à-vis* other cities, it, being free and independent, as is (virtually) the Homeric head of household, must protect those who ask for its protection; must, not out of devotion to some abstract idea of duty; not *merely* because the gods protect suppliants, though this, if believed, is a guarantee against wilful maltreatment by the host himself: but because to fail to protect the suppliant is unworthy of a free unit which must be strong enough to support itself in order to exist. To fail is to be no better than a slave; hence to fail is *aischron*.

If one must be killed, then, no matter what the rights or wrongs of the case may be, one must die fighting. To go out to meet one's enemies unarmed would be to die *aischrōs*, even if one has wronged them;[b] it is cowardly, *deilon*, for Orestes, having killed his mother, to let the Argives stone him, *kallion* to fight;[c] and nothing is *kallion* than to do one's enemies some harm:[d] all of which fits into the pattern of the Homeric *agathos*-standard without difficulty.

In one respect, indeed, these writers are less 'advanced' than Homer. *Kalon*, which in Homer commended the co-operative virtues, has now evidently become the true contrary to *aischron*, and is linked generally[e] to the *agathos*-standard.[5] Since this usage, though not Homeric, is 'traditional' when compared with that of the 'moralizers' of the next chapter, it will in future be referred to in this manner, like the Homeric uses of *agathos*, *arete*, and other words.

In peace, there are games to be won. The standards which apply here are naturally to be seen almost exclusively in Pindar and Bacchylides; but these poets do not write only for tyrants, and their standards are clearly of more general application. Here too it is *kalon* to succeed, *aischron* to fail. So Pindar says[f]

Songs and stories have brought down to us the noble deeds, *kala . . . erga*, of men of former years,

and *kala erga* prove to be successes at boxing. *Elenchein* may be

[a] Chapter XI, pp. 230 ff.   [b] E. *H.F.* 1384 ff.   [c] E. *Orest.* 777 ff.
[d] E. *Bacch.* 877, cp. *Troad.* 401 f.; Aesch. *Pers.* 444.
[e] For an exception even in Pindar, cp. below, p. 182.
[f] Pind. *Nem.* 6. 29 ff.

used, as in Homer, to characterize defeat: so at Pytho Thrasydaeus and his father[a]

Put to shame, *elenchein*, the assembled Greeks by the speed of their running.

Here 'put to shame' simply means 'defeated': the thought, like the word, is Homeric. Naturally, *arete* appears in such contexts. Pindar says[b]

Any man becomes happy, *eudaimōn*, and a theme for poets[6] who conquers (in the games) by means of his hands or the *arete* of his feet, and wins the greatest of prizes by his daring and strength.

Daring, strength, and success are the qualities commended by *arete* in this context too.

Another of the uses of *agathos* in Homer was to commend the skilled counsellor. This usage persists:[c]

For from the gods come all means of attaining to *aretai* for mortal men: through their agency are men wise, *sophoi*, by nature, mighty of arm, and fluent of utterance.

This passage is important, for it is from such ideas as those of wisdom and fluency of utterance that the civic uses of *arete*, to be discussed in subsequent chapters,[d] must be developed. In view of this, the manner in which the phrase 'mighty of arm' is sandwiched between them is significant; as are the words of the Chorus[7] to Prometheus:[e]

It is *aischron* for a wise man, *sophos*, to make a mistake (about his own interest).

There is nothing 'immoralist' in these passages; but in them *arete* is naturally linked to strength, daring, and success; and if a civic use of the term is to be developed from them, their implications for the future are dangerous.

Again, in Homer *agathos* and *arete* commended a class which was in fact wealthy; while in Theognis *agathos* had evidently begun to denote a class which was merely wealthy.[f] This social flavour of the words naturally persists. Pindar says of Hiero that he is[g]

Gentle to the citizens, not envious of the *agathoi*, and a man worthy of admiration from foreigners.

[a] Pind. *Pyth.* 11. 49 f.   [b] Pind. *Pyth.* 10. 22 ff.   [c] Pind. *Pyth.* 1. 41.
[d] Cp. especially Chapter XI.   [e] Aesch. *P.V.* 1039.
[f] Above, pp. 77 f.   [g] Pind. *Pyth.* 3. 70.

If we subtract 'citizens' in some sense of the word, and foreigners, who are left as the *agathoi* whom Hiero does not envy, or to whom he does not grudge their *arete*? Surely the wealthy upper classes, whom a tyrant might well fear,[8] lest they, conceiving their *arete*—wealth and birth—to be as great as or greater than his own, should conspire to overthrow him. This use continues to be prominent in Athens, as may be seen from an anecdote which Xenophon records or invents in the *Oeconomicus*. Socrates[a] says to Ischomachus that a horse may be *agathos* even though it has no money, provided it has an *agathē psuche*, provided, that is to say, that it possesses the qualities of character and the abilities which a horse ideally should possess; and he is led to hope by this that it may be permissible for him to become *agathos* on the same terms, even though he is poor. This is clearly still a surprising thing to say in the fourth century.

There is a sense in which *arete* may be opposed to wealth, as was the case in Theognis;[b] but in such contexts *arete* means neither 'poor but honest' nor 'poor but courageous'. The traditional standard here contrasts being comfortably off and a good fighting man (and possibly a good athlete as well) with being wealthy but a merchant, and neither of use as a fighting man nor inclined to spend money on winning successes in the games.[c] In Pindar and Aeschylus above all we find the values of the tyrant on the one hand and the hoplite classes[d] on the other. For them, to be *agathos* entails not merely toil but also expense (for it is expensive to train to win races, particularly chariot-races, and the hoplite must furnish his own armour); as Pindar says of the games:[e]

Ever for the sake of *aretai* do toil and expense strive to achieve a deed whose outcome is shrouded in danger and uncertainty; but when men are successful they seem wise even to the citizens, *politai*.

This quotation, with its emphasis on toil and expense, and on a

---

[a] Xen. *Oec.* 11. 3 ff., cp. E. *H.F.* 634 ff.
[b] Cp. Pind. *Ol.* 2. 53; Eur., frags. 542, 1029 Nauck. Theognis, above, p. 77.
[c] Cp. Pind. *Nem.* 9. 32.
[d] The heavy-armed soldiery. As they had to provide their own armour, it was inevitable that the richer citizens should form the hoplites.
[e] Pind. *Ol.* 5. 15, πόνος δαπάνα τε, cp. *Isth.* 1. 42, 5. 10.

way of life which the people in general, *politai*, cannot share but, given a successful outcome, will approve, is typical of *arete* in the first half of the fifth century, and of its dominant use thereafter.

This being so, actions which one may be forced to do as a result of poverty or defeat are still naturally termed *aischra*. So the Trojan princess Polyxena, on hearing that she is to be enslaved, laments that she will never be able to fare well, *eu prattein*, again, and says,[a]

Counsel me to die sooner than meet with *aischra*, for such a fate does not become me. Any man who is not accustomed to taste of woes, *kaka*, bears them indeed when he must, but takes it ill that he should bring his neck beneath the yoke. Such a man would be more fortunate dead than alive; for to live ignobly, *zēn mē kalōs*, is a great burden.

Slavery is a terrible thing; but to apply *aischra* and *zen mē kalōs* to slavery is not to censure the institution *morally*, but to bewail its disadvantages as a way of life.[9] Conversely, if one is going to do wrong, it is most *kalon* to do wrong in order to obtain a tyranny; and if Agamemnon bewails the ruler's life, a subject can reply that it is in such a life that the *kalon* lies.[b] Here too we see the persistence of traditional standards.

The only quiet moral virtue commended by *agathos* in Homer was chastity in women. This use, too, naturally still survives. It has been shown that fair fame is the end of life; accordingly, when Euripides' Helen complains that she has a bad reputation though she has done nothing wrong, and that this is worse than having deserved one's reputation, this is not a characterization of Helen as a cynic, or at all events not merely this.[c] Another woman might not have drawn the conclusion, but the conclusion is there to draw: no woman of the period must be found, however innocently, in a compromising situation, for it is reputation which counts above all. So, in the *Iphigenia at Aulis*, Achilles tells Clytemnestra, who has visited him with irreproachable motives, to take great care in leaving his tent[d]

And do not shame, *aischunein*, your father's house. For Tyndareus does not deserve to be badly spoken of, *kakōs akouein*, since he is a powerful man among the Greeks.

[a] E. *Hec.* 373 ff.   [b] E. *Phoen.* 524 f., *I.A.* 20.
[c] E. *Hel.* 270 ff.   [d] E. *I.A.* 1030 ff.

If Clytemnestra is seen leaving Achilles' tent (in an excited state), people will talk; if they talk, Tyndareus will *kakōs akouein*; *kakōs akouein* is *aischron*; and *aischron* is the most powerful term of value. That *arete* is similarly used is shown by the brusque words of Pericles in the Funeral Speech[a]—words which evidently reflect a definition of woman's *arete* current at the time, since they have little relevance in the context: a woman's *arete* consists in being spoken of as little as possible among men, whether for praise or blame. Accordingly, to be spoken of, at all events for blame, is a diminution of a woman's *arete*.

In fact, if we confine ourselves for the moment to traditional uses,[b] the general standard of *arete* seems identical with that of Homer; and accordingly, as in Homer, *a man* need be ashamed only of his failures, not of his breaches of the quiet virtues. So, when Aeschylus says[c] that Agamemnon perished *aischrōs*, the most evident implication is that what happened was *aischron* for Agamemnon, since he did not die bravely in battle as a warrior should, not that it was *aischron* for his murderer; just as when in the *Persae*[d] the men on the island of Psyttaleia died *aischrōs* by an ill-famed death—since they were cut off and unable to resist adequately—it was *aischron* for the men (and for the Persians in general) that they should have perished in such circumstances; and when in the *Prometheus Bound*[e] Prometheus says that he will see Zeus fall very *aischrōs* and very speedily, it is *aischron* for Zeus that this should happen. For the Greeks it is certainly not *aischron* to have defeated the Persians, on the island of Psyttaleia or anywhere else, just as it is not *aischron* for Prometheus to contrive (or not to prevent) Zeus' fall; and it is not even so obviously *aischron* for Clytemnestra to have killed Agamemnon, though Clytemnestra is a woman, as it is for Agamemnon to have been killed in such a manner. In all these cases, the situation is as it is in the *Odyssey* when Telemachus takes steps to ensure that Odysseus' disobedient serving-maids should die most pitiably:[f] no censure is there intended upon Telemachus, for to be brought into a pitiable condition is, by the most

[a] Thuc. ii. 45. 2.
[b] For 'moral' uses, even in Pindar and Aeschylus, see below, pp. 172 ff., 181 ff.
[c] Aesch. *Cho.* 493 ff.   [d] Aesch. *Pers.* 444.
[e] Aesch. *P.V.* 959. Cp. *Cho.* 345 ff., where the whole context of this belief is visible.
[f] *Odyssey* xxii. 472, ὅπως οἴκτιστα θανοῖεν.

powerful of traditional standards, shameful only to oneself, and to anyone whose (loyal) dependant one may happen to be. Even Clytemnestra's condition becomes most evidently *aischron* when, in the next world, she wanders unavenged.[a]

(iii) *The Shameful and the Ugly*

Thus far, for the convenience of exposition, these usages have been distinguished and classified. The distinctions, however, answer to nothing real in the material; and hence the nature of the most important standard of this society, with its consequent effect on moral responsibility, can only be discovered by allowing these usages to coalesce and exist together. The whole derives its peculiar flavour from *all* the actions and situations for which the society of the period was accustomed to express approval or disapproval through these terms.

Before we discuss the result, however, it is necessary to note the use of these terms beyond the sphere of action. *Aischron* and *kalon* are also used to decry and commend visible objects. One of the war-poems of Tyrtaeus indicates very clearly the relation of such usages to those considered so far. Tyrtaeus begins by saying that it is *kalon* to die for one's country,[b] and continues some lines later by saying that flight is *aischron*. He also stresses the horrors of being a refugee, and the advantages of defending one's own; and thus far the use of *aischron* and *kalon* seems very like those discussed above. He then, however, considers old and young men in battle. In referring to the old he describes a wound calculated to shock and disgust anyone at any time, and says that it is *aischron* to the eyes;[c] but turning to the younger men, he says that since the young man is *kalos*, he is so no matter what happens to him: he is *kalos* when he falls among the foremost fighters (even if he suffers such a wound). We might be tempted to translate the earlier instances by 'noble' and 'shameful', the later by 'beautiful' and 'ugly'. But the point of the poem would then be lost: the later instances too, though they are distinguished as '*aischron* to the eyes', act as motives for and against action *in precisely the same way* as the former ones. The old man ought not to suffer such wounds in precisely the same way as one ought not to flee from the enemy, for both are

---

[a] Aesch. *Eum.* 98.   [b] Tyrtaeus 10 Bergk.
[c] αἰσχρὰ τά γ' ὀφθαλμοῖς.

aischron: and Tyrtaeus uses *kalos* unqualified to commend both the actions and the physical beauty of the young men. Though decisive examples rarely occur, it seems evident that for this period even these two uses, the 'moral' and the 'visual', of *aischron* and *kalon* are not distinguished;[10] and if these are not distinguished, much less can the others be. An *opposition* between the two uses first occurs in the last decade of the fifth century.[11] Accordingly, at an earlier period, though it is much less misleading to translate *aischron* by 'shameful' than by 'wrong', it is still misleading; for when a single term of value in Language A spans two situations (*a, b*) which are distinguished in Language B, it is misleading to say that Language A uses the same word to mean both *a* and *b*: it is truer to say that Language A has no word for either *a* or *b*, but rather a different system of values, with the different world-view which accompanies it.

C. TRADITIONAL *ARETE* AND MORAL RESPONSIBILITY

(i) *The Sanction*

It is now clear that the traditional *arete*-standard persisted throughout the fifth century. Accordingly, as in Homer, the problem of the relation of *dikaiosune* to this system of values remains of the utmost importance. If we temporarily leave out of account any new developments in values, the only possible method of relating *dikaiosune* to *arete* is as a means to a desired end, namely material prosperity for oneself and one's family; and that justice *is* the means to this end must be guaranteed by the gods. An inevitable divine justice, dispensed in this life, is the essential foundation of this morality.[12] It must be so: we have as yet seen no other effective inducement to pursue the quieter virtues. I have said[a] that this problem becomes acute when one man or one group has the power to be unjust on the grand scale. Such is the tyrant; and a passage of Pindar shows the view of traditional values which might be held by anyone in this position:[b]

If any man who has been fortunate in winning prizes of renown, or in possessing the strength which wealth brings, restrains baneful insolence in his mind, he deserves to be praised by the citizens.

[a] Above, pp. 61, 66 f.   [b] Pind. *Isthm.* 3. 1 ff.

Zeus, mighty *aretai* come to mortals from you. The prosperity of those who revere the gods lives longer; but prosperity does not for all time dwell abundantly with men whose wits are crooked.

There are two inducements to justice here: in the first place, the citizen-body, opposed, as in the quotations above,[a] to the wealthy classes and the tyrant, should praise any man of these upper classes who has prospered in any way, if he shows restraint. That is to say, *in these circumstances and when accompanied by these other highly desirable qualities*, restraint is praiseworthy. This is not even to say that it is *kalon* for an *agathos* to be *dikaios*; for a precondition of such a judgement would be that the equals of the *agathos*, not merely his inferiors, should prize such self-restraint: and it is much further from saying that it is *kalon* to be *dikaios tout court*. Indeed, Pindar does not say that the opinion of the ordinary citizens should act as a restraint; he says that, *if* the successful man shows restraint, the ordinary citizens should praise him: a very different thing.

Accordingly, the real inducement to the tyrant to be just is still that, if he respects Zeus, his *olbos*, his material prosperity, will last far longer than if he does not.[b] Justice remains a means to an end: an end which must be attained in this life. The dangers of this were pointed out in Chapter IV:[c] and in view of the manner in which a tyrant is likely to obtain his power in the first instance, the theory that the highest material rewards may be obtained by being just is unlikely to find much support. This is still a major problem for Greek values: that Plato should spend so much time in proving that tyrants are not really 'prosperous', *eudaimones* or *olbioi*, is not surprising.

(ii) *Success and Failure*

Even if the gods are believed to underwrite justice, difficulties of values remain. One of the poems of Simonides shows the effect which the principal system of values might still have upon moral responsibility. He writes:[d]

It is hard for a man to become truly *agathos*, four-square in hands

---

[a] Pind. *Pyth.* 3. 70, *Ol.* 5. 15, p. 159 f.

[b] So Pindar can hold that it is the mark of a wise man, *sophos*, to be just: *Pyth.* 5. 11 ff.   [c] pp. 68 ff.

[d] Simonides 5 Bergk. See Appendix for a discussion of some alternative interpretations of this poem.

and feet and mind, wrought blameless. Nor does the saying of
Pittacus seem to me to be well said, though it was uttered by a
wise man. He says it is hard to be *esthlos*. Only a god could have
this privilege. For a man it is impossible not to be *kakos* if irresistible
disaster overtakes him. For when he fares well, *eu prattein*, every man
is *agathos*, but *kakos* when he fares badly, *kakōs*. Accordingly I will not
seek for what is impossible and throw my share in life fruitlessly
away on the vain hope of finding a man without blame, among
those of us who enjoy the fruit of the broad earth; but if I find him
I will tell you. I praise and make my friends anyone who does
nothing *aischron* of his own free will, *hekon*; but against necessity even
the gods do not fight.

When Simonides writes *agathos*, it is clearly the traditional
agathos-standard to which he is referring: here the strong, brave
soldier, the speedy runner, and the good counsellor. We seem in
the opening lines to be concerned with military and athletic
success rather than wealth; but when Simonides goes on to say
that only a god can be really *agathos* or *esthlos*, and that this
depends on success, *eu prattein*, all the glittering implications of
agathos are brought to mind. For Simonides is merely recording
a fact about traditional values: if a man 'fares well', whether in
winning a battle or a race, or in becoming prosperous, he is
agathos; whereas if he does not 'fare well' (except in the special
case of dying bravely in battle),[13] he is *kakos*. Accordingly, if
'irresistible disaster' comes upon any man, he must needs be
kakos, whether deprived of the trappings of riches or of the
power to resist his enemies successfully. No man is 'without
blame': if one evaluates a man from the point of view of prosperity and success, there is always something with which one
can find fault. One could always have more money. The manner in which *agathos* and *kakos* have been used in the poem up to
this point shows that they are to be taken thus; and the examination of other uses at the period has shown that there is no
reason *a priori* why they should be taken otherwise. This is
important in considering the remainder of the poem; which,
being 'enlightened' by the standards of the late sixth and early
fifth centuries, may most conveniently be discussed in a later
chapter.[a] Here it suffices to state that, inasmuch as the traditional values which persist into the fifth century depend, for

ᵃ Below, pp. 196 f.

adequate reasons already given, upon prosperity in peace and success in war, intentions can be little considered. In the field of the most important values, *moral* responsibility still does not exist.

This becomes clearer if the manner in which the judgement 'this is *aischron* for me' functions in this society is considered in detail. If I say 'this is wrong and I am guilty' I mean 'I have done this *wilfully*'.[14] 'This is *aischron* for me', however, is far more complex. In *any* society in which the criterion is 'what people say', a situation may be *aischron* even though nothing *aischron* has in fact been done, so long as it is believed to have been done. One is ashamed none the less. This is the fate which Achilles fears may befall Clytemnestra in the *Iphigenia at Aulis*, and which has befallen Helen in the *Helen*.[a] Again, supposing that something *aischron* has been done in this society, there are several possibilities. One may feel shame at something which one has oneself done: which is what Helen feels, in the *Orestes*,[b] when she says that she is unwilling to show herself before the Greeks. Secondly, one may feel shame as a result of something done to one: as is the case when Iphigenia refuses to show herself to Achilles on learning the truth about her 'marriage'.[c] Thirdly, one may feel shame at something someone related to oneself does: as Orestes would have felt shame, had Electra in fact been the poor man's bride.[d] Fourthly, one may feel shame at something which someone related to oneself suffers: as the family of Ajax would feel shame after his death,[e] if Tecmessa came down in the world.[15] Only in the first group is personal responsibility *likely*; for the doings and sufferings of those related to oneself remain *aischron* whether or no one could do anything about them oneself. And since, as has been shown, even the first group is concerned entirely, or almost entirely, with the evaluation of success and failure, though the agent is here personally involved, his intentions are unlikely to be considered: no one *intends* to fail.

The most important system of values, then, gives no more encouragement to the development of the concept of moral responsibility than it did in Homer. The quieter virtues remain

---

[a] E. *I.A.* 1030 ff., *Hel.* 270 ff., cp. p. 161.   [b] E. *Or.* 98.
[c] E. *I.A.* 1341.   [d] E. *Elec.* 43 ff., cp. Aesch. *Supp.* 996.
[e] S. *Ajax* 505.

linked to this system by divine guarantee only. This, and the processes of law, are the only guarantee of the weaker against the stronger; and if the stronger should be in a position to get his own way, only divine sanctions remain. Yet these are, after all, the 'good old days' to which Aristophanes, in his role of moralist, looks back.[16] Accordingly, despite theological difficulties, divine sanctions must have sufficed to keep even the most powerful of citizens within bounds, in Athens at all events; where, indeed, in the early fifth century the gods seem very obtrusive in thought, though this impression may be due to the personality of Aeschylus alone. The system will work if two conditions are fulfilled: firstly, if men in general believe sufficiently strongly that their success depends on their *dikaiosune*; and secondly, if it is assumed that the proper field for displaying active *arete* is the field of battle and the games, leaving civic life as the field for *dikaiosune*. Given the paramount position of *arete*, it is not easy to provide a reason for this allocation of spheres of influence, should anyone attempt to question it. Accordingly this system, in the most literal sense, will not bear thinking about; and this is the period in which the sophists were to do precisely this.

NOTES TO CHAPTER VIII

1. Pindar is here in effect expressing his (or more probably his employers') version of 'This is *arete*' (cp. Chapter IV, pp. 73 ff.). He does not say that *aretai* which involve no danger are not *aretai* at all, for his attitude to life is not that of the elegiac poets; but by saying 'if something *kalon* is achieved with much labour' he implies that the true *kalon* is that which results from toil and effort in war or in the games. Hence, since ideally *arete* is to do *kala*, and *kala* are what is done by the *agathos* qua *agathos*, one may conclude that the true *aretai* are those which involve toil and effort. Pindar is presumably only contrasting hard-won success with success easily attained; but it is interesting to note how readily this dismissal of such *aretai*, which is merely the traditional attitude, could be used to dismiss *dikaiosune* and similar quiet excellences, should they attempt to usurp the title of *arete*.

2. Cp. S. *Ajax* 619, 1357, *Trach.* 177, 645, *Phil.* 1420 ff.; E. *Her.* 625, *Supp.* 850, 912, *I.T.* 114 f., &c.; Hdt. i. 95, 169, vii. 53, 234, &c., especially in the phrase *anēr agathos genesthai*, 'to become, or show oneself, an *agathos*', common in the historians and orators. We may compare *andragathiā*, the quality of the *agathos*, Hdt. i. 136, iv. 65, vi. 128, which, though it may be freely opposed to the claims of high birth, i. 99, v. 39, vii. 166, is never used to commend the co-operative excellences. For

Herodotus' use of *arete*, cp. Hdt. i. 52, iii. 120, v. 49, &c.; and for *agathos* and *arete* in Thucydides, Thuc. ii. 87. 9, iv. 40. 2, iv. 95, v. 69. 2. For the general flavour of the word, note that Lysias finds it necessary to employ *arete* twenty-two times in the *Funeral Speech*, whereas the word does not occur at all in his *Murder of Eratosthenes*, which is concerned with adultery. The qualities commended are those of Heracles and Ajax: of Heracles, S. *Phil.* 1420 ff.; E. *H.F.* 335, 655; Lysias, *Epitaph on the Corinthian Auxiliaries*, 6 and 15, and cp. the Choice of Heracles in Prodicus, D/K frag. 2. These qualities, in so far as they are moral, are those of the knight-errant, who protects the weak from the wrongs of others; but they do not raise the question of his own behaviour in civic life. Other incidents in Heracles' career, all expressions of *arete*, make it clear that he would be a rather disturbing next-door neighbour.

3. *Aretai* are 'deeds of valour (successes)' even in Thucydides, cp. i. 123, iii. 67. 2.

4. Cp. also *O.C.* 897 ff. Theseus, when Creon attempts to carry off Antigone and Ismene by force, calls for reinforcements 'lest I may become a mockery to this stranger if I am overcome by force'. *O.C.* 929 f., however, represent a new development in thought, which cannot conveniently be discussed in this chapter; cp. Chapter IX, Note 16.

5. I have quoted examples from Euripides, to show that this use continues throughout the century. Lest it should appear that they are instances of a new 'immoralism', I add here some material from Aeschylus. When Aegisthus, *Agam.* 1610, says, 'It is *kalon* for me even to die now that I have seen Agamemnon in the net of justice', he is not speaking as only a bad character would speak, but using language as any man of the period would have used it. It is a mark of *arete*—and hence *kalon*—to *administer* what one believes to be justice, not to submit to it oneself; cp. Heracles in Note 2 above. Again, when it is said of Eteocles, who has been killed defending Thebes, that he has died where it is *kalon* for young men to die, the relation of this to the basic use of *arete* is apparent. (Contrast the situation of Polynices, *Septem* 581.) The use of *arete* to commend prosperity is paralleled by such uses of *kalon* as at *Agam.* 846, and *Cho.* 807, &c. At *Cho.* 739 it is said of the supposed death of Orestes that it has turned out *kalōs* for Clytemnestra, but altogether *kakōs* for those who are loyal to the dead Agamemnon; which again shows how far *kalon* is from the quiet values.

6. So Sandys and Puech. Gildersleeve renders γίνεται σοφοῖς as 'is accounted in the eyes of the wise'. If this rendering is adopted, 'wise' is evidently persuasive, rather than a reference to a specific class of men, and hints that not all men subscribe to this standard. Cp. *Ol.* 5. 15, discussed on p. 160.

7. Though the context is far different, this line shows how the most important values fanned the anger of those who, considering themselves to be *sophoi*, were exposed by Socrates. The situation is annoying in any circumstances; here, however, it is *elenchos* indeed, and *aischron*, a failing to satisfy the requirements of *arete* (for wisdom, however interpreted, is of course an element of *arete* from Homer onwards).

8. Cp. Hdt. iii. 80, where Otanes says that tyrants generally display envy towards the *aristoi*. This is evidently not moral, but a criticism of the tendency of tyrants to base their power on the support of the common people, whose champions they so frequently proclaimed themselves to be. Since the discussion of Hdt. iii. 80 is a sophistic set-piece (cp. p. 178 below) Otanes is presumably expressing a sophistic generalization on the habits of tyrants; and Pindar is saying in effect that Hiero is a most unusual tyrant.

9. For the attitude to social disadvantage generally, cp. S. *Ajax* 505; E. *And.* 645 ff.; E. *Phoen.* 1691. This justifies the assortment of motives which induce Orestes to kill Clytemnestra, e.g. Aesch. *Cho.* 297 ff. That Prince Orestes and Princess Electra have 'come down in the world' as a result of Clytemnestra's behaviour is *aischron* for them. Cp. E. *Elec.* 304 ff., and an anecdote of Socrates, Xen. *Mem.* ii. 7. 4, showing a change in this standard under the stress of war. *Aischron* is the most powerful term of value; hence any means are justifiable in order to remove this stigma.

10. This may seem to go too far. Surely, it may be said, no one could blame a man for being *aischros* physically; after all, Protagoras (Plat. *Prot.* 323 D), says that no one blames men for defects which they have by nature or by chance, and he takes as examples men who are *aischroi* (physically) or small or weak. Possibly 'blame' is the wrong word, though Protagoras' statement in Plato cannot be taken as necessarily valid for any period before the sophists, and does not necessarily ensure that there shall be a general change of attitude afterwards: Plato, in the *Gorgias* myth, 523 C 5, cites, among the reasons why justice goes astray on earth, that men who have morally bad *psuchai* are clad in bodies which are *kala*, and in the trappings of lineage and wealth. The last two certainly confused Greek justice, as Chapter X will show; so presumably the first also played its part. If this is so, then to be *aischros* physically must have been an equal disadvantage: that externals could go against a man in court is shown by Lysias, *For Mantitheus* 19, Demosthenes, *Against Pantaenetus* 52. The latter passage is an excellent footnote to Aristotle's *megalopsūchos*, *E.N.* 1123ᵃ34 ff., showing clearly why Aristotle pays such attention to e.g. the possession of a deep voice. (Cp. Chapter XVI, Note 14.) Any or all of these attitudes may be adopted in any society: in Greek the language encourages and *justifies* their adoption; and since actions which are *aischra* are so whether performed voluntarily or not, the Greek need not have felt that these were in any way special cases.

11. S. *Phil.* 475 f. It will be shown below (Chapter IX, p. 189) that Sophocles is at some pains in this play to contrast new standards with old. This too may be a new development.

12. Cp. Chapter VII, pp. 138 ff. Even in the closing stages of the *Eumenides*, 934 ff., the reformed Furies are still to punish the wrongdoer *or his descendants* for his crimes, despite the fact that they have already said, 269 ff., that there is punishment after death too.

13. Hence presumably the great insistence that a man 'showed himself to

be *agathos*' (ἀνὴρ ἀγαθὸς γενέσθαι) in referring to those who die in battle (cp. Note 2 above). This is the only aspect of traditional *arete* in which one's *arete* is not placed beyond dispute by one's own success. Cowards and brave men both die in battles; hence all who deliver funeral orations must reiterate that the *arete* of the deceased is beyond doubt.

14. This is of course an oversimplification; but there is no need *here* to discuss the implications of carelessness, or situations in which one would say 'I *feel* morally responsible' in our system of values.

15. Cp. the very significant lines of *Iliad* iii. 241 f. Helen does not see her brothers Castor and Pollux on the Greek side and, not knowing that they are dead, supposes they are ashamed: 'They are not willing to come down into the battle, for they fear the *aischea*, insults, and reproaches which are my lot.'

16. e.g. *Clouds* 961 ff. The Just Argument speaks thus: 'I will speak of the former mode of education when I flourished and counselled what was just, and *sophrosune* was the custom.' A society could well hold these values together with the Homeric ones, provided no excessive strain were put upon the system. Even if Aristophanes' lines are nostalgic, the form which the nostalgia takes is significant.

IX

THE INFILTRATION OF 'MORALITY'

A. *AGATHOS* AND *KAKOS*

THE last chapter closed in a gloomy tone. Hitherto, however, we have deliberately confined the discussion to 'traditional' values. Certain other aspects of the *agathos*-standard in fifth-century writers suggest once again that the problem has solved itself. Some encouragement can be found in Aeschylus, and even in Pindar.

What is needed is a use of *agathos* to commend, or a use of *kakos* to decry, a man who falls short in respect of the quiet virtues. The latter at least is to be found in Aeschylus. In the *Suppliants*[a] we find:

> Zeus . . . watches over these things, and holds the balance, assigning to the *kakoi* their unjust deeds, *adika*, to the law-abiding, *ennomoi*, their righteous deeds, *hosia*.

Kakos is explicitly opposed to *ennomos*, and to be *ennomos* must entail observance of (some) co-operative virtues.

Not surprisingly, the same use of *kakos* is found in Sophocles. In the *Ajax*,[b] Athena, counselling mankind to avoid *hubris*, maintains that

> The gods love men who are *sōphrones* and hate those who are *kakoi*.

These passages show a remarkable change of linguistic usage. The sentiment is not new, but its expression is startlingly so. Till Aeschylus, the *kakos* has been characterized, not by insolence, but by docile and subservient behaviour suited to an inferior. Achilles' treatment of Hector's body[c] was not the act of a *kakos*, bitterly though the gods disapproved of it; it was something which, in this late book of the *Iliad*, was too horrible

---

[a] Aesch. *Supp.* 402 ff.   [b] S. *Ajax* 132 f.   [c] Cp. p. 38.

for even an *agathos* to claim to do: a very different thing. The relation between (say) *anosios* and *kakos* has been rather: 'If you are *anosios*, impious, and *agathos*, which is perfectly possible, the gods may be angry and bring you to ruin, *kakotes*.[a] The gods have not punished men for being *kakoi*, poor craven failures. There was no need: such things are their own punishment.

The gods are explicitly mentioned in the above passages. Such mention is not necessary: in the *Oedipus at Colonus*,[b] Oedipus says

How can I be *kakos* by nature? I acted in self-defence; and so, even had I known who Laius was, I should not have been *kakos* in killing him.

Here again *kakos* is (implicitly) opposed to *dikaios*; just as, later in the play, it is used as a synonym for *ekdikos*, lawless.[c]

Such a usage is clearly a great advance. To decry the unjust, however, is not enough. One must also commend the just; and for this purpose there is no word so powerful as *agathos*. *Agathos* and *kakos* are, strictly, correlated terms; accordingly, a change in one might appear to entail a change in the other. Logically, this is true; but least of all in questions of value are men logical. The evidence of previous centuries, again, gives no reason to suppose that a similar change in *agathos* will take place. After all, in Homer the suitors could be termed *kakoi*, ineffective fighters and weaklings in drawing the bow, though they were, socially speaking, the *aristoi* of Ithaca and its neighbourhood; but there is nothing to suggest that, even had the (lower-class) Thersites been, *per impossible*, brave and handsome, he would have been termed *agathos* as a result. The other implications of *agathos* are too strong.[d]

The evidence in fact suggests that this change in the use of *kakos* was not readily followed by a similar change in the use of *agathos*. *Agathos* and *arete* commend traditional values in Aeschylus;[1] and in Sophocles, though the 'co-operative' use of *kakos* is the *prevailing* one, there is no instance in the extant complete plays of the use of *agathos* (*arete*) as a synonym for *dikaios* (*dikaiosune*).[2] This will serve as a brief statement of the position; but its implications require further examination.

[a] For this use of *kakotes* (in direct opposition to *eudaimoniā*, prosperity) cp. Hdt. vi. 67. 3.
[b] S. *O.C.* 270 ff.   [c] *O.C.* 919 ff.   [d] Cp. p. 36 above.

In the *Philoctetes*,[a] the Chorus says that now, after all his sufferings, Philoctetes

Will come to be prosperous and great, since he has met with the child of *agathoi*,

in meeting with Achilles' son Neoptolemus, who has undertaken to help him. If we take these lines in isolation, there is nothing here which we can say firmly is not contained in traditional standards. Even in Homer it was expected of the *agathos*, the man of good family,[3] that he should help the suppliant. This, however, in two senses: the *agathos* had to protect against the attacks of others the suppliant whom he had taken under his protection, for this was (and as we have seen, still is in the fifth century) an expression of his *arete*;[b] but to accept the suppliant in the first place, and to refrain from maltreating him oneself once accepted, was sooner the mark of the pious or 'prudent' man, the *hosios* or *pepnumenos*, than of the *agathos*.[c] But the *agathos*, the powerful man, was the man to whom suppliants would naturally come; and hence it was, in a sense, the mark of the *agathos* to accept and help them. We need have no more than this here. Indeed, we may have less: Neoptolemus has already promised to help Philoctetes, and the Chorus may mean by these lines merely that an *agathos*, a powerful man, has the *capacity* to give a great deal of help to Philoctetes. Nor is there anything else in the use of *agathos* in Sophocles to suggest a more 'advanced' interpretation.[4]

So much we may say of the use of *agathos* in isolation. Here, however, we have to consider it together with the use of *kakos* discussed above, and to inquire in this light whether Aeschylus and Sophocles have advanced at all upon Homeric and traditional usage. It is difficult to give a firm answer to this question. If, disregarding the warning above, we attempt to force strict logic upon these writers, we must admit that there is some advance: if *kakos* is used in the manner discussed above, then, if the *agathos* behaves in a manner which is unjust or impious, these writers are willing to term him *kakos*; and they would certainly term *kakos* on these grounds any man who was not *agathos*, of good family. They are less 'advanced' than Theognis, evidently, for they would certainly not admit that any man

---

[a] S. *Phil.* 719 f.   [b] pp. 35, 157 above.   [c] p. 65 above.

whatever becomes *agathos* in virtue of his *dikaiosune* alone; but surely if Neoptolemus did not help Philoctetes, he would be not merely *anosios* but *kakos*; and this is an undoubted advance. We may, it seems, say at least that Aeschylus and Sophocles demand certain co-operative excellences from the *agathos* much more insistently than do traditional standards.

To say this would be rash. The examples of *kakos* used in a moral manner in Aeschylus are generalizations. We do not find them used to influence a decision directly or to solve a problem of values: and we shall see below[a] that Aeschylus does not use the new 'moral' use of *aischron* to solve a very pressing problem in the manner of the two later dramatists. Further, when *kakos* is used in the *Septem*[b] to influence the decision of Eteocles, the Chorus contends that he will not appear *kakos* even if he does not fight his brother. Clearly *kakos* decries cowardice here; and a few lines earlier Eteocles had used *aischune* of the shame of cowardice. Such a usage is far more typical of Aeschylus; and it seems safest to say that these moral generalizations which employ *kakos* were not properly co-ordinated into Aeschylus' moral scheme. To say this is not to disparage Aeschylus unduly: we shall see that the fifth century as a whole had little better success. Sophocles uses *kakos* (and *aischron*, as will appear below) more freely in the moral sense, and can make definite points with it, as Oedipus does in the passage quoted above; but it is to be noted that though the uses of *kakos* quoted above suggest that injustice in the widest sense is decried, the only 'quiet' excellence which Sophocles may be demanding of the *agathos* as *agathos*—and that only in the latest two of the extant plays— is that of helping the suppliant. That is to say, the justice commended is the quality of those who have justice in their own hands, not that of equals before the law. Accordingly, it is safest to claim no more than that we have here the very beginning of the attempt, which becomes much more important later, to make the practice of the quiet virtues one of the attributes of the gentleman; and this claim depends on the use of *kakos*, not on that of *agathos*.

Sophocles, then, seems to make no real attempt to break with tradition in his use of *agathos*. Such a modification, even had Sophocles wished to make it,[5] was certain to prove difficult.

<hr />

[a] p. 185.   [b] Aesch. *Septem* 698.

That it did so is suggested not only by the absence of such usage in Sophocles, but also by its rarity in such authors as do use it. Euripides, where naturally the new use of *kakos* occurs,[6] shows this clearly. Two quotations, one employing *arete*, the second *agathos*, will serve both to display the usage and to suggest that it cannot be unpremeditated. In the fragments alleged to belong to the *Heraclidae*,[7] the following passage occurs:

> There are three *aretai* which you must practise, my child. Honour the gods, your parents, and the common laws of Greece, and in so doing you will have for ever an excellent, *kallistos*, garland of *eukleia*, fair fame.

That it should be expected of a man that he honour the gods and his parents and obey the laws, whether the 'common laws of Greece' or others, is not new, though, as has been seen, the connotation of traditional *arete* might sometimes confuse these expectations; but that these actions should be termed *aretai* and, in view of the manner of expression, the *cardinal aretai*, is both new and surprising. It is to be expected as a result that a man will be termed *agathos purely in virtue of his practising these aretai*, which are all 'quiet' or 'co-operative' virtues. More than this, however, may be deduced from this passage. The lines are schematic and didactic in form, and it seems as a result highly likely that Euripides has imported the manner of expression from current sophistic thought. Though their context is lost, the shape of the lines makes it clear that they must have been produced with intent to surprise the audience; which, to judge from the earlier use of *arete*, they can scarcely have failed to do. This is quite unlike the unpremeditated use of *kakos* in Sophocles; accordingly, though the thought may have influenced the linguistic usage of its (sophistic) authors, there is no reason to suppose *a priori* that it will influence the general linguistic usage of the poet who has borrowed it or of his audience; and it is in fact rare in Euripides.[8]

Euripides' use of *agathos* in this new manner gives a similar impression. In the extant complete plays, it is not until the *Electra* that *agathos* appears in a quiet sense *used of a man*;[9] and here the manner of the utterance points not only to its novelty, but also to the difficulty in making such a change in habits of thought. Orestes has discovered that the Husbandman has not

attempted to consummate his marriage with Electra, whom
Aegisthus had given to him in marriage on the grounds that
such a husband would not be encouraged by the match to
attempt to seize the throne which he had usurped from Agamemnon. Orestes is amazed by the Husbandman's self-control,
and begins to reflect upon the nature of *euandriā*, a type of word
which, commending the kind of man most valued, in traditional
thought pre-eminently denotes and commends courage.[10] He
begins[a] by saying that human beings do not always breed true,
and that one will often find that the offspring of a *gennaios*, a
nobleman, is a mere cipher,[11] and vice versa. Since birth is an
inadequate guide, he wonders what guide there may be. Wealth?
No. Poverty? No: 'Poverty is a diseased condition, and teaches
a man to do harm, *kakon*, as a result of need.' No Greek regarded poverty as a sign of virtue. The weapons a man carries
(since earlier the charioteer-kings, and more recently the cavalry
and the hoplites, had the strongest claim to be *agathoi*)? No: one
cannot tell whether a man is *agathos* (even in the sense of
brave) merely by looking at his weapons. In short, Orestes
dismisses all these indications, since the present case proves
them to be pointless:

For this man, who neither has a high position among the Argives,
nor is puffed up by the fame deriving from noble lineage, but is a
man of the people, has proved to be *aristos*. Will you not come to
your senses,[b] you who wander about full of empty opinions, *kena
doxasmata*, and in future judge men by their mode of life, and hold
those to be noble, *eugeneis*, who lead moral lives?

Aristos here clearly commends self-control, a complete departure from traditional usage. The quieter virtues are to have their
place, and men are to be judged by what they do, not by what
they seem to be. The violence of this sudden turn to the audience
is to be explained by the fact that it is his own habits of thought,
as well as those of his audience, that Euripides is trying to
eradicate.[12] The political implications of this and similar passages will be explained in the next chapter.

Despite the vehemence of Euripides, this seems to be the
only passage in the extant complete plays in which *agathos*, in

[a] E. *Elec*. 367 ff.
[b] This is evidently the sense, though the exact means of reaching it is not clear,
cp. Denniston, ad loc.

reference to a man, is identified with or analytically related to the quiet co-operative virtues.[13] Nor are examples any more frequent in other writers. In the whole of Herodotus—who uses *kakos* and *kakotes* in the new manner quite unselfconsciously[14]— there is one example of *aristos* used in this manner, and this a highly significant one. The passage from the *Electra*, from its highly schematic nature, again seems to be a borrowing from some sophist; and the passage from Herodotus is similar. In the third book he records a discussion held by the seven Persian conspirators, after they had slain the Magi, on the best form of government for Persia, Otanes advocating democracy, Mega-byzus aristocracy, and Darius monarchy.[a] Even Herodotus' contemporaries poured scorn on the historical truth of this account;[b] and it is clear that Herodotus has merely taken a contemporary discussion on the merits of these three forms of government and set it in Persia. That is to say, the passage may be termed 'sophistic'. In it, Otanes argues against monarchy as follows: it is a bad thing, since the monarch can do as he pleases without fear of punishment, and even the *aristos* of all men, given such powers, would abandon his customary modes of behaviour. With such opportunities, not even the *aristos* could control himself: if one may say this, clearly it is characteristic of the *agathos* here to be self-controlled. But here only; this 'sophistic' usage has no relation to the use of *agathos* anywhere else in Herodotus: which emphasizes the sharpness of the cleavage between old and new.[15]

In Thucydides, this use of *agathos* may progress even further, as is indicated by one passage in particular:[c] the Corinthians, rebutting the Corcyreans' speech at Athens in request of an alli-ance, say of them

If they were *agathoi*, as they claim to be, the less they could be assailed by their neighbours, the more clearly could they have dis-played their *arete*, by giving and receiving what was just, *dikaion*.

To be *agathos*, to display *arete*, may now be *among other things* to observe without compulsion the claims of *dikaiosune* both in inter-state relations and within the state.[16] In Thucydides, too, this is a startling thing to say, as subsequent chapters will make clear. The thought behind it will then appear: here it suffices

---

      [a] Hdt. iii. 80.   [b] Ibid., *ad init.*   [c] Thuc. i. 37. 5.

to say that, in the thoughtful and intellectual Thucydides, the identification of *agathos* (*arete*) with *dikaios* (*dikaiosune*) seems *on some occasions* to be complete.[17]

It seems evident that the new use of *agathos* is directly related to sophistic thought, using this phrase to signify the more or less systematic thought on political matters which, for reasons which will be discussed below,[a] flourished in Athens at this time. The source of the new use of *kakos* should, one would suppose, be the same; and presumably the sophists had some part to play in its development. But it was shown above[b] that the new use of *kakotes* seems to appear in the *Purifications* of Empedocles, a work heavily influenced by 'Orphism' or Pythagoreanism, whose belief in a 'real' future existence would make possible a use of the most powerful terms of value in a sense which did not entail success *in this life*. Aeschylus' use of *kakos*, too, might have been affected by this.[c] Again, the traditional use of *agathos* and *kakos* is, as was shown in Chapter III,[d] related to the insecurity of Greek life: it might not be coincidental that this new use of *kakos*, in writers who had not the beliefs about the next world held by Empedocles and Aeschylus, appeared at a time when Athens, now mistress of an empire, could look forward to more material prosperity than any Greek state had ever known, and could hence afford to give more prominence to the quieter virtues; even though, as will be shown in the next two chapters, Athens' new condition also produced quite different (and disastrous) developments in this same complex of values. The provenance of these values is of much less importance than their effects; but that several different influences should tend in the same direction is interesting.

B. *AISCHRON* AND *KALON*

(i) Values 'Out of Step'

Before discussing *aischron* and *kalon*, we must draw attention to an aspect of Greek moral thought and practice which is, from this point onwards, of great importance. The Greeks, as is shown by the writings of the elegiac poets, and even earlier by

[a] pp. 220 ff.   [b] p. 143.   [c] p. 144.   [d] pp. 34 ff.

Homer,[a] were wont to lay much more emphasis on the characteristics of the approved type of man and his excellence, the
agathos and his *arete*, than on those of his individual actions.
Thus anyone who engaged in theory was much more likely to
ask first 'What is *arete*?' or 'Who is the *agathos*?' than to ask
'What is the *aischron*?' or 'What is the *kalon*?' The reason for
this approach, both in theory and in practice, seems clear: the
former questions appear much less abstract, much more 'practical', than the latter. The importance of this difference of
emphasis lies in the strange results to which it may lead in
practice. *Agathos* is the highest term of praise for a man, *kalon* for
his actions. Hence it follows logically that the *agathos* does *kala*;
and thus, if the characteristics of the *agathos* are determined, it
might appear that the characteristics of *kalon* are determined
too. Here again, however, logic cannot have the last word.
We have seen that even words so closely linked as *agathos* and
kakos may have different criteria of application in the same
writer; and the difference of emphasis given to *agathos* and *arete*
as compared with that given to the individual action ensures
that *agathos* and (say) *kalon* may become out of step even more
readily.

To say 'out of step', however, does not indicate which is the
more likely to take the lead; for the emphasis on *agathos* does
not entail that it should lead the way. If changes came about
solely as a result of meditation, this might be true. It is conceivable that some thinker should work out in detail his definition of the *agathos*, the type of man most needed by his society,
and then alter the usage of *kalon* and *aischron* to commend and
decry such actions as his definition of the *agathos* demands: we
see Plato behaving very similarly in the *Laws*.[b] If he were not
such a radical thinker as Plato, however, he might go no further
than his definition of *arete*: and in this case, should the definition
be accepted generally, it would be necessary subsequently to
alter the usage of *kalon* and *aischron*. This is one conceivable
train of events; but if no thinker is to be found, changes may
occur imperceptibly in practice; and in this case, simply because
of the greater emphasis on the *agathos* and his *arete*, and the
consequent knowledge of their defining qualities, it may well
be easier to say, of an action not previously held to be *aischron*,

'This is *aischron*, therefore you as an *agathos* should not do it', than it is to say in reference to the same action 'In doing this you are *kakos*', when the man has all the traditional grounds for regarding himself as *agathos*. But whichever term succeeds in taking the lead at any given time—and it is likely that in a time of moral confusion both tendencies may exist simultaneously (in different individuals) in the same society—the fact that the two groups of words, logically connected, have become in some respects unrelated must create strains in the system of values until they are correctly related again. This problem will be prominent in the discussion of the subsequent chapters.

(ii) *The New Uses*

In the case of *aischron*, as in that of *kakos*, there are some indications of a new use in Aeschylus, while Pindar displays one 'advanced' use of *kalon*. It seems to be *aischron* to tell lies by this time. At all events, Io makes this claim[a] when she asks Prometheus to foretell her future sufferings, and implores him not to hide the truth out of pity for her; but Io expresses the judgement as her own opinion, and even were it generally accepted as valid in such a case, this does not necessarily entail that it would be *aischron* to tell lies in order to secure one's own success and prosperity. Again, Aeschylus can use the word '*aischron*-counselling'[b] of the state of mind which induced Agamemnon to sacrifice Iphigenia; but here too to use a compound adjective is less pointed than to say roundly that the action was *aischron*. A third passage seems to confirm that Aeschylus finds difficulty in using *aischron* in this manner: Paris, he says, shamed, *aischunein*, the table of hospitality when he abducted Helen.[c] For whom is this *aischron*? For Menelaus, certainly:[18] adultery is always *aischron* for the offended husband, for, whether the wife is regarded as a chattel or as something more, it is the part of an *agathos* to keep his own dependents and possessions safe. Normally the act is not *aischron* for the adulterer. The man who commits adultery with the wife of his host, however, is in a special case: the relationship of guest and host by its very nature demands co-operation, not competition, and even in Homer[d] the use of *kalon*, though not of *aischron*, reflected this situation. Accordingly,

---

[a] Aesch. *P.V.* 685 f.
[c] Ibid. 401.
[b] Aesch. *Agam.* 222, αἰσχρόμητις.
[d] Cp. pp. 43 ff.

in saying that Paris shamed the table of hospitality, Aeschylus
may be implying that the act was *aischron* for Paris too. If so,
this is certainly more 'advanced' than the traditional position:
but it cannot be assumed that Aeschylus could have made the
point explicitly, much less that he could have used *aischron*
freely to decry breaches of the co-operative virtues outside this
very special relationship. (It is worth noting that Herodotus, in
telling the story of Paris, confines himself to terming his action
'most impious', *anosiōtaton.*[a])

Pindar may go a little further in saying to Hiero[b]

Nevertheless, since to be envied is better than to be pitied, do
not disregard actions which are *kala*: govern your people with a
just helm, and hammer out your speech on a truthful anvil.

Here, corresponding to the judgement that it is *aischron* to tell
lies, it seems to be *kalon* to tell the truth; but it also seems to
be *kalon* for the ruler to be *dikaios* (once again to his inferiors,
not to his equals). Pindar does not exactly say this; the three
exhortations could be taken as parallel, and *kalon* restricted to
success; but it seems somewhat harsh to do so. In fact, such a
use is similar to Sophocles' use of *agathos* discussed above: it is
hinted that it is *kalon* for the powerful man to be just to his
inferiors—particularly when he is in a position to dispense that
justice—not that justice is *kalon per se*.

The words of Pindar and Aeschylus give us no right to assume
that they imply more than is said. In view of the linking of
kalon and *dikaion* found in Homer and discussed in Chapter
III,[c] it may be felt that there is no reason to doubt that
dikaiosune is said to be *kalon* without restriction here; but, as was
shown in the last chapter,[d] *kalon* is not normally linked with
quiet values in the writers of the earlier fifth century. In so far
as there is a link here, it looks forward to what is new, as do the
Aeschylean usages discussed above. Furthermore, such usages
are most untypical of these writers; and while they imply
changes in the *agathos*-standard, they do not force into the open
the conflicts of values which inevitably follow from such changes.
Neither writer in fact states explicitly that a success may be
aischron, if unjust. To find *aischron* used to decry such a success

---

[a] Hdt. ii. 114. 2. He also terms Paris 'most *kakos* of mankind'; but such a use is
quite normal in Herodotus, cp. p. 178 and Note 14.

[b] Pind. *Pyth.* i. 85.   [c] pp. 43 ff.   [d] pp. 156 ff.

would be a development as important as the new uses of *agathos* and *kakos* already noted.

This we find in Sophocles, significantly in a late play. In the *Philoctetes*, when Odysseus asks whether Neoptolemus intends to return the bow which he has obtained from Philoctetes by trickery, Neoptolemus replies[a]

Yes, for I obtained it by shameful means, *aischrōs*, and unjustly, *ou dikēi*.

A few lines later he adds

I have committed a shameful error, *hamartiā aischrā*; but I will try to remedy it.

Neoptolemus has undoubtedly gained a victory over Philoctetes: a victory which, if he keeps the magic bow, will result in the capture of Troy. Yet in the first passage *aischrōs* is linked overtly with *ou dikēi*, to decry this unjust victory. Neoptolemus terms the action *aischron*, and his behaviour makes it clear that this *aischron* weighs with him more than the *kalon* of success. The second passage suggests that such usages as these have gained some currency. Under traditional values, a *hamartia aischra* is a mistake which has led to a failure: Agamemnon's *hamartia aischra* is not his depriving Achilles of Briseis, but his miscalculation of the effect of the loss of Achilles' support.[b] As a result, Agamemnon, *qua agathos*, could not distinguish mistake from moral error. To be able to use such a phrase as *hamartia aischra*, in a situation where a success has been gained, indicates a firmly rooted change in values. That is to say, it indicates that there has been a change in linguistic habits in at least a section of society: it does not indicate that all have adopted the change, nor that those who have adopted it have fully worked out its implications, nor yet that they would abide by their new usage under conditions of stress. The new usage is sufficiently rooted to be understood without explanation, but only a minor assault might be needed to overset it.

As one would expect in Sophocles, such linguistic changes are not argued. In Euripides, however, may be seen individual attempts to argue, in the interests of a different standard, that certain actions traditionally considered *aischra* are not so. Thus,

---

[a] S. *Phil.* 1234, 1248.
[b] pp. 50 ff. above. The phrase is not used, but the idea is present.

in the *Suppliants*,[a] Adrastus, on learning that Theseus has himself assisted in burying the Argives lying dead before Thebes, exclaims

It was a terrible burden and one that carries *aischune* with it.

To this the messenger replies

What is there *aischron* for men in one another's woes?

We may compare a passage from the *Phoenissae*.[b] The blind Oedipus, to dissuade Antigone from following him in his flight from Thebes, say*s*

For a daughter to be exiled with her blind father is *aischron*.

Antigone replies

It is not *aischron*, but noble, *gennaion*, at all events if she is a virtuous woman, *sōphronein*.

The views of Adrastus and Oedipus express traditional values: such actions have indeed always been *aischron*. In both cases here, however, we find a reference to a higher standard,[19] an attention to facts rather than appearances. To see what is new here, we may contrast these passages with a superficially similar one in Sophocles' *Antigone*.[c] Creon asks Antigone whether she is not ashamed of having tried to bury Polyneices in defiance of his orders, and she replies

It is not *aischron* to show respect for one's own brother.

This reply is quite different. It is undeniably true under traditional values, but it does not end the argument, for Creon can make other judgements about the situation which are equally valid under traditional values: Polyneices is not only a brother but also a traitor, a defeated traitor; and to care for traitors is normally *aischron* and deserving of the utmost punishment. The replies in the Euripidean examples, however, are not envisaged at all by traditional values. If accepted, they must—as they do—end the argument, for the situation is thereby exhibited in a completely new light.

This emphasis on the facts of the case, morally evaluated, this general tendency for *aischron* and allied words to reprehend breaches of the quieter moral virtues, *seems* a great advance. It creates, however, difficulties of a very far-reaching kind; but before these can be discussed, the difficulties caused by the

---

[a] E. *Supp.* 767 f.   [b] E. *Phoen.* 1691 f.   [c] S. *Ant.* 510 f.

attempted solution of a somewhat different problem must be considered.

C. *AISCHRON* VERSUS *DIKAION*

In the last chapter, in the course of demonstrating that the possession of a good reputation with its advantages was still the avowed end of life, certain examples were quoted to show that no term of value was more powerful than *aischron*; and among the examples were several in which *aischron* was not, as in the example from the *Philoctetes* just quoted, linked with *dikaion* but opposed to it, as a standard which overrode *dikaion*. A passage from Sophocles' *Electra* was there quoted.[a] In Euripides' *Orestes*[b] a similar passage occurs. The Chorus says of Apollo's advocacy of Orestes' killing of Clytemnestra that it was performed justly, *dikāi*; to which Electra replies, 'But not honourably', *kalōs d' ou*. Naturally, as was said in the last chapter, this settles the matter, for there is no higher term of value to invoke. Again, in Euripides' *Electra*,[c] the Chorus replies to Clytemnestra's defence of her actions

Your words are just, but your justice, *dike*, is *aischron*.

The judgement, and the result, are the same: the argument goes no further.

These three passages are of great importance. They express the solution of the two poets to the problem set by the crime within the family which, in the house of Atreus and elsewhere, calls forth an act of retributive justice from another member of the family which in its turn calls forth another act of retributive justice, in a chain which can only be broken by the extinction of the accursed house. In such a situation, the man who slays in retribution seems both *dikaios* as avenger and *adikos* as murderer and parricide: clearly a problem which needs solution.

The solution of Aeschylus involves no such opposition of *dikaios* and *aischron*. The trial of Orestes on the Areopagus proves him to be *dikaios* and so breaks the chain; and Clytemnestra's attempted defence of her actions takes a different form.[d]

---

[a] S. *Elec.* 558 ff., cp. p. 156.   [b] E. *Orest.* 194.

[c] E. *Elec.* 1051, δίκαι' ἔλεξας· ἡ δίκη δ' αἰσχρῶς ἔχει.

[d] Cp. p. 121 above, *Agam.* 1468 ff. and *Cho.* 910 f. For the justification of Orestes, cp. *Eum.* 614 ff.

Aeschylus does not attempt—perhaps could not have attempted[a] —to employ the new uses of *kakos* and *aischron* as a deterrent, for he relies on the processes of justice, human and divine. The solution of Sophocles and Euripides, however, to which these passages are crucial, is different: he who deals retributive justice within his own family would be both *dikaios* and *adikos*; but in the circumstances given, Sophocles and Euripides maintain that in fact justice should not be exacted. There is a higher standard which may be set against the claims of strict justice. The feelings of the two playwrights are admirable, and the solution is, for the moment, a solution; but the choice of *aischron* as the term to express the claims of morality against *dikaiosune* is less admirable, even if it was in fact the only conceivable word which could be used.

That it was the only conceivable word is clear. Drawn as it is from the more powerful, competitive, system of values, in which system it is the only adjective commonly used to decry courses of action, it readily overrides as no other word could a word drawn from the quieter system. Furthermore, the manner in which such actions must be termed *aischron* is evident. To do so is to say that they are unworthy of the *agathos*; and as the conduct of the *agathos* embraces not merely successes and failures but a whole way of social—though not, traditionally, quiet moral—life, these actions are stigmatized as 'not done'.[20]

D. SOME EFFECTS

The manner in which *aischron* may be thus extended is in no doubt; but the disadvantages of so extending its use should be equally clear. At the end of the last chapter it was said that the traditional Greek scheme of values, though little suited to civic life, might continue to work provided that the competitive system of values could be restricted to war or the games, the quieter system to peace; that is to say, provided that men, when faced with a decision in civic matters, inquired what was *dikaion*, not what their *arete* demanded. Divine sanctions might ensure this; but to realign the system of values, to identify or link analytically the *agathos* and the *dikaios*, the *adikon* and the *aischron*, and hence assert that justice is the most important— or at least a very important—quality in a man, is a solution

[a] Cp. pp. 175, 181 f.

greatly to be preferred. As will be seen,[a] this solution has its
difficulties; but, given the traditional Greek scheme of values,
to *oppose aischron* and *dikaion*, however good one's motives,
raises many more. It is done with the best of intentions: true.
The word so used effectively prevents, or should prevent, an
action which is abhorrent to the user: true. *Aischron* is used
'morally' here: apparently true. But all the traditional uses of
aischron are fully alive, as has been shown. The word *aischron* is
only one word through all its usages, and no real distinction
can be drawn between one usage and another. Such words
condemn deficiencies in the *arete*-standard as a whole; and all
the traditional uses of *arete* are still alive too. It is in effect *the
whole* of this standard which, always taking pride of place over
the quieter virtues, is now *explicitly* opposed to those virtues *in a
civic context*. To do this is to imply that a man should avoid what
is *aischron* at all times rather than do what is merely *dikaion*;
which, so far as words go, is the rule of life followed by Agamemnon in the *Iliad*;[b] and the words still possess all their traditional
flavours. As will be seen, unfortunate results follow; results
which were neither intended nor foreseen by the poets or by the
other thinkers on whom they depended, but results which were
to be expected, particularly if the circumstances of history
should actively favour them.

It has already been said that the traditional system of values
will in the most literal sense not bear thinking about. Here
thought has produced results which were in the long run
disastrous; and it seems very likely that the whittling away of
extraneous *aischra*, illustrated above, is related to thought which
bore a no less sinister fruit. In this case the danger lies not merely
in the nature of the language but also in the nature of contemporary thought. Some *aischra* are, it seems, not *aischra*, even
though general opinion would have it so, and even though
general opinion has been till now the arbiter of what is *aischron*.
Evidently the idea of *aischron* has been 'loosened up' by some
means; and, since a natural manner of expressing the distinction between the two classes of *aischra* is to say that some are
aischra by nature while others are only *aischra* by convention, the
antecedents of this type of thought seem clear. The contrast of
phusis, nature, with *nomos*, convention or law, is at this time a

commonplace of one stream of sophistic thought. This dichotomy *may* have been invented with good intentions, for the sophistic movement was an intellectual movement, and it is the mark of all such to seek truth and reject mere opinion; and to contrast the natural with the merely conventional is a convenient method of expressing this search. There may be good intentions in the background; but all the surviving specimens of this thought help, and are intended to help, to give intellectual respectability to the pretensions of the 'immoralists' and power-politicians of late fifth-century Athens,[a] by laying emphasis on the 'natural man', who seeks to satisfy his own natural desires as opposed to 'the man bound by convention', who allows law and moral restraints to prevent him from doing so. As we find it in our sources,[21] the contrast between actions which are *aischra nomōi*, shameful by convention, and those which are *aischra phusei*, shameful by nature, is the contrast between the new 'quiet moral' *aischra* and the traditional *aischra* of failure; and naturally to draw this contrast is to dismiss out of hand 'quiet moral' *aischra* as not really *aischra* at all. The strength of this position should now be evident: the use of *aischron* to decry breaches of the quiet virtues was recent, can have possessed only slender roots in the language as yet, and, as will be seen, inevitably gave rise to serious problems. It is hardly surprising that the *aischra* of failure should appear more genuine, not only to the 'immoralist' but to the 'ordinary Greek'. Accordingly, though Euripides was able to benefit from a 'loosening up' of *aischron*, when we examine the general context in which this 'loosening up' took place, any advance apparently gained from the ability to contrast 'real' with 'conventional' *aischra* in the interests of morals was almost certain to be lost later. Even had there been no speculation on *phusis* and *nomos*, to contrast any set of *aischra* with any other, as Euripides in effect does in the passages discussed,[22] would have been dangerous, given the whole range of *aischron*. Anyone might feel able to select for himself those actions and states which are 'really' *aischra* and those which are not; and this, in view of the emphases of Greek values, would lead most naturally to the rejection of the new 'quiet' use of *aischron*. In the light of the speculation on *phusis* and *nomos*, the danger is many times multiplied.

[a] See below, pp. 232 ff.

The results of this type of thought, however, must be left to a later chapter. Here it suffices to point out certain effects which must follow simply from the infiltration of the quieter values into a system of competitive values, if all the old values continue to exist alongside the new ones. Since courage and justice, competition and co-operation, may well seem to demand opposing attitudes to the same action—particularly if, as is here the case, there has been as yet no attempt to integrate these two systems of values, now using the same terms, into one system—it may well come about that words from this one group of terms are needed both to commend and to decry the same action. This we find in the *Philoctetes*.[a] Odysseus has almost succeeded in persuading Neoptolemus to cheat Philoctetes, promising him 'two gifts' if he does so. These gifts prove to be

You would be called at the same time both wise, *sophos*, and *agathos*.

With this inducement, Neoptolemus replies:

So be it. I will do it, and cast off all sense of shame, *aischune*.

Neoptolemus will cast off his *aischune*, and he has said in the preceding duologue that he considers the cheating of Philoctetes to be *aischron*. But as a result of doing this *aischron*, he is to be called *agathos*: and the basic statement of Greek values is that the *agathos* does *kala* and shuns *aischra*. This clash is doubtless deliberately contrived by Sophocles. He points thereby the clash of character;[23] but as may be seen in this chapter, and as will become even clearer in subsequent chapters, the confusion of values of which Sophocles here makes use is part of the moral scene at this period. The manner in which Platonic logic is able to exploit this confusion will be shown in Chapter XIII. First, however, the presuppositions which lie behind this shift in values, and its continuity with traditional values, must be shown.

NOTES TO CHAPTER IX

1. And in Pindar. It has been held that the four *aretai* of *Nemeans* 3. 72 ff. are the cardinal *aretai* of Platonic and later thought; but Wilamo-witz is clearly right (*Pindaros*, p. 279, and cp. Schwartz, *Ethik der*

[a] S. *Phil.* 119 f.

Griechen, p. 52) to reject this. The four *aretai* of this poem are the three modes of behaviour, however interpreted, which are fitting for the three different periods of a man's life, with the addition of *phronein*, to be prudent, which, like *sophronein*, p. 258 f., need by no means be a 'moral' excellence. For the most recent survey of the cardinal *aretai* in Greek thought, cp. Ferguson, *Moral Values in the Ancient World*, pp. 24 ff.

2. In discussing the tragedians (cp. Note 13 below) I have usually avoided fragments, since the exact flavour of these is frequently unclear. Experiment will readily confirm this: cp. e.g. Eur. frags. 8, 53, 75, 644 Nauck. Here, however, Sophocles frag. 103 might be cited on the other side; for the passage *seems* to equate *esthlos* (l. 3) with *eusebes* (l. 6). It is notable, however, that the poet is unable to escape from words describing birth (βλαστόντας, l. 2, γεγῶτας, l. 4, γεγώς, l. 10) when using these terms of commendation. He is in fact unable to free himself from the ideas of 'class' and 'birth' here. (It should further be noted that F. G. Schmidt, *de ubert. orat. Soph.* i. 9, cited by Nauck ad loc., argued—with considerable probability—on general grounds of style that the passage should be attributed to Euripides. In view of the uncertainty which surrounds it I have not felt it necessary to take this passage into account in discussing Sophocles in the text.) The passage indicates the strength of the bonds of traditional language even in a case where a writer is trying to escape from them. (For a use of *kakos* to oppose the 'social' use of such terms, cp. Soph. frag. 752.)

3. To term a person *eugenēs*, well-born, in Sophocles may give one reason to hope for good behaviour, but certainly does not entail it. For this cp. S. *Phil.* 874, again of the behaviour of Neoptolemus. It may of course refer only to birth, leaving open the question of behaviour, cp. *O.C.* 728.

4. The use of *agathos*, *aristos* in *O.C.* 1100, 1458, is similar, with nothing added but flattery.

5. He seems to have been quite content with traditional usage. Possibly (cp. Note 23) he saw too clearly the effects of the *other* new usage of *agathos*, cp. Chapters X–XIII.

6. Cp. E. *Hipp.* 654 (where *kakos* is opposed to *eusebes*), 945, 1024, 1071, 1075, 1077, 1191, 1251, 1320, all of the suspected crime of Hippolytus. At 942, we have 'those who are not-*dikaioi* and *kakoi*'. In the *Ion*, 370 and 441, *kakos* is used of Apollo's behaviour to Creusa; and in the *Electra*, 551, we find 'many who are *eugeneis*, of high birth, are *kakoi*' in a quiet moral sense. We may compare such phrases as '*kakos* towards one's friends', *Medea* 84, in the sense of *kakos philos*, 'a bad friend': a usage which may be compared with Thuc. i. 86, where the ephor Sthenelaidas says that the Athenians were *agathoi* (brave) against the Persians, but are *kakoi* towards the Spartans now. Here again *kakos* is used in a quiet sense, and we have an interesting coupling of traditional and new values.

7. There is at all events nothing in the lines to render it impossible that Euripides should have written them, cp. following note.

8. It occurs also in the *Ion*, 440 ff., where Ion adjures Apollo to pursue *aretai*, meaning that he should not beget children and then abandon

them. It seems clear, too, that in the earlier *Hippolytus arete* was used to commend Hippolytus' chastity—for, Eur. frag. 446 Nauck, *arete* is equated with *sophrosune*, in explicit reference to Hippolytus, though in the later *Hippolytus*, despite the frequency of the corresponding use of *kakos* (cp. Note 6 above) *arete* is not so used.

9. For earlier passages in fragments, cp. Note 13. Of course, even if we possessed every play of Euripides complete, to say 'this is the first occurrence of such and such a use in Euripides' would be to say something of comparatively small value, for there is no sign that either Euripides or any other of the writers of the second half of the fifth century whose writings survive to any considerable extent themselves originated any of the usages which they reflect. The significant element in the two passages of Euripides discussed in the text is the air of novelty which they possess, which is eloquent of the *general* standards of the period.

10. Cp. *andragathiā* in Hdt. i. 99, 136, iv. 65, vi. 128, &c.

11. A significant phrase. The *agathos* contributes something to society, the *mēden ōn*, the man who 'is nothing', does not.

12. Cp. *Hipp.* 409 ff., *Androm.* 766 ff. Both passages show tension, but adhere to traditional usages.

13. Again I have avoided fragments; but a usage very close to that in the text appears in Eur. frag. 495, 40 ff. Nauck (Melanippe):

ἐγὼ μὲν ⟨οὖν⟩ οὐκ οἶδ' ὅτῳ σκοπεῖν χρεὼν
τὴν εὐγένειαν· τοὺς γὰρ ἀνδρείους φύσιν
καὶ τοὺς δικαίους τῶν κενῶν δοξασμάτων,
κἂν ὦσι δούλων, εὐγενεστέρους λέγω.

'I do not know by what standard one ought to judge *eugeneia*, nobility: I hold that the brave and the just are more *eugeneis*, even though they be born of slaves, than those who are merely outward show, *kena doxasmata*.' The method of approach is precisely that of the *Electra*. Here the poet takes *eugenes* and, relying on the flavour of 'noblesse oblige' which the word may possess (cp. Note 3), attempts to make it into a term of quiet morals. (The occurrence of *kena doxasmata* in both passages—in rather different senses—is interesting.) This passage may be compared with Eur. frag. 336 Nauck, which indicates that Euripides had already expressed similar sentiments in the *Dictys* in 431 B.C. The lines there are less full, but no less surprising: and it is interesting to note that such insights tend to occur at periods of stress, the stress of the beginning of the Peloponnesian War in 431 B.C. being indicated also by the—traditional, but here very emphatic—use of *kakistos* in frag. 347, also from the *Dictys*, to decry the man who praises other cities to the detriment of his own. We may compare and contrast Eur. frag. 282, esp. 22 ff., where Euripides' views on the uselessness of athletes are similar to—and presumably imitated from—those of Xenophanes (frag. 2 Bergk, cp. p. 74 above), but the requirements of the citizen, as opposed to those of the athlete, are more fully worked out. It is to be noted, however, that in this passage Euripides does not maintain that the *dikaios* is *agathos*. The relevant lines are:

ἄνδρας χρὴ σοφούς τε κἀγαθοὺς
φύλλοις στέφεσθαι, χὤστις ἡγεῖται πόλει
κάλλιστα σώφρων καὶ δίκαιος ὢν ἀνήρ,
ὅστις τε μύθοις ἔργ' ἀπαλλάσσει κακὰ
μάχας τ' ἀφαιρῶν καὶ στάσεις· τοιαῦτα γὰρ
πόλει τε πάσῃ πᾶσί θ' Ἕλλησιν καλά.

'We should crown with garlands men who are wise, *sophoi*, and *agathoi*, both the man who leads the city *kallista*, being prudent, *sophron*, and *dikaios*, and the man who abolishes harmful deeds, *kaka erga*, by his words, preventing battles and civic strife; for such actions are *kala* both for the whole city and for all the Greeks.' This passage, in virtue of its Panhellenism, is 'advanced' (cp. Chapter XVI, pp. 338 ff.); but in other respects it is less so than the other passages quoted. Here 'both the man who . . . and the man who . . .' amplifies *sophoi* and *agathoi*, and it is evident that *arete* and *sophia* are displayed in being a skilled politician, in securing the city's success, and in banishing war and strife. Euripides acknowledges that such a man should be *sophron* and *dikaios*; indeed, it may be necessary that he should have such qualities if he is to fulfil this function: but it is not clearly stated that these qualities are part of his *arete*. They are subordinated grammatically; and since Chapters X and XI make it clear that they are subordinated in the mind of the ordinary man, it is unnecessary to assume that Euripides means the audience to suppose that *sophrosune* and *dikaiosune* are part of *arete*. Still less is it said in this passage that the *dikaios* is *agathos* purely in virtue of his *dikaiosune*. Frag. 388, ψυχῆς δικαίας σώφρονός τε κἀγαθῆς, 'a mind which is *dikaios* and *sophron* and *agathos*,' indicates the normal alignment of values at this period: even where *dikaiosune* and *sophrosune* are valued, they are not held to be *aretai*, and *agathos* and *arete* may be used with them to commend a quite different set of excellences (cp. also frag. 672). This is really no more advanced than Aesch. *Septem* 610, σώφρων δίκαιος ἀγαθὸς εὐσεβὴς ἀνήρ, 'a man who is *sophron*, *dikaios*, *agathos*, and *eusebes*,' where being *agathos* evidently does not imply the possession of any of the other qualities mentioned. This mode of expression continues to occur: cp. Chapter XVI, Note 17.

14. Cp. Hdt. v. 92., iii. 80. 4 (sophistic), iii. 148. 2. He has, of course, also the traditional uses of *kakotes*, cp. vii. 168. 4, viii. 109. 2.

15. For *arete* used in a 'sophistic' manner by Herodotus, cp. Hdt. vii. 237. 2, where Xerxes says that one citizen never gives another the best advice, unless he has progressed far in *arete*. The words are both out of character and unjustified by traditional standards; Herodotus has put into the mouth of Xerxes a 'sophistic' redefinition of *arete* current at the time. The traditional effect of *arete* in a city appears at iii. 82. 3, where, even in a context which, as was said in the text, is a borrowing from some sophist, it is said that when a number of men exercise their *arete* in civic affairs, the result is dissension and stasis. Again, even in iii. 80, Herodotus *also* uses *agathoi* to denote 'the better classes', for whom tyrants normally feel envy. These examples show that the new uses of *agathos*

and *arete* have not been integrated into Herodotus' (nor, as will be seen, into general) usage as a whole.

16. For relations within the state, cp. Thuc. iii. 82. 7 (Corcyra). The usage still only appears in moments of stress. For a passage in tragedy similar to that from Thucydides quoted in the text, cp. *O.C.* 929 f. Theseus says to Creon that if he carries off Antigone and Ismene by force, without resort to just negotiation, 'You are bringing shame (*aischunein*) upon a city which is not worthy of it—your own.' This too is a complete departure from traditional standards, and the form of the expression (the translation represents the Greek word-order) shows that it is meant as a *coup de théâtre*. For a traditional treatment of the situation, cp. p. 157 (Demophon in the *Heraclidae*).

17. For Thucydides has *also* all the traditional uses of *agathos* and *arete*, cp. i. 129. 3, ii. 35, ii. 87. 9, vi. 40, viii. 48. 6, &c. As he writes what is 'suitable' for each speaker, i. 22, it cannot be supposed that he endorsed all the varied views which appear in the speeches, only that they were 'in the air'.

Not surprisingly, *aischron* may behave as a term of quiet morals in Thucydides. Cp. i. 38. 5, also from the Corinthian accusation of the Corcyreans, and iii. 58, where the Plataeans urge that if the Spartans acceded to the Theban demand that the Plataeans should be killed, the concession would be *aischron* (opposed to *sophron*). In both cases the speakers have a strong interest in using the new values; and cp. v. 111. 3, where the Athenians too have strong—though different—motives for urging the Melians to abandon the traditional use of *aischron*, and iii. 63. 3 and 67. 2 (the Theban case at Plataea). For the traditional use in Thucydides, cp. especially vi. 10. 2, vi. 11. 6, and vi. 48.

18. Cp. Chapter V, p. 99. As was shown there, the emotions aroused by this disgrace were strong enough to affect the idea of 'pollution' illogically.

19. The sophistic origin of the former passage is suggested by the idea of 'the brotherhood of man', which is not an 'ordinary Greek' thought. For the idea, cp. Democritus (Democrates), frag. 107a Diels–Kranz. For sophistic insistence on truth, cp. Hdt. vii. 10, certainly a 'sophistic' passage.

20. It is of course to stigmatize them much more powerfully than 'not done' would suggest, for it is to bring them within the purview of the most powerful system of values, to which 'not done' does not belong; but the phrase suggests the flavour.

21. On this topic, cp. Heinimann, *Physis und Nomos*, and Sinclair, op. cit., pp. 48 ff.

22. He does not use either *phusis* or *nomos* here. Possibly the 'immoralist' flavour was too strong; but the thought associated with these terms must have 'loosened up' *aischron* and *kalon*.

23. Sophocles does not employ *agathos* or *arete* in a quiet moral sense, but his use of *agathos* does reflect the New Thought of the sophists in some respects. With the passage quoted in the text we may compare *Antigone* 31, where Antigone refers to Creon as *agathos*. Jebb, ad loc., calls this usage 'ironical' and compares *Philoctetes* 873, where Philoctetes calls Agamemnon and Menelaus 'the *agathoi* army-leaders'. Both passages—and cp.

also *Trachiniae* 541—take established uses of *agathos*, in the *Philoctetes* that commending skill and courage in war, in the *Antigone* the new usage which commends the skilled power-politician (cp. Chapter XI), and implicitly contrast the person termed *agathos* with a quieter and more compassionate form of behaviour not normally commended by *agathos*. If to do this is irony, then these passages are ironical. Certainly they seem to draw attention to deficiencies in the *agathos*-standard commonly in use. Sophocles seems never to approve of the politically efficient New Man whom this use of *agathos* commends, as indeed is indicated by the outcome of both *Antigone* and *Philoctetes*. (It may have been in part his disapproval of this aspect of sophistic thought which led him to avoid the new 'quiet' use of *agathos*, cp. pp. 173 ff. above, for the two usages, as Chapters X and XI will show, are closely connected.)

X

THE GOOD CITIZEN AND THE JUST MAN: ASSEMBLY AND LAW COURTS

A. THE *DIKAIOS* AS THE MORE EFFICIENT ADMINISTRATOR

IN the last chapter, among other examples in which the *agathos* seemed to be equated with the *dikaios*, a passage was quoted from the *Electra* of Euripides in which Euripides, thinly disguised as Orestes, rejected many other qualities in virtue of which men have hitherto been termed *agathoi*, and claimed that the Husbandman was the true *agathos*. The Husbandman, poor and of humble birth,[1] had yet behaved with great self-control; and was apparently termed *agathos*, despite his lack of the traditional qualities, merely in virtue of his self-control. If only the lines quoted in the last chapter are considered, there seems to be no reason for such a change; but in view of the past history of *agathos* and *arete*, a strong reason seems necessary: and the passage[2] in fact continues[a]

For such men administer well, *eu oikein*, both their cities and their own households, whereas those who are nothing but senseless lumps of muscle are mere ornaments of the market-place, for a strong arm does not even endure a spear-thrust any better than a weak one. No; such ability lies in a man's nature and in his excellence of spirit, *eupsūchiā*.[3]

The self-controlled man is *agathos* because self-controlled men are best at the organization of their cities and their own houses in the interests of prosperity: these new *aretai*, justice and self-control, have been enrolled on precisely the same terms as the old ones. It was said above that *dikaiosune* might become part (or even the whole) of *arete* could it be realized that the quieter virtues are essential to the stability and prosperity of society;[b] and society seems at last to have realized this.

[a] E. *Elec.* 386 ff., above, p. 177.   [b] Above, p. 70.

The new usage seems very democratic in tendency. The extent of the change in attitude will be clearer if a poem which, by traditional standards, is enlightened, is compared with Euripides' lines. The beginning of the most important surviving poem of Simonides was discussed above.[a] That poem continues as follows: having said that to be continuously *agathos* is impossible, Simonides goes on

Any man suffices me who is not *kakos* nor utterly *apalamnos*: and (or 'at any rate'[b]) a man who knows city-benefiting justice is a 'sound' man. I will not find fault with him; for the race of the *ēlithioi*, foolish, is limitless. All things are *kala* with which *aischra* are not mingled.

It has already been shown that the traditional use of *agathos* and *kakos* appears in this poem, as one would expect from its date. Whatever interpretation is adopted, these lines are difficult; but the perverse interpretation given by Plato in the *Protagoras*[c] seems correct in one point at least: in writing these lines Simonides envisages a condition in which a man, while not *agathos*, is not to be termed *kakos* either. *Kakos*, as the earlier portion of the poem showed, is used in this poem to decry the man who has lost certain external advantages, or has failed in war or the games, while *apalamnos*, apparently parallel, presumably has its original sense of 'helpless', 'useless'.[4] The men with whom Simonides says he will not find fault are not *agathoi*; they are not, therefore, the men on whom the city's security and prosperity primarily depends, and presumably form no important part of its fighting force; yet they are not entirely useless to society, and they know city-benefiting justice. The exact implications of Simonides' words are difficult to discover: a poet may make his points by juxtaposition rather than by closely reasoned argument, and it is not clear whether the acknowledgement that the man who 'knows justice'—i.e. is just—is a 'sound' man is an explanation of the previous clause or a separate point; whether, that is, it is his city-benefiting justice which makes a man not utterly useless, or whether being not utterly useless implies having moderate property which, when combined with justice, makes a man 'sound'. It seems unlikely, however, that a Simonides—clearly no radical thinker—could

[a] Simonides 5 Bergk, cp. p. 165 f.   [b] Reading γε for τε.
[c] Plat. *Prot.* 346 D 6 f.

have left a man's property out of account altogether in reckoning a man's value to society. It is probable, in fact, that Simonides is commending the class immediately below the *agathoi*, and that from these he demands the justice which he terms in a most enlightened manner 'city-benefiting'. But whatever the exact interpretation, the important aspect is the different manner in which these men, who are just but not wealthy, are valued in these two poets. For Simonides to be just, however much it may benefit the city, is to be a 'sound' man *in contrast to* being *agathos*; for Euripides it is to be *agathos*, the most glittering of all Greek terms of value.

The difference is striking. It is the difference between the values of tyranny or oligarchy and those of democracy; and it is a difference not based on sentiment but on practical realities. The primary function of any state is to survive, and to prosper as well as it may; and in a small state such as a Greek city-state, in competition with its neighbours for the produce of a not very wealthy land, this primary function can never be long out of mind. To ensure survival, the will and the ability to resist, coupled with good counsel, are the most evident necessities. In a hoplite-oligarchy, or any society in which the individual must buy his own fighting equipment, the most effective striking force is supplied by the rich; and, given the prestige derived from this in a society with the traditional Greek values, it is the rich who, even in a society which is a democracy in name, will give advice in the assembly and hold the most important offices.[5] In the maritime democracy of Athens, however, all this is changed: the poor man, not the rich, mans the navy, the most important striking force of the state, and, his equipment being provided for him, can meet the rich on at least equal terms on that score. Observers from the Old Oligarch onwards[6] are agreed that this is the justification for Athenian democracy. On this basis we might say that it is inevitable that, as soon as he realizes his importance in the state, the poor man will offer his advice in the assembly as well as the rich. Since both poor and rich now participate both in defence and deliberation, *agathos* must surely cease to be a term denoting and commending a social class and instead denote men of all classes with certain specific attributes which make them valuable to the state; and if the co-operative excellences prove to be among these attributes, they will be enrolled forthwith among the *aretai*.

Once more there is a temptation to pronounce the battle won and the problem solved, on the most satisfactory terms available. Admittedly, some of the examples of the new use quoted in the last chapter show no signs of needing any such justification as we have here. They appeal, in fact, to the idea of 'gentlemanly behaviour' in *agathos*, *arete*, and *kalon*, and try to persuade the Athenian *agathos* that quiet moral behaviour is an essential attribute of gentlemanly behaviour. Such persuasion continues, and indeed finds a distinguished culmination in Aristotle;[a] but in a crisis of values such as that which developed at the end of the fifth century reasoned proof rather than persuasive definitions is desirable; and such proof can only proceed on the lines which we find in the *Electra*. The proof, however, is only a solution if it is believed; and the preceding paragraph is blatantly theoretical. The lines of Euripides on which it is based show both by their tone and by their content that Euripides is pleading for the realization of an ideal, not recording a fact. It is in fact the hoplites, the wealthy, and the strong who are termed *agathoi*, and who are consequently, as a result of this prestige, able to sway the assembly. Euripides is appealing for a change in attitude. To show the reasons for the actual situation, and the extent to which events compelled a change, will be the task of this chapter.

B. THE *AGATHOS POLITES*

(i) *The Assembly*

What in fact emerges from this passage of Euripides is that, as will be confirmed abundantly below, the *agathos* has become the good citizen, the *agathos polītēs*. Again we might well suppose that this is to make *dikaiosune* a defining property of the *agathos*, since most people would now consider 'the good citizen is just (law-abiding)' to be an analytic proposition, and some might hold that it expressed an identity. This, however, in view of the past history of *agathos*, requires further examination: all

[a] Cp. Chapter XIII *ad init.* (the position of Socrates in the *Crito*) and Chapter XVI.

that may be said with confidence is that in terming the *agathos* '*agathos polites*', Athenian usage relates the *agathos* overtly to his city. There are other relationships than quiet moral ones.

To discover what is expected of a man by Athenian democracy before it will term him *agathos polites*, it is natural to turn first to speeches delivered in the assembly, or rather to the versions of those speeches which appear in Thucydides. In 415 B.C. the Athenian Assembly, profiting by the comparative peace in mainland Greece, was proposing to engage in a huge expedition to Sicily, ostensibly to assist the inhabitants of Segesta who had asked for their help. The cautious and conservative general Nicias, who had been appointed one of the commanders of the expedition, wished to dissuade the Athenians from the project, for which they had already voted, but which he considered rash. He denied that he was afraid for his own skin, but maintained[a]

That a man who displays some forethought for his own safety and that of his property is none the less an *agathos polites*, for such a man would, in his own interest, be most anxious that the city's affairs too should prosper.

The *agathos polites*, like Euripides' *agathos*, is explicitly linked to the successful handling of the city's business. In his peroration,[b] Nicias, in a last effort to persuade the Athenians to change their minds, again refers to the 'good citizen'. Turning to the prytanis,[c] he says

And you, prytanis, if you consider that it befits you to care for the state, and you wish to become an *agathos polites*, put the matter to the vote and take the opinion of the Athenians again; and if you fear to upset the former decision, reflect that you will not be blamed if you break the law[d] with so many to abet you, and that you will become a doctor to the city which has deliberated badly, *kakōs*, and again that the man who governs well, *kalōs*, is the man who benefits his native land as much as possible, or at least does it no harm deliberately, *hekon*.

Here too it is the mark of the *agathos polites* to secure the advancement of his city at all costs, even that of oversetting the laws.[7] That Nicias' advice is the only sane advice, if the city

[a] Thuc. vi. 9. 2.   [b] Thuc. vi. 14.   [c] i.e. president.
[d] i.e. in taking a second vote on a matter already decided.

has in fact decided foolishly in such a matter, is irrelevant here; what is important is the balance of one value against another in popular thought at this period.

One more example from Thucydides is relevant. In the Funeral Speech, Pericles turns to consider those dead who in life fell short of the highest standards, and says[a]

Again, the end of these men seems to me to show clearly in what the *arete* of a man consists, whether it gives the first indication of its presence or a final confirmation. For it is right that those too who are worse, *cheirones*, in other respects should display[b] courage, *andragathia*, in the face of the enemy on behalf of their native land; for having wiped out the harm, *kakon*, they did by the good, *agathon*, which they have now done (by fighting bravely), they have conferred a greater benefit upon the city than the harm they did by their individual actions.

Though in one sense nothing is said which need surprise anyone in a funeral speech, the passage is interesting. In view of the closing words, Pericles is presumably referring to criminals; even in the contortions of the Funeral Speech, it is straining language too far to suppose that the reference is to those who were 'worse', *cheirones*, socially and economically and hence, being unable to help the city to the full, are hyperbolically said to have harmed it. Accordingly, when men die bravely in battle, 'having become *agathoi*' in the cant phrase,[c] any previous breaches of the law may be forgotten, for they have done the state more good than harm. This statement, we might say, is completely unexceptionable in a funeral speech. The men are dead, after all, and their account may be made up; and funeral speeches are not meant to be taken 'au pied de la lettre'. But to oppose *agathos polites* to the *dikaios* has its dangers; there are other ways in which the *adikos* may show himself to be *agathos*, ways which do not involve his death: and the balance sheet of good and harm done to the city is particularly sinister. Since to be *agathos* is and always has been more important than to be *dikaios*, this encomium may be taken 'au pied de la lettre'.

---

[a] Thuc. ii. 42. 2.

[b] If προτίθεσθαι here means 'put forward as a screen', not simply 'display', the point is made even more clearly.

[c] ἄνδρες ἀγαθοὶ γενόμενοι.

(ii) *The Law Courts*

The above examples show the new phrase in general use; to see it, and the simple *agathos* in the same sense, influencing particular decisions more closely, we must turn to the law courts. First, however, some general remarks are necessary. It is impossible to read a Greek forensic speech without being struck by the curious practices which are permitted, and the curious pleas which are considered relevant. One may reflect briefly that this is a natural result of the popular nature of these courts, and pass on; and there is some truth in this. It is, however, possible to draw certain conclusions relating to popular standards from these pleas. True, highly emotional appeals are made to the jury in Athenian trials. One should not, however, be discouraged by this from the attempt to find the standards implicit in these appeals; for moral judgements are not a matter of intellect alone, and the presence of even violent emotions does not entail the absence of standards. Such standards may well be revealed by the oddities mentioned above; and accordingly these may repay more detailed investigation.

If, in reading a Greek forensic speech, one has in mind the practice of a modern court of law, the most prominent oddity in Greek practice is the never-failing mention, where such have been performed, of the speaker's services to the state, not as a mitigating circumstance when he has been found guilty, but as a plea intended to justify his acquittal. Such words as one might expect to find in the mouth of politicians justifying their actions before the assembly are uttered by ordinary citizens in ordinary cases of all kinds.

The words of Lysias in his speech against Eratosthenes are of great interest here. Eratosthenes was one of the Thirty Tyrants in the revolution of the closing stages of the Peloponnesian War, but he is not being impeached for this political offence[8] but on the criminal charge—as we should distinguish it—of having killed Lysias' brother Polemarchus during the Reign of Terror. Yet Lysias is compelled to say during the course of his speech[a]

And note that he cannot even resort to the expedient, so habitual among our citizens, of saying nothing to answer the accounts of

[a] Lys. 12. 38.

the accusation but making other claims about themselves, by means of which they sometimes deceive you.

This is an unusually severe attack; but even here Lysias does not take it upon himself to reprehend this type of plea in plain terms; for 'by means of which they sometimes deceive you' does not mean 'sometimes you allow these illegitimate pleas and are thereby deceived' but 'sometimes they make claim to other excellences which they do not possess and thereby deceive you'. The context makes this clear, and also the nature of the claims made: Lysias argues that such a plea cannot be relevant here, since it would be fruitless for Eratosthenes and his friends to pretend that they had killed more enemies than citizens, that they had taken more ships than they had surrendered, or that they had won over a city to be compared with Athens, which they enslaved. Lysias does not deny the relevance of such pleas generally; he merely says that they do not apply here.

There is then a plea which in normal circumstances may be used to overset what we should consider to be strict justice. Other passages in the orators make the nature of this plea clearer. In the twenty-fifth speech of Lysias, the accused quotes a list of 'liturgies' (services to the state) which he has performed, and says openly that he spent on them more than the minimum requirements[a]

In order that I might be thought *beltiōn*, better, by you and, should some misfortune overtake me (i.e. should I be brought before a court) I should have a better chance in court, *ameinon agōnizesthai*.

To spend money in order to be thought 'better' and have a better chance of success in lawsuits: it would seem that nothing could be more opposed to impartial justice, which the jury in fact swore to observe.[b] Yet the speaker can state his motives plainly, and clearly hope to prejudice the jury in his favour by so doing. There are, too, other means to the end of appearing 'better': in the thirtieth speech of Lysias[c] the accuser asks rhetorically what reasons the jury could possibly have for acquitting the accused. Has he proved himself *agathos* against the enemy, and served bravely in many battles by land and sea? No. Has he—for many have obtained 'pity', *sungnōmē*, for

---

[a] Lys. 25. 13.   [b] Dem. *In Timocr.* 746, cp. Lys. 14. 40.
[c] Lys. 30. 26, 27.

this reason too—distinguished ancestors? No. Has he made many contributions to the city's finances? No. Yet again, none of these pleas is said to be out of place in a court of law. It is simply insisted that the present defendant is in no position to benefit from them.

Nor is this merely absent-mindedness. Such things may be said even when justice is mentioned. In Lysias' thirtieth speech it is said[a] that people have enumerated the *aretai* of their ancestors and the benefits which they have conferred upon the city themselves, and have thus gained *sungnome*, even though they seemed to have committed injustice. The jury may be swayed by other considerations than the simple question 'has the accused broken the law or not?'

What these are must be considered. First, however, it must be shown that the jury were not merely swayed by pity in these instances. It being notoriously common practice to produce one's wife and children in court, to wake the sympathy of the jury,[9] it might be supposed that simple pity for a citizen who had shown himself to be a worthy member of society in other respects was the motive. After all, the word *sungnome*, which might be translated 'pity', appears in two of the examples discussed above. To ask for *sungnome* in an Athenian court, however, is not to admit one's guilt and plead for mercy. It, or some other word of similar meaning, may be closely coupled with an assertion of the justice of one's cause. So, in the third speech of Lysias, the speaker presents the evidence and says[b]

Remember these things and give a just verdict, *ta dikaia*.

That is, he claims that justice is on his side. Yet a few lines later he claims that neither he nor his ancestors has ever done Athens any harm,

And so I might with justice, *dikaiōs*, be pitied by you and by the rest of the citizens.

He claims to be in the right: and yet he stresses the good will to the city of both himself and his ancestors, and still asks for 'pity'. Accordingly, 'to show pity' may in the courts be equated simply with 'to decide in my favour': it has precisely the same

[a] Lys. 30. 1. Note, 30. 2 ff., the *social* as well as moral stigma attached to Nicomachus' father. This too is relevant in court.
[b] Lys. 3. 47 ff.

implications as *ameinon agonizesthai* in the other example quoted above.[a]

In fact, in making such pleas as these the speakers are not asking the jurors to let their hearts run away with their heads. The pleas are related to others which appeal to emotions far more reliable than pity. In these courts it is the regular practice to show, when asking for justice, that it is also advantageous to the city, *sumpheron (lūsiteloun) tēi polei*. So, in the twenty-first speech of Lysias,[b] the speaker claims that if the jury is persuaded by him, they will give a just verdict, *ta dikaia*, and will also choose what is profitable, *ta lūsitelounta*, for themselves. The speech is an argument against the confiscation of the family fortunes. The speaker argues that since he gives away most of his money to the state in 'liturgies' anyway, and can be relied upon to look after his own, the citizens will benefit from it more if he is allowed to keep it himself than if it were made public money, when it would be less zealously administered. Again, at a later date, Aeschines,[c] even while prefacing his remarks with the claim that a democracy differs from all other forms of government in being controlled not by whim but by law, tells the jury that if they support his view, which *is* the strict legal one,

You will vote for what is both just, *dikaia*, and in accordance with your oath, *euorka*, and advantageous, *sumpheronta*, to yourselves and to the city.

What might happen in an extreme case if justice were to clash with the city's advantage is shown by the twenty-seventh speech of Lysias.[d] It is said that the defendant Epicrates and his friends have maintained in the past that unless the jury condemned those who were pointed out to them, the money which the city needed for paying wages would run out. To condemn on such grounds may be *sumpheron*, but is certainly not *dikaion*: for popular values do *not* normally hold that what is *sumpheron* for the city *is dikaion*. Lysias maintains that from this the jury received *aischune*, while Epicrates and his friends took the benefit; for the money has run out anyway. This particular decision is

---

[a] Lys. 25. 13, p. 202.

[b] Lys. 21. 12. One might compare earlier Aesch. *Eum.* 667 ff.

[c] Aeschin. *In Ctes.* 8. Though the implications of this trial are political, it is not in form a political trial.

[d] Lys. 27. 2.

aischron: it is, however, an extreme case, and furnishes an example of the type of situation[a] which, as will be seen, produced a
temporary change of values in the law courts. What is important here is that the citizens seem to have chosen, not justice, but what was *sumpheron tēi polei*. One may blame the chaos
of the times; but there is no inconsistency with the attitudes
which the speakers quoted in the earlier passages expect.

If these two groups of examples, that in which the speaker
attempts to represent himself as *agathos* and that in which he
attempts to represent a decision in his favour as *sumpheron tēi
polei*, are taken together, the standard of the popular courts of
Athens becomes clear. It is precisely that of the assembly: to
gain favour *there* a man must show himself to be an *agathos
polites*, willing to spend himself and his possessions to promote
the city's prosperity; and to gain favour for his proposal he
must naturally show that it is conducive to the city's prosperity.
In court too he must show that he is an *agathos*, in terms exactly
similar to those of Thucydides' *agathos polites*, by drawing attention to his various services to the state, and also that his proposal, 'acquit me' or 'condemn him', is in the city's (material)
interest. There is no reason to be surprised at this, if the nature
of the Athenian popular courts is remembered. They were
courts of the people in the fullest sense: the enormous juries
which tried cases were in effect committees of the assembly, the
assembly in which all were used to sitting and voting on the
safety and prosperity of the state; and these juries could be
addressed, like the full assembly, simply as 'men of Athens'.
Accordingly, it is misleading to import ideas derived from a
different type of court.

C. *ARETE* AND *DIKAIOSUNE* IN COURT

(i) *Trierarch and Choregus*

There are, then, excellent reasons for the state of affairs
which we find in the courts of Athens. The juryman, however,
swore to give a just verdict; and yet, as a regular practice, the
prosecution allows the defence to bring forward the plea that
the speaker is *agathos* or *agathos polites*, opposing it merely with

---

[a] Though not one drawn from the period of the Thirty. The speech seems to
date from about 390 B.C.

facts designed to prove that the speaker is not *agathos*, instead of objecting to the plea as a blatant attempt to pervert justice. This may seem odd; but there is in fact nothing odd here at all. Neither Lysias nor anyone else says this at this period, because it cannot be said. If the defining characteristics of the *agathos polites* do not include being *dikaios*—and here they evidently do not—it is pointless to say: 'I am *dikaios*, and that man is only *agathos*. You must decide in my favour.' The *agathos polites* has inherited the most powerful term of value in Greek, and it is pointless to attempt to outbid it with a weaker one. Only if *dikaiosune* is shown to be an essential part of or means to *arete* can it meet *arete* on equal terms. This is true, whatever may be the exact connotation of *arete* at any time, for while the connotation of terms of value may vary, their respective values or emotive strengths do so to a much smaller degree. The *agathos* is now the *agathos polites* (whether the phrase is used or not on each occasion), and is linked *overtly* to the promotion or preservation of the security or prosperity of the state. Accordingly, in order to link *dikaiosune* with *arete*, it is essential to show that *dikaiosune* is necessary to the attainment of this end; and while Euripides and the thinkers on whom he is drawing may believe this to be true, such thought may well be beyond the capabilities of a popular court.

It is evident that there is nothing in this either immoral or amoral: the Athenian jury is merely acting in accordance with received standards. But though the whole derives from traditional standards, the practice, with the results it entails, may be new for all that. This must be a matter of inference, for we possess no forensic speeches of a significantly earlier date; but the inference is not *a priori* impossible.[10] As was said above,[a] the traditional system of values works quite well on the assumption that a man is *agathos* in war and, regarding *dikaiosune* as subject to divine sanctions, *dikaios* in peace. If, when he comes into court, both the man who is *agathos* on a basis of wealth, birth, and prowess and the jury which tries him believe that the gods are concerned that justice be done, strict justice in terms of law may well be done.[11]

This sanction no longer applies. Yet even if, from theological confusions or some other cause, it is now less believed that the

[a] Chapter VIII, p. 168.

gods concern themselves with men's justice and injustice, the passage quoted from Euripides above indicates that the importance of the quieter virtues to civic stability on purely naturalistic grounds is now realized to such an extent that the man who is poor but self-controlled may be termed *agathos*—in a play. Why, it may be asked, is such not the case in the lawcourts? Euripides' values are 'democratic' in tendency; and these are democratic courts.

The answer, disastrous as it may be in the long run, is simple, and lies in the manner in which these new values must be explained and expressed. If one is a democrat in a democratic society, and finds those who are traditionally held to be the 'best' citizens—i.e. men of wealth and good family—not to one's taste, the manner in which one will redefine the term *agathos* is clear. The cry must be 'It isn't what a man is that matters, but what he does'; and both in the passage quoted above, and in passages in which he says that a slave need be no 'worse' than a free man, for only his name is shameful,[a] Euripides evidently supports some such view.

What matters is what a man does: what then is he to do? Traditionally, the *agathoi* always earned this commendation because they were in fact the most valuable men, the men most able to secure society's safety. Accordingly, the *agathos polites* must do the same: he must *agatha poiein* his city. That this is not in itself a moral phrase needs no illustration here:[b] it means simply 'to benefit', as *kaka poiein* means 'to harm'. Accordingly, if justice is to figure in the qualities which society demands of the *agathos polites*, it must be believed that justice and self-control in the individual significantly benefit the city, while injustice significantly harms it. Even Euripides in this passage does not go quite so far; he says that *if* a man is just he is the sort of person who will be able to administer well, *eu oikein*, his house and his city, not that his justice is in itself a benefit to the city, an *agathon tēi polei*.

This is a question not in morals but in political theory, and it is unreasonable to expect a popular assembly at any period, least of all one in which political theory is in its infancy, and in fact understood by none, to work out the implications for itself,

[a] Cp. *Ion* 854, *Helen* 730 f., Frags. 511, 831.
[b] Cp. Chapter XII, pp. 249 ff.

even if such an assembly were subject to no external influences whatsoever; that is to say, even if the state is in fact a society in which there is no temptation on practical grounds to value one person more than another, other than morally. It requires little to show that not even Athens, materially most favoured of all Greek city-states at this time, was in such a position. What then must the citizen do for his city, and therefore what must the good citizen do well? In the first place, he may at any time be called upon to fight for his city, a unit not so large that the service of one man will not be noticed; and it should be remembered that these standards were developed during the Peloponnesian War, a period in which Athens more than was usual even in Greek states was fighting for her existence and prosperity. Most citizens, however, can perform this service at some time in their lives, in the triremes or elsewhere. There are others which only a man of substance can perform. The common people who form the crews of Athens' triremes do not provide their own weapons, and are the most powerful striking force in the community: true. This fact is democratic in tendency, but it requires qualification. Though the state provides the hull of the trireme, to fit it out as a ship of war the services of a trierarch are needed. The ramshackle finances of Athens do not enable the state to fit out the navy for war, nor (for example) to provide the money for choruses at festivals. The individual citizen must perform these beneficial services, *agatha*, for his city; only a man of substance can perform them;[12] and hence such men have, by the most democratic reasoning, more claim to be termed *agathoi* than their fellows. To be trierarch advances the security of the city; to be choregus, or to win races at the great games, as Alcibiades did with such éclat, advances its prestige. That prestige too is an *agathon* has been abundantly demonstrated: all these men, then, are *agathoi*, are worthy of the confidence and esteem of their fellow citizens, and possess all the claims upon them which a man termed *agathos* has always possessed. The claim of the *dikaios* to be *agathos* has little chance in such circumstances.

Thus, partly as a result of a misfire in democratic theory, partly as a result of the stress of war,[13] questions of responsibility are hopelessly confused in the Athenian popular courts. The relevant questions, as we should term them, are overridden;

with the support of traditional values—extrapolated—the requirements of law are overset; and if the relevant questions cannot gain a hearing, it is unreasonable to expect the relevant answers to be given.

(ii) Success and Failure

This is a serious problem; but it is not the only problem. The competitive values of the overriding standard traditionally and necessarily tend not to excuse failure. Nicias may have said[a] that the *agathos polites* was the man who benefited his state *or at least did it no harm deliberately*; that is, he may have said it in a version by Thucydides, a devotee of the New Thought—which, as we have seen,[b] is sensitive to questions of responsibility—at a time when Athens, full of confidence, was discussing fresh conquests. But in the rough and tumble of a popular court, in the baffled anger of defeat or the vindictiveness of suppressed revolution, the result may be different. In Lysias' thirteenth speech, against Agoratus, he imagines Agoratus as pleading that he acted *akon*, under compulsion, and replies[c]

But, gentlemen, I do not consider that you ought not to requite yourselves upon a man who has done you harm, *kaka*, so great that it is impossible to conceive a greater, even if he was under the greatest possible compulsion, *hōs malista akon*.

Agoratus' crime was to have accused and secured the condemnation of democratic leaders under the Thirty Tyrants. Lysias alleges that Agoratus did *not* act under compulsion, but then adds the words quoted.[14] There are crimes, of which this is one, for which no society can allow any defence. This is accordingly a special case; but *akon* spans both compulsion and mistake,[d] and the words are readily applicable to any failure to secure an end which the state desires: and there are indications that the words would be applicable in such circumstances. Demosthenes, after his military failure in Aetolia,[15] feared to return to Athens lest the Athenians should vent their anger upon him; an anger natural to any society, whatever its scheme of values, but one which in this society is justified by the

[a] Above, p. 199. [b] Chapters V and VI.
[c] Lys. 13. 52, and cp. 29 and 31. [d] Cp. especially Chapter XV.

society's values to such an extent that, had Demosthenes been arraigned before the courts, he would have been left with nothing to reply.

D. A BRIEF ENLIGHTENMENT

Yet since this is merely an extrapolation of traditional values, and since those values are justified on the same grounds as has always been the case, exhortation is of no use against this position: if one is dissatisfied, one can only, like Aristophanes, arch one's back and spit. One might threaten disaster; but unless this is to be divinely sent (and as it is lack of belief in this which seems to have brought about this crisis in values, such a threat could have little weight), it requires more skill than any writer of the period possessed to discover *and explain to a popular court* in what respect the condoning of a breach of law was more dangerous than the offending of a citizen of great value (reckoning value in talents and minae) to Athens.

But though the danger may be difficult to discover and explain, it is one which is certain to force itself on public notice *in practice*. The most prominent example of the *agathos polites*, reckoned in terms of skill, wealth, performance of 'liturgies', success in the games and similar activities, was undoubtedly Alcibiades: and this appalling combination of talent, efficiency, and political opportunism must have caused many to reconsider their accepted standards.[16] The mild revolution of 411 B.C., and much more the Reign of Terror of the Thirty Tyrants, both conducted by men who were indisputably *agathoi polītai* in the sense illustrated above, made the problem still more acute. By some means or other the *agathos* must be redefined.

There are clear signs of one attempt. Lysias in the thirteenth speech says[a] that Agoratus is the enemy both of the prosecutor and of the whole people, for he has killed men who were well-disposed, *eunoi*, to the citizen body; and immediately below he uses the phrase '*agathoi* with regard to the citizen body'. The phrases used[b] refer to the common people: the *agathos* here is the good citizen and the good democrat. The words could always have been so used, but civil strife has made some of their implications clearer; so we need not be surprised to discover

---

[a] Lys. 13. 1 and 2.

[b] εὖνοι τῷ πλήθει τῷ ὑμετέρῳ, ἀγαθοὶ περὶ τὸ πλῆθος τὸ ὑμέτερον.

that it was the *agathoi* who went home and did not vote for Theramenes' proposals to entrust the government to the Thirty.[a] When the tyrants were in power, Athens' rulers were the worst of men, *ponērotatoi*; but now the Athenians engage in politics with men who are *aristoi*.[b] Again, it is said of one man that he reached such a pitch of *arete* that he felt more anger at the wrongs done to the people than gratitude to those responsible for his return from exile.[c]

This use of *arete* has its new elements, particularly its complete lack of oligarchic flavour. Despite the apparently democratic implications, and probably the democratic intent, of the phrase *agathos polites*, those who could claim to be *agathoi* in this sense were sooner the traditional *agathoi*, who could perform the services required, than anyone else;[17] but it is now *agathos* to be a democrat *per se*. Apart from this, however, there is no reason to suppose that benefiting, *agatha poiein*, the city will include any *agatha* that were not recognized before: 'not having plotted against the city' seems a poor thing to bring forward as one's qualification for *arete* in comparison with 'having fitted out a trireme', so that the situation in court seems unlikely to be very different, unless one of the parties is a traitor or a revolutionary. Yet at this moment of stress the point was seen, as is shown by one or two pleas. In Lysias' eighteenth speech we find the words[d]

But *now* you would all admit that political harmony, *homonoia*, is the greatest *agathon* for a city, and that discord is the cause of all *kaka*.

This truth the Athenians, like the Corcyreans,[18] had had ample opportunity to meditate. Its recognition calls for a change of emphasis in the definition of the *agathos*, as Lysias himself realizes in the twenty-sixth speech,[e] the scrutiny of the qualification for office of a man debarred from holding office as a result of his family's share in the tyranny of the Thirty. Lysias anticipates the usual defence that both Evander and his father have performed 'liturgies', and replies in advance that the father would have been 'better', *kreittōn*, had he not spent his money in this manner:

a Lys. 12. 75.   b Lys. 12. 94.   c Lys. 18. 9.
d Lys. 18. 17.   e Lys. 26. 4.

For having gained the trust of the common people by this means, he destroyed the democracy; and these actions are more to be remembered than the votive offerings which commemorate his 'liturgies'.

Accordingly, to have subverted the democracy is, not surprisingly, to have inflicted a serious *kakon* upon the city (or upon the common people). The converse, that *not* to have subverted the democracy is an important *agathon*, is much more difficult to comprehend. On *one* occasion, however, in these forensic speeches, this view appears. In the twenty-first speech of Lysias,[a] we have this plea:

Do not think only of public 'liturgies', but also consider men's private pursuits, bearing in mind that the most laborious of all 'liturgies' is to be always to the end moderate and temperate and to be neither overcome by pleasure nor elated by gain, but to show yourself to be such a man that none of the citizens either finds fault with you or dares to summon you into court.

This passage is doubly interesting: it shows a new attitude, and at the same time proves that the evaluation of the old attitude given above is correct, for one does not assimilate private virtue to public service unless it is public service which is regarded as most laudable.[19]

It is difficult to evaluate the effect of this new attitude upon moral responsibility. On the one hand, if the quieter virtues are treated as a 'liturgy', they, like the other 'liturgies', are held to be conducive to the stability and prosperity of the city, and thus anyone who performs this 'liturgy' has a claim to be *agathos* in virtue of so doing. Admittedly, Lysias does not argue that it should be held to be the only 'liturgy'; he could not deny that the other 'liturgies' benefited the city: but since he maintains that it is the most laborious of the 'liturgies' he should presumably believe that its performance should give a man a greater claim on the goodwill of the jury than any other. The defects of this defence, viewed as a solution to the problem of moral responsibility, lie deeper. In the first place, it is not the justice or injustice of the particular act on trial which is thus thrust into the foreground, but the general tenor of the defendant's life. Secondly, though Lysias' words appear to be general,

[a] Lys. 21. 19.

we must consider them in the context in which they were uttered. Like all the other pleas, they must be seen against the background of the revolution of the Thirty: Lysias means—or at all events the jury will most readily assume that he means —by 'to be moderate and temperate' that to be wealthy and despite this remain a good democrat is difficult, and worthy of the highest praise. Against such a background the words could hardly be interpreted otherwise; and *dikaiosune* in general can hardly be expected to benefit greatly from them. The speaker in this case has performed other 'liturgies':[a] Lysias has merely provided the well-to-do democrat with one more plea to enable him to escape from the charge on which he is being tried.

E. THE RELAPSE

Admittedly the last plea considered above does represent an insight from which a higher valuation for *dikaiosune* might in theory have been developed. Such a development, however, seems unlikely *a priori*; Lysias, despite his experiences under the Thirty, only rarely approaches the point of view discussed above; and in fact when circumstances returned to normal even these lessons were forgotten. The orators of the later fourth century might, and sometimes did, draw on the thought of Isocrates and Plato, as earlier authors had drawn on that of the sophists; but since, as will be seen, even Plato had pronounced difficulties in solving the problem of the relation of *dikaiosune* to civic *arete*, it is not surprising that no satisfactory solution could be brought into the law courts. These orators may be treated briefly, for their problems remain unchanged, and they have no real solution for them. Lycurgus, said to have been a pupil of Isocrates and Plato,[b] condemns, in his prosecution of Leocrates,[c] the introduction of irrelevant public topics, and says that only the strict rights and wrongs of the case in hand should be considered. He insists that the witnesses should confine themselves to the facts of the case;[d] and yet when he considers the support which Leocrates' friends will give Leocrates, and the certainty that they will cite their own 'liturgies' as a

[a] Lys. 21. 16.
[b] Plutarch, *Lives of the Ten Orators*, Lycurg. *ad init.*
[c] Lyc. *In Leocr.* 11.   [d] Ibid. 20.

claim on the favour of the jury, Lycurgus is even now unable to say that such claims are illegitimate.[a] He can only say that such 'liturgies' as Leocrates' friends have performed—horse-breeding, and acting as choregus—are not really services to the state. So far the thought of the century could help him. With these, however, he explicitly contrasts being a trierarch, building walls to protect the city, or subscribing money from one's own property in the interests of public safety. These *are* services to the state, and

In these one may see the *arete* of the donors, in the former only the wealth of the spenders.

Such services *are* expressions of *arete*: this cannot be denied. Hence those who perform them are *agathoi*, and have claims upon their fellow citizens, to some degree on behalf of their friends, much more on their own.[b] The situation, together with its dangers, is unchanged.[20] Accordingly, it is natural to find Hyperides, in prosecuting Athenogenes for fraud, attempting to prove that Athenogenes is a traitor, and so *kakos*;[c] and that orators still attempt to show that justice and expediency coincide.[d] Lastly, in Demosthenes' speech against Conon, the prosecutor, after the usual mention of trierarchies performed, utters the following words:[e]

For even if we were admittedly even more useless and worse, *achrēstoteroi* and *ponēroteroi*, than these men, we are not for that reason, I suppose, to be beaten and assaulted.

The words *achrestoteroi* and *poneroteroi* refer to inability to perform the important civic functions; and it is clear from the manner in which the point is made that the family of Conon has in fact performed more 'liturgies' than that of the prosecutor, and that this is likely to count against the latter.

Accordingly, even if we may regard the passages discussed in the previous section as constituting a kind of enlightenment, it is evident that this was short-lived. In these later orators the values of the popular courts have returned to normal, and with them the confusion of ideas of responsibility.

---

[a] Lyc. *In Leocr.* 139.   [b] Ibid. 140, cp. Hyperides frag. 23.
[c] Hyp. *In Ath.* 29 ff.
[d] e.g. Dinarch. *In Demosth.* 111 and 114.
[e] Dem. *In Con.* 44.

NOTES TO CHAPTER X

1. Note, however, that the Husbandman claims to be of a noble family which has come down in the world, 34 ff. He remarks that noble birth is soon overlooked when one has no wealth to support it.

2. These lines (386/90) were excised by Wilamowitz (*Anal. Eur.*, pp. 190 ff.) as being irrelevant. Denniston, *Electra*, ad loc., agrees that the lines are irrelevant, but adds 'But it does not follow with certainty that Euripides could not have put it in.' I have no doubt at all that the lines should stand where they do: they are the explanation of the foregoing lines, which at this period certainly stand in need of explanation.

3. Note that though Euripides has at some length defined *euandria*, the quality of the *agathos*, in terms of quiet virtues (by a process of elimination), pp. 176 f., he nevertheless uses *eupsuchia*, the possession of good psychic qualities, to commend courage in the lines immediately following.

4. It is derived from παλάμη, the hand viewed as a means of making war or engaging in crafts, with a negative prefix. Wilamowitz, *Sappho und Simonides*, p. 175, denies that the sense in this poem is that suggested in the text: a denial which depends on the rest of his argument, for which see Appendix, pp. 355 ff.

5. Such people will also naturally possess the necessary political skill, handed down within the family, at a time when such matters are little understood generally; or rather not the necessary political skill, but all that is available: and they will also benefit from the general prestige of the *agathos*, and from tradition and habit.

6. Ps.-Xen. *Ath. Pol.* 1. 2. The writer admits that it is right (*dikaiōs*) that the common people should have power since 'these are the men who give the city its strength, much more so than the hoplites, the men of good birth, *gennaioi*, or the 'useful', *chrēstoi* (another synonym for *agathoi*). Traditionally, the hoplite classes are the most important striking force in the state, and hence are *agathoi*. Since this is the case no longer, they have lost the basis of their claim to be *agathoi* (or *chrestoi*). The author retains the traditional usage; but the situation must have led to great despondency and confusion among the Athenian upper classes, and to a search for new justifications for their claim to be *agathoi*, cp. pp. 236 ff. below.

7. The tone of this speech, the willingness to go against law—though admittedly in a good cause—may seem odd in the mouth of a timid conservative like Nicias, but Thucydides may have felt it suitable to the occasion, even if not to the person. It is possible that Nicias may have said some such thing; but both the references to the *agathos polites* here have the air of being 'set pieces': and even if Nicias expressed these sentiments, he may not have used these words. (Many of Thucydides' speeches, notably the Debate on Mytilene, have the air, like Herodotus' Debate on Government, iii. 80, quoted in Chapter IX, of being sophists' set pieces, in this case on 'the true meaning of expediency in politics', re-arranged to suit the particular circumstances.)

8. Tyranny is per se *adikia* from the earlier fifth century, cp. Hdt. iii. 142. 1, vii. 164.

9. So that Socrates can score a definite point by *not* resorting to appeals of this kind, Plato *Apol.* 38 E. Socrates' defence as a whole, of course (cp. Chapter XIII *ad init.*), disdains the method of approach illustrated in this chapter, and relies on *dikaiosune*. If Socrates' defence bore any resemblance to Plato's version of it, it is hardly surprising that he should have been condemned. For an instance of the practice mentioned in the text, cp. Hyperides, *Against Philippides* 9.

10. Aristophanes, *Acharnians* 676 ff., bears witness to a tumult in the courts, resulting from changes. Clever young men are dragging the Old Men of Marathon into court and obtaining verdicts against them which he holds to be unjust. Presumably the reference is to the new skill of forensic oratory in general; but the passage as a whole seems to indicate that justice once held sway in the courts in a manner in which it does so no longer.

11. In murder trials, the element of 'pollution' and the wrath of the spirit of the dead may sometimes produce a heavy emphasis on justice, cp. *Tetralogies* Cb 8, Cd 10. This emphasis, born of the idea of 'pollution', is not without its disadvantages. In primitive thought, it is not sufficient to intend to fulfil the terms of an oath. One must in fact keep it, cp. *Iliad* x. 332: Hector's *epiorkon* (a word which elsewhere denotes a false oath) is an oath unfulfilled as a result of events completely beyond his control. In ordinary trials in Athens, as this chapter makes clear, the jurors' oath weighed lightly with them. In these murder trials, however, the oath is reinforced by the thought of 'pollution', and the jury are called upon to give, not a just verdict on the evidence, but a decision which is just in fact. Cp. Cd 10, where it is said that 'pollution' will come upon the jury if they in fact condemn an innocent man. (A different view is taken in *Tetralogies* Aa, but the former view is by far the commoner.) Aeschines, *Parapresb.* 87 mentions a safeguard: the man who wins his case at the Palladion must affirm with the most solemn formalities that those jurors who have voted on his side have voted what is true and right and that he himself has spoken no falsehood, calling down destruction upon himself and his household if this be not true: 'A right provision, citizens, and one worthy of a democracy. For if none of you would wish to taint himself with justifiable homicide, *phonos dikaios*, surely he would take the utmost care not to taint himself with culpable homicide, *phonos adikos*, by taking away a man's life, property, or civic status: acts such as have caused some men to kill themselves, and others to be put to death by the state.' Evidently to condemn an innocent man on a capital charge would traditionally be *adikos phonos*, whatever the state of the evidence. Demosthenes, *In Aristocratem* 96, however, says of those who, in cases in which the oath is emphasized, come to a decision which, while in accordance with the evidence, is wrong, 'Do those who come to such a decision not abide by their oaths, then? They do. How? I will tell you. They swore to give judgment with just mind, and the opinion of their mind [ἡ δὲ γνώμης δόξα, a contorted

phrase, and one which may betray the difficulty Demosthenes experienced in making the point] is induced by what they hear. As a
result, when they give their votes in accordance with their opinion,
they act piously, *eusebein*. For everyone acts piously who does not give
his vote contrary to his true opinions as a result of enmity or friendship
or any other unjust reason.' The point of view is unexceptionable; but
it is a point which has to be made, even in the time of Demosthenes.
Where there is no such particular fear of the supernatural, however, the
standards which apply are quite clear from this chapter.

12. According to Demosthenes, *Against Aphobus*, p. 833, every Athenian
who possessed three talents or more was liable for 'liturgies'. For the
manner in which the Athenians fitted out their ships, cp. Hdt. viii. 17;
Thuc. ii. 24, vi. 31; Aristoph. *Knights* 916; Isocrates, *Against Calli-
machus* 59 f., &c.

13. But even though in peace the strains would be less, many 'liturgies'
would still have to be performed, and the situation would still exist in
some degree. Note the manner in which Lysias is able to turn the
normal plea against Alcibiades the Younger, 14. 43 ff.

14. I am not of course denying that the plea of *force majeure* was normally
applicable: to go no further, that Agoratus should make such a plea
proves that such a defence was normally good. Naturally, too, mistake
or accident was a good defence, and had long been so, cp. Draco's
murder law and the attempted plea of Socrates, *Apology* 25 D ff., where
he argues (sophistically, cp. Chapter XIII, p. 269) that if he corrupted
the young he must have done so unintentionally: 'and if I am corrupting
them unintentionally, *akon*, it is not the custom to bring a man into
court for such unintentional errors, but to take him aside privately,
and teach and admonish him'. The distinctions can be drawn, and
Chapters V and VI have suggested that at the end of the fifth century
much thought was devoted to refining and improving them. The danger
is (cp. following note) that, since the *arete*-standard takes precedence,
these distinctions may be overridden by the demands of success, or of
benefiting the city.

15. Thuc. iii. 98. 5. We may compare the trial of Miltiades for his failure
to take Paros, Hdt. vi. 136. Miltiades was impeached 'for deceit', τῆς
ἀπάτης εἵνεκεν, which can only mean that he had said that he could
take Paros when *in fact* he could not; that is, he was impeached for his
failure. The trial of Pericles, Thuc. ii. 59 ff., is similar, as also is that of
the generals after Arginusae for their failure to recover the dead, Xen.
Hell. i. vii. 8 ff., though here the matter is complicated by religious
beliefs. Greek values justify these attitudes in political trials; even under
traditional values (cp. Miltiades) *arete* was bound to take first place in
a trial of this nature, and doubtless generals and politicians have no
real defence to offer should they fail; but it is the mark of the new
values to import these standards into ordinary trials, where they have
no place, with the results set out in the text.

16. In the case of Alcibiades, the perplexity of the Athenians is reflected in
Aristophanes, *Frogs* 1422 ff. (For a biography of Alcibiades, cp. Benson,

The Life of Alcibiades, London, 1928, and Hatzfeld, *Alcibiade*, Paris,
1951.)

17. Possibly the new usage implied the admission that men who were
wealthy but not of good birth were *agathoi*, but (cp. Chapter IV, pp.
75 ff.) it was almost impossible to exclude these anyway.

18. We may compare Thuc. iii. 82. 7 for a quiet moral use of *agathos* in
relation to the stasis in Corcyra, a use which (cp. i. 37. 5, discussed
above, pp. 178 f.) only appears in this writer in conditions of stress.
Thucydides was clearly very sensitive to *all* the arguments about values
current in his day, and could employ them, and the linguistic usages
which accompanied them, with great dramatic and rhetorical effect.

19. This new attitude, as is said in the text, is really not a solution to this
problem at all. It is the nearest approach to a solution which we find in
the courts, but there may be indications of a better solution in contemporary thought in Thuc. iii. 67. 2. The Thebans, accusing the
Plataeans to the Spartans, say, 'Do not listen to the account of their
former *aretai*—if indeed there were any—and so be moved to pity; for
such *aretai* ought to be of help to those who are wronged, but their
existence should be an occasion for double punishment if their possessors do anything *aischron*, since they are committing errors in defiance
of what is becoming to them.' Here the reference is to suitable treatment
of a defeated enemy in war, but, given Greek values, the words can
readily be applied to any trial; and these words may well be the reflection of contemporary thought of more general application. The solution is much better than that of Lysias: to acknowledge past *aretai* as
aretai, but claim that they are irrelevant, is much more fruitful than to
say that other activities are more important *aretai*, since it is not obvious
that such activities are essential to the state, at a time when there seems
to be no danger of stasis. That is to say, such a solution is better in
theory; but there could be no chance of convincing a popular court that
anything is more important than *arete*, however interpreted; and the
method of approach adopted by Lysias is the only practical one, even
though it is in fact no solution.

20. Lycurgus in fact maintains that no one can claim to save a traitor like
Leocrates; but *arete* is *arete*, and even if its claims might fail in this one
instance, it is evident that they must be heard in all other cases, and
further that even in the case of traitors Lycurgus must argue the point.
Lycurgus can whittle away extraneous *aretai* (and cp. Hyperides, *For
Euxenippus* 37), but if a man has really benefited the city on a large
scale, this is *arete*, and its claims must be met. For a further example, cp.
Dinarchus, *Against Aristogiton* 8. Dinarchus cannot argue that such
pleas are illegitimate: he too must show that they do not apply here.
Certainly, Dinarchus in the same speech (15) can say that Demosthenes
and Demades were punished for corruption—'and rightly, *dikaiōs*, too,
though you were conscious that much, if not all, of their political career
had been of service, *chrēsimon*, to the state'. This might suggest that the
plea that one is an *agathos polites* could be rejected by the jury as illegitimate. Dinarchus, however, could not have admitted their past services,

had Demosthenes or Demades themselves been on trial. *Then* he would have branded them both as traitors and unskilful politicians, as in *Against Demosthenes* 111, where he argues that Demosthenes' political career has been a disaster to the city, and 113, where he argues in effect that anyone who rises to support Demosthenes is a traitor: the only means of rendering support ineffective. Dinarchus' words in *Against Aristogiton* 15 are accordingly a rhetorical trick, cp. also *Against Demosthenes* 14, where the reference is to Timotheus. One cannot admit that the *present* defendant has performed valuable services.

XI

THE ADMINISTRATOR, THE IMMORA-
LIST, AND THE ORDINARY MAN

A. THE ADMINISTRATOR

THE last two chapters have illustrated a remarkable change in
values, together with the theory on which it was based, and the
virtual impossibility, in the particular context of the law courts,
of maintaining the supremacy of the new values in practice,
since the theory so much more readily supported a quite different system of values. We have noticed the difficulty of seeing
in such a context the relation of private injustice to civic success
or failure, especially when other aspects of a man's life seem
to contribute much more to that success or failure; but nothing
has yet been said which refers in particular to Athens' own
situation and problems. The problems which have been considered might have arisen in any Greek state, large or small,
subject or despot.

In the second half of the fifth century, however, Athens was
far from being an ordinary Greek state. The Delian League
of Aegean cities whose formation she had inspired after the
Persian Wars had become gradually metamorphosed into an
empire, in which Athens' subject states could not disregard her
wishes. Her position of power gave Athens opportunities which
were denied to the smaller cities; and since it is the task of this
chapter to examine the point of view of the administrator and
the (so called) immoralist in relation to that of the 'ordinary
Athenian', it is desirable to examine the values which guided
Athens in the administration of her empire. Those values must
be sought primarily in the speeches of Thucydides. These,
being set speeches, are doubtless much more coherent than those
actually delivered in the assembly. Such coherence, however,
does not destroy their usefulness for the present purpose: the
values of the period are just as apparent in these as they could
have been in the actual speeches, and their coincidence with the

values of the 'ordinary men' who appear in Plato's earlier dialogues[a] indicates their authenticity.

The values of the Athenian assembly[1] are clearly demonstrated by the speeches delivered before it by Cleon and Diodotus, during the discussion of the treatment appropriate to the revolted Mytileneans in the fifth year of the Peloponnesian War. Cleon, asking for severe punishment for the islanders, lays emphasis on their injustice, *adikia*; for so he evaluates their revolt against Athens.[b] This, however, is not the mainstay of his argument. He begins by saying that he has always known that a democracy such as Athens is unable to govern, *adunaton archein*. To say this is to belittle its *arete*,[c] and hence the most powerful of insults. He further says that those who do not change their minds for the most part administer their cities better—i.e. more efficiently—*ameinon oikein*;[d] and that anyone who wishes to oppose his motion would have to show that the injustices of the Mytileneans were beneficial, *ōphelimoi*, to Athens.[e] Like the pleaders in the law courts, he insists that his motion unites the just, *ta dikaia*, and the advantageous, *ta sumphora*: and in conclusion implores his hearers not to betray themselves.[f] The core of Diodotus' arguments against this position is as follows: if the Athenians make their decision hastily and in anger, they are unlikely to act with good counsel, *euboulia*: and, he insists, it is not about the *adikia* of the Mytileneans but about the *euboulia*[2] of the Athenians that they are debating, or should be.[g] Whatever the facts of the case, the islanders should neither be condemned *nor* acquitted unless the course of action is advantageous, *sumpheron*, that is to say an *agathon* for the city. The Athenians are not sitting in judgement in court upon the Mytileneans, when they would have need to consider what was just, *ta dikaia*—a statement which, as has been seen, is not altogether true. The Athenians, he insists, are deliberating on the manner in which the Mytileneans may be of use to them:[h] and the manner of treating the Mytileneans which is the most beneficial to Athens is not, as Cleon had maintained, to treat

---

[a] Below, pp. 226 ff. [b] Thuc. iii. 38. 1 and 39. 1.
[c] Cp. Meno's definition, *Meno* 73 c 9, below, p. 229.
[d] Thuc. iii. 37. 3. [e] Ibid. 38. 1.
[f] Ibid. 40. 7. For the idea that not securing one's interests is self-betrayal, cp. *Crito* 45 c 5 ff., p. 230 below.
[g] Thuc. iii. 42. 1 and 44. 1. [h] Ibid. 44. 3.

them harshly. Accordingly, the *dikaion* and the *sumpheron* are separated: and in such a case it is treated as only natural that the assembly should pursue the *sumpheron*.

The words are blunt: they express, however, not the values of a depraved post-Periclean ochlocracy, but the values of Pericles himself, as may be seen by comparing his last speech[a] with the debate on Mytilene.[3] In the present instance, their application results in the following of the milder course; but, as Diodotus says, the more ruthless course might have been *sumpheron*: in which case, justice or no justice, it should be followed.

A brief survey of the Melian Dialogue illustrates this. The Athenians throughout advise the Melians to take counsel for their own safety, even though it entails becoming subjects of Athens.[b] Their own values and their own motives are in no doubt. They say that they will have nothing to do with fine words: justice is for equals, the possible is what the stronger aim at, and the weaker must acquiesce.[c] They say that they are there to benefit their own empire. They wish to rule over the Melians without trouble.[d] In face of this, the Melians, baulked of their effort to threaten divine vengeance by the Athenian claim that the gods are on the side of the big battalions, and told by the Athenians that they are not in a position to expect justice, are forced to conduct their argument in terms of what is *sumpheron*: they try to prove that it is *sumpheron* for *both* sides that the Athenians should neither force the Melians into submission nor destroy them outright.[e] One can only conduct an argument if both sides agree on terms: a principle which will become important later.

These examples demonstrate the values of the Athenian democracy. The course followed is that which is thought to be advantageous, *sumpheron* or *agathon*, for the state, when the state is dealing with other states, just as when she is trying her own citizens in her own courts of law. What is needed to determine what is in fact *sumpheron* for the state is naturally a skill, whether denoted by *euboulia* or by some other word, a skill which has, of course, no relation to the standards of the quieter virtues. To what extent such behaviour is immoral by Greek

[a] Thuc. ii. 62 ff., cp. p. 234 below.　　　[b] Thuc. v. 87, 101, 111.
[c] Ibid. 89.　　　[d] Ibid. 91.
[e] Ibid. 98.

standards will be discussed below:[a] here it is sufficient to emphasize that this is a system of values based on calculation, and can be no other.

Thus far it seems unnecessary that *euboulia* should imply anything more than an eye to the main chance. Athens' situation as an imperial power, however, provided not only unusual opportunities for self-indulgence, but also serious administrative problems. The smaller Greek states, with no subject peoples and an insignificant revenue, could doubtless be administered by a combination of experience, inherited from father to son by a few prominent families, and simple improvisation, without becoming involved in serious difficulties. Athens, however, had a large annual income from her subjects, and some at least of the legal problems of those subjects had to be settled in her own courts: a move presumably designed at least in part to simplify litigation,[4] but one which must inevitably have created serious problems of administration in Athens.[5] In such matters improvisation might well be baulked by the complexity of the problem, and inherited experience fail to meet a situation for which in the whole of Greece there existed no precedent.

Nor is this all. We have to remember that not only in Athens but also in the subject states the claims of *arete* had to be heard. Here the situation is complex. A recent article[6] has demonstrated that the common people of the subject states were frequently more friendly towards Athens—that is, towards the Athenian common people—than towards their own richer citizens. That such an attitude is in fact commended by current Greek standards of value is shown by the present chapter: 'to help one's friends and harm one's enemies', which, as will appear, is the goal, in politics may be interpreted as helping one's own class—or the class with which one identifies oneself as a politician—and harming other classes. Accordingly, it is natural that the *demos* of a subject city should feel more hostility towards its own *agathoi*, at all events where these were powerful, than to the Athenian *demos*. In saying that the subject states were disaffected, then, we should mean that the upper classes, the *agathoi*, were so. They had excellent reasons for this attitude: not only was their own *demos* doubtless 'harming its enemies'—

---

[a] See below, pp. 232 ff. The Athenians claim, Thuc. v. 105, that they are merely following traditional practice.

the *agathoi*—with the help of the *demos* of Athens, they them-selves, *qua agathoi*, were the traditional possessors of *arete*. Now *arete*, as we have seen, is the quality by which men and states maintain themselves as free and independent—and in this it is *kalon* for the *agathos* to succeed, *aischron* to fail.[7] The upper classes of the subject states, then, had two excellent reasons for dis-affection.

But we may go further. It might appear that Athens could have solved this problem by suppressing the old *agathoi* in her subject states completely. Surely then the solidarity of the empire would have been assured. This is highly unlikely. *Agathos* is such an attractive word that, had the rich been no longer in a position to term themselves *agathoi*, the *demos*, or its politically articulate leaders,[a] would have inevitably laid claim to the title of *agathoi politai*; and we have seen nothing in the *arete* of the democratic Athenian assembly to suggest that its exercise en-couraged co-operation with, much less subordination to, any other state. In the particular circumstances of her empire, Athens had many friends in her subject states; but unless the concept of *arete* had been radically redefined, she could never have had willing subjects, unless these were more afraid of some other enemy than of Athens. To picture a solidarity of the proletariat in the fifth-century Aegean would be quite un-realistic.

Accordingly, that any of Athens' subject states—or the *agathoi* in them, however interpreted—should revolt, given the oppor-tunity, is simply in accordance with the most important Greek values. These values make co-operation difficult, subordination or subjection an insult to manhood.[8]

When this difficulty is added to the former, it becomes evident that the Athenians needed much more than an eye to the main chance. Native wit might have enabled a Themistocles to improvise what the situation needed[b] in the early years of the century; to see, for example, the need to divert the Laurium silver to the construction of triremes, and to persuade the Athenians to agree;[9] but in the second half of the century more

---

[a] In pp. 219 ff. above we see that it may be *agathos* not to engage in stasis. Any internal political calm would almost certainly lead to the exercise of *arete*, tradi-tionally interpreted, in external affairs.

[b] αὐτοσχεδιάζειν τὰ δέοντα, Thuc. i. 138.

than native wit was needed to solve the niggling problems of day-to-day administration. The skill of the counsellor had always been prized, from Homer onwards; but now a new kind of man with a new kind of skill was needed.[10] If needed, he and his kind were certain to be valued when found; and hence it is reasonable to expect, in Athens above all, the emergence of a new kind of *arete*—a use, that is, of the highest term of value to commend a new kind of activity, or even the promise of such an activity. There is no reason to suppose that the Athenians solved their problems; but the very existence of such problems guaranteed the title of *agathos* to anyone who promised or seemed able to show them the means to a solution.

Now there is nothing 'immoral' here: the skill is needed; *arete* is the most powerful word available to commend it; and *arete* has always commended the ability to produce certain results. The man with the desired skill has a perfect right to be termed *agathos*. All this with the best intentions; but we have seen already that the best intentions are rarely sufficient in Greek moral thought. *Arete*, as this chapter will show, is now in fact used to commend the production of certain results in government and administration. Since the first aim of government and administration is to secure the safety and prosperity of the state, it is evident that *agathos* and *arete* will be used to commend those who succeed in this aim. The justification of this use of *arete*, then, is identical with that of traditional *arete*. But all the traditional qualities of the *agathos* were still required: Athens had still to be able to defend herself at any time, albeit now rather with her navy than with her land forces, and could feel no temptation to value courage and success in war any less than she had done in the past. Hence—as we have seen—*arete* still has all its traditional flavour. The danger is obvious: it is almost inevitable that this new use of *arete*, even if it originally merely commends a political skill, will come to commend not simply those who secure in the field of politics the ends secured by traditional *arete* on the field of battle, but those who secure them in the *manner* of traditional *arete*. Such *arete* requires courage, initiative, and the willingness to take risks to achieve a desired end. It has no relation to quiet co-operative values, and hence is unlikely to be conducive to peace and justice between states or within the state.

The danger was not avoided. Despite the quiet moral use of
arete which was seen in Chapter IX to be developing, the
traditional use of the term is the normal one in Athenian politics.
Doubtless the Athenian assembly would have behaved in the
same manner anyway; but the new terminology, the extension
of traditional values, supported them in their actions.

B. 'THE ORDINARY MAN'

More will be said of this below.[a] The chief purpose of this
chapter, however, is the comparison of the values of the 'ordinary
Athenian' with those of the 'immoralists'; and for this purpose
the earlier dialogues of Plato must be examined. Here the
argument sometimes takes its rise from the expressed desire of
an 'ordinary man' to become *agathos*, or from his desire that his
son should become so. This clearly means a desire to be an
agathos polites, not in the sense of the forensic speeches, where the
proof that one was *agathos* depended on the performance of
unpleasant or expensive tasks on the city's behalf, but in the
sense of becoming a politician skilled in word and action, to the
same end of promoting the prosperity of the city.

It is in this sense that the young men of the period wish to be
made 'better'; it is with this purpose that they come to the
sophists, or anyone else who claims to be able to teach the desired
skill; and it was presumably for this reason, however much
Socrates in the *Apology*[b] may deny that he taught anything, that
young men came to Socrates himself, not merely for the pleasure
of hearing their elders and betters confuted by the Socratic elenchus.[11] This sense of 'better' can readily be illustrated. In the
Theages—which, though doubtfully Platonic, is useful since it
demonstrates the situation most clearly—Theages, doubting
that one can be taught to become *agathos*, says that he has heard
that Socrates maintains that

The sons of these politicians, *polītikoi*,[c] are no better, *beltīous*,
than the sons of shoemakers.

It is the politicians' sons whom one would expect to be 'better'
than the shoemakers' sons, because 'better' means 'better in the

---

[a] Below, pp. 232 ff.   [b] Plat. *Apol.* 19 D ff., 20 E.
[c] Themistocles, Cimon, and Pericles have been mentioned.

political craft'. So Theages infers[a] that it would be foolish to hope that one of the politicians would hand on to *him* his wisdom, *sophia*, when he does not benefit his own son in this way.[12] Again, Socrates suggests that Theages, in order to become *agathos*, be taken to one of the men who are *kaloi kāgathoi* in respect of politics.[b] Later, too, he says that he is not surprised that Demodocus wants to have his son educated, since a man should aim at nothing so much for his son as that he should become as *agathos* as possible; and this is interpreted as becoming an *agathos polites*.

In this dialogue the politicians are taken as the repository of political skill; and at first political knowledge in the young democracy must still have been confined to the old families who had been prominent in earlier days. The new democracy created a great demand for this knowledge, a demand which the political families may well not have been eager to supply; and the spreading of such knowledge, and its refinement and improvement in the light of Athens' unprecedented position and responsibilities, must have been the most important function of the sophistic movement. That such skill was taught by sophists is clear: Hippocrates, in the *Protagoras*, wishes to be made wise, *sophos*, by Protagoras; and Socrates, after some discussion,[c] induces Protagoras to define his teaching as follows:

What they learn is sound judgment, *euboulia*, about their own affairs—how best they may manage, *arista dioikein*, their own households—and about the affairs of the city—how they may be most competent, *dunatoi*, to handle its business both in speech and in action.

Socrates then asks:

Do I understand you correctly? You seem to mean the political art, *polītikē technē*, and to be promising to make men into *agathoi politai*.

To this Protagoras agrees.

It is, then, *politike techne* or political excellence, *politike arete*,[d] that the young men of Athens require in order to become

[a] (Plato) *Theages* 126 D., cp. *Prot.* 319 E.
[b] For *kalos kāgathos*, cp. p. 337. The phrase suggests that political knowledge is believed to be confined to the upper class here.
[c] Plat. *Prot.* 318 E ff.
[d] Plat. *Prot.* 319 A, 319 E, 321 D 4 (*sophia . . . politike*), 322 D 7, 323 A 6.

agathoi politai; and this entails skill in managing one's own household and in transacting the affairs of the state. The end in both cases is clear and desirable: prosperity and stability. Only the means are required: what is to be taught is a skill, a *techne*. This is inevitable: the state's first function is to survive, and the ancient household, too, was much less protected by the state: its head had to look first of all to its existence.[13]

This skill in budgeting and defence, in home and in state, is no more moral than the skills commended by traditional *arete*. *Dikaiosune* must be linked to it, if at all, as a means; and this depends on the answer to the question: 'Must the prosperous householder, the successful politician, be just?' Whatever the answer, the 'must' is not moral, but means 'Is it a necessary means to his prosperity?' An answer given by an 'ordinary man' appears in the *Meno*.[14] Meno is attempting to satisfy Socrates' request for a definition of *arete*. To help him, Socrates asks the following questions:[a]

> Socrates: Were you not saying that the *arete* of a man is to administer his city well, *eu dioikein*, the *arete* of a woman to do the same for her household?[15]
>
> Meno: I was.
>
> Socrates: Well, is it possible to administer anything well—city or household or anything whatsoever—if one does not do it in a temperate and just manner, *sophronōs* and *dikaiōs*?
>
> Meno: It is not.
>
> Socrates: And if they administer it temperately and justly, will they administer it with justice and temperance, *dikaiosune* and *sophrosune*?
>
> Meno: It is inevitable.
>
> Socrates: Women and men alike, then, need the same qualities if they are to be *agathoi*: *dikaiosune* and *sophrosune*.
>
> Meno: Apparently.

This passage makes the position which the ordinary man believes himself to hold quite clear. Meno seems to be portrayed as the intelligent man in the street, so far as moral questions are concerned. He wants to run his city—and to have his house run—'well', *eu dioikein*, in the sense of *arista dioikein* in the *Protagoras* passage; efficiently, that is, with no moral overtones whatever; and he is prepared to admit that justice and self-restraint are necessary to this desired end, and hence that these qualities are desirable in a derivative sense. This should be emphasized. The impossibility of administering well unless one does so justly does not derive in any way from any relationship —analytic or synonymous—subsisting between *eu* and *dikaiōs*. There is no such relationship. Whether or no it is possible to administer 'well' and unjustly is an experimental issue, not a question of language. To say that Meno is prepared to admit that *sophrosune* and *dikaiosune* are necessary in this sense is not to say that he does so reluctantly; but it is to say that there is no doubt in Meno's mind which is the end and which is the means. The *agathos*—the man displaying this *arete*—is still the individual functioning to the top of his capacity in the city's interest and his own, and making the same claims as he has always made. This is made even clearer by an earlier definition of (male) *arete* offered by Meno:[a]

If you want a definition of the *arete* of a man, that is easy enough: the *arete* of a man is to be capable of taking part in politics,[b] and while doing so, to be capable of helping one's friends and harming one's enemies, while taking care to suffer no harm oneself at their hands.

This passage is significant: it is Meno's *first* definition of *arete*; and it is to be noted that the word which Plato depicts as coming most readily to mind in this connexion is 'capable'. *Arete* remains a capacity, an ability, a skill. When driven from this position, Meno says of *arete*[c]

What else is it than the capacity for ruling men?

Doubtless he means this in the sense proper to a democracy, but a democracy with an empire. Later, too, he defines *arete* as[d]

To desire what is *kalon* and to be able to obtain it.

This too is capacity, whatever Meno means by *kalon*. Lastly,[e] he defines *arete* as

The power to obtain *agatha*,

the capacity of providing (for oneself and friends, in view of earlier definitions) a supply of 'good things'. The Meno of the

---

[a] Plat. *Meno* 71 E 2 ff.   [b] ἱκανὸν εἶναι τὰ τῆς πόλεως πράττειν.
[c] *Meno* 73 C 9.   [d] *Meno* 77 B 4.   [e] *Meno* 78 C 1.

dialogue, essentially well-meaning, readily admits that *dikaiosune* is *an arete*—though only when the point is put to him by Socrates—and that when he says 'the power to obtain *agatha*', he means the power of doing so in a pious and just manner, *hosiōs* and *dikaiōs*.[a] Any sober citizen will doubtless admit this when prodded by a Socrates, and doubtless (with the reservations made below) act upon it in practice, in his relations with his fellow citizens, despite the pleas which are offered in the courts; but the priority of the values which commend 'the individual in efficient action' is abundantly clear.

One reservation must be made at once. It is evident that, not merely in the rough and tumble of the courts, but also in the more reflective surroundings depicted in the earlier dialogues, the ordinary man's conception of the 'good citizen' is inadequately 'civic'. The *agathos polites* is expected to help his friends and harm his enemies within the city: thus his primary loyalties are *overtly* to a group smaller than the state, in the last resort to his own family.

This fact increases the dangers inherent in the idea of justice as a means to an end, for it multiplies the occasions on which the standard of *dikaiosune* as administered—in theory—in the courts may clash with the standard of *arete*. There can be few if any more convincing portraits of the ordinary decent Athenian than Plato's portrait of Crito. No man could be further from being a sophist, much less an immoralist sophist. Accordingly, his advice to Socrates in prison is interesting. Crito's opinion of Socrates' refusal to escape from prison when he has the chance is quite clear:[b] he regards Socrates' action as self-betrayal.[c] Socrates claims to have practised *arete* all his life. Well, surely a man who is *agathos* and brave, *andreios*, as Socrates thus claims to be, will choose to live and protect his children, rather than let them suffer the unhappy fate of orphans. Further, if Socrates does not escape, Crito fears that others may believe that this was the result of some cowardice and unmanliness, *kakia* and *anandriā*, on the part of Crito and Socrates' other friends; which would of course be *aischron* for them. Put into the mouth of Crito, these words can only represent ordinary Greek values.

These standards are, in one sense, not surprising, in view of what has been said in previous chapters. We are here given a

---

[a] Plat. *Meno* 78 D 4 ff.   [b] Plato *Crito* 45 C 5 ff.   [c] σαυτὸν προδοῦναι, 45 C 6.

glimpse, unusual as a result of the nature of our sources, of the ordinary Athenian paterfamilias in relation to other heads of families and to the state.[a] It may appear surprising, in a state allegedly governed by law, that the *agathos* should be expected to be courageous, *andreios*, in resisting that law, and that it should be represented as cowardice, *anandria*, to comply with the law in certain circumstances. There is really no cause for surprise: the actions commended by *agathos* in other contexts are pre-eminently those involving physical courage; and, if there is a typical form of behaviour for the *agathos* within the city, it is not unreasonable that it should be valued in the same terms by an ordinary man such as Crito. To express this in terms of *andreios* and *anandria* is simply to say the same thing more explicitly, for to call a man *andreios* is to say of him that he is a true *anēr*, man, and hence *agathos*.

If this passage is added to the others, the concept of *agathos* and *arete* which, at the end of the fifth century, the ordinary man possessed, is clear. It has been seen that the *agathos polites* 'administers well' his city and his own household, both in an efficient sense. Whether called *agathos polites* or *agathos*, he is a self-sufficient unit, able to defend both himself and his friends, and harm his enemies; as a paterfamilias, able to protect his children, his property, and his wife; and when it is threatened by an external enemy, able to defend his city. The city's claims *may* override others in times of stress;[16] but where the city's interests are not threatened, or seem irrelevant to the case in hand, there is nothing in these standards of value to prevent the *agathos polites* from attempting to thwart the laws of the city on behalf of his family and friends, with whom he has closer ties.[17] That Socrates was unjustly condemned is irrelevant; taking Meno's 'ordinary language' definitions, and the balance of *dikaiosune* and *arete* throughout earlier Greek, it is clear that Crito was bound to urge Socrates to save himself, *qua agathos* and *andreios*, whether he believed Socrates to have been wrongly condemned or no. The question after all is: 'Must the householder be just—either in the sense of general quiet morality or in the sense of 'obedient to the laws'—in order to be prosperous? Where it seems as evident as in this case that the prosperity of the family depends directly on being disobedient to the laws,

[a] Cp. also *Tetralogies* Aa 8, p. 109, n. 14.

to be disobedient to the laws is simply to act in accordance with the generally accepted scale of values. Hence Crito's difficulty in seeing the point of Socrates' refusal.

It may well be asked whether Crito and Meno are different kinds of 'ordinary man', since Crito, while evidently agreeing with Meno that *arete* is 'the power to obtain *agatha*', here evidently refuses to add 'in a pious and just manner'. There is no reason to suppose this. Meno only adds 'in a pious and just manner' when pressed to do so by Socrates. Being a well-meaning man, he doubtless believes that he would act on this. He is, however, treating *arete* in the abstract; and even here the priority of 'success', the provision of 'good things', is clear. Crito is faced with an urgent practical problem; and in such cases the essentials of a system of values appear. Meno and Crito could very well exist in the same skin, since the apparent illogicality of their position, such as it is, is precisely the illogicality of the ordinary man, especially in a turmoil of values such as exists at this period.

C. THE IMMORALIST, AT HOME AND ABROAD

It is in the light of the values of the 'ordinary Athenian' that the position of the 'immoralists' must be examined, for it is only in this light that the true nature of the 'immoralist' position, and its full strength, can be appreciated. We meet these 'immoralists', sophists or pupils of sophists, as opponents of Socrates in some of the earlier dialogues of Plato, where they are characterized by their ruthless self-seeking and their claims that injustice is a preferable course of action to justice. These claims are frequently expressed in terms of the distinction between *phusis*, nature, and *nomos*, convention, which has already been mentioned.[a] So in the *Gorgias*, Callicles says[b]

By nature, *phusei*, everything is more shameful, *aischion*, which is also more harmful (to oneself), *kakion*, that is to say suffering injustice; but by convention, *nomōi*, committing injustice is more shameful. For to suffer injustice is not an experience which befits a man, but one fit only for a slave for whom death is preferable to life; a man who when he is wronged and insulted is incapable of helping either himself or anyone else for whom he cares.

[a] Above, p. 187 f. and Chapter IX, Note 21.   [b] Plat. *Gorg.* 483 A 7 ff.

Later, referring to the man who, lacking the devices of rhe-toric, is unable to defend himself skilfully in court,[a] Callias asks Socrates[b]

Do you think, Socrates, that a man who is thus situated in a city, and is unable to help himself, is 'honourably', *kalōs*, situated?

Again, in the *Republic*,[c] it is the nub of Thrasymachus' argument that to act unjustly is to be more powerful, more worthy of being called a free man and a master over others, than is to act justly: the just man may be unable to defend himself and his family, which is *aischron*. The unjust man is more independent and self-sufficient.

The great strength of this position should be evident. The 'immoralists' are claiming to be acting in accordance with the standards of 'real', as opposed to conventional, *arete*; and this *arete* is precisely that traditional *arete* which, as the case of Crito demonstrates, is still the standard on which the ordinary Greek relies in a crisis. No Greek of this period or of any earlier period—no Greek whom we have yet considered, at all events[d] —could deny the primacy of the need to be free, self-sufficient, and able to defend oneself, one's family, and one's friends. The situation in which he lived guaranteed his attitude. Nor is it only the end which is agreed. Even if, as a member of a mer-cantile state should, the ordinary Athenian agrees that honesty is the best policy, not infrequently there will be occasions when it seems more conducive to independence and self-defence to be unjust than to be just. Crito was acting, if not in accordance with the highest standards available at the time, certainly according to the prevailing and most deeply rooted ones.

Thus, with the best will in the world, any Greek of this period was bound to find it very difficult to confute the 'immoralists'. Exhortation was useless; for the 'immoralists' and the power-politicians had plausibly pre-empted the most valued terms; and as the views of Crito and Callicles have shown, ordinary

---

[a] In the Athenian courts, the free citizen had to defend himself, though he might have his speech composed for him by a professional speech-writer.

[b] Plat. *Gorg.* 522 c 4 ff.   [c] Plat. *Rep.* 344 c.

[d] That one should not score unjust victories over others was accepted by the 'moralizers' of Chapter IX. That one should accept 'defeat'—in the courts or elsewhere—in the interests of justice is doubtless a corollary, but one that has not yet been faced. For Socrates' position, cp. Chapter XIII, pp. 260 ff.

man and immoralist would often agree on the exact interpretation of those terms, not merely on their general flavour. Plato
was to offer an answer; but to realize the seriousness of the
problem it is only necessary to consider Athens' foreign policy.
That there was an opposition foreign policy, at all events until
the ostracism of Thucydides son of Melesias, seems clear:[18] there
were those who did not wish Athens to prosper at the expense of
her subject-allies. We may indicate the manner in which this
policy may have been expressed by repeating the Corinthian
complaint against the Corcyreans, discussed in Chapter IX:[a]

If they were *agathoi*, as they claim to be, the less they could be
assailed by their neighbours, the more clearly could they have
displayed their *arete*, by giving and receiving what was just, *dikaion*.

The Athenians might have displayed *arete* in the same way
towards their subject-allies. As was said in Chapter IX, however, such a use of *agathos* and *arete* has no relation to traditional
standards, but is part of the new 'quiet' use of these terms there
discussed. That there should be *dikaiosune* between travellers and
the states or households which they visit is an expectation as old
as Homer;[b] but quietly not wronging a man or a group has not
been commended as *arete* till now.

Such a violent change of usage was bound to cause difficulties. This was shown to some extent in Chapter IX; but it is
only now that the weakness of the new *arete*-standard can be
fully demonstrated. The Corcyreans, the Corinthians complain,
consult their own interests at the expense of others. This is
precisely the policy of Athens; and the manner in which Pericles
characterizes those who vainly advocated an alternative policy
displays its strength. In his last speech, in an Athens ravaged by
plague, he says of the Empire:[c]

You may not abdicate from your ruling position—supposing that
anyone at this time out of fear wishes to play the *agathos* by remaining
inactive, *apragmosunēi andragathizesthai*. You hold your empire in the
guise of a tyranny, which it may be unjust, *adikon*, to obtain, but is
dangerous to relinquish.

The ordinary man will not be dismayed by the thought that he
possesses a tyranny, 'prosperous injustice', *adikiān eudaimona*;[19]

[a] Above, p. 178.   [b] Cp. Chapter IV, pp. 65 ff.
[c] Thuc. ii. 63. 2.

for prosperity, *eudaimoniā*, is what he wants, and it is only 'wretched' to be the *subject* of a tyrant. He will certainly not adopt the opposing view, that of peace and justice: for Pericles has characterized this by *apragmosunēi andragathizesthai*, one of the most outrageous oxymora possible in Greek. *Dikaiosune* is a quiet, co-operative virtue; accordingly, Pericles terms it *apragmosune*, inactivity. *Andragathiā*, on the other hand, as may be seen from Herodotus[a] and from the sense of *agathos* throughout earlier Greek, in its traditional usage entails courage, daring, and initiative, and may stand as a synonym for *arete*. To characterize the new standard of *arete* in such a manner as to indicate that it violates the old standard in every detail is to pour scorn on it with a demagogy so brilliant that the position could not for a moment stand against it. The phrase, however, merely brings the difficulty into sharp focus; it is in fact a difficulty so serious that it must be felt at every attempt to use *agathos* or *arete* in the new manner.

D. THE DANGERS OF AGREEMENT

The 'immoralists', the politicians, and the 'ordinary Athenians', then, are agreed on their basic values. They disagree only on the point at which *adikia* becomes a better means to the desired end than *dikaiosune*. This in itself creates a problem which Plato might well have felt the need to try to solve; and the problem was to grow even more acute before Plato inherited it. For its values, revealed as clearly in Thucydides and Lysias as in the earlier dialogues of Plato, the Athenian democracy paid in blood. The values by which the democracy could justify its rule over the Empire, the idea of the *agathos* as the man—or the state—capable of ruling over others, furnished equal justification for the actions of the Thirty Tyrants, and for those of the much milder Five Thousand. Callicles the 'democrat'[20] in the *Gorgias*, Thrasymachus in the *Republic*,[b] both commend *pleonexiā*, the grasping for more, in the *agathos*. Here too traditional values are on their side: to be *agathos* does give a man a claim to preferential treatment, the treatment of the

[a] Cp. Hdt. i. 99, 136, iv. 65, v. 39, vi. 128, vii. 166.
[b] Plat. *Gorg.* 483 c 2, *Rep.* 344 A 1, &c.

Homeric kings.[a] In the law-courts, as has been seen, it gives him
a claim more powerful than that of strict justice, at all events
now that justice has lost its divine sanctions; while in the state it
wins him 'honour', *time*, a *time* which will not necessarily consist
merely in being well spoken of, but may well bring him more
tangible advantages.

None of this is opposed to traditional values; but the situation in Athens made traditional values peculiarly dangerous at
this time. The old *agathoi*, the hoplites and the cavalry, were,
in Athens' maritime democracy, no longer the most valuable
fighting force in the state. Especially since the débâcle of
Coronea and the consequent abandonment of a policy of empire in mainland Greece, the navy sufficed to hold down
Athens' subjects, and keep the seas clear for her imports of
food. The Long Walls made Athens virtually an island; and
Pericles' strategy of treating her as such, as the course of the
war made clear, left the hoplites and cavalry little to do but
watch from those walls while the enemy burned their farm-
steads at leisure. The situation would have caused frustration
and resentment in any society; in a society holding traditional
Greek standards, it removed from the traditional *agathoi* the
fundamental grounds of their claim to be *agathoi*. If to this be
added the fact that, as often as the interests of the hoplites and
cavalry were opposed to those of the 'naval mob', they must
have been in a minority, the hidden strains set up in Athens
can be imagined.

In such a situation, these classes must have searched for new
grounds to justify their continuing to regard themselves as
agathoi. Theognis has been seen, in similar circumstances, going
through the same evolutions. The identification of *dikaiosune*
with *kalokāgathiā*, the qualities of a gentleman, in Xenophon,[b]
and some, though by no means all, of the usages discussed in
Chapter IX, may have been made easier by this desire:[21]
Theognis came to roughly the same conclusion.[c] If, however, a
justification more in keeping with traditional values could be
found, there would certainly be some to accept it. The answer
was found in the new skill of the sophists, the *techne* which gave
a man the claim that he possessed political *arete*, the quality of

[a] Cp. Chapter III, pp. 34 ff.   [b] See below, p. 337.
[c] Above, p. 78.

the *agathos polites*. The rich men's sons had more leisure to
listen to sophists, and the money to pay them. They were thus
in the best position to acquire this *arete*; they must have considered themselves the ruling class by right; and at the end of
the Peloponnesian War it was evident that the democracy had
bungled matters, that it had *not* preserved the stability and
prosperity of the state, that it was deficient in *arete*. The Thirty
might well regard themselves as more capable of ruling, *hikanō-
teroi archein*, than the democracy which had brought Athens to
ignominious defeat; and the democracy itself had taught them
to what ends rule should be turned. The democracy squealed,
as democracies will; but it is difficult to see what cause it had
for complaint.[22] With the possible exception of situations in
which the success of the city as a whole against a foreign enemy
is in question, to be *agathos*, as the *Crito* and *Meno* demonstrate,
is to work for the prosperity of oneself, one's family, and one's
friends. To fail is *aischron*, as Crito insists to Socrates; and a
passage in Aeschines[a] underlines the point. One of the consequences imprecated upon those who break their vow to
guarantee the Plain of Cirrha[23] is that they should suffer

Defeat . . . in war, in the courts, and in the assembly.

The cases are treated as parallel; and if this is so, then, since
defeat in war is *aischron*, so is defeat whether in the courts or in
the assembly. This being so, there is the strongest inducement
to wipe out this disgrace *by whatever means*, unless some even
stronger deterrent can be found.

These values not only lead inevitably to revolution: they commend it, to any person or group which finds itself continually
worsted in political life. If a man sees no hope of turning the
tables on the stronger party, he may howl for justice; but if he
sees any opportunity of wiping out this *aischron*, he will surely
take it; and the tables once turned, what reason has he to be
just himself, if the gods care nothing whether he is just or no,
and it is *kalon* to seek one's own interest and that of one's
friends? Protagoras[b] may commend justice to a whole state, to
ensure its continued existence; he may relate myths which
maintain that injustice leads inevitably to political upheaval
and civic disintegration; but, like Tyrtaeus[c] in urging the men

[a] Aeschin. *In Ctes.* 111.   [b] Plat. *Prot.* 322 A ff.   [c] Tyrtaeus 10 Bergk.

of Sparta to war, he must show that it is not merely *kalon*, and advantageous to the city in general, that a man should fight and not run away in the one case, and be just in the other, but also that *personal* disadvantage is much more likely, or preferably inevitable, if one runs away or commits injustice. Tyrtaeus proved his point fairly easily. Protagoras had a much more difficult problem, which Plato was to spend a lifetime trying to answer.

What has happened is evident. Though Plato never names the disease in so many words, he prescribes the cure, or at least the first-aid precautions, accurately enough in *Republic* ii and iii when he attacks Homer. Homeric values have returned; or rather, since the basic framework of Homeric values has persisted unchanged, these values have been stripped of their accretions: the long-lived accretion of belief in divine retribution, the recent one of quiet moral *aretai*. This being so, the values of the *Iliad* remain, naked and unashamed. Scratch Thrasymachus and you find King Agamemnon. The system of values which worked quite satisfactorily in the loosely knit Homeric society has prevailed, and is now forced into the foreground, in the much more closely integrated civic society of Athens. The 'ordinary Athenian' Crito in advising Socrates to resist the law finds himself in exactly the same position as the 'ordinary Heroes' in *Iliad* xxiii[a] in attempting to apportion the prizes and settle the disputes after the chariot race. Races, to be run, need rules; states, to function satisfactorily, need laws. In both cases there must be co-operation, agreement to abide by the rules even to one's own detriment. Yet the most important values by which both Crito and the Homeric Heroes direct their lives are not co-operative but competitive ones. Only confusion can result; and ultimately the situation of *Odyssey* xxiv must be reached: where Odysseus, having killed the suitors for the sake of his *arete*,[24] because it would be *aischron* not to do so, faces the relatives of the suitors, who must attack him, because it would be *aischron* for them not to do so, and whom Odysseus must resist, because it would be *aischron* for him not to do so. A struggle, as Homer says,[b] must have resulted had not Athena appeared in person and settled their differences: a

a Cp. Chapter III, p. 56.
b *Odyssey* xxiv. 528.

solution which the Athenians of the fifth and fourth centuries were never fortunate enough to experience.

The problem is inevitable, once these values have returned unopposed; but it is not a moral problem, in the sense of a problem created by a wilful abandonment of standards acknowledged to be the highest. The problem results directly from the rejection of the belief in divine retribution, and the consequent disappearance of the checks on the competitive values; and to find oneself unable any longer to hold a belief is not a sign of moral turpitude. In such a situation, moral suasion is useless, for such suasion can only expect success if it uses the most powerful terms of value. The 'immoralist' and the ordinary man already use these terms to justify their own actions; and mere suasion can hardly hope to deprive them of such terms, in face of the awful plausibility of their position.

The influence of this situation on moral responsibility is clear. In life in general, as in the courts, the requisite questions can still not usefully be asked, for actions are evaluated primarily in terms of a system of values which raises only questions of success and failure.

The problem is serious; but as a result of its very nature it contains the seeds of a solution. In the hands of a Protagoras[a] political *arete* may be a skill turned to civic ends, even if the idea contains confusions which entail the whole problem of this chapter, for Protagoras is depicted as a well-meaning sophist; a Meno[b] may hold, with Protagoras, that *dikaiosune* is essential to the efficient exercise of that skill, even if the case of Crito proves that he could not adhere to this opinion in a crisis; a Callicles or a Thrasymachus may believe that *dikaiosune* is merely an impediment to its exercise. *But it remains a skill*: and for the exercise of any skill certain minimal standards are necessary. Callicles and Thrasymachus are immoralists in a sense, but they are in no sense nihilists. There are standards which they cannot and will not abandon, for they are the basis of their claim to be *agathoi*, and hence to do what they do. Thrasymachus has been criticized when, in *Republic* i,[c] he does not 'slip out into an easy nihilism', a position which by its very nature is incapable of logical refutation, but instead, by insisting

---

[a] Plat. *Prot.* 318 E ff., cp. p. 227 and footnote.   [b] Cp. pp. 228 f.
[c] Plat. *Rep.* i. 340 B 4 ff.

on the expert status of the ruler, allows Plato to refute his position at least to Plato's own satisfaction. He does not slip out into an easy nihilism for the sufficient reason that he and his kind are not nihilists.[25] They have standards; and in the existence of these standards, on which they and the ordinary man are agreed, lies the hope of a solution. Anyone who accepts standards of any kind must also accept any results which can be shown to follow from their acceptance. Thus Plato, or any other moralist, has a basis upon which he may attempt to erect his proofs of the necessity of the co-operative virtues to individual and civic well-being. The task is a difficult one; but at least there is a point from which to begin.

The standards accepted are the traditional ones, the standards of Homer; but as a result of the thought and practice of intervening periods many words and phrases unknown to Homer have come to be attached to this system. Before considering the successive Platonic attempts to solve the problem of relating *dikaiosune* to the competitive *aretai*, it will be necessary to set out and explain some of these phrases; and this will be the task of the next chapter.

NOTES TO CHAPTER XI

1. On this topic, and for a discussion of Thucydides' values in general, cp. Shorey, *On the Implicit Ethics and Psychology of Thucydides*, TAPA 24, pp. 66 ff.; J. de Romilly, *Thucydide et l'impérialisme athénien, passim*; and Grene, *Man in his Pride*, pp. 24 ff.

2. On *euboulia*, cp. Sinclair, op. cit., p. 37.

3. Cp. esp. ii. 62. 3, 'and it is more *aischron* to be deprived of an empire when one already possesses it than to fail in obtaining it in the first place', ii. 63. 1, 'the *time* which we derive from our rule,' and above all ii. 64. 3, where the immortal memory of Athens, even should she fail, is to be sustained by the fact that she ruled over more Greeks than any other Greek city at any time. These remarks are precisely the same in tone as those of Cleon and Diodotus, and depend on the same scale of values.

4. Possibly not wholly for this reason. The assembly, being also the members of the juries, may have felt that they had a vested interest in the matter. On this topic see Thuc. i. 77. 1, and Gomme, *Thucydides*, ad loc.

5. Aristophanes' joke, *Eccles.* 982 ff., is presumably based upon real delays in the courts; it is not merely an allusion to the age of the Hags.

6. G. E. M. de Ste.-Croix, *The Character of the Athenian Empire*, Historia iii, pp. 1 ff.

7. Cp. Grene, op. cit., p. 43.

8. This is the scale of values on which the Melians naturally fall back, Thuc. v. 100, as their chief reason for not submitting tamely to Athens' rule. The Athenians, v. 101, attempt to suggest that for a smaller state safety is more important than freedom, but traditional values are on the side of the Melians. Cp. also Diodotus' words, iii. 46. 5: he regards it as 'only to be expected' that a state which was once free and is governed by force should attempt to regain its freedom at the first favourable opportunity.

9. The original proposal for the disposal of the silver, Hdt. vii. 144—that it should be divided amongst the adult male citizens—indicates the simple nature of Athenian finances before the days of the League.

10. It is presumably for this reason that *dikaiosune* appears to the Athenians —to those, that is, who value it—at this period to be a skill, a *techne*. (At all events, Plato considers no other possibilities.) As may be seen from the fifth book of the *Nicomachean Ethics*, the word *dikaiosune* brings readily to mind the thought of just distribution and just decision, from the point of view of the person making the decision (*E.N.* 1131ᵃ10 ff.). In such circumstances, particularly in the case of a state facing such baffling problems as was Athens, so much more than good will is needed that good will may seem, particularly to those who are theorizing on the subject, comparatively unimportant. Anyone who thought seriously about the organization of the Athenian Empire must have seen *dikaiosune* in the light of these unprecedented problems.

11. After all, though Socrates maintains in the *Apology*, 19 D ff., that he does not *teach*, his reason for testing the *arete* of those who claim to possess it is to ensure that the *psuche* of others is as *agathe* as possible, 29 E. His mission, he believes, is to persuade others to practise *arete*, 31 B, and his *arete* is related to, and justified by, the same considerations as everyone else's. All other good things, *agatha*, both for the individual and for the state, come from *arete*, 30 B: that is to say, the quiet virtues— for of course Socrates' *arete* includes the quiet virtues—are related to *eudaimonia*, the most satisfactory condition for a man, (as a matter of faith) in the manner of Chapter X.

12. On this topic cp. Sinclair, op. cit., pp. 55 ff.

13. Traditional values are based from Homer onwards on the assumption that the household is virtually autonomous, cp. Crito's words on p. 230.

14. Cp. Eur. *Electra* 360 ff., discussed in Chapters IX and X. The relation of justice to the desired end is the same, but Meno—though he admits that justice is *an arete*, 73 D 9—is far from holding that the man who is poor but self-controlled should be termed *agathos* on this account.

15. The apparent exclusion of men from domestic economics is not adhered to elsewhere, cp. *Protagoras* 318 E ff., quoted above.

16. They *may* override other claims, but generally held values by no means entail this. We have seen, pp. 223 f., that in the Athenian Empire one's friends—whom one helped—might readily belong to another state, one's enemies—whom one wished to damage—to one's own; and the narrative of the closing stages of the Peloponnesian War, Xen. *Hell.*

ii, suggests the same conclusion. Earlier, Aristides the Just had preferred to defend his city, Hdt. viii. 79, though the words which Herodotus puts into his mouth seem to derive from later thought; cp. also the offer of Cimon at Tanagra, Plutarch, *Cimon*, 17. 3. The career of Alcibiades is the most prominent example of a man who did not put his city's interests before those of his friends. From our standpoint, such action may seem base; but given Greek terms of value the priority of the city's claim is not self-evident. (On this topic cp. Pusey, *Alcibiades and* τὸ φιλόπολι, Harvard Studies in Classical Philology, 1940, pp. 215 ff.)

17. Plato's desire to abolish the family in the ruling classes of the *Republic* presumably derives in part from these ineradicable associations of *arete* in the Greek state as normally organized.

18. Thucydides was ostracized in 444/3 B.C. The manner in which Pericles speaks seems to indicate that there was some opposition even in the early years of the Peloponnesian War, but that—except in times of general despair, such as that which followed the plague—such opposition was inconsiderable. Certainly no prominent man supported the allies' cause after Thucydides' ostracism. (In Plutarch, *Pericles* 12, Thucydides and his supporters are represented as opposing the popular plan of building temples in Athens with the allies' tribute: 'Athens had no right to deck herself with thousand-talent temples.')

19. The words *adikian eudaimona* appear in Eur. *Phoenissae* 549. The words are used by Iocasta as a disparagement of tyranny, but given the alignment of Greek values there seems no possibility of disparagement in these terms having any effect, since *eudaimonia* is a term so much more powerful than *adikia*. At 557, Iocasta says that the gods may take this prosperity away as they gave it, which is a much more powerful threat; but, apart from the general fading of belief in divine retribution, we have to remember that it was generally believed that it was possible —and for the tyrant especially possible—to purchase the goodwill of the gods by sacrifice, cp. pp. 134 f. Line 549 is thus another instance of the —abortive—'moralism' discussed in Chapter IX.

With *apragmosunēi andragathizesthai* cp. Cleon's *ek tou akindūnou andragathizesthai*, Thuc. iii. 40. 4, 'to play the *agathos* in safety'—another oxymoron, for traditional *arete* always involves risks. The occurrence of *andragathizesthai* to make just this point in these two passages, and only here in literature of comparable date, suggests that the word was coined, whether by Thucydides or the power-politicians, for this particular purpose.

On this topic, cp. de Romilly, op. cit., p. 143.

20. I term Callicles a 'democrat' on the basis of *Gorgias* 481 D 4 ff., and the gibe about Callicles' attitude to the assembly which there accompanies it. Callicles presented himself to the assembly as a democrat: that his real values are such as we should term 'undemocratic' is far from surprising, since Chapter X has shown that even the courts, whose juries were democratic in intent, made use of values highly undemocratic in practice.

21. Reasons are given for the identification in Xenophon, *Symposium* 3. 4,

for it is always best to be able to justify one's usages, but cp. the other passages cited in Chapter XVI, pp. 337 f., and Chapter X, p. 198 above.

22. On this topic, cp. Sinclair, op. cit., p. 74.

23. The curse dates from the time of Solon, Aeschin. *In Ctes.* 108, but we have seen nothing to suggest that popular values had changed even in the time of Aeschines.

24. The justification of the pre-eminence of *agathos* is seen in *Odyssey* xxiv. The suitors were unjust, certainly; but when Antinous' father Eupeithes says that Odysseus took away with him many *esthloi*—all of whom he has lost by war or shipwreck—and now on his return he has killed the *aristoi* of the Cephallenians, Halitherses and Medon, stress the crimes of the suitors as they will, can do nothing to outbid Eupeithes' evaluation of the matter. Odysseus himself acknowledges the basis of these values in xxiii. 121: 'We have slain the bulwark of the city—the *aristoi* of the youths of Ithaca,' on whom its defence might have rested. For this act there can be no justification from the mere fact that justice was on his side.

25. On the 'non-nihilism' of Thrasymachus, cp. Kerferd, 'The Doctrine of Thrasymachus in Plato's Republic,' *Durham University Journal*, December 1947.

XII

GROUND FOR AGREEMENT

A. INTRODUCTION

THE general shape which the moral theory of Plato had of necessity to take is now evident. In order, however, to make clearer the analysis of some of his arguments, which will be the task of the next chapter, it is convenient first briefly to record the key terms used in these arguments, the group of values, competitive or co-operative, to which they belong, and the extent to which they are valued, or not, by all. This is necessary, since certain of the phrases used by Plato have a misleading resemblance to certain other phrases used in modern English/ European values; and any tendency to identify the two, as frequently happens in translation, leads naturally to the transformation of an argument which is not particularly uplifting but ruthlessly logical[a] into an argument which, though admirably moral, contains admissions and statements which no one would reasonably make in the position being defended.

The most highly prized terms may be divided, for convenience of exposition, into those which commend the type of man most highly valued and those which commend the type of life such a man will lead.

B. THE MOST HIGHLY VALUED MAN

To take first the man himself: it has been shown that the *arete* of the *agathos* or *agathos polites* of the late fifth century is a skill, a *techne*. In view of the emphasis on success, this has always been true in a sense;[1] but the codification of the knowledge required, so far as the sophists had succeeded in doing this, forces this aspect into the foreground. It is only to be expected that some more particularizing adjective than *agathos* will be current to commend those who display such skill. This adjective is *phronimos*: a word which, though not now coined for the first

---

[a] In intention, at all events; but cp. Chapter XIII.

time,[2] is, from the time of the composition of the earlier dialogues of Plato, or rather that of the first appearance of the thought which these dialogues reflect, used as a term to define the *agathos*. Since all men prize political skill, it is not surprising to find that all men prize the adjective *phronimos*, which may be rendered 'intelligent in practical matters', and define such virtues as they approve in terms of the noun *phronēsis*, the intelligent handling of one's own interests, however conceived. So in the *Laches*,[a] Laches readily agrees that courage, *andreiā*, is endurance accompanied by *phronesis*; and in the *Protagoras*[b] Protagoras assents to a similar position. Admittedly when in the *Laches*, a few pages after the earlier passage quoted,[c] Nicias refuses to call children or animals brave on the grounds that they are not *phronimoi*, Laches accuses him of deserting ordinary language, and Socrates says that he must have been listening to the hair-splitting sophist Prodicus; but it is difficult to see why Laches should object, since Nicias' view follows directly from the agreed definition of *andreia* already given: and in fact no one seriously attempts to sustain the opposite view at this period.[d]

The *To Nicocles* of Isocrates[e] shows clearly the relation between *phronimos* and political skill. Isocrates regards it as monstrous that the worse, *cheirous*, should rule the better, *beltious*, and amplifies this by

And that the more foolish should give orders to those who are more *phronimoi*.

This use of *agathos*, to which *phronimos* is so closely linked, like all other uses from Homer onwards, expresses a strong claim for preferential treatment.

The 'immoralist' practitioners of the political art naturally agree in their valuation of *phronimos*. The resolute 'immoralist' Callicles says in the *Gorgias*[f]

By better, *beltious*, I do not mean shoemakers or cooks, but those who are *phronimoi* in that they know how the affairs of the city would be well managed, *eu oikein*, and not only *phronimoi* but also manly, *andreioi*, being (thereby) capable, *hikanoi*, of carrying out in

[a] Plat. *Lach.* 192 c, cp. Gorgias frag. 6 D/K.
[b] Plat. *Prot.* 350 B.   [c] Plat. *Lach.* 197 A.
[d] When theorizing, that is; for this is of course a departure from ordinary language.
[e] *To Nicoc.* 14.   [f] Plat. *Gorg.* 491 A 7 ff.

action the plans they form; men who will not grow weary from 'softness of spirit'.

Many of the key ideas appear in this passage; and from it the high position of *phronimos* is clear. A man may be induced to abandon his claim that the stronger[a] is the *agathos* by the ridiculous consequences which such a proposition can be shown to generate;[3] but it is only to amend 'stronger' to 'more *phronimos*'; and this position he will not abandon. Here accordingly is a term, non-moral but entailing certain standards, on whose high value all are agreed; a term which, as a result, Plato can usefully employ in moral argument.

In such circumstances, it is likely that other words which denote intellectual virtues will be highly valued; for example *sophos*, wise. That 'wisdom' should be interpreted in practical terms is natural, for there exists as yet no corpus of abstract thought sufficiently large to demand the exclusive use of such a word; and that it should be non-morally interpreted is hardly surprising. Indeed, it may be sharply opposed to moral terms, as in the Philoctetes.[b] To Odysseus'

Neither what you say nor what you have a mind to do is *sophon*,

Neoptolemus replies

But if it is *dikaion*, this is better than *sophon*.

It should not be concluded from this passage that *dikaios* is really valued more highly than *sophos*. The lines are an instance of the abortive 'moralism' discussed in Chapter IX. Sophocles, in attempting to exalt the claims of *dikaiosune* above those of *sophia*, was attempting to resist 'immoralism' by persuasion and exhortation. That the attempt failed is clear from the last two chapters. Indeed, *sophos* is in effect a synonym for *phronimos* at this time, as the following words of Menelaus[c] indicate:

If I do not set my affairs in the best order possible, I am an incompetent and no *sophos*.

Sophos naturally shares the high position of *phronimos*, and thus this term too may prove useful to Plato.[4]

Sophrosune is differently situated. From the days of Homer

---

[a] ἰσχυρότερος. [b] S. *Phil.* 1246 f.
[c] E. *Androm.* 378 f.; and for *sophia* used of practical skill, cp. (Plato) *Theages* 126 D, p. 226 above.

prudence in one's own interests has been commended as *sao-phron*.[5] This prudence may entail the quieter virtues, and yet *sophrosune* not be a moral word; but it had by this time become so much attached to the practice of such virtues, even from the most prudential of motives, that it seems less likely *a priori* that this word should prove attractive to the 'immoralists'. It is, after all, such men as Bellerophon and Hippolytus who are *sophron* in the moral usage of the term; and no 'immoralist' wanted to imitate them. Nor would one expect the ordinary man to value *sophrosune* very highly: the normal use of *arete* does not readily bring *sophrosune* to mind. Yet *sophrosune* is also directly opposed to the state of madness, and further, both in mercantile contexts and elsewhere, is used to commend 'shrewdness', when it seems closely to approach the sense of the valued *phronimos*. In Herodotus[a] it is said to be more *sophron* for the seven conspirators against the Magian usurper to associate more men with the plot in the interests of success. It is here opposed to acting *aboulōs*, without due consideration; and clearly there can be no vestige of quiet morals in such a usage.

Of course this division, like others made elsewhere, answers to nothing real in the material. The use of *sophron* in all these instances reflects one general world-view; but it might appear that too much of the flavour of the quiet virtues adhered to this word to make it of interest to the 'immoralist', and hence to Plato in his attack on the 'immoralist' position.

This seems in fact to be the case. *Sophron* may belong to the most highly prized group of values. In the *Protagoras*[b] the following exchange takes place between Socrates and the sophist:

Socrates: Do you think that some men *sophronein* in committing injustice?
Protagoras: Agreed.
Socrates: And you mean by *sophronein* '*eu phronein*', 'reason well'?
Protagoras: I do.
Socrates: And by *eu phronein* '*eu bouleuesthai*', 'come to a sound conclusion', in committing injustice?
Protagoras: Agreed.
Socrates: Is this the case if they fare well, *eu prattein*, in committing injustice, or if they fare badly?
Protagoras: If they fare well.

[a] Hdt. iii. 71. 3.   [b] Plat. *Prot.* 333 D, cp. *Charm.* 171 D.

Here, since Socrates couples *sophronein* by simple agreement with *eu phronein* and *eu prattein*, both highly valued[a] and both used to commend the individual in efficient action, it is evident that *sophronein* is similarly valued and similarly used, and hence belongs to the same group of terms as *agathos* and *phronimos*. In the *Gorgias*,[b] however, Socrates constructs an argument to *prove* to Callicles that the *sophron psuche* is the *agathe psuche*.[c] If it is necessary to prove this, the words evidently belong to different groups of terms. *Agathe psuche* is highly valued; accordingly, *sophron psuche* is not.

The character of the people concerned in these passages is highly significant. Protagoras, himself an advocate of *dikaiosune*, espouses the cause of injustice, in the sense in which the ordinary man is wont to see the matter, for the sake of argument; whereas Callicles is the complete immoralist. The ordinary man is, to judge from Crito, just or unjust as suits his own—modest—interests, and is supported in this behaviour by the system of values he finds current. He finds himself a citizen with others in a state, men whom he either has no desire to exploit as individuals,[6] or knows at all events that he has little chance of treating in such a manner. For such a man 'prudence' is naturally an important idea. The 'immoralist' and self-styled practical politician, however, feels no need of prudence. He is 'able to get what he wants', as Callicles in effect said above; so why should he be prudent? To be *phronimos* may be to be thrusting and bold, if the situation calls for such action: the associations of *sophron* are far too quiet. This word, then, in a sense distinguishes the practice of the ordinary man and the 'immoralist', whose chief aims and values coincide; and for this very reason it is of much less use to Plato in moral argument, for it has no constant value.

The *agathe psuche*, the possession of 'good' qualities of character, is another desirable. Though the idea of having a 'good' *psuche* is not new, it gains new importance at this time from the great emphasis laid on the distinction between *psuche* and *soma*, body,[7] and also from the use which Plato is able to make of this distinction in argument.[d] If one has a *psuche*, it is clearly in one's interest to have a 'good' one, since it is natural to want everything one possesses to be *agathos*, good of its kind. The phrase will naturally behave in the same manner as *agathos* and *arete*, and commend the—psychological—qualities of the type of man favoured by the speaker; accordingly, there is no reason to suppose *a priori* that *agathe psuche* will have a quiet moral flavour. So in Aeschylus the phrase '*aristos* in respect of one's *psuche*' is used of being courageous, and *kake psuche* decries the cowardice of Aegisthus.[a] These are the standards of traditional *arete*; and so naturally Callicles—who, as an 'immoralist', is a traditionalist—defines the type of man he admires as one who can carry out his purposes without having to give up through 'softness'—*malakiā*, a near-synonym for *kakia* when used of a man— of his *psuche*. Accordingly, to behave as this 'immoralist' desires is to display that one has an *agathe psuche*. The phrase, then, is valued by the 'immoralist', and denotes the man who pursues ends of which the ordinary man also approves.[8] Hence this too is likely to prove useful to Plato in argument.

C. THE MOST VALUED EXISTENCE

Naturally, the group of valued words used to characterize a man contains many more words and phrases, including words denoting social position and all words relating to courage and manliness, both of which sub-groups can readily be derived from the prevailing flavour of traditional *arete*. The above, however, will suffice; and we may now turn to those words which commend the environment and way of life which the *agathos* desires, and which his qualities should enable him to attain. These words are *agathon* (*agatha*), *eudaimonia*, *eu prattein*, *agathos bios*, and similar words.

The pursuit and enjoyment of *agathon* and *agatha*, 'good things', or as a second-best the avoidance of *kakon* or *kaka*, is the chief aim of the Greek from Homer onwards. This is a fact of psychology, not of morals, for *agathon* is not a moral term. No one can resist the bait of *agathon*. Admittedly in the *Meno*[b] Meno says that some people desire *kaka*, and even amplifies this a few lines later[c] by saying

Some desire *kaka* since they think that they are beneficial, others even though they know that they are harmful.

Socrates, however, readily induces him to admit that the first

---

[a] Cp. Aesch. *Agam.* 1643 and Chapter VIII, p. 156.
[b] Plat. *Meno* 77 c 1 ff.   [c] Ibid. 77 D 3.

group act under the impression that the *kaka* are really *agatha*, while the second group cannot exist, since no one wants to be damaged, and hence to be wretched and miserable, *athlios* and *kakodaimōn*.

It is evident even from this passage alone that *agathon* has a close relationship with *ōphelimon*, beneficial. What is *agathon* must, as is said in the *Protagoras*,[a] be beneficial to human beings, or at all events—taking into account Protagoras' objection—beneficial, *ophelimon*, to *something*. Since Plato seems willing to assert, as he does in the *Republic*,[b] not merely that what is *agathon* is beneficial but also that what is beneficial is *agathon*, *agathon* and *ophelimon* have the appearance of synonyms; and indeed Plato is capable of substituting one for the other in argument without justifying the change, and apparently without thinking about it.[c]

We are not here concerned to discuss whether this apparent identification is a real one, or with the implications of such an identification for philosophical theory, but with the advantages which such a word as *agathon* proves to have for Platonic practice. Since it is evident that *agathon* has at the very least a strong flavour of 'beneficial', that it means, in fact, 'good for', there can be no doubt about these advantages. The weakness of *kalon* and *aischron* in argument, or in commending or decrying action, is that, in the usage of this period, they have, for reasons already given,[d] acquired the stigma of commending and decrying some things which are only *nomōi kalon* and *nomōi aischron*; a fate to which they were peculiarly prone, since the nature of the *kalon*-standard had always been determined by popular approval. *Agathon* can have no such disadvantages. Nothing can be beneficial 'by convention': it either is beneficial or it is not.[9]

Since what is beneficial is desirable, it follows that to desire *kaka* in full knowledge that they are *kaka* is in Greek stark lunacy. As Meno says, one can only desire *kaka* under the mistaken supposition that they are *agatha*, that they will be beneficial. Even a hedonist must agree: he must identify the pleasant with the *agathon*, and if Plato can prove that the two are not identical, he must follow the *agathon*, at least on reflection.[e]

[a] Plat. *Prot.* 333 D ff.
[c] Compare Plat. *Gorg.* 474 E 7 with 475 A 3.
[d] Cp. Chapter IX, p. 187 f.
[b] Plat. *Rep.* 608 E.
[e] Plat. *Gorg.* 495 A ff.

The question at once arises: if *agathon* means 'good for'—
good for whom? And as soon as the question is asked, it becomes
clear that, though the word may be useful for the moralist, its
use will not be easy. True, in the law-courts great emphasis is
laid upon the *agatha* which a man performs for his city; but they
are, as has been seen, not something which a man desires to do,
but something unpleasant or expensive for whose performance
he expects a reward. True, in the *Protagoras*,[a] Protagoras says

If anyone does not possess the *agatha* which come to men as a
result of practice and training and teaching, but possesses the *kaka*
opposed to these, it is against these, I think, that anger, punishment,
and admonition are directed. These include injustice, impiety, and
in short everything which is opposed to political *arete*.

This use of *agatha* and *kaka* seems moral enough, or at all events
capable of being translated into moral sentiments. It is, however, these qualities *in other people*, in the general context of the
state, that are being termed *kaka*, their opposites, *agatha*: and it
is good *for us* that other people should be just to us. One might,
however, while saying that justice in other people is good for
oneself, quite consistently maintain that one's own justice is
allotrion agathon, another man's good, and prejudicial to one's
own interests,[b] and so intimate that one proposed to have as
little to do with it as possible. The *agathon* which the Greek pursues is not 'something which is good for the majority, even if it
harms me, and therefore I will put up with it'. It is no use to tell
him, even in a military context, where a certain self-sacrifice
might be expected, that he must stay and fight because it is
to the advantage *of all* for him to do so, even if he is killed. One
must also point out that he is much more likely to be killed if he
runs away; or that even if he runs away and escapes, his city
will be ruined, and hence that he himself will lose his livelihood.[c] *Agathon* to be pursued, must be '*agathon for me*': and given
the position of *agathon* in the values of Greece, the full force of
saying that justice is another man's *agathon* can be appreciated.

The condition in which a sufficient number of *agatha* is possessed and enjoyed is denoted by *eudaimonia* and its synonyms or

[a] Plat. *Prot.* 323 D 6.
[b] Cp. Plat. *Rep.* 343 c (Thrasymachus) and 392 B, where it is in fact coupled
with οἰκεία δὲ ζημία.
[c] Cp. Tyrtaeus 10 Bergk.

near-synonyms. It is accordingly the word which denotes the
end of life to the Greek of this period. Hence to advocate any
quality or course of action the moralist must show that it is an
essential part of, or means to, *eudaimonia* or being *eudaimon*. So
when, in the *Gorgias*,[a] Socrates, having proved to his own satisfaction that the quiet virtues are necessary and desirable, says
that if anyone is to confute him

He must show that it is *not* through the possession of *dikaiosune*
that the *eudaimones* are *eudaimones*, and through the possession of
kakia[10] that the *athlioi*, wretched, are *athlioi*,

he is stating the case in the manner in which it must be stated;
and it is for this reason that the poets must not be allowed
to say[b]

That many men are unjust and yet *eudaimones*, while many just
men are *athlioi*, and that injustice is profitable.

Eudaimonein, the verb corresponding to *eudaimonia*, has several
important synonyms. *Eu prattein*, to 'fare well', readily denotes
the end of life; so that in the *Euthydemus*[c] Socrates can say

Do all men wish to *eu prattein*? Or is this not one of the absurd
questions which I was afraid I might ask? Surely it is foolish to ask
such questions: for which of mankind does not wish to *eu prattein*?

To suggest that anything other than *eu prattein* could be the end
of life is nonsense; and in the subsequent argument *eu prattein*
and *eudaimonein* are treated as interchangeable.[d]

Agathos bios, the 'good' life, and *eu zēn*, to live 'well', are also
important synonyms for *eudaimonia*. So in the *Republic*[e] Plato can
say that the inquiry about the condition of the tyrannical man
who succeeds in becoming tyrant over a city is about the most
important subject, the *agathos bios* and the *kakos bios*; and he is
discussing the 'prosperity' or otherwise of the tyrant's life. He
might have replaced *agathos bios* by *eudaimonia*; and there is
accordingly no necessary flavour of quiet morals about the
agathos bios. As one has a *bios*, one would naturally like it to be
the best possible, just as one would like one's possessions to be
the best possible; and to call a *bios* 'agathos' is to say precisely

---

[a] Plat. *Gorg.* 508 A 8.   [b] Plat. *Rep.* 392 B.
[c] Plat. *Euthyd.* 278 E, cp. *Meno* 77 C 1 ff., quoted above, p. 249.
[d] Plat. *Euthyd.* 280 B 6 and 280 c 6.   [e] Plat. *Rep.* 578 C.

that it is a good specimen of *bios*. *Bios*, a word which will render 'livelihood' as well as 'life', refers to a man living an active life. It denotes the sum total of a man's activities; and when combined with *agathos*, to these activities in their highest, which is to say most efficient, expression; which is *eu zen*,[a] to live 'well', *eu prattein*, to fare well, and *eudaimonein*, to be prosperous, to possess an abundant supply of *agatha*.

It is evident—indeed, the point hardly requires making—that no Kantian idea of 'Duty' can exist in such a system of values as this: what one 'ought' to do is what it is necessary to do in order to be *eudaimon*. So in the *Republic*[b] Socrates says

We must consider whether the just really live 'better', *ameinon zen*,[c] than the unjust and are more *eudaimones* . . . for the discussion is not about any casual subject, but about the manner in which one 'ought', *chrēnai*, to live.

The manner in which one 'ought' to live is the manner in which one will be most *eudaimon*; hence this question must be answered before one can discover how one 'ought' to live. There is no possibility of Plato's setting 'duty' against *eudaimonia*. Nor has there been any possibility at any time in Greek thought before Plato: the incentive to pursue the quiet virtues has always been that to do so is a surer method of attaining prosperity—*eudaimonia* or some other word—than not to do so, whether the downfall of the wrongdoer and the prosperity of the upright was guaranteed supernaturally or by the processes of law. The recent attempt to make quiet virtue a characteristic of the *agathos* or *kalos kāgathos*, the 'gentleman',[d] promises no better: one 'ought' in one's own interest to pursue a course of action which is likely to lead to one's success, but one can have no duty to succeed, and hence no duty to be an *agathos*, for so many of the defining characteristics—success, wealth, &c.—do not depend on the will of the individual alone for their acquisition. The Greek moral scene does not provide, and never has provided, even the raw material from which a categorical imperative could be fabricated.

[a] *Eu zen* is equated with *eu prattein* and *eudaimon*, *Rep.* 354 A.
[b] *Rep.* 352 D 2.
[c] Comparative degree of *eu zen*.
[d] Cp. p. 198, and for an analysis of the difficulties inherent in this attempt, Chapter XVI.

D. THE MOST POWERFUL TERMS AND THE MORALIST

The words considered above, then, clustering round *agathos* and *eudaimonia*, characterize the qualities which all[11] at this period set before themselves as desirable, the ends which they proposed to themselves, and, more generally, the kind of life which they hoped to lead. Accordingly, since no other terms are powerful enough to set against them, it must be in these terms that any moralist must commend any course of action which he sees fit to commend; for only if he uses these terms will anyone take the trouble to listen.

To demonstrate the desirability of the co-operative virtues in these terms will not be easy, for they all commend the competitive excellences. Yet there are elements in the moralist's favour. For all parties, life is a skill, as was said above, and it is clear that that skill is to be devoted—not surprisingly—to the attainment of success. Skills require standards, and success is a 'real' thing, or may be treated as such, since all agree on its nature. True, this success is viewed in the grossest materialistic terms; but material advantage is not sought for itself alone. A man desires *agatha* for himself, his family, and his friends; but he does not desire to keep these *agatha* under lock and key, rusting and festooned with cobwebs. *Eudaimonein, eu prattein*, and similar words have about them the strongest possible flavour of 'wealth'; a flavour which is not now given to them for the first time.[a] But wealth is desired by these men for its uses. These uses are gross: a man may desire, like Callicles, to 'live the life of the stone-curlew',[b] and gratify every natural[c] desire to the limit, or he may wish to keep house on the grand scale and be a power in politics. In any case, he holds fast to the idea of liberality and free, unfettered living inherent in such words as *agathos* and *kalos kagathos*; he wishes to *eu zen*, to *eu prattein*; he does not wish to withdraw from society for the better enjoyment of his vices, nor yet to be a miser; and this ensures that *eudaimonia* is, and *agatha* contribute to, a full and active life, however conceived. It is with this background that *eudaimonia* commends 'a completely satisfactory life with no regrets';[12] and viewed in this light, the idea of *eudaimonia* may be of great value to the moralist and political thinker.

[a] Cp. Aesch. *Cho.* 700 ff.; E. *Med.* 598, *Alc.* 653 ff.
[b] Plat. *Gorg.* 494 B. [c] For this see below, pp. 271 f.

E. THE TRIPLE STANDARD OF BEHAVIOUR

It is into this world-view that *dikaiosune* must be fitted, in
such a way that it will be valued not only by the man who is,
temporarily or permanently, the underdog, but also by the
successful man. Not only *dikaiosune*, however: a third standard,
as has been seen, has appeared in Athens. Traditionally, to be
agathos is *kalon*, while *eudaimonia*—the idea, whatever the word
used—is the reward, divinely guaranteed, of *dikaiosune*; and
since the word in fact used to commend a man's success was
arete, the *dikaios*-standard, provided that the gods did their part,
was closely linked to the *agathos*-standard. These values are
natural to an agricultural community, in which one must be
willing and able to keep one's enemies from destroying or steal-
ing the growing crops, or the livestock, while being in the last
resort dependent on other factors for the eventual success or
failure of the crops so defended.[13] Athens, however, thriving on
self-seeking, *pleonexia*, no longer believing that the gods punish
injustice, and gaining most of her livelihood from pursuits
other than farming, might well attribute the credit for success,
eudaimonia, as a whole, to the skill, *arete*, of the man who gained it.

Agathos and *eudaimonia* having thus joined forces, and *dikaiosune* being doubtfully valued as a doubtful means to the desired
end, the position of *kalon* might have become precarious in any
case. The fruitless attempt to link *dikaion* with *kalon*,[a] however,
has made matters even more confused: *kalon*, attached traditionally to the competitive system of values in a use which is
still fully alive, but now associated in addition with the co-
operative values, is left in an invidious position between the two.

Accordingly, Plato finds himself with three standards by
which to evaluate action. Of any action it may be said that it
was performed *eu*, *kalōs*, or *dikaiōs*. Since *eu*, being the adverb
corresponding to the adjective *agathos*, is the only word of the
three which is indubitably attractive, Plato must attempt to
link the other two to this standard. In the *Crito*[b] it is said that
one's object must be not simply *zen*, living, but *eu zen*. Any

---

[a] Fruitless, that is, so far as Plato's opponents are concerned; but see Chapter
XVI.

[b] Plat. *Crito* 48 B ff., cp. *Gorg.* 521 c, where the sequence is *adikōs . . . aischrōs . . .
kakōs*.

Greek would agree to this, as Crito does. But Socrates continues:

Are we still agreed that to live *eu*, to live *kalōs*, and to live *dikaiōs*, are one and the same thing?

In translation, this sounds harmless enough: living 'well', 'honourably', and 'justly', though not necessarily synonymous, seem to us not violently opposed ideas. In Greek, each step is a difficult one, and refers to a different standard. *Eu zen* is simply 'efficient', 'enjoying life at its best', and hence universally attractive; *kalōs zen* invokes the standard of 'what people will say', and since people have been saying such bafflingly different and difficult things, this standard has lost much of its power; while *dikaiōs zen*, as a term of quiet morals, has no initial attraction whatsoever for the successful man.[14] Accordingly, to subsume the other two standards under that of *eu zen* is certain to be extremely difficult. If the moralist can achieve this, however, he has the strongest possible means of advocating *dikaiosune*; for if *dikaiōs zen*, to live justly, is *eu zen*, to enjoy life at its best and fullest, and *adikōs zen*, to live unjustly, is *kakōs zen*, to have a wretched and miserable existence, everyone, as Socrates says,[a] will be on the watch to prevent himself from committing injustice, and so harming himself and impairing his *agathos bios*.

Plato's various attempts to achieve this may now be examined.

NOTES TO CHAPTER XII

1. Cp. Chapter III, p. 57; and with the discussion of this chapter generally cp. E. Schwartz, *Ethik der Griechen*, chap. ii.
2. It is used, S. *Ajax* 259, to refer simply to the recovered sanity of Ajax.
3. Note the successive definitions of Callicles, *Gorgias* 488 D ff., at 488 D, 489 C, 490 A, and the final appearance of his real position, 491 B.
4. We have some indication of its possible usefulness in, for example, Euripides, *Andromache* 1161 ff., where Euripides uses *sophos* in a persuasive definition to commend quiet moral behaviour.
5. In *Iliad* xxii. 462, Apollo would not be *saophron* if he fought with Poseidon βροτῶν ἕνεκα . . . δειλῶν, 'for the sake of miserable mortals'. That is to say, 'the game would not be worth the candle'.

[a] Plat. *Gorg.* 480 B ff., 507 C 9 ff., *Crito* 48 B 3 ff., *Rep.* 443 E.

6. Though, as a member of a political group within the state, he need have no compunction about treating his opponents in such a manner, particularly if these values should lead, as they almost inevitably do, to open stasis.

7. On *psuche*, cp. Burnet, *Essays and Addresses*, London, 1929, pp. 126 ff.

8. *Gorgias* 491 B 4. For the *agathe psuche*, cp. *Gorgias* 507 A, cited on p. 248. One must naturally insist that the course of action one favours issues from and maintains an *agathe psuche*. When, *Gorgias* 477 B 5, the confused and half-hearted Polus is unwise enough to admit that *adikia* is *ponēriā*, badness (i.e. by traditional usage, wretchedness) in the *psuche*, he is, though Plato uses a different method of clinching the argument, already defeated. Callicles and Thrasymachus, as will be seen in Chapter XIII, are much more wary. We may compare *Republic* 366 C, where the good-hearted Adeimantus inquires—in the hope that Socrates will solve the problem—how anyone with *dunamis psuchēs*, capacity or power in his *psuche*, could be expected to be *dikaios*. The man with the *agathe psuche* is the man who can 'get things done' in his own interest.

9. Cp. Plato, *Theaetetus* 177 D: no one has the hardihood to claim that *agatha* are merely *agatha* by convention.

10. The substitution of *kakia* for *adikia*, which makes the second limb in a sense analytic—since *kakia* in traditional usage means 'in a poor condition' with no reference to quiet morals—is justified, since Socrates has just 'proved' the equivalence of *adikia* and *kakia*.

11. All, that is to say, who swayed general decisions. As Chapter IX has indicated, and Chapter XVI will also show, there is an undercurrent of 'moralism' dependent on the values there illustrated. But though this proves useful, as will be seen, to Aristotle, Plato, at a time of crisis, could not use a system of values which depended so largely on assertion and exhortation, when his opponents had such a plausible position; particularly since there is no sign that anyone had worked out the 'moralist' position in detail, and the cases of Meno and Crito, pp. 228 ff., suggest that the best intentions vanish in a crisis.

12. The word *eudaimonia* should not be hastily translated 'happiness', for in common usage the idea of material prosperity is much more evident in *eudaimonia* than 'happiness' would suggest. Indeed, in an extreme case *eudaimonia* may even be opposed to happiness: in the *Medea*, 598 f., Medea says: 'May I never have a *eudaimon bios*—i.e. prosperity—which is painful to me, nor an *olbos*—a synonym for *eudaimonia*—which grieves my mind.' These lines are at once an implied criticism of the purely materialistic standard of *eudaimonia* and an acknowledgement that this is the normal use of the word. Of course, had Euripides wished to put forward his own version of the fully satisfactory life, he would have used *eudaimonia* to commend it; for 'all men are agreed that *eudaimonia* is the end, and use *eu zen* and *eu prattein* as synonyms for *eudaimonia*; but they disagree about the nature of *eudaimonia*', Aristotle, *E.N.* 1095^{a}18 ff. (Aristotle in fact says 'almost all men', but this seems to be merely a philosopher's caution in the face of empirical generalizations.) It is the

general picture of a satisfying life of activity and 'prosperity', coupled with the difficulty of specifying this accurately, and the very high emotive power of *eudaimonia*, which renders this term so useful to the moralist.

13. The reference to the harvest is direct in *Odyssey* xix, 109 ff., quoted in Chapter IV, p. 66.

14. True, in the *Gorgias*, 483 c ff., Callicles uses the idea of *phusei dikaion* and *phusei adikon* to denote the 'natural justice' by whose right the stronger takes what he will and the weaker goes to the wall; and in the *Republic*, 338 c, Thrasymachus defines justice as 'what is in the interest of the stronger', basing his claim on the observation that the ruling class of any state enacts laws and administers justice—or so Thrasymachus claims—in its own interest. Such a definition of justice would render *dikaiosune* attractive to the immoralist. Normally, however, it is not so redefined. Even Creon does not claim that his commands are *dikaia* per se: he says that his subjects should obey him 'in matters small and just and the opposite', S. *Ant*. 667. (Contrast, however, Pindar frag. 169. 3.) The attitudes of Callicles and Thrasymachus are really only a squib so far as they are concerned: the argument on which Thrasymachus sets most store is that which terms *adikia* an *arete*, *Rep*. 348 B 6 ff.

XIII

PLATO: LOGIC AND ELENCHUS

A. THE SHAME OF SOCRATES

In his opposition to the system of values current in his day, or rather to the interpretation put upon those values, Plato was attempting to solve an urgent practical problem, since such values had led inevitably in practice to revolution and disaster. Even had Athens flourished, however, devotion to his master Socrates might well have led him in the same direction. Socrates had died in prison, at the hands of the executioner; further-more, he had refused to escape when escape was possible—a refusal which to a mind accustomed to other standards may appear heroic, but which by the common standards of the day could only seem foolish and *aischron*. Socrates, having been poor, and hence a failure, all his life, had proved unable to defend himself in court as an *agathos* should, and by his death had left his family unprotected. A Crito might well remonstrate, and a Callicles jeer at a man so evidently *kakos*, *athlios*, *anandros*, and *kakodaimon*. Nothing could be more *aischron* than Socrates' life and death; and yet this was the unpromising subject whom Plato, in the closing words of the *Phaedo*,[a] chose to term the most *agathos*, *phronimos*, and *dikaios* of all the men of his time whom we have known.

Such a claim was, to say the least, unlikely to be accepted without good proof. Simple assertion could achieve nothing. Socrates must be shown to have exhibited in his life *when properly considered* those qualities as a result of which men are termed *agathos* and *phronimos* to a greater extent than his opponents. Nothing less would suffice.

Accordingly, Plato's chief problem in ethics is the problem which has existed in Greek values from Homer onwards: namely, that of affixing *dikaiosune*, and the quiet virtues generally, to the group of values based on *arete* so firmly as to make future

---

[a] Plat. *Phaedo* 118 A 16, and contrast, for example, *Gorg.* 486 A.

severance impossible. The problem of the extent of a man's responsibility for his individual acts can appear of little importance in these circumstances: before such refinements as these, which lie within the field of quiet morals, can be usefully discussed, the respectability of the field of quiet morals as such must be established. On the manner in which this is established, however, depends closely the manner in which responsibility for individual acts is viewed; and hence Plato's solution, or solutions, is of the utmost importance to the question of moral responsibility.

B. THE JUSTIFICATION OF SOCRATES

(i) *The* Apology

The first justification for his actions is that given by Socrates himself in his defence as we have it. *His* scale of values is quite clear. He accords great importance to *dikaiosune* by linking it with *arete* and the *agathos*.[1] In the situation in which he now finds himself—in court, on a capital charge—he clearly values it above everything else; and when he maintains[a] that to defend himself without thought of strict justice would be illiberal, *aneleutheron*, his words are clearly related to the attempt, illustrated in Chapter IX, to make the practice of the quiet virtues one of the social attributes of the gentleman. The difficulties of this have been indicated. Socrates, however, does not confine himself to such claims: carrying the war into the enemy's camp, he points out in effect that to be *agathos* in war may involve remaining in a position of danger because a superior officer has given the order; which, claims Socrates,[b] is what he is doing now. He is under the orders of 'the god'[c]—since the Delphic oracle had pronounced that there was no one wiser than Socrates,[d] and he felt it incumbent upon himself to discover the meaning of this utterance—to continue philosophizing and asking questions of the Athenians, whether the Athenians approve or no; and it would be *aischron* to desert his post. Furthermore, his *daimonion*—the mysterious power which, Socrates claims, has always restrained him even in the smallest matters when he was not acting *orthōs*, correctly[e]—has not

---

[a] Plat. *Apol.* 38 E 3. [b] Ibid. 28 D and 39 A. [c] Ibid. 28 D ff.
[d] Ibid. 21 A. [e] Ibid. 40 A ff.

restrained him as he made his speech. Accordingly, he will not alter his attitude; 'will not', not 'may not', for he is convinced that any course of action which his mysterious inner voice[2] permits him to pursue is *beltion* for him;[a] and *beltion* can only mean 'better' in the sense of 'more advantageous'. Thus, Socrates believes that it is both more *kalon* and more advantageous for him to behave as he has done.

For this position Socrates willingly died. Plato, however, could clearly not let the matter rest here. The failure of the advocacy of *dikaiosune*, whether as social grace or as means to prosperity, has been shown: his contemporaries were unlikely to believe that the forms of defence which Socrates has rejected— those discussed in Chapter X—were illiberal. And to refer to courage in war, and particularly to the virtues of the Homeric Hero,[b] can only be dangerous, since the qualities prized by Plato's opponents could so readily be claimed to be precisely those virtues. It is the fact that he possesses his *daimonion* which gives coherence and strength to Socrates' position; and for this very reason Socrates' justification of his position will not suit Plato as moralist and political philosopher. The *daimonion* is peculiar to Socrates. Furthermore, that what the *daimonion* permits is beneficial, *agathon*, is for Socrates an article of faith, not reason. The *daimonion* is non-rational; and indeed it must be, since, failing the full-scale Platonic solution, reasoning about the basic Greek values only too readily produces standards quite contrary to those of the *daimonion*. It endowed Socrates with a faith whereby he could live—or die; but it endowed Plato with nothing on which he could build a political or moral theory by which men in general could live and die. The Greeks generally would only do something unpleasant if it was quite clear that they would benefit *tangibly* thereby, or at the very least that calamity faced them if they did *not* do it.

(ii) *The* Crito

Such is the background to Socrates' attitude in the *Apology*. In the *Crito* his continued refusal to escape from prison and go

---

[a] Plat. *Apol.* 41 D.

[b] As Socrates does, ibid. 28 c 6. The opposition of *arete* to the idea of 'womanish behaviour', 35 B, is also dangerous, in view of the traditional excellences of Greek man.

into exile is defended on grounds different from, but compatible with, these. At the end of the dialogue[a] Socrates imagines the protests of the—personified—laws of Athens should he in fact run away. The argument runs essentially as follows: No city can continue to exist in which private individuals frustrate the decisions of the courts (and the stability of the city is taken to be the end of the actions of the citizens, at which all should aim). If you, Socrates, frustrate the decision of the court in this matter the city will be weakened. Furthermore, Socrates, by living in Athens—and you have lived here for seventy years, though you could easily have gone elsewhere—you have in effect agreed to obey us. Again, it was only through our agency that you were born, reared, and educated.[b] We, accordingly, are your parents, and you are our offspring and slave, *doulos*.[c] So, if we think it *dikaion* to destroy you, how can you claim that it is *dikaion* for you to resist? No,[d]

In war, in the law-courts, and everywhere else, a man must do whatever the city and his fatherland command, or persuade them where the *dikaion* in fact lies; it is impious to use force upon one's mother or father, and much more impious to use it upon one's fatherland.

Thus, though Socrates may have been unjustly condemned, by men but not by the laws—for, the laws insist, it is the jurors, not they, who have condemned Socrates[e]—he would be acting unjustly if he now refused to accept the verdict, for he would be doing violence to the laws.[f]

This is an interesting theory. It has two stages. First of all, the stability of the city is taken as the acknowledged end. If this is acknowledged, then, if to flout court decisions weakens civic stability, court decisions must not be flouted. But if, as is evident both from Crito's objection in particular[g] and the general nature of Greek values from Homer onwards, the individual household also has its claims, which demand to be heard first, then some higher principle must be invoked. Accordingly, a type of contract theory is offered. To live in any state is to make an agreement *with the laws* to obey them; an

---

[a] Plat. *Crito* 50 A 8 ff.   [b] Ibid. 50 D ff. and 51 C 6 ff.
[c] Ibid. 50 E 3 f.   [d] Ibid. 51 B 8 ff.   [e] Ibid. 54 C.
[f] Ibid. 51 C 7.   [g] Above, Chapter XI, pp. 230 ff.

agreement which, as Socrates says, must include the clause 'to abide by whatever verdicts the state passes',[a] since otherwise any man wrongly condemned could claim that he had obeyed the laws, and hence that he was indeed unjustly condemned, and might hold that he was thereby released from his obligations.

This theory seems to be groping towards an imperative, such as that furnished to Socrates by his *daimonion*, which will apply to the citizen-body as a whole; an imperative which will hold in all circumstances for any given state. It is unjust to disobey the laws, even when the laws are unjust; one must persuade, not force.

The theory, if accepted, would give to 'this is *dikaion*' and 'this is *adikon*' the same degree of finality as 'this is *agathon*' and 'this is *kakon*' in normal Greek. 'This is *agathon* for me' would now naturally be outbid by 'but it is *adikon*', since it is not the case that contracts are to be kept only when to do so is to one's own advantage.

In some respects this is Plato's most interesting political theory. Though formally sound, however, it contains obvious obstacles to its general acceptance in practice by those whose views have been examined in earlier chapters. The core of the theory, since it is intended to explain Socrates' position, is the idea that it is unjust to resist an unjust decision of the courts; and that in such a situation it is not the laws who are wronging a man, but his fellow citizens.[b] The law, in fact, can do no wrong, since it never does anything, except enter into this contract. This is the drawback: in an ordinary contract there are conditions, foreseeable and specified, in which the contract becomes null and void. In this contract, however, nothing which the state does can void the agreement; and in this respect it is unlike a contract, but, as the laws are imagined to say in the passage quoted above, like the relationship which subsists between a master and his slave.

There could be no surer way of convincing Socrates' detractors that what he had done was *aneleutheron*, unworthy of a free man, the action of a *kakos*, than to liken him to the slave of anything, even the laws; for, given traditional values, a slave cannot be *agathos*, and hence to be a slave must be *aischron*. No one, 'immoralist'[3] or ordinary man, could tolerate this. No political theory can be stated in these terms and gain general acceptance at this period: nothing could be more shocking to traditional values.

The contract theory, however, is strictly only the second step here. The first step is of interest in its own right. It has been shown that, on the civic plane, *eudaimonia* is regarded as the end of life; and that this may be equated with smooth running, stability, and prosperity. This being the case, if we accept for the moment the claim that civic *eudaimonia* should take precedence over personal *eudaimonia*, anything which conduces to the smooth running and stability of the state is desirable and should be done, while anything which prevents or inhibits smooth running and stability must be avoided. The condemnation of Socrates is unjust; but to weaken the judicature, as Socrates would do were he to escape against the will of the Athenians, conduces to dissension and failure in the state: accordingly, Socrates must acquiesce in his unjust condemnation. The argument here justifies the execution of unjust sentences honestly arrived at; but it would also, quite legitimately on the basis of these values, justify the execution of unjust sentences cynically arrived at; and, by looking to the end alone, justifies the complete ignoring of motives and intentions, since evidently the ultimate criterion of any punishment inflicted on any citizen is the effect which such treatment will have on the efficiency of the state as a whole. These conclusions are not drawn; but they follow from Socrates' premisses, from the presuppositions of the immoralists, from those of the sophists and ordinary men who interested themselves in political philosophy, and from the standards obtaining in practice in the Athenian courts.[4]

These conclusions follow logically; but any Greek would naturally find them distasteful when applied to himself or his friends, and would fall back on the position of Crito,[a] stressing the importance of the *eudaimonia* of the individual and his household. It is in these terms that the justification of Socrates' position, and more generally of the quiet moral values, must be attempted; for the *arete* and *eudaimonia* of the individual are the ultimate values.

One attempt is sketched in the earlier section of the *Crito*.[b]

---

[a] Above, pp. 230 ff.   [b] Plat. *Crito* 47 A 10 ff., esp. 47 E.

Socrates distinguishes the body, *sōma*, from 'that part of us which injustice damages, and justice benefits'; and which is more important[a] than the body. Crito agrees that man possesses such a part; and also that

Acting efficiently, *eu*, honourably, *kalōs*, and justly, *dikaiōs*, are one and the same thing,

and that

Committing injustice is both harmful, *kakon*, and shameful, *aischron*, for the man who commits injustice.

Now once Crito has agreed to these propositions, he clearly cannot object to Socrates' refusal to escape, provided that he agrees that it would be *adikon* for Socrates not to remain;[b] for to act *adikōs* is then clearly against one's own interests, as was shown at the end of the last chapter. Crito does agree, and therefore must necessarily accept the conclusions.

He agrees; but no proof of the propositions is offered; and it is reasonable to suppose that Plato at this period, and hence that Socrates, had no proof to give. The facts of language on which the assertions are based are evident: once unjust men are termed *kakoi*, once *adikia* can be termed *kakia* or *ponēriā*, such men and such acts are linked to the system of values which commends success and decries failure. In traditional usage, to be *kakos* is undeniably more *aischron* and more *kakon* than to be *agathos*, since failure is undeniably more disadvantageous than success, and, given the Greek world-view, necessarily more shameful. Now, however, men are termed *kakoi*, or said to possess *kakia* or *poneria*, for different reasons, in the usage of Chapter IX. In these circumstances, there are only two logical attitudes to adopt: like Socrates, one may insist that these new instances of *kakia* can be characterized in the same manner as the old as both more *kakon* and more *aischron* for their possessor than the corresponding new usages of *arete*; or, like the thoroughgoing 'immoralist', one may insist that these new instances are not instances of *kakia* at all. For one can only justify the extension of the use of *kakia* in this remarkable manner on the assumption that in some sense the same criteria may be applied

---

[a] τιμιώτερον.
[b] As Socrates goes on to prove to him, Ibid. 49 E 5 ff., discussed above.

in the new instances as in the old. Thrasymachus[a] denies that the criteria have any resemblance. Socrates here insists that they must have such a resemblance; but he offers no proof, and does not even name the *psuche* as the more precious element in us which is damaged by injustice.[b] He is, in fact, relying on the linguistic usage of the day in asserting that the *adikos* is *kakos*; and furthermore on the linguistic usage of a restricted group, or on a linguistic usage which is only too readily abandoned, as the evidence of previous chapters would suggest. Hence he insists that only the opinion of the *phronimoi*[c]—clearly using this emotive word as a persuasive definition to denote those thinkers and their followers who in fact agree with him and use language in a similar manner[5]—should be regarded in deciding such questions of value. A Thrasymachus might well be unimpressed.

C. THE OPPONENTS OF SOCRATES

(i) *Polus and the Ordinary Man*

Plato's ethical writings, up to and including *Republic* i, are naturally in great part devoted to the attempt to replace this reliance on the language of a group among other groups by arguments of logical respectability. The ease with which Plato accomplishes this, or seems to, naturally depends on the coherence of the attitude which he is attacking at any given time.

The muddleheadedness of ordinary values, represented by Polus in the *Gorgias*, receives short shrift. Socrates, Callicles, Thrasymachus, and traditional values are all agreed that what is more *aischron* for any agent is also more *kakon* for that agent, widely though the course of action which they would recommend by these terms might differ. Polus the confused 'immoralist' does not agree: committing injustice is in his eyes more *aischron*, shameful, suffering injustice more *kakon*, harmful.[d] He clearly wishes to advocate injustice: acknowledging the existence of the new 'moral' use of *aischron*,[e] he opposes to it the 'real' value of *kakon*, thereby intimating his intention of pursuing the *agathon*, benefit to oneself, of committing injustice,

---

[a] Plat. *Rep.* 348 c 3 ff. An *arete must* be profitable, traditionally; and Thrasymachus denies that justice is profitable.

[b] i.e. in *Crito* 47 c ff.   [c] Ibid. 47 A.

[d] Plat. *Gorg.* 474 c 5.   [e] Chapter IX *passim*.

and disregarding the fact that such action may be held to be *aischron* as unimportant. To attempt to change the alignment of a group of terms of value is always dangerous; and it requires much more clarity of thought than Polus possesses. Socrates immediately presses him to agree to the apparently harmless proposition that there is a reason why men apply *kalon* to those situations to which they do apply the term; and Polus does agree. *Kala*, he says, are so termed either because they are pleasant, *hēdu*, or because they are beneficial, *ophelimon*; hence if one thing is more *kalon* than another—Socrates deduces—it must be so because it exceeds the other in the pleasure or the benefit which it affords, or in both, and if anything is more *aischron* than another, it must exceed the other in the pain or the harm, *kakon*, which it causes, or in both. This follows directly from the agreed definition; and Socrates readily shows that, since committing injustice, which—Polus has admitted—is more *aischron* than suffering injustice, is not more painful than suffering injustice, it must be more harmful, and cause more *kakon*, *to the man who commits injustice* (since 'harmful to the agent' is the sense in which *kakon* is understood throughout). Hence committing injustice is both more *aischron* and more *kakon* than suffering injustice, and will naturally be avoided by all who know the true facts of the case.

Polus goes down almost without a fight. The reason for this, and the nature of his mistake, should be clear from what has gone before. The mistake lies naturally in the agreed definition. Polus *may* agree that there is a reason why *kala* are so termed; but to Socrates' suggestion as to the nature of that reason he should have replied: 'No, Socrates. I maintain that the reason that *kala* and *aischra* are so termed is that people in general conspire to do so. Admittedly in the past *aischron* has generally been used to decry military, social, and other failures, and *these* situations do exceed their converses in the amount of pain or harm caused to the person who experiences them; but there has recently been a considerable extension of usage, and I see no reason why the criterion of 'pain or harm' should be held to apply to all cases. That, Socrates, is what you have to prove: it would be folly if I were to admit it without a struggle.'

Polus, in fact, reflects in his person the confusion of values existing in Athens at this period. The evaluation of *kakon* and *aischron* on which he proposes to act entails that *aischron* be for him a term of very little emotive value henceforth. It is, however, very difficult to drain a word of emotive value, even for oneself; and as soon as Socrates presses him, Polus naturally allows to *kalon* and *aischron* the full flavour which they have traditionally possessed, as part of the most powerful system of values commending success and decrying failure. The words I have put into the mouth of Polus are a logically possible reply; but given a tradition which endows *aischron* with such emotive power, it is highly unlikely that a Polus will succeed in finding it. This becomes even more evident, and the reason for Polus' confusion more comprehensible, if it is recollected that *all* of the traditional uses of *aischron* and *kalon* are still fully alive.[a]

The confusion, as Socrates' own comment on his refutation of Polus implies,[b] is one at this time existing in 'ordinary Greek'. Plato naturally finds it easy to exploit such confusions and ambiguities. These result generally, like those of Polus, from the infiltration of the quiet moral excellences into the group of terms based on *agathos*; an infiltration which, whether welcomed or abhorred, is confusing. One type of argument to which it may lead is seen in *Republic* i.[c] Polemarchus, who earlier defined justice as helping one's friends and harming one's enemies,[6] has been manœuvred by Socrates into saying

Well, at all events one should harm those who are both one's enemies and also 'bad', *ponēroi*.

Socrates propounds the following argument against this position:

Socrates: When horses are harmed, do they become better, *beltious*, or worse, *cheirous*?
Polemarchus: Worse.
Socrates: In respect of the *arete* of dogs or that of horses?
Polemarchus: That of horses.
Socrates: Shall we not say, then, that men, on being harmed, become worse in respect of human *arete*?
Polemarchus: Certainly.
Socrates: But is not *dikaiosune* (the?) human *arete*?
Polemarchus: It must be admitted to be so.
Socrates: Then it must also be admitted that men who are harmed become more unjust.

[a] Chapters VIII, X, XI *passim*.   [b] Plat. *Gorg.* 475 E 7 ff.
[c] Plat. *Rep.* 335 B ff.

This absurd piece of reasoning is offered in opposition to the
normal Greek view that the man who is *agathos* and *dikaios*
should help his friends and harm his enemies: clearly if to harm
a man simply makes him more unjust, and hence more likely
to harm oneself, it is not in one's interest to harm one's enemies.
Socrates does not draw precisely this conclusion here, insisting
rather on the illogicality which this argument seems to generate,
that it is the mark of justice to make men more unjust; but in
the *Apology*[a] he defends himself against the charge of 'having
made the young men worse' on similar grounds. The illogicality
is once again generated by the confusion between the traditional
and the modern. To harm one's enemies is clearly to damage
their *arete* in the traditional sense, by maiming them in person
or in property; and clearly this renders them *less* able to re-
taliate. But once the new usage has admitted *dikaiosune* as human
arete—whether as the only *arete*, as the chief *arete*, or as one
among many—Plato feels himself able to substitute *dikaiosune*
for *arete* in the argument, and so produces this absurd conclusion.[7]

Seen against this background, the position of Thrasymachus
and Callicles and that of Socrates appear as different answers
to the same problem set by ordinary language. The infiltration
of the quiet moral values has transformed a moderately homo-
geneous collection of traditional *aretai* into a heterogeneous
mess of conflicting claims, desiderating apparently two different kinds of men, commended by the same group of terms.
The mess cannot be allowed to remain a mess; and two solutions are possible. Callicles and Thrasymachus reply in effect
that since the 'logic' of the new *aretai* is so different from that of
the old, since they are commending such a different type of
man, the new *aretai* are not *aretai* at all. Socrates' reply is quite
different: he assumes that the 'logic' of the new *aretai* must be
the same as that of the old, and thereby authorizes himself to
make quite illegitimate substitutions, as here. Since the assumptions, when tacitly made, are so tempting, it is not surprising
that a moderate man should see no objection; and doubtless
Socrates and the earlier Plato were satisfied too. Yet in the
Gorgias,[b] at all events, Callicles, on taking over the argument
from Polus, says that Socrates has cheated by playing on the

confusion between things which are *aischra* by convention, *nomōi*, and things which are *aischra* by nature, *phusei*. If we interpret 'conventional' and 'natural' as 'innovating' and 'traditional', this is perfectly true; so that it seems likely that Plato in some sense realized what he was doing in the *Gorgias*.

(ii) *Callicles and Thrasymachus*

It is from this surely unsurpassed confusion of standards that much of the efficacy of the Socratic elenchus is derived. The success of the methods discussed above in confusing the muddle-headed or goodhearted is complete; but for those who are neither, men who feel no shame at calling injustice an *arete* if it seems to have the characteristics of an *arete*, different means are necessary. The hardheaded must be made to believe that the values which they prize above all—that is to say, skill devoted to securing personal prosperity, their own and their friends' success in politics, and the prosperity of the city in which, it is assumed, they and their friends will be dominant politically[8]—entail consequences and standards of behaviour quite other than those they had supposed. This, before *Republic* ii, Plato tried to accomplish by logical means; the means which he used upon Callicles and Thrasymachus.

Callicles makes his position quite clear.[a] Ordinary men

Praise *sophrosune* and *dikaiosune* through their own lack of manliness, *anandria*;

for if a man were born a king's son, or if he were himself a man capable of providing himself with a tyranny or some other position of power,

What in truth could be more *aischron* and more *kakon* for such a man than *sophrosune* and *dikaiosune*?

Why should such men take upon themselves as master, *despotēs*,[9] the laws, words, and rebukes of the majority of mankind? For . . .

Luxury, intemperance, and licence, provided that they have the means[b] to gain their ends—these are *arete* and *eudaimonia*.

[a] Plat. *Gorg.* 492 B 1 ff.
[b] Either in the sense of 'wealth', or in that of 'courage and practical intelligence, *phronesis*'; so Thompson, ad loc.

The other claimants to *arete* are merely men's conventions, 'against nature', nonsense, worth nothing.

This position seems quite coherent. *Aischron* and allied words are not opposed to *kakon* and allied words: no simple contradiction can be generated. Callicles' words are not even violently paradoxical: he has as much right to redefine *arete* as have (say) Xenophanes, Tyrtaeus, and Theognis, and, as has been shown, the way of life which he commends can be more readily demonstrated to be an expression of traditional *arete* than can its converse. Plato's task is difficult; but since the 'immoralists' have definite standards, he has a point from which to begin.

Callicles has expressed his approval for those who, being *phronimoi* in respect of handling the city's affairs, can get what they want; and his contempt for *sophrosune*, self-control.[a] The rejection of *sophrosune* in this manner sounds like complete nihilism; but though Callicles is not worried by Socrates' comparison of his ideal life with that of the stone-curlew,[b] and will if pressed accept as *eudaimonia* the life of a man perpetually gaining pleasure from scratching his itch, when Socrates asks him about the *eudaimonia* of the pervert whose desires are fully satisfied, and who therefore has what he wants, Callicles asks Socrates whether he is not ashamed, *aischunesthai*, of bringing the conversation round to such topics. Callicles is genuinely shocked. He, like Socrates, regards such a life as 'terrible and *aischros* and wretched'[c]—or if he does not, he does not regard it as an expression of his *arete*, which is the question at issue here. He and his kind do not want to satisfy unnatural desires. They merely want *carte blanche* to exercise all their natural desires to the full in the city; and they cannot understand why Socrates will not discuss the matter with them on their own ground.[d] Though he is shocked, however, Callicles for the moment continues to assert that *eudaimonia* is 'obtaining pleasure in any way whatsoever', that the *agathon* is the pleasant.[e] Socrates first[f] attacks this position with a fallacious argument on the nature of pleasure and pain;[10] an argument which Callicles feels to be fallacious, and to which he replies by sulking. Socrates persuades him to continue, and attacks again. Callicles has insisted

---

[a] αὐτὸν αὑτοῦ ἄρχειν, ibid. 491 D 7.
[b] Ibid. 494 B 6.
[c] Ibid. 494 E 4 ff.
[d] Ibid. 490 C 8 ff.
[e] Ibid. 495 A ff.
[f] Ibid. 495 C ff.

that the *agathos* is the *phronimos*, and that the *agathon*, the end of
life, is the pleasant; and hence, since the man who is most
agathos is the man who can obtain the most *agathon* by means
of his skill, he must be the man who obtains the most pleasure.
Now since it is undeniable that there are situations in which
cowards, fools, and children—*aphrones*, lacking in practical intelligence, all—obtain as much pleasure as the *phronimos*, Callicles' insistence on *phronesis* seems to entail that he must abandon
his equation of the *agathon* and the pleasant,[11] for clearly feeling
pleasure does not depend on being *phronimos*. It seems to entail
this: in fact Callicles could escape simply by saying that though
pleasure is the aim of both the *phronimos* and the fool, and though
one need not be *phronimos* in order to enjoy oneself, it *is* necessary to be *phronimos* to put oneself consistently in positions in
which one may enjoy oneself; against which position this is no
argument.

Thus far all that has really been shown is that there are some
pleasures about which Callicles feels squeamish, and that in
order to secure one's own end, whatever that may be, as successfully as possible, skill is required. One needs a *technē* to
provide *agatha* for one's body and one's *psuche*; that is all that
Plato has proved.

This is still not noticeably moral. But the subject of the
dialogue is rhetoric, and this theme is once again introduced.
Earlier in the dialogue, Gorgias had claimed that rhetoric is a
techne, an 'art',[12] and indeed the greatest of the *technai*. The claim
is natural to a sophist who professes to teach the art of practical
politics in a city governed by a democratic assembly; and
rhetoric is certainly a *techne* in 'ordinary Greek', for *techne* means
'skill' or 'organized body of knowledge' in the widest sense.
Plato, however, in reply introduced a 'philosophical' redefinition of a *techne* as a skill aiming at an *agathon*, distinguishing it
from an *empeiriā*, a 'knack', which merely aims at pleasure;[a]
and he instanced as examples cookery, an *empeiria* which minis-
ters to the body, and medicine, the *techne* which deals with the
same subject matter. He now revives this definition, and com-
bines it with his 'proof' that pleasure is not the *agathon*, which
ends as follows:

---

[a] Plat. *Gorg.* 462 D 8, reintroduced 500 A 7. Gorgias himself, *Helen* 14 D/K,
compared rhetoric to medicine.

So we ought to do everything else and pleasant things too for the sake of things which are *agathon*, not things which are *agathon* for the sake of pleasure.

Clearly all that Plato can even *claim* to have proved here is that a man ought to seek *agatha* for himself rather than pleasure for himself: he might pursue other people's pleasure with a view to obtaining *agathon*, benefit, for himself thereby; and this, it might seem, is what the (unscrupulous) orator does. Callicles, one might say, could well allow rhetoric to be an *empeiria*, titillating the senses of the audience, and subserving the *techne*—presumably the political art—which cares for the self-interest, the *agathon*, of the *agathos*. To say this, however, is to forget the nature of the sophistic movement: it is an intellectual movement, and hence, since *techne* as defined by Plato is intellectually more respectable than *empeiria*, rhetoric must be a *techne*; and therefore (in a phrase which is insufficiently analysed in this dialogue) it must aim at the *agathon* of its subject-matter, the *psuche*, as a doctor aims at the *agathon* of his subject-matter, the body.[a]

To make Callicles insist on *techne* is probably legitimate: Plato knew his opponents, and could be under no obligation to refute positions which in fact were held by none.[13] He continues by pointing out that the characteristics of a good product of *techne*—say a house—are arrangement, *taxis*, and order, *kosmos*; that this is true also of the medical *techne*; and that in the body *taxis* and *kosmos* are health, and 'the rest of the *arete* of the body'.[b] From this it is only a short step to say:[c]

Arrangement and order in the *psuche* are termed lawfulness and law, as a result of which men become law-abiding and orderly, *kosmioi*; and this condition is *dikaiosune* and *sophrosune*.

Accordingly, it is argued, the orator who is *agathos* and possessed of his *techne* will attempt to produce *taxis* and *kosmos* in his subject-matter, his audience; and this is *dikaiosune* and *sophrosune*. Later,[d] reverting to the discussion of the qualities which the *agathos* ought to possess himself, Plato makes use of the agreement that the state of anything which is termed its *arete* is that which possesses *taxis* and *kosmos*, to argue that as a result the

---

[a] Plat. *Gorg.* 500 A ff. [b] Ibid. 504 B 7. [c] Ibid. 504 D.
[d] Ibid. 506 D 5 ff.

agathe psuche is the *kosmiā psuche*, the *psuche* with *kosmos*, and that
—by the usage of 'ordinary Greek', as above—this is the *sophron
psuche*. Hence the possessor of a *sophron psuche* has an *agathe
psuche*, is *agathos*, and therefore *eudaimon*.[a] Thus, to show himself a skilled practitioner of his art the orator must implant the
quiet virtues in his audience, to show himself an *agathos* generally
he must possess them himself.

Now clearly if Callicles were wide awake he would retort
that, unless Socrates can prove the contrary, he is merely
punning on the word *kosmios*. There is a sense in 'ordinary
Greek' in which it is a near-synonym for *sophron*, but Socrates
has not shown that this is the sense in which the *agathe psuche* is
kosmia. Granted, Callicles might say, a good house must be
kosmia, orderly; but one can see whether it is so or not in relation to a clearly defined purpose. Certainly the orator should
aim at making his audience 'orderly': but why should *kosmios*
mean anything other than 'docile and obedient'?[14] Certainly
the *agathos* should aim at being 'orderly' himself—'for I have
standards, Socrates, though they are not yours'—but why should
kosmios mean anything other than 'skilful and courageous',
'orderly', that is to say, in the sense of 'never declining into
mistake about one's self-interest or cowardice in securing it'?
Such 'order and arrangement' suits Callicles' view of the respective roles of audience and 'immoralist' orator and politician admirably; and Plato is as yet in no position to prove the
contrary.

This proof then is really no proof at all; a fact which Plato's
contemporaries must have realized, since in *Republic* i Thrasymachus—Callicles *redivivus*—puts some of the objections which
Callicles should have put. The same moves are made. Just as
Callicles could not admit that rhetoric was a mere 'knack'
when he might claim that it was a *techne*, so Thrasymachus
insists on the infallibility of the ruler properly defined;[b] and as
he had done in the case of Callicles, Socrates attempts to prove
that the practice of a *techne* requires the practice of the quieter
virtues. His first argument runs as follows.[c] Any *techne* is perfect,
and lacks nothing of its own *arete*, excellence. That is to say, for
the purposes of this argument no skill termed a *techne* need
devote time to improving itself or consulting its own interests,

---

[a] Plat. *Gorg.* 507 c 3 ff.   [b] Plat. *Rep.* 340 c.   [c] Ibid. 342 A 1 ff.

but may confine its attention to the interests of its subject-matter. *Technai* rule over their subject-matter. The art of ruling rules over subjects: therefore the true artist in ruling, the man who uses the *techne* of ruling properly, consults the interests of his subjects, not his own.

This argument is rather less plausible than that employed against Callicles; and Thrasymachus finds the right answer, asking whether Socrates supposes that shepherds consult the good of their sheep, rather than their own good; or, he might have added, that the Athenians had consulted the good of their subjects, rather than their own good, in governing their empire. This is the right answer, though Thrasymachus might have expressed it better. We may imagine the argument as written by Thrasymachus:

Thrasymachus: Socrates, you are drawing parallels from other *technai* in order to prove to me what the practice of the *techne* of the ruler should be?
Socrates: I am.
Thrasymachus: It is the function of the shepherd's art to produce good sheep, that of the ruler's art to produce good subjects?
Socrates: It is.
Thrasymachus: But are not 'good sheep' those which fetch the best price in the market?
Socrates: I suppose so.
Thrasymachus: That is to say, good sheep are those which suit the purpose of the shepherd best?
Socrates: Agreed.
Thrasymachus: In that case, Socrates, for all you can say to the contrary, good citizens are those which suit the purpose of the ruler best. The shepherd consults his own interest in practising his *techne*: why should not the ruler do the same?

Had Thrasymachus put the point in this matter, the ambiguity latent in the definition of a *techne* as a skill which aims at the *agathon* of its subject-matter and renders it *agathos*—the ambiguity on which Socrates played in the *Gorgias*[a]—would have been brought into the open. Even as the point is put, Socrates has to face the problem which he should have faced before; but the argument as imagined above would have rendered his solution even less plausible than it is.

[a] Above, p. 273.

He attempts to solve the problem as follows.[a] It is not *strictly*
the business of an art to make money, but to perfect its subject-
matter. Accordingly, the shepherd in pursuit of the shepherd's
art is not concerned with making money. In order to be most
efficient at making money, one should pursue the art of making
money; quite a different art, and not to be confused with the
shepherd's art. Socrates also adds the point that ruling cannot
be profitable, since rulers have to be paid; a quite irrelevant
point, since it clearly refers only to democracies, not to the
tyranny, or membership of a tyrannical oligarchy, which Thrasymachus covets. The other two points, however, can safely be
accepted by Thrasymachus, so long as Socrates makes only
logical deductions from them. The deduction which he in fact
makes is quite illegitimate: that since the money-making art
takes care of profit, the other arts are left to make their products
as 'good' as possible in a purely altruistic sense. Had Thrasymachus or Socrates ever considered the relation of the art of
money-making to the art of being a shepherd, the absurdity
of this would have become clear at once. There are three possible relationships: the two may be simply equals, the money-
making art may be subordinated to the shepherd's art, or the
shepherd's art may be subordinated to the money-making art.
If they are equals, no decision between their rival claims is
possible; and since they deal with the same subject-matter—
sheep—rival claims will be continual. This cannot be the relationship. If the money-making art is subordinated to the shepherd's art, then the true interest of the sheep must always take
the first place; if the money-making art demands mutton for
sale, the shepherd's art will refuse it, since it is evidently a bad
thing for a sheep to be mutton. It is only when the sheep dies
full of years and honour that the money-making art can dispose
of the carcass; unless indeed the shepherd's art decides that it is
better for the sheep to have a decent funeral. It is evident, in
fact, that all such arts are subordinate to the money-making
art; that it is the good of this art, not that of the sheep, which is
considered. If the money-making art demands mutton, even if
it demands mutton produced in a manner very painful and
harmful to the sheep, its demands must be heard. 'Good sheep',
as we imagined Thrasymachus saying above, are sheep which

___
[a] Plat. *Rep.* 341 B ff.

fetch a good price in the market.'Thrasymachus could readily draw parallels with the government of states. The fact that in a democracy officials are paid because *in this case* they are prevented from ruling in their own interest is quite irrelevant to a general discussion of government.

The argument which follows, however, is one of the more interesting of those to be found in the earlier writings of Plato.[a] Thrasymachus has asserted that injustice is an *arete*, that it betokens sound judgement, *euboulia*, that it is *kalon* and powerful, *ischūron*; and though he cannot quite bring himself to say that *dikaiosune* is *kakia*, he has termed it 'a very noble foolishness'.[b] Socrates admits that had Thrasymachus said—as Polus did[c]— that injustice was profitable, but admitted it to be *aischron* or *kakia*, his task would have been easier; and then attacks the position in the only way in which logic can attack any position, by attempting to show that injustice has implications which are inconsistent with those of sound judgement, *euboulia*. Thrasymachus is induced to agree to the following propositions: No doctor attempts to outdo the diagnosis of another doctor, if that diagnosis is correct; and as Thrasymachus has insisted that the argument should be about ideal practitioners, it must be correct. Nor does he attempt to improve upon the correct dosage, though if a man who is not a doctor attempts to prescribe, he will certainly attempt to improve on his (incorrect) advice. A man who is not a doctor, on the other hand, may well try to outdo both the doctor and the layman in these matters. The doctor possesses knowledge, is *epistēmōn*, therefore *sophos*, therefore *agathos*; the man who is not a doctor, the contrary. But it is the mark of a just man not to attempt to outdo another just man, but only the unjust; the mark of an unjust man to try to outdo all and sundry. Accordingly, the just man is more like the *epistemon*, *sophos*, and *agathos* than is the unjust.

What cogency this argument possesses is derived from the confusion of the views put into the mouth of Thrasymachus; views which may have been typical of the period, but which are certainly not the best that can be done for his position. Thrasymachus claims that the unjust man is *phronimos*, that he is *agathos* at managing the affairs of the city, that he has a *techne*. He uses his political skill for his own selfish ends; but it remains

[a] Ibid. 348 c ff.   [b] πάνυ γενναίαν εὐήθειαν.   [c] Above, pp. 266 ff.

a skill for all that. The admissions put into his mouth by Plato forget this fact. The unjust man, *adikos*, with whom Plato is concerned ought to be as 'ideal' as the *dikaios*; and in the sense in which one doctor will not try to outdo another, in attempting, that is, to improve upon a perfect diagnosis of disease and prescription of treatment, the perfect *adikos*, the skilful seeker of his own interest, will not attempt to outdo another perfect *adikos*, for each will come to the same conclusion as to the maximum amount of personal gain to be wrung from any situation. That their interests might conflict is irrelevant: two sculptors cannot carve a statue from a piece of stone big enough for only one of them, nor two doctors amputate the same limb.

If the Thrasymachuses of Athens are really only concerned to score immediate successes against their fellows, just and unjust alike, then Plato's argument will serve *ad hominem* in practice. Thrasymachus, however, evidently has a stronger position, that which Plato pretends to be refuting here. He is refuted only because his perfect *adikos* is not perfect enough: he makes mistakes about his interest, his *sumpheron*.[15]

Thus Platonic logic fails to refute the extreme 'immoralist' position, as indeed it must fail, if that position is internally coherent. As a result, *dikaiosune* refuses to adhere firmly to *arete*, the *sophron psuche* cannot be shown to be the *agathe psuche*, and to pursue justice is not evidently to secure one's *eudaimonia*. If logic fails—and despite the drawing of so many specious conclusions in these dialogues its failure must have been realized— other methods must be tried. The *Crito*[a] had tried to solve this problem by considering the individual in relation to his city: the *Republic* and the *Laws* were now to attempt the same task, but on more acceptable terms.

NOTES TO CHAPTER XIII

1. *Apol.* 32 E 3, 'I took the part of justice as an *agathos* should.' In 39 A 10 ff. he links *poneria, kakia, mochtheria,* and *adikia*. All but *adikia* belong traditionally to the *arete*-group, so that this too implies that *dikaiosune* is linked with *arete*. Though it is of course extremely unlikely that the *Apology* bears any close detailed resemblance to Socrates' actual words, it seems highly probable, in view of the evidence of Chapter IX, that the *values* manifested by this speech are those of Socrates.

[a] Above, pp. 261 ff.

2. On which cp. Dodds, op. cit., pp. 184 f.

3. Callicles, *Gorgias* 492 E ff., declines to be subject even to himself: 'How could anyone become *eudaimon* if he were the slave, *doulos*, of anyone whatsoever?' By 'anyone whatsoever' he means 'even himself'. Callicles is not a complete nihilist, for he has definite standards, cp. pp. 270 ff.: he is merely expressing his disapproval of the 'quiet' connotation of the phrase αὑτὸν αὑτοῦ ἄρχειν, used to commend 'self-control', i.e. *sophrosune*.

4. For in all cases where the *eudaimonia* of the state is in question, this naturally takes precedence over what is merely *dikaion*, cp. Chapter X, &c. (This remains true even if the Athenians were on rare occasions squeamish about the results, cp. pp. 204 f. above.) The 'immoralists', once in charge of the state, would naturally, as the Thirty did (cp. *Apol.* 32 C; Lys. *In Eratosth.* 5 ff.), execute individuals in their own interest: a procedure which, on the theory of the *Crito*, it seems unjust to resist, at all events so long as such executions are carried out with a show of legality.

5. For of course Chapter IX indicates that Socrates' thought was part of a wider movement: Socrates' distinction was that he was willing to die for his beliefs.

6. This requires some explanation. It is evident that from Homer onwards this is not the *first* picture suggested by *dikaiosune* and allied words, for *dikaiosune* is a co-operative virtue, and helps to hold society together. And here it is not the first definition offered by these 'ordinary men'. Cephalus, the father of Polemarchus, says in effect that *dikaiosune* is to speak the truth and pay back what one has received from anyone. It is only when Socrates points out that it might not be *dikaion* to return a sword to a madman from whom one borrowed it when he was sane that Polemarchus, who has succeeded to Cephalus' role in the discussion, modifies the definition to '*dikaiosune* is to return to every man what is due to him'; and *then* Socrates by further questioning is able to induce him to say that *agathon* is due to friends, *kakon*, to enemies, and hence that *dikaiosune* is to help one's friends and harm one's enemies. This—re-tributive—justice, the justice meted out by an *agathos* to other indivi-duals, is the justice of Heracles, in virtue of which he is termed *agathos*, not *dikaios*. There is no reason why the 'immoralists' should not accept *this* justice, for it is an expression of traditional *arete*, and lends itself well to the morals of faction and party strife. Accordingly, the *dikaiosune* against which Thrasymachus inveighs is a completely different quality: there is a change in the sense of *dikaiosune* in the course of *Republic* i. The *dikaiosune* attacked by Thrasymachus is of course what the ordinary man has in mind when he thinks of justice, as is evident from Cephalus' definition: *dikaiosune* suggests fairness, truth, and co-operation. Pole-marchus, 332 A, only mentions friends; it is Socrates who brings enemies into the discussion. The argument against Polemarchus reveals serious deficiencies in the popular standard of *dikaiosune*; but the manner in which the argument is presented indicates that these do not lie in those aspects of *dikaiosune* which come to mind first. If pressed, any ordinary man of the period—or earlier—might admit that it is just to harm one's

enemies; but if asked to define *dikaiosune*, he will do it in the manner of Cephalus.

7. Of course, the argument is absurd whether one supposes Plato to mean that *dikaiosune* is *the* human *arete* or one of the human *aretai*. If it is one of the *aretai*, clearly it is not the one which is damaged if one maims one of one's political enemies; and if it is *the* human *arete*, then clearly to maim one's enemy does not diminish this *arete*, and hence does not make him 'worse' at all. Even if confined to traditional *arete*, the argument is invalid, for traditional *arete* is complex. If one cuts off a man's arm, this diminishes his *arete* traditionally; but good birth is one traditional *arete*: ergo, if a man loses his right arm, he becomes 'worse', therefore of lower birth than he was before. This is no more and no less absurd than the argument found in the *Republic*.

8. It is this which gives rhetoric its prominence as 'the finest of the *technai*', 448 C: though some of the possessors of political *arete* might covet a tyranny or a close oligarchy, most must have realized that their dominance would have to be secured by democratic means in a democratic society; and here the power of swaying an assembly would be of the greatest use.

9. Note not only *anandria*, which must be the mark of a *kakos*, but also the idea of having the law as a *despotes*, which must entail, as in the *Crito*, cp. pp. 262 f., being oneself a slave, *doulos*.

10. That the argument is fallacious is clear. It is a substitution-argument, using alleged logical equivalents as follows: 'being thirsty' = 'being in pain', 'drinking' = 'feeling pleasure'; the conclusion being that 'drinking when thirsty' = 'feeling pleasure while being in pain' in respect of one and the same part of oneself. Accordingly, since Callicles has already admitted, 495 E 3 ff., that no two qualities which can be thus co-present can be the *agathon* and the *kakon*, Plato concludes that since pleasure and pain can be co-present in the same part of a man with reference to the same activity, they cannot be the *agathon* and the *kakon*, as Callicles had maintained. Plato is cheating: it is 'drinking when thirsty' that Callicles should have admitted to be pleasant— thereby destroying the argument—not drinking *per se*; for drinking at other times might be neutral or even painful, and in fact *per se* can have no constant pleasure-pain rating. The argument is built very neatly, cp. 496 E 1 ff. 'Drinking' is glossed as 'satisfaction of thirst'; hence thirst is assumed, and Plato can suavely insert 'when one is thirsty, that is' at E 3, having thus 'justified' this quite illegitimate substitution.

11. He will of course not abandon his equation of the *agathos* with the *phronimos*, for this is one of the basic tenets of his philosophy.

12. A *techne* is defined, *Gorg.* 465 A, as a skill which can give an account of the real nature of things: that is to say, the medical *techne* can give an account of the real nature of the medicines it employs, and their effects; whereas cookery can give no such account of the effect which different foods have on the body. This of course is a philosophical redefinition of *techne*; in ordinary Greek both cookery and rhetoric may be termed *technai*.

13. Just as in *Republic* i he is under no obligation to refute Thrasymachus as a nihilist if Thrasymachus and his kind were not nihilists; cp. Chapter XI, pp. 239f., n. 25.

14. After all, Plato's argument, that Pericles must have been a bad statesman if the people of Athens tried and fined him after he had been in charge of them for many years, *Gorg.* 516 A ff., comes very close to this view, though evidently Plato would not require the citizens to be docile merely in order that their rulers could exploit them. This aspect of Plato's thought is discussed in Chapter XIV, pp. 299 ff.

15. If *Republic* i was really circulated as a separate dialogue, and these flaws were pointed out by Plato's contemporaries, this imperfection of the *adikos* here may account for the zeal with which Glaucon 'polishes the statues' of the just and the unjust man in *Republic* ii. 361 D 5 ff.

XIV

PLATO: IDEAL STATES

A. A CHANGE OF APPROACH

THE position is now this: if Plato is to be successful in solving
the problem of linking *dikaiosune* indissolubly with *arete*, he must
cease to try to show that the claims of *dikaiosune* are derived from
any contract which makes men its slaves, or to chop logic in a
manner which can never be psychologically cogent, whatever
its apparent logical validity. A new approach is needed; and a
possible, though difficult, method is available. We have seen
that in one sense the ordinary man and the 'immoralist' agree,
in another sense utterly disagree, with Plato about the most
important values of human life. Their agreement is much more
extensive than need be the case: the emotive power of any term
of value may remain constant while its use—the range of actions
or events which it commends or decries—changes utterly. Plato,
Meno, and Callicles might agree in using *arete* and *eudaimonia* to
commend the most important qualities in a man and his way
of life while disagreeing utterly on the nature of those qualities.
In fact, as we have seen,[a] there is considerable agreement. All
use *arete* to commend a skill or skills, as it has always done, and
eudaimonia to commend an existence which is smooth-running,
stable, and completely satisfying, as it has always done. This is
agreement, important agreement; but its nature should not
be overlooked. To say that a man should skilfully pursue a
stable and efficient life which will fully satisfy his desires is to
describe neither the skill nor the way of life. It is to create certain expectations, which may be fulfilled in many different ways.
Accordingly, Plato may attempt to meet ordinary man and
'immoralist' on their own ground in a manner different from
that employed hitherto. Ordinary man and 'immoralist' agree
in wanting *agatha*, 'things which are good for them', to enable
them to lead a full life, to *eudaimonein*, to *eu prattein*: Plato must
delineate to them a different set of *agatha* which *indisputably*

[a] Chapter XII *passim*.

leads to a life which will be fuller and more satisfying, and hence more worthy of being termed *eudaimonia*, than that which they have till now favoured. Ordinary man and 'immoralist' desire a skill, which may enable them to make no mistake in identifying and securing their *agatha*: Plato must induce them to admit that the skill which they really need is not such as they had believed, but a different, *more efficient* skill which will secure their *agatha* much more certainly than the skill they had favoured. Plato may be able to show that internal *agatha*, things which are 'good for' a man on the psychological level, are much more important and conducive to the stability and efficiency of man and state than any external *agatha*; and that the skill needed to secure these *agatha* is much more highly specialized than had been supposed. If Plato can show this, he has fulfilled the general expectations of this system of values in a manner which 'immoralist' and ordinary man, dislike it as they may, must admit to be more satisfactory than their own. In these circumstances, they must agree to Plato's conclusions; and not only to these, but to any further consequences which follow from them. Just as Plato could not appeal to the better nature of the 'immoralist' by having recourse to more powerful values—for there are none—so the 'immoralist' and the ordinary man can oppose no such values to Plato's argument. They must show that argument to be invalid or acquiesce in the consequences.

B. THE *REPUBLIC*

(i) *The Method*

After *Republic* i, Plato deserts logic-chopping, and in the remaining nine books attempts to link *dikaiosune* with *eudaimonia* in the manner described above. That is to say, he delineates in considerable detail a type of man and a type of state which—he believes—will be agreed to be *eudaimon*, and then claims that *dikaiosune* and the other co-operative *aretai* are essential to the *eudaimonia* of both. Here we may evaluate his success against 'immoralist' and ordinary man separately; for though they are agreed on their ultimate values, as has been shown, their everyday interpretation of them differs. The ordinary man wants to administer both his household and the city efficiently, though he

expects some reward—to which he has an undeniable claim—
from his fellow citizens for his services to the city.[a] The 'immoralist' wishes to exploit the city in the interests of himself
and his immediate associates, can 'get what he wants', and
need desire the prosperity of the city only in so far as it thereby
becomes a fatter prey. True, the practice of the ordinary man
and the 'immoralist' may be indistinguishable in a crisis;[b] but
Plato may none the less find it easier to prove his point to the
satisfaction of the former.

In the *Republic*, Plato deliberately poses his problem in extreme terms. The ordinary man in his ordinary life naturally
benefits in any society from a reputation for justice and fair-
dealing, even if other qualities are more important: honesty is
likely to be the best policy for most men at most times, and
justice, if not desirable in itself, may well be desirable for such
results. Here, however, justice is to be praised neither on these
grounds nor on the grounds of possible advantages after death.[c]
Socrates is to advocate justice solely on the grounds that it is a
constituent of or essential means to *eudaimonia* here and now, on
this earth, even if a man has the worst possible reputation, and
is hated and reviled by his fellow citizens: it must be an inherent, 'real' source of benefit, in no way dependent on public
opinion. As a result, *dikaiosune* should have, initially, not even
the minor attraction which it has in ordinary language: unless
Socrates can show[d]

What each in itself does to its possessor, in virtue of which
dikaiosune is *agathon*, a beneficial thing, *adikia*, *kakon*, a harmful thing,

dikaiosune has here no attraction at all.

Plato's purpose, then, is to demonstrate that justice is a 'good
thing' for its possessor. Since the *Crito*, however, he has been
content to argue about individuals, not cities; and it might
appear sufficient to demonstrate that *dikaiosune* is necessary to
the *eudaimonia* of the individual, for after all *dikaiosune*, in its
usual sense, must be exercised in society: one cannot keep it to
oneself. In fact, Plato employs a subterfuge to enable him to
consider *dikaiosune* in the state first: it is easier to see in the state,
which is larger, and must be qualitatively the same in both.

[a] Cp. Chapter XII *passim*.
[c] Plat. *Rep*. 360 E ff.
[b] Cp. Crito, pp. 240 ff.
[d] Ibid. 367 B.

This subterfuge is necessary. Plato's *dikaiosune* is peculiar; and
we shall see that his argument derives great—and illegitimate—
benefits from this approach. The argument must be greatly
abbreviated here; and in setting it out I shall draw attention
rather to the presuppositions which lie behind it than to the
manner in which Plato expounds it himself.

Beginning with the state, Plato argues that a perfect—most
eudaimon—state consists of three classes: the wise, who govern
it; the brave, who defend it; and the remainder, who do all the
other things—banking, writing poetry, cleaning the streets,
and so on—which people do in cities. In this ideal state, the
classes are to be mutually exclusive: though the governors are
to be selected from such of the defenders as prove suitable, no
one can belong to both classes at once. Accordingly, Plato can
argue[a] that each class has its own proper function, and hence
ideally its own proper *arete*, excellence: the governors, *sophia*,
wisdom; the defenders, *andreia*, courage; and the rest—since
they have no public or political function to perform—*sophrosune*,
moderation and self-restraint, which must also be displayed by
the other two classes, since no class is to trespass on the functions
of any other. Having apportioned these qualities, Plato claims[b]
that *dikaiosune* exists in a state when each class performs its own
function and 'minds its own business':[c] *dikaiosune* is political
harmony thus achieved.

Plato next argues[d] that the *psuche* of each man must also be
tripartite, insisting that the qualities of the state can only be
derived from qualities manifested by the individuals which
compose it, and adducing a number of arguments designed to
prove that these qualities proceed from distinct elements in the
soul. Each of these three elements—the intellectual, the spirited,
and the appetitive—must then, like the three classes in the state,
have its own function and its own *arete*: the intellectual, *sophia*;
the spirited, *andreia*; and the appetitive, *sophrosune*. As in the
state, *dikaiosune* exists when each element performs its own function: *dikaiosune* is psychological harmony thus achieved.

It is not my purpose to attack Plato's psychology[1] but to
ascertain to what extent Plato has succeeded in solving his
problem, if this psychology is accepted as valid. Evidently the

[a] Plat. *Rep.* 427 D ff.   [b] Ibid. 433 A ff.   [c] τὰ αὑτοῦ πράττει.
[d] Ibid. 435 c ff.

quiet virtues are related to *eudaimonia* by this means, for *dikaio-sune* and *sophrosune* now denote and commend the successful performance of certain functions by both soul and state. In both, the successful performance of its function by any element is evidently its *arete*, its excellence, and hence its most desirable condition; for when it is performing perfectly it may truly be termed *agathos*, a good specimen of its kind. Equally, the perfect performance of its function is evidently the *eu prattein*, the 'faring well', the *eudaimonia* of each element, for such performance must give complete satisfaction with no regrets. *Dikaiosune* is the condition in which each of the elements is performing its function perfectly, is displaying its *arete*, excellence, is *agathos*, a good specimen of its kind, *eu prattei*, is in a state of *eudaimonia*. Thus, *dikaiosune* is an *arete* and an essential condition of *eudaimonia*; which is what Plato set out to prove.

The above argument is not precisely that of Plato; but Plato could have stated the argument in this manner, and would have had to do so had he depicted Socrates as arguing with Thrasymachus here. In fact *Republic* ii–x consists of a conversation with Glaucon and Adeimantus, good-hearted men who believe *dikaiosune* to be 'better' than *adikia*, and have asked Socrates to provide intellectual justification for their belief. It must be this change of tone which betrays Plato into carelessness. When, having constructed his *eudaimon* state, he begins to look for *dikaiosune* in it, he says,[a]

I expect, then, that we shall find that if the city has been correctly founded it is perfectly *agathos*. And if so, it is clear that it is wise, *sophos*, and brave, *andreios*, and 'prudent', *sophron*, and just, *dikaios*.

This method of putting the point begs the question.[b] If Thrasymachus or anyone else admits that a state which is *agathos* must be *dikaios* and *sophron*, he has admitted that these qualities are *aretai* and hence desirable, and Plato has no need to prove his point. In fact Thrasymachus maintained that *adikia*, not *dikaiosune*, was an *arete*;[c] and in view of the traditional connotation of *arete*, Glaucon and Adeimantus ought to have the desirability of justice demonstrated to them before they accept *dikaiosune*

---

[a] Plat. *Rep.* 427 D.   [b] Cp., for example, Shorey, *Republic*, Loeb series, ad loc.
[c] Above, p. 277.

as such. In fact, Plato has introduced a 'moralizing' use of
arete[a] which is quite irrelevant here. Plato should have put the
point thus:

> Socrates: You are agreed that this is a *eudaimon* city?
> Glaucon: Yes.
> Socrates: It has been correctly founded, and is therefore fully
> stable and efficient?
> Glaucon: It has and it is.
> Socrates: It must then be *agathos*, a good specimen of its kind?
> Glaucon: It must indeed.
> Socrates: It has, then, many excellences, *aretai*?
> Glaucon: Undoubtedly.
> Socrates: Let us consider what these are.

Thereupon Plato could have pointed out the excellences of his
city which he does point out, all of which contribute to its
smooth running or defence and stability, and hence are undoubtedly *aretai*; and then could have 'recognized' these *aretai*
to be (say) *sophrosune* and *dikaiosune*. Then, if Thrasymachus
agreed that the city adumbrated is *eudaimon*, and (later) that
the corresponding man is *eudaimon* too, he would have to admit
that *dikaiosune*—thus defined—is an *arete*. Plato was asked to
demonstrate that *dikaiosune* is beneficial, and hence desirable;
and at least at first sight he appears to have done so.

(ii) *The Nature of the Trick*

Questions, of course, are begged. I shall confine myself here
to those which are immediately relevant. It is evident that
Plato has tricked Thrasymachus somehow: in fact, in two ways,
the first derived from his apparently harmless insistence on
considering *dikaiosune* and *sophrosune* in the state before turning
to the individual. All Thrasymachus' political prejudices immediately come into play. Though his opinion is never can-
vassed, since his part in the narrative section of the *Republic* is
negligible, it is natural that, as a self-styled political expert, he
should assume that in any society he would be an *agathos*.
Naturally, then, *qua agathos*, he would be eager to agree with
Plato that in a city there should be[b]

Agreement of the better and the worse as to which should rule the
other.

a Cp. Chapter IX.   b Plat. *Rep.* 432 A.

This is Plato's definition of *sophrosune* in the city. It is equally natural that Thrasymachus should agree that those who are most competent to perform any task in the city should perform it, without interference from the unqualified, for the same reason; and this is Plato's definition of civic *dikaiosune*. Having agreed with Plato on these points, Thrasymachus would naturally agree that subservient subjects—who, as the above quotation shows, are the 'worse' element in the city—are good subjects, and that a city in which all are agreed to let the brave defend and the experts rule is a good city. In each case he could use *agathos* to express his approval, not of course in any quiet moral sense, but to commend the city as one functioning in a manner convenient to him as ruler. This tacit agreement to evaluate the city from the point of view of a ruling political expert enables Plato to maintain that *sophrosune*, thus defined, is the *arete*, excellence, of the third class of citizens. This of course does not entail that such *sophrosune* is the end which the third class would naturally set before itself, merely that it is the form of behaviour which a ruler would find convenient; but of course Plato never admits that he is evaluating *sophrosune* and *dikaiosune* as *aretai* from the point of view of the ruling class, and so can conveniently assume that he has proved that *sophrosune* is the *arete* of the third class from the point of view of that class; and hence, as was said above, that *sophrosune* represents the highest function of this class, its *eu prattein*, its *eudaimonia*. The trick is exactly similar in the case of *dikaiosune*.

There is, of course, no reason why Thrasymachus should object to this. The *sophrosune* and *dikaiosune* which Plato has proved to be *aretai*, *aretai* to which all the classes of the city should conform, bear no resemblance to *sophrosune* and *dikaiosune* as ordinarily understood. *Sophrosune* is the acknowledgement of the rulers that they should rule, of the defenders that they should defend, and of the rest that they should acquiesce; and *dikaiosune* is the state of affairs in which this is put into practice. The *manner* in which the rulers should rule is not indicated at all: if a qualified political expert exploits his subjects to the utmost, and they acquiesce, both are behaving with *sophrosune* and *dikaiosune* in the sense in which these have been shown to be *aretai*, conducive to the smooth running of the state. Thrasymachus should be delighted: now, should he find himself tyrant,

he can explain to his subjects that so long as they are subservient they are manifesting their own particular *arete*, that
they are functioning to the top of their capacity, and hence that
they are *eudaimon* really, however the matter may appear to
them.

The foregoing represents what Plato can legitimately claim
to have proved on the basis of the agreed connotation of *arete*
and the analysis of the city which he has constructed in *Republic*
ii–iv. The exposition, however, is not in the form of argument
but of narrative. In these books, Plato sketches in a city which
is *sophron* and *dikaios* in the ordinary usage of Greek; and at the
end of this 'finds' *dikaiosune* and *sophrosune* in his city in the sense
discussed above. He uses this form of exposition to reinforce his
pun on *arete*, which should command Thrasymachus' cynical
approval, with a further pun on *sophrosune* and *dikaiosune*: he
assumes throughout that his *sophrosune* and *dikaiosune* have all
the implications which these terms possess in ordinary Greek.
Such passages as the 'question-begging' quotation discussed
above[a] facilitate this: it is now clear that Plato benefits much
more from this apparent carelessness than was immediately
apparent. Though Plato could construct a good logical argument in the manner suggested, he cannot legitimately make the
deductions from it which he does make. Thrasymachus of course
should violently reject any identification of Platonic with ordinary Greek *dikaiosune*.

Since no one in the Republic is permitted to see this point,
Plato may assume, on turning to the individual *psuche*, that
personal *eudaimonia* depends on the possession of *sophrosune* and
dikaiosune in the ordinary sense; whereas in fact he has merely
proved that the intellect should direct, the appetites acquiesce:
the instructions which the intellect is likely to give to the appetites—or which it should give to them—cannot be thus
determined. Of course, if Plato could *prove* that *dikaiosune* and
sophrosune in the ordinary sense were necessary to the stability
and prosperity of the city, they could be enrolled as *aretai*; but
Plato does not do this, and it is difficult to see how a convincing
method of proof could be fitted into the scheme of the *Republic*.

---

[a] Above, pp. 286 f.

(iii) *The Compatibility of Individual and Civic* Eudaimonia

Let us suppose, however, that Plato can deceive Thrasymachus with these puns, as he does in the dialogue. He has now
to show that individual *dikaiosune* is always an *agathon*, that in
all circumstances a man will obtain more *eudaimonia* from being
just than from anything else which he could do in a given set of
circumstances. This in the last resort Plato is unable to do. In
Book IV[a] he admits that it is impossible to make each citizen
as *eudaimon* as he would like to be: his purpose is to make the
whole city *eudaimon*. True, he insists that the guardians of his
state have a life which is more *eudaimon* than that of an Olympic
victor; but what can Plato reply to Thrasymachus—or even to
Glaucon and Adeimantus—if he asks why they should not be
more *eudaimon* still, since this is possible? Not more *eudaimon* in
the sense of living by exploiting their fellow citizens, since—
allowing Thrasymachus to be taken in—this would upset their
psychic harmonies by impairing their *sophrosune*, and make them
less *eudaimon* in the true sense; but when Plato introduces the
idea of the philosopher-king, the man who studies objective
political truths in the abstract and then makes use of them to
govern the city, it is clear that to philosophize as much as
possible is the most *eudaimon* existence for a man, the life which
is most truly an *agathos bios*: these men are less *eudaimon* as
kings than as philosophers. Yet they must return from their
pure philosophy 'into the cave' to engage in politics, a life
which is 'more wretched' than the best of which they are
capable. Plato presents this[b] as an advantage of his system:
since the philosophers have a better life to return to 'outside
the cave' of the affairs of this world, they will not be tempted to
set any value on political power as an end in itself, and hence
will be just and disinterested rulers. They will treat the time
which they spend in governing the city not as something *kalon*
but as something 'necessary'.[c] This, by the principles with
which Plato set out, is scandalous. Thrasymachus, accepting
the idea that *dikaiosune*, in the sense of maintaining one's
own psychological harmony, is or entails *eudaimonia*, can in-
stantly inquire why the philosophers should engage in government at all. Plato replies that since the city produced them,

---

[a] Plat. *Rep.* 420 E 7 ff.   [b] Ibid. 519 D ff.   [c] Ibid. 540 A ff.

since they did not arise spontaneously, they have an obligation
to the city. But if Plato were to say that it would be unjust for
them not to engage in government, he would be merely punning on the word 'unjust'. Injustice, in the sense in which Plato
has shown that it should be avoided, is the upsetting of a man's
psychological harmony. But it is nowhere suggested that the
desire for philosophy and contemplation can become too strong.
To philosophize is an absolute good. The philosophers would
be more *eudaimon* if they remained aloof from politics: accordingly, Plato can offer no real reason why they should go
back. Admittedly the city would be better governed, and hence
more *eudaimon*, if they went back; but Plato cannot explain
why, if one's own *eudaimonia* is the end of life, one should prefer
the city's—or anyone else's—*eudaimonia* to one's own. Certainly
Thrasymachus is unlikely to accept any explanation. The ordinary man might be prevailed upon to aim at the city's *eudaimonia*; but there are only two available motives for such action.
He might believe that it is *kalon* to act in this manner; but Plato
says expressly that the philosopher-kings will not believe this.
Secondly, he might hope to receive benefits in return for the
agatha conferred upon the city;[a] but the only possible benefit
which the city could confer upon the philosopher-king is per-
mission to return to his philosophy, and this they would not
need if they took no part in politics in the first place. Accordingly, the ordinary man has no reason to accept Plato's account
either.

It is evident that Plato has created this last difficulty for
himself. Admittedly, the metaphysics of the Forms leads him
to believe that the visible world is less 'real' than the entities
apprehended in abstract thought; and it may follow necessarily from this that the contemplation of these entities is more
fully satisfying, and hence renders a man more fully *eudaimon*,
than any political or moral activity in the visible world. But
since man is not entirely intellect, it does not follow necessarily
that such contemplation will ensure the *eudaimonia*, in the sense
of psychological harmony, of the whole man. Since Plato's
assertion that the life of pure philosophy is fully and continuously satisfying is merely an assertion, it may be thought
that Plato could have solved this problem merely by asserting

[a] Cp. Chapter X.

that the whole existence of his rulers, both as philosophers and as kings, was the most *eudaimon* existence possible for a man. Such an assertion would of course be a solution; but to suppose that it is a solution open to Plato is to forget the nature of the movement of which both Thrasymachus and Plato form a part. It is an intellectual, not a moral, movement, and the intellect must always take precedence. Politically speaking, Thrasymachus is an intellectual bandit; but we have seen that, though he may not realize it, his values entail that he is an intellectual first and a bandit afterwards. Plato is an intellectual moralist and political philosopher; but his values entail that he is an intellectual first and a moralist and political philosopher afterwards. Plato has deepened the idea of a skill to secure *agatha*; it is not surprising either that a Thrasymachus should—if convinced—be willing to accept it, or that it should be a skill completely unrelated to the co-operative virtues.

(iv) *The Results*

It is now evident that Plato has failed to solve his problem. *Dikaiosune* and *sophrosune*, in the sense in which these terms are ordinarily understood, have not been shown to be essential to *eudaimonia*; and in the peculiar Platonic sense they not merely fail to prove that the best citizens should govern justly, but even that they should govern at all. It is, however, worth while to inquire what follows if we accept Plato's account of *eudaimonia* in soul and state, and are willing to suppose that the rulers will be willing to restrict their own *eudaimonia* in the interests of the whole. All Plato's contemporaries agreed that the end of life was *eudaimonia*, a completely satisfactory life with no regrets, however interpreted. Thus, unless they could show that this vague concept should be interpreted quite differently, they had of necessity to accept any consequences which followed from Plato's *eudaimonia*. There is one most important consequence. The harmony, psychological and political, which is *eudaimonia* in soul and state, can only be produced by a process of very careful conditioning and very careful control, and can only be discerned by experts of a very remarkable kind—the philosopher-kings. Accordingly, the citizens must be very carefully conditioned and controlled, and a very remarkable kind of expert sought; and when found, he must be allowed full scope to do whatever he likes in the interests of the citizens' *eudai-monia*, as delineated by Plato. The conclusion may be unpalatable, but it follows from the premisses, and unless one is willing to abandon the premisses, which involve the most powerful terms of value in Greek, or can find some flaw in the reasoning, one must abide by the conclusion. This may be stated briefly here; the discussion of the *Laws*[a] brings it much more into the foreground.

Here we must consider to what extent *dikaios* has become firmly affixed to *agathos*, if we admit that Plato has proved what he claims to have proved. *Dikaiosune* has been shown to be one of the four *aretai* of the soul; and since every citizen must possess *dikaiosune* and *sophrosune*, to be *agathos* is to be *dikaios*. Justice is, however, only one of the four *aretai* of the soul; and in the *Republic* it—and *sophrosune*—have no ascendancy over the others. This is important; for it is only natural to say of the rulers of this state that they are the most *agathoi* of the citizens, not because they are more just than the others,[2] but because they are wiser; and we have indeed seen that those who are less wise may be termed 'worse'.[b] In Plato's clockwork state this does not matter, for Plato can hold all four *aretai* in balance, and postulate that all the inhabitants who are wise are also *dikaios* and *sophron*. Unless the state of the *Republic* is accepted as a whole, however, the ethical thought contained in the work does not serve to solve the problem of values with which we are concerned; for since we have here a deepening of the ordinary Greek values of the period rather than a realignment, any ordinary Greek state containing ordinary Greeks and no philosopher-kings will still be tempted to value political skill and benefits above other qualities; and though in an ideal state where the inhabitants are just and self-controlled as well this does not matter, the dangers in more normal circumstances have been abundantly illustrated.[c]

C. THE *LAWS*

(i) *A Revaluation of* Aretai

In the *Laws*, however, a work in which he pays much more attention to means than in the *Republic*, Plato appears in a

---

[a] Below, pp. 296 ff.   [b] Above, p. 287.   [c] Chapter X *passim*.

different guise. In the *Republic*[a] he had said that the rulers were to be those who had become *aristoi* in philosophy and in respect of war. The judgement really entails that *andreia*, courage, and *sophia*, wisdom, will be—as in the sense in which they are known to ordinary language they have always been—the most highly regarded qualities. In the *Laws*, however, though to be *agathos* naturally includes success in battle, for the conditions of life have not changed, it is evident that Plato has been thinking about the relative importance of the *aretai*. The Cretans and Spartans, whom 'upper-class' and philosophic Athenian opinion had so much admired, are now held to be mistaken, inasmuch as their education is directed purely to warlike ends, to the development of *andreia*. One should on the contrary resort to a form of education[b]

As a result of which a man would be not only *agathos* in war, but also capable of administering his city; the type of man who, as we said at the beginning, is really more skilled in war than the warriors of Tyrtaeus; the man who honours courage as the fourth grade of *arete*, not the first, whether it is manifested in individuals or in the city as a whole.

Courage is to be ranked fourth of the *aretai* in merit; and, on a somewhat different calculation, the brave deeds of the soldier are to be ranked second:[c]

So touching this matter let there be laid down this law coupled with laudation, a law which counsels the people to honour to a lesser extent those *agathoi* who preserve the city whether by acts of courage or by stratagems of war; for the greatest honour is to be given to those who are able to observe to an outstanding degree the written pronouncements of their good legislators.

The law-abiding citizen comes at long last into his own;[3] and the emphatic phraseology shows the violence of the change in standards. Plato now means by *agathos polites*, it seems, something approximating to the modern 'democratic' idea of the good citizen, for he characterizes him[d] as

The man who knows both how to govern and to be governed.

'To know how to be governed' seems a curious phrase; but if Meno's definition of *arete*,[e] a definition which the *Republic* does

---

[a] Plat. *Rep.* 543 A 4.   [b] Plat. *Laws* 666 E.   [c] Ibid. 922 A.
[d] Ibid. 643 E.   [e] Above, p. 229.

not decisively reject, is compared, the reason for the form of the expression is clear, as is the extent of the change of values which has taken place.

Dikaios, then, has firmly taken its place in the forefront of Greek values in the *Laws*; and once again it might appear that the problem is solved. *Dikaiosune* raises the right questions; that has been repeated many times in the present work: and the claims of *dikaiosune* will now be heard. Only the elimination of any inconsistencies, and the refinement of any crudities, will now be necessary for the attainment of a satisfactory concept of moral responsibility.

This seems inevitable; and indeed we find Plato, as Protagoras had done,[a] insisting on a relationship between punishment and voluntary action:[4] for example, he makes regulations drawing a distinction between those who lose their weapons in war voluntarily, *hekon*, and those who lose them involuntarily, *akon*,[b] a distinction which popular usage evidently failed to draw, as is clear both from the amount of space which Plato devotes to it and from the implications of the *aischron*-standard which have been explained in earlier chapters. Reasons have been given for this state of affairs; but now that *dikaiosune* has been firmly fixed both to *kalon*[5] and to *arete* by Plato, it seems reasonable to suppose that this distinction will be drawn in the future, and that the claims of responsibility will be considered.

(ii) *The Price of Success*

After so many unsuccessful solutions, however, we may well be chary of asserting that the problem is solved. Plato has solved *his* problem: if the code of the *Laws* is accepted, the state will function, at least in theory, and be stable, suitably prosperous, and hence *eudaimon*. We need not inquire here whether he has *proved* that civic and individual *eudaimonia* are compatible, or that *dikaiosune* is an *agathon*. The *Laws* claims to be the legal code for a state; hence Plato can enact what he believes to be beneficial without proving that it is so, and naturally may direct his enactments to securing the *eudaimonia* of the state as a whole as his chief consideration; though he certainly believes that these are in the 'true' interests of the individual as well.[c]

---

[a] Plat. *Prot.* 323 c.   [b] Plat. *Laws* 944 c 4 ff.
[c] Below, p. 309 and Note 17.

Plato has solved his problem. From the point of view of moral responsibility, however, he has solved it at a price. *Agathos/ eudaimon* and *dikaiosune* are firmly linked; but since, as was inevitable, *agathos* is the stronger partner, *dikaios* has adopted the 'logic' of *agathos*, not the reverse: as a component of *eudaimonia*, *dikaiosune* is an *agathon*, with the 'logic' of an *agathon*. Its only claim to be linked to *arete* is still the essential contribution which it makes to civic (and personal) prosperity and stability. Plato justifies his re-ranking of *dikaiosune* thus:[a]

For I certainly expect that if you follow the argument which I put forward just now, you will discover that what caused the downfall of these kingdoms . . . was not cowardice or ignorance of warfare on the part of the rulers or of those who should have been their subjects, but that what ruined them was 'badness', *kakia*, of all other kinds, and especially ignorance about the greatest of human interests.[6]

The co-operative virtues have come into their own, since the lack of them causes the ruin of states. From the manner in which they must be justified, an inevitable result follows, which may be expressed in a variety of ways. On the civic level this *arete*, like traditional *arete*, being the prime necessity for the existence of the state, is something which the state cannot afford not to possess: it is *the* unqualified good, and any means are justified in securing it;[7] while on the personal level, since any *arete*, excellence, must be a desirable, *dikaiosune* and any other quality now termed *arete* are an unqualified good for the individual citizen as well as for the state, and the individual should acquiesce in the use of any method which may secure his possession of these desirables.

This it is which justifies the attributes of the states of the *Republic* and the *Laws*, and of the ruler of the *Politicus*; and this it is which must have made any reply to Plato so difficult for his Greek contemporaries. For example, in the *Politicus*[b] Plato inquires whether a ruler may compel his subjects, or whether they must be willing to be governed. His reply is quite explicit:

It is, then, a necessary consequence that among forms of government that one is pre-eminently right and is the only real form of government in which the rulers are found to be truly possessed of

---

[a] Plat. *Laws* 688 c.   [b] Plat. *Polit.* 293 ff.

knowledge, not merely to seem to possess it, whether they rule with law or without law, whether their subjects are willing or unwilling, whether they themselves are rich or poor. . . . Provided that they act in accordance with knowledge, *epistēmē*, and justice and preserve and benefit the state by making it better than it was, this, we must say, is the only correct, *orthē*, form of state.

Violence is justified, if necessary, as it would be in the case of a physician, to force the city to act in a manner which is more *dikaion*, more *agathon*, and more *kalon* than formerly. It is, however, suggested that violence would be unnecessary, and that the tyrant, the king, oligarchy, aristocracy, and democracy have all arisen because men have felt distaste at their one perfect ruler[a] and have refused to believe that there could ever be anyone worthy of such a power, or willing and able to rule with *arete* and true knowledge, *episteme*, and dispense what is *dikaion* and *hosion* to all . . .

For they admit that if such a person as we describe should actually arise, he would be honoured and would continue to dwell among them, directing in all prosperity and stability, *eudaimonōs*, a perfectly correct, *orthe*, form of government.

This is the condition of the hypothetical rulers of the *Republic*; and as we have said, no Greek of the period could dissent from the conclusion by opposing higher values to it. Nor could he say that Plato was misusing the terms: Plato has given him a state with the qualities—efficiency, stability—he desires, using to commend it the terms he approves. The only course open to any Greek of the period who wishes to reject the conclusion, if he can discover no flaws in the argument, is to deny that a ruler with such qualities can exist; for Plato himself says that if there is no scientific ruler available[b]

No citizen shall dare to do anything contrary to the laws, and he who does so shall be punished with death and the most extreme penalties; and this is most correct, *orthon*, and most *kalon*, as a second best.

When Plato wrote the *Laws*, at the end of his life, he had himself come to the conclusion that a scientific ruler in his sense could not exist. The difficulty is both one of comprehension,

[a] Ibid. 301 c.   [b] Ibid. 297 d.

and of the good will needed to act upon the truth comprehended:[a]

And secondly, even if a man fully grasps the truth of this as a principle of *techne*, should he afterwards gain control of the state and become an irresponsible autocrat, he would never prove able to abide by this view and to continue always fostering the public interest in the state as the object of the first importance, to which the private interest is secondary; rather his mortal nature will always be urging him on to grasping and self-interested action.

A scientific ruler is humanly impossible;[8] but if by a miracle one should occur, the conclusion of the *Republic* and the *Politicus* still stands:[b]

No law or ordinance is mightier than knowledge, nor is it right for reason to be subject or in thrall to anything.

Failing a miracle, no man can be autocrat; but the second-best state of the *Laws* leaves as little freedom to its subjects as that of the *Republic* and *Politicus*. Everything must be fettered by law;[c] the law can allow no room for private freedom. Every *techne* must submit its standards to the political *techne*;[d] and if the poet cannot be persuaded to write about the right things as *agatha*, and in the right manner, he must of course be compelled to do so,[e] for he is not concerned, as the state must be, with the psychological and moral effects of his writing. No individual may act on his own initiative: a point which is explicitly made with respect to action in war.[f] Such a code, Plato recognizes, must be accepted willingly by the inhabitants;[g] but once the initial agreement is made, the inhabitants of the Law-state, in the same manner as the subjects of the philosopher-king, have ceded all claim to act of their own free will.[h] They may not need to be coerced, but they make no choices of their own. What they are to do is laid down in the laws or in the proems to the laws which, using the *kalon*-standard, exhort the citizen[i] to do what is laid down on the law that follows. The good citizen treats these as binding upon himself: there is

---

[a] Plat. *Laws* 874 E ff.   [b] Ibid. 875 C.
[c] Ibid. 804 D, cp. 792 D ff., on music.   [d] Ibid. 802 E.
[e] Ibid. 660 A, 801 C.   [f] Ibid. 942 A, cp. 780 A.   [g] Ibid. 752 C, 746 A.
[h] Using the phrase, of course, in an 'ordinary language' sense.
[i] For the method, cp. *Laws* 880 A.

no need to make choices, for civic stability and *eudaimonia* do not require that choices should be made. To this end all is directed: though Plato says that mere survival is not enough, that one must 'live well' in addition, the city which *eu zēi*[a] is definable as being more stable than the one which merely survives. Plato's city is not faced with the alternative of standing firmly by its convictions or, by a sacrifice of some standards, surviving as it otherwise could not; for Plato certainly believes that his state is more capable of survival than any other of comparable size.[b]

To most people, such a state must appear repellent. When we turn to the individual, however, the position seems even more alarming. It is not necessary, indeed it is not desirable, that the citizen should make choices: accordingly, in producing the ideal citizen for the Platonic state, whether that of the *Republic*, the *Politicus*, or the *Laws*, Plato naturally devotes himself to the production of a citizen who has neither the need nor the desire to make choices: a policy which may be justified merely by pointing out that personal *eudaimonia* has no more need than civic *eudaimonia* of the making of choices. Since to be *agathos* has never been to make choices so much as to produce results, such a change could not seem so violent to a Greek.

D. THE BACKGROUND TO PLATO'S THEORY OF PUNISHMENT

(i) *Some Implications of Ordinary Greek*

The manner in which these conclusions affect the responsibility of the individual citizen must be considered more closely: for which purpose a brief survey of some other passages of the earlier Plato is necessary. Plato starts in all things, as he must, from the position of the sophists, whose chief claim was that they made men better, *beltious*. This word has clear implications. It has been shown that at all periods, for powerful reasons, *agathos* commended in a man the ability to produce certain results rather than the possession of good intentions. This element of *agathos* naturally persisted, as has been seen, into the new use

---

[a] Cp. Chapter XII, p. 252.   [b] Cp. *Laws* 697 B ff., 739 E, 960 B.

which it obtained as a result of the thought of the sophists. In
the *Apology* Socrates says to Callias that if his sons had been
colts or young bulls,[a] there would have been no difficulty in
finding a trainer for them; but as it is, they are men: does
Callias know who has knowledge of—and hence can impart—
human and political *arete*? (Callias replies that he does, and
names a sophist.) Here we have an evident comparison between
training animals and training men; and there is nothing in the
history of *agathos* and *arete* to suggest that the comparison is in
any way strained: the Greek can well term man 'the best of the
animals'.[9]

However, though this is one legitimate manner of thinking of
the *agathos* in Greek, it need not in ordinary language, which
thrives on illogicalities, exclude others. The Greek may be able
to compare human education with training animals, for the
reasons given; but it is unnecessary to assume that the comparison was pushed to the limit; and in the manner in which the
sophists and the earlier Plato used it, the comparison seems
unlikely to lead to dangerous consequences. In the *Euthydemus*,
for example, it is said that the function of the political *techne*
is not, as is commonly supposed, to make men wealthy, but to
make them[b]

Wise, *sophoi*, and give them a share of knowledge, if indeed this
techne is to benefit them and make them *eudaimones*.

So long as the ideal is to make men *sophoi*, all is well, for *sophos*
is still employed in the 'ordinary Greek' sense, to denote political skill in a sense in which any reasonably intelligent man
may acquire it. Despite the animal-analogy, the teacher gives
his pupil a skill which he is then regarded as himself exercising
intelligently, not automatically.[10]

Thus far all is well; but as soon as the thinker turns his attention from the individual to the state, the latent dangers emerge.
The *agathos* has always been valued for the contribution he
makes to the state's stability and security: from Homer onwards
he may readily be considered as a unit functioning more or less
successfully in his environment—a unit which must succeed to
secure its own and society's continued existence. It is for this

[a] Plat. *Apol.* 20 A 6 ff. For the form of expression, cp. (*Theages*) 121 B.
[b] Plat. *Euthyd.* 292 B 4.

reason that men may be regarded as comparable to colts or young bulls without straining ordinary Greek; but when they are *explicitly* so regarded, the results from the point of view of individual responsibility must be held to be deplorable. The statesman becomes the skilled citizen-trainer, and one may estimate a man's quality as a statesman by comparing the manner in which his citizens treat him at first with the manner in which they treat him when he has had them in hand for some time.[a] The statesman and the sophist have no right to complain if their charges ill treat them. As with training lions, it is the result that counts: intentions are quite irrelevant on both sides.

(ii) *Platonic Additions*

Thus it follows readily from 'ordinary Greek' usage that the statesman and the sophist should condition their charges to have the right reactions; for it is far safer than to make them *sophoi* and ensures far more surely that the units will function properly in their environment. The soil is properly prepared for Platonic psychology and Platonic metaphysics; and when these are added, the transformation is complete. The man who best blends gymnastics with 'music' and applies them most successfully to the soul is the man whom we should most rightly pronounce to be the true musician, far rather than he who brings the strings into harmony with one another.[b] The purpose of the blending is to ensure the correct reactions in the lower parts of the soul. This activity might be devoted merely to preparing the ground for the implanting of reason, *logos*, and knowledge, *episteme*. The *Republic*, however, makes it clear that this is not the case. Possession of the Platonic *logos* and *episteme* is for the few: only the philosopher-kings are capable of it, even the defenders having to be content with mere true opinion.[11] The latter are to be properly conditioned specimens and, as it were, 'guardians of the flock';[c] for which function they require no more. Again, when the philosopher-king is introduced, he is to be compelled to 'practise stamping on the plastic matter of human nature, in public and in private, the patterns which he sees in the world of Forms'; and Socrates claims[d] that such a

---

[a] Cp. Plat. *Gorg.* 516 A 5, 517 B 5.   [b] Plat. *Rep.* 412 A, cp. *Polit.* 306 ff.
[c] Plat. *Rep.* 451 C.   [d] Ibid. 500 D, cp. *Phaedr.* 270 B ff.

man would be a skilled producer[a] of *sophrosune, dikaiosune*, and 'demotic' *arete*[b] in general in the ordinary citizens. A good 'end-product' is all that matters.

The effect of all this is to produce a society in which only a few in the full sense know what they are doing. In the *Laws*, however, having concluded that the philosopher-king is an impossible ideal, Plato is left with a society of 'ordinary men' whom he must make as reliable as possible in a city which is to be as stable as possible. In order to show more clearly what Plato hopes to achieve by conditioning these men, the state of the unconditioned man must be briefly considered.

(iii) *Plato and Free Will*

The desire to condition any man might appear to imply the belief that one is tinkering with an automaton, that man is an ingenious piece of clockwork. This, however, Plato certainly does not believe. His citizens are, left to themselves, perfectly capable of making plans for their own lives. In saying that man is the puppet of the gods,[c] Plato does not assert that the gods pull the strings and that man must needs follow where they lead, in the sense that each individual action is fully determined from above. The sole relation of the 'strings' to the gods seems to be that the gods have planted them in us, and we can do nothing about their presence. In that sense men are at the mercy of the strings, but in no other. We do not move in a given direction as a result of some compromise between the strings, some ghostly parallelogram of forces. We have a golden string called 'calculation', *logismos*, and with this, expressed publicly as law, we must always co-operate; for 'since calculation is good, but gentle rather than forceful, its leading string needs helpers to ensure that the golden element within us may vanquish the other kinds'. 'We' must co-operate with the golden cord. There is an 'I' in us in addition to the cords, just as in Homeric psychology there is an 'I' over against *thumos, kradiē*,[12] and the other psychological functions; and if 'we' can co-operate or no at will, any form of automatism is out of the question. Indeed, one

---

[a] δημιουργός.
[b] i.e. *arete* based on conditioned 'right opinion', not on knowledge of the Forms.
[c] Plat. *Laws* 645 A ff.

of the advantages for the moralist of a psychology based on calculation is that it discourages belief in any kind of determinism; for it is difficult to believe that one is not free to calculate correctly or incorrectly.[13]

Thus, in principle, every man, according to Plato's psychology, is capable of directing his life according to the dictates of reason.[14] The question is simply whether Plato feels able to allow him to do so; and observation leads Plato to believe that the man who is capable in fact of long resisting his desires in the interests of reason is very rare indeed.[a] Now if human nature is incapable of long resistance to the buffets of passion, and the conflict is seen as one between rational and irrational desire—which, considering the nature of the Greek *agathon*, must be the case—the obvious solution is, if possible, to ensure that rational and irrational desire pull in the same direction, that of the 'golden cord'. This is the purpose of Plato's system of education and conditioning. From earliest days the child in the Law-state will be taught the nature of 'true' pleasures and 'true' *agatha*. The same things will be shown to be 'truly' noble and 'truly' beneficial. The laws will teach him to put into practice the general requirements of the 'good life', life at its most efficient and stable; and as a result, or so Plato believes, his desires will coincide with the dictates of reason. These people will not be automata: they will know what they are doing, and unless they are too stupid to understand their own laws, which are to contain explanations of their provisions,[b] why they are doing it; but if their conditioning is a success, they will never have to make a moral choice. Ends are fixed by their conception of *agatha*, and as to what things are *agatha* they will have 'indelible opinion'; and so complete is the code of laws that they will rarely need to choose the means, since it will be necessary simply to consult the code. Plato's psychology leaves room for free will; but Plato's code of laws calls upon the inhabitants of any city which adopts it to resign its free will, in exchange for those things which it prizes most highly, for *eudaimonia*. Plato has solved his problem in terms of Greek values.

[a] Ibid. 918 c. Cp. the pessimistic reason given for the composition of the *Laws*, 874 E ff.
[b] Ibid. 721 A ff.

E. PUNISHMENT AND RESPONSIBILITY

(i) *The Theory*

We are here, however, concerned not merely with the relative importance of values, but with moral responsibility. That it too is a problem is acknowledged by Plato in the *Laws*. He has shown that to be *dikaios* is an *agathon*, that it is necessary to *eudaimonia*. Accordingly, the attainment of *dikaiosune* becomes a desirable goal, and one might suppose that its attainment raised merely problems of calculation; that is to say, that any error must be intellectual error, a mistake as to one's own best interests. By constructing his ideal states Plato has achieved to his own satisfaction what he was trying to achieve by logic in the earlier dialogues. In either case, provided that Plato's results are accepted, it appears that *oudeis hekon hamartanei*, that no one 'makes a mistake' on purpose. As soon as the co-operative virtues are acknowledged to be *aretai* or *agatha*, and so desirable, the 'Socratic paradox' becomes a mere statement of fact.

From the point of view of punishment, this conclusion sets a serious problem for the legislator, as both the Stranger and Cleinias acknowledge in the *Laws*.[a] Cleinias, indeed, is sophisticated enough to realize that a plea which has universal application cannot be taken into account, for he does not suppose that, even if all 'error' is involuntary, *akousion*, no punishment at all can be imposed; but he clearly does suppose that as a result there can be no *differentiation* of punishment, that in these circumstances no other criteria could be relevant. Plato tacitly disagrees: though he does not express the matter in this way, he in fact introduces such criteria, as will be shown below. He could instead have abandoned the Socratic dictum '*oudeis hekon hamartanei*' altogether. At all events, this seems to be possible: Plato's psychology does not entail that moral error is purely intellectual, and he is fully aware of this. Ignorance, he holds, is only one of the three possible causes of 'errors', *hamartēmata*, the other two being passion, *thumos*, and desire.[b] Further, the 'puppet of the gods' is at liberty to favour which of the cords he pleases; and the *Laws*, like the *Republic*, contains an excellent

---

[a] Plat. *Laws* 861 E ff.   [b] Ibid. 863 B ff.

characterization of the 'acratic' man,[a] who knows the good and fails to do it at the behest of desire or passion. This, one might suppose, was exactly 'to make a mistake on purpose'; and Plato thus seems in a position to abandon the Socratic dictum.

In fact, on the contrary, he recognizes it explicitly in the *Laws*[b] and says with great and repeated emphasis that he will not abandon it, and that a solution must be found which does not entail its abandonment.[15] There are at least two reasons for this. The first is clear from the manner in which the discussion is introduced. Plato reiterates that all *kakoi* are involuntarily *kakoi*, poor specimens of their kind, and draws from this the conclusion that men are always involuntarily *adikoi*, unjust, since all *adikoi*—as has been agreed—are *kakoi*.[c] Plato could easily analyse the phrase 'involuntarily *kakos*' in terms of the psychology of passion and desire mentioned above; but since the whole practical and protreptic strength of his position is that *kakia* is abhorred by all *tout court*, he doubtless felt unwilling or unable to abandon this brief, neat, and uncomplicated statement. The second reason, which depends on Plato's perpetual distinction between what a man 'really' wants, *eudaimonia*, and his transitory desires, will become clear in the course of the discussion.

Since Plato is unwilling to abandon the Socratic paradox, a theory of punishment must be devised to suit it; and Plato finds it quite possible to devise such a theory. Other legal codes distinguish between voluntary and involuntary 'errors' or crimes, between *hekousia* and *akousia hamartemata* or *adikēmata*. Plato cannot do this, but in effect introduces new criteria. He brings into the discussion the term 'harm', *blabē*; and of this he says that it may be readily *hekousios* or *akousios*. But not all harmful acts, *blabai*, are acts of injustice: if anyone harms another man not deliberately but *akon*, Plato insists, the act is not to be termed *adikēma akousion*, but (not *adikema* at all) merely *blabe*. Whereas if a man benefits another, and the benefit is not 'correct',[d] this *is* to be termed *adikia*. One must not consider whether any harm has been done, but whether the man who benefited or harmed another had 'a just disposition and character', *ēthos*

---

[a] Ibid. 689 A, cp. Leontius, *Rep.* 439 E.   [b] *Laws* 861 D 2 ff.
[c] Ibid. 860 D.
[d] i.e. not in his own or the state's 'true' interest.

dikaion.[a] One must distinguish *blabe* and *adikema* from the point
of view of the treatment appropriate to each. The manner,
which is not what might be expected, will be discussed below.

This is not a mere change in linguistic usage, designed (say)
to improve legal terminology, with no metaphysical overtones:
if it were, it would be difficult to understand why Plato, having
stated so vehemently that *oudeis hekon hamartanei*, and having
declined to alter his opinion under any circumstances, should
'explain' this in such a way that no one is to be held to have
done wrong unless he did it on purpose, *hekon*. The explanation
of the linguistic clash is clear enough: *hekon* is being used on two
quite different levels. It is quite legitimate—if confusing—to
say that no one (really and truly) *hekon hamartanei* and at the
same time that only those who (in ordinary language) commit
harm *hekon* are to be held to be unjust. Plato need not have
realized that he was punning on the word *hekon*, for he has contrived an apparent distinction between *adikema* (or *hamartema*)
akousion, involuntary injustice or error, and *blabe hekousios*; but
the attempt to apply *adikema akousion* and *blabe hekousios* to the
same individual action should quickly have convinced him that
the words were not used in the same sense.

Nevertheless, once an 'ordinary language' use of *hekousios*
and *akousios* has been introduced, it might be hoped that a
theory of reward and punishment which drew what we might
consider to be 'normal' distinctions would follow. This, however, requires closer examination. The most interesting phrase
of those quoted above is 'the man who has an *ethos dikaion*, a just
character'; for this, it soon appears, is not a misleading way of
saying 'provided he had no criminal intent, which can best be
inferred from his general way of life'. The meaning becomes
clearer when Plato defines justice and injustice.[b] He terms
injustice, *adikia*, 'the tyranny in the soul of pleasure and passion
and grief and jealousies and desires, whether it does any harm
or not'; whereas if his opinion of what is best, *ariston*, rules a
man, even if it should fail, *sphallesthai*, in some respects, what is
done amiss by such a man is to be termed not involuntary
injustice but just. An act is to be termed *dikaion* when it is done
by a *dikaios*.

---

a ἤθει καὶ δικαίῳ τρόπῳ χρώμενος.
b Plat. *Laws* 863 E ff.

The implications of this system are not clear unless 'even if it should fail in some respects' is understood; and this may be clarified by a passage from the *Sophist*, which is evidently related. There[a] the Stranger says that there are two types of *kakia* in the soul. These prove to be the conflict between reason and the passions, characterized as cowardice and incontinence and injustice, which are like a disease; and on the other hand ignorance, *agnoia*, which is like a deformity, *aischos*, in the soul. Of the latter the Stranger says that it is the condition of a soul striving towards the truth; and for it[b] teaching is the cure, for the former, punishment. Punishment, then, in the *Sophist*, is restricted to cases of conflict between reason and the passions.

'Ignorance', however, must be defined more clearly. The Stranger now divides it into two parts, *amathiā* and *agnoia*. *Amathia*, the more important part, is defined[c] as the condition of thinking one knows something when one does not, which, says Plato, is the cause of almost every failure, *sphallesthai*, of the intellect in all men. It is distinguished from simple *agnoia* by the treatment appropriate to each. *Agnoia* may be removed by 'instruction', by the teaching of facts and techniques;[16] whereas *amathia* requires 'education', *paideiā*, which, it is said, is accomplished by means of exhortation and elenchus. Evidently *amathia* must be interpreted as 'not knowing what is in one's interest' in the full Platonic sense, not knowing, that is, what is (really and truly) *agathon*.

There can be no doubt that the *Sophist* and the *Laws* express the same view of punishment here. In both, as in the *Republic*, *adikia* is the conflict, *dikaiosune* the agreement, of the lower desires with reason. But whereas in the *Republic* it seems to be assumed that *dikaiosune* in this sense inevitably leads to a state of *eudaimonia* (as is natural on the assumption that the reason of the philosopher-kings is in touch with objective truths of value) in these dialogues it is recognized that a psychological calm or harmony may be united with what are for Plato mistakes about the basic facts of human existence. Such mistakes are not compatible with *eudaimonia*; and on the political level Plato might have termed these *adikia* too, since they harm the well-being of the state. In fact he adopts what seems prima facie a most

---

[a] *Sophist* 227 E ff., 228 B 3 ff., 228 E 2.   [b] Ibid. 229 A 8.
[c] Plat. *Soph.* 229 C 5.

enlightened attitude for a 'closed' society; for if 'even if he should fail, *sphallesthai*, in some respects' is compared with 'every failure, *sphallesthai*, of the intellect' in the passage from the *Sophist*, and the two versions are compared generally, it becomes evident that 'even if he should fail in some respects' too is to be taken in a very general sense. If a man's reason and desires are not in conflict, *whatever his basic view of life*, he is to be termed *dikaios*, provided that his actions are based on reason, not passion or desire. Teaching, exhortation, dialectic: these are his needs, not punishment, which is designed to reform the rebellious lower elements of the soul.

(ii) *The Effects*

This may be 'enlightened'; but it is with the effects of this system upon the concept of moral responsibility that we are concerned here. The system might appear to be very sensitive to the requirements of moral responsibility: voluntarily harmful actions, *hekousioi blabai*, have been defined and distinguished from involuntarily harmful actions, *akousioi blabai*, and punishment has been assigned to the one, education to the other. Perhaps the theory is not so detailed as might have been hoped; but doubtless the details could be filled in. Such a supposition is completely unjustified. The true nature of this system is revealed by Plato's treatment of atheism. There are, he says, two kinds of atheists:[a] the one, while not believing in the gods, has a just character, an *ethos dikaion*, hates unjust men and injustice, and has a great affection for justice and just men, the other, in addition to his atheism, is licentious and self-seeking. The latter does the most harm, for while the former may corrupt others if he is not corrected, since he speaks freely of his beliefs, the latter, being cunning and deceitful, may become a tyrant or a popular leader; in which position he may do much more harm. These men, who are not merely atheists but include also those who hold the type of beliefs censured in *Republic* ii, are to be terribly punished;[b] but it is not with these that we are primarily concerned here. The former class is more significant. By definition, they have an *ethos dikaion*; hence any harm they do is involuntary, *akousios blabe*, as has already been said.[c] It is natural, on Plato's principles, that they should receive

---

[a] Plat. *Laws* 908 B.   [b] Ibid. 909 B.   [c] Above, pp. 305 f.

education, in order that they may 'think correctly', *sophronein*, and that they should be segregated in a 'house of correction', *sophronisterion*, is perhaps reasonable too. But if the treatment is unsuccessful, they are to be executed; and it is this which makes clear the true nature of Platonic legislation. We are not concerned here to discuss the humanity or otherwise of such enactments, merely with their effect upon the concept of moral responsibility; and this is immediately apparent if we compare the treatment which Plato proposes for *adikoi* when drawing the distinction between *hekousios* and *akousios blabe*.ᵃ After listing the punishments appropriate to a man who is *adikos*, who does harm, *hekousios blabe*, under the influence of passion or desire, he says that anyone whom the nomothete perceives to be incurable must be executed, as an example to others and in his own 'true' interests.

The situation is now clear: harm done by a man with a just character, an *ethos dikaion*, is *akousios blabe*, even if the 'mistake' of such a man concerns the basic principles of life; but both he and the criminal who commits *hekousios blabe* must be killed if they prove incurable. In so far as 'responsibility' can be used of such a system as this, ascriptions of moral responsibility are not affected by terming one class of actions involuntary, *akousioi*, the other voluntary, *hekousioi*. Only the method of treatment is affected by such ascriptions; and here the suitable method is definable not by the intentions of the agent, but by the results which the treatment will produce. Only success in producing *eudaimonia* in the state, and secondarily in the individual, is to be considered.¹⁷ Hence Plato's classification of 'errors' in terms of *hekousios* and *akousios blabe* is a mere concession to ordinary language: a meaningless concession, since it implies a consideration of intentions which is in fact irrelevant. Plato might as well have classified these as 'punishable' and 'teachable', or 'hard' and 'soft' errors, or applied any other label which took his fancy. The labels are irrelevant; for the two classes, even in their present condition, exist only on sufferance. Plato's psychology leads him to believe that two *different* forms of treatment are suited to these two classes of action; but if the same kind of treatment, psychological or other, should prove the most efficient in both classes, the two classes would have to be merged,

ᵃ Plat. *Laws* 862 D ff.

and the last justification for Plato's distinction, in terms of *hekousios* and *akousios blabe* or any other terms, would vanish.[18] The ultimate sanction both for *adikia* and for that *dikaiosune* which is harmful to the state is the same: a change not in theory but in the view of the means whereby that theory may best be put into practice would make the two classes one throughout. Intentions must be irrelevant to such a system.

Plato's 'closed' society perpetually raises this problem. Its *eudaimonia*, its successful functioning and that of its citizens, takes precedence. Hence though Plato, as was said above,[a] insisted on a distinction between cowardice and mistake in war, and may well have believed that such a distinction could readily be sustained, it is doubtful whether this could ever be long so in practice. Mistake, just as surely as cowardice, may endanger the city's *eudaimonia*; and if the mistake is sufficiently important, this will be realized. Plato himself says that, while the man who commits sedition is 'the worst enemy of the city', the man who *fails* to notice that sedition is being committed must be considered as 'second in respect of badness, *kákē*'.[b] The use of *kákē* implies that such a man is a *kakos polites*, whether as a result of a mistake or of a moral lapse. Hector would have felt quite at home.[c] The reasons for Plato's position are obvious; but as Plato has already[d] defined the *agathos polites* as—preeminently—the law-abiding citizen, it is unfortunate that the idea of failure should have to be reintroduced.

Plato, of course, is not incapable of drawing a mental distinction between mistake and moral error. He expressly distinguishes the coward from the unfortunate man in war. The necessary concepts exist, and in many cases Plato draws a distinction; but if the claims of individual and civic *eudaimonia*—the latter, as has been said, taking precedence over the former—are held to be paramount, if, that is, the implications of this system are pushed to the limit, it is evident that, as in the cases above, he is incapable of abiding by it in any sense which makes it a fruitful distinction.

The analysis of Plato's theory of punishment shows that the implications would be pushed to the limit: if a man's existence

a Above, p. 295. b Plat. *Laws* 856 B.
c Cp. *Iliad* vi. 442 ff. and xxii. 104 ff., discussed in Chapter III, p. 47.
d Above, p. 294.

proves inimical to the *eudaimonia* of the state, for whatever reason, he must be removed. Nothing may take precedence over civic *eudaimonia*.

F. PLATO AND THE 'ORDINARY GREEK'

This, the developed system of the *Laws*, is only made explicit in that dialogue; but it should by now be clear that this system of rewards and punishments is *implicit* not only in the whole of Plato, but in the whole of Greek values from Homer to Plato, in the sense that, given the priorities of ordinary Greek values, some such system as this is the only logical result. Accordingly, this system is not simply a result of *Plato's* desire for a form of society in which such punishments are inevitable. Plato has merely systematized the assumptions lying behind what a Lysias may say in a moment of crisis,[a] and what men have tacitly accepted as the basis and justification for the most powerful system of values from Homer onwards, and has drawn the logical conclusions from these assumptions. For, as has been seen, the first necessity was always held to be that the social group should continue to exist, and that group's continued existence *vis-à-vis* its fellows was always so precarious in the period considered that mistakes could rarely be tolerated where its existence was in question; while the manner in which the sanction of public opinion was imposed merely served to render more unlikely any practical distinction between mistake and moral error. As has been said,[b] while divine sanctions upheld the quieter values, all may have been well; but given the collapse of the belief in such sanctions—at all events in the articulate classes—in the latter years of the fifth century, the only satisfactory solution of the resulting crisis of values was the insertion of the quieter values into the most valued group. That, at all events, is the only practical solution which has so far appeared; and to adopt it is to insist on the importance of these quieter values to the stability and prosperity of society, and hence in this field too to imply that, given the paramount importance of stability, there should be no toleration of 'mistakes' of any kind capable of affecting that stability. If a 'closed' society is—among other things—one which does not distinguish between mistake

[a] Cp. Chapter X, p. 209.   [b] Cp. Chapter VIII, pp. 167 f.

and moral error, then the ideas clustering round *agathos* and *arete* have always been those of a closed society—values whose implications either a crisis or philosophical speculation might always force into the foreground. Had Plato been able to confine himself to the logic-chopping of the earlier dialogues, these implications might not have become evident; but once such argument had failed, and the systematic construction of a political theory had become the only possible solution, it was inevitable that the full implications should emerge. From the *Apology* onwards Plato's ethic steadily developed and became more subtle; but increased subtlety, allied to the necessity for system-building, could only render explicit what was already implicit in ordinary standards.

In fact, the Platonic state in one form or another, with its inevitable effects upon moral responsibility, seems the only natural outcome of Greek values; but before such a conclusion is adopted, the position of Aristotle must be considered.

NOTES TO CHAPTER XIV

1. The attack would hardly be worth while: the psychology of the *Republic* seems to be determined by the form of the Ideal State, not the State by Plato's psychology.

2. Since they know *why* they should be 'moral' as well as *that* they should be so, their justice may be said to be of a higher order; the difference, however, is not one which is relevant in a court of law. (Despite what is said in the following paragraphs of the text, the danger is present even in the *Laws*, cp. p. 964. It remains true, however, that Plato is much more careful in the later dialogue.)

3. *Agathos* may clearly be applied to the soldier too, for it cannot reasonably be taken from him in the circumstances of Greek life; which shows the importance of Plato's 'law coupled with laudation'.

4. The doctrine is presumably Protagoras' own; for it is hard to see otherwise why Plato should have attributed to him such an estimable (and novel) point of view.

5. The *kalon*-standard is of course linked firmly to *agathon*, and so made 'real', cp. *Laws* 654 A ff.: the good man must be able to sing *kalōs*; accordingly his songs must be *kala*: and such songs are those which portray or express 'things which pertain to the *arete* of *psuche* or body'. Cp. *Laws* 801 E, *Republic* 457 B; also Xen. *Mem.* iv. 6. 9.

Despite this, the *kalon*-standard in the sense of 'what people may say' reasserts itself surprisingly in the later Plato. There is a curious statement at *Laws* 950 B. 'And reputation in the eyes of others, whether for goodness or the reverse, is a thing which should never be lightly esteemed. For the majority of men, though far removed from goodness themselves, are not equally lacking in the power of judging whether others are bad or good; and even in the *kakoi* there resides a divine and correct intuition (cp. *Meno* 99 B–C) whereby a vast number even of the extremely *kakoi* distinguish aright in their speech and opinions between the better and the worse. . . . The most correct and important rule is this: that the man who pursues a good reputation should himself be truly good, and that he should never pursue it without goodness, if he is to be really a perfect man.' This is very odd. The last sentence is clearly moral, not prudential. Plato is not saying: 'the people will find you out if you aim at a good reputation without being good, and therefore you should aim at a good reputation as a safety measure.' He is giving a prescription for becoming a perfect man in a 'real' sense (cp. and contrast Heraclitus frag. 135 Diels, together with frag. 29). Yet the former is what Plato ought to be saying, in the light of the rest of the paragraph; for if the vast majority of men can tell good from bad intuitively, pretence is pointless. (Plato is not, of course, maintaining that the judgements of ordinary people are correct because they are the judgements of ordinary people: he can only mean that such are generally objectively correct.) Nor is Plato maintaining simply that his properly conditioned citizens will be capable of this type of intuition: the point is made primarily in reference to judgements about the Law-state made by other states which have not had the advantage of this conditioning. Plato cannot mean all that he seems to mean. If he did, there would be no point in conducting the type of ethical inquiry on which he has spent his life, and which is still regarded as valid in the *Laws*. If most people can divine which are good men, a statistical survey of their opinions will reveal the characteristics of the good man; and this Plato does not and cannot believe. Only the utmost rigour of the elenchus can produce such results. On the other hand, the motive which led Plato to write this paragraph is clear. He recognizes the importance which reputation has in Greek society: in the *Republic* he insisted that the most just man is the most *eudaimon*, reputation or no reputation, but also in the end that the just man will also have the best reputation. Given the *kalon*-standard of ordinary Greek, a good reputation is in Greece even more essential than in most societies to a man who does not intend to live like a Socrates; and the gentlemen-smallholders of Plato's city are not to do this. Plato's recognition of this fact leads him to go too far, and say what he cannot mean; and this bears witness once again to the power of the *kalon*-standard, the standard of others' opinion. Plato's real—i.e. more considered—opinion at the time of writing the *Laws* is made clear in the passage quoted at the beginning of this note.

6. This passage is surely related to Athens' failure in the Peloponnesian War: a failure which could not plausibly be ascribed either to lack of initial prosperity on Athens' part, nor yet to a deficiency in courage or skill (at all events at the beginning of the war) on the part of her troops. This, coupled with the stasis of the closing stages of the war, had

rendered it necessary to re-examine the means by which stability and prosperity might best be assured.

7. Given the position which *arete/eudaimonia* holds relative to all other values, the end must *logically* justify the means; and therefore, even if the implications are sometimes distasteful, no logical attack is possible.

8. The implications of ordinary Greek values, which tended to stress the claims of the individual household, were shown above, Chapter XI, p. 230, with reference to the *Crito*. In the *Republic*, Plato's rejection of family life and personal property for the ruling classes helped to solve this problem, one of theory as well as practice (though, cp. p. 290 above, the *eudaimonia* of the rulers as individuals remained a problem). In the *Laws*, Plato has abandoned such radical solutions. The family is the unit on which the Law-state is based, cp. especially 928 E, where it is said that expulsion from the family entails expulsion from the state. The implications of ordinary Greek being thus likely to appear in his state, Plato has not merely the psychological drives common to all men, but also traditional Greek values, to contend with. He might well despair.

9. Cp. Plat. *Gorg.* 516 B 5, also Xen. *Cyrop.* viii. 3. 49, and cp. Xen. *Mem.* i. 6. 14. It is sometimes said that Aristotle's biology is responsible for the form of Aristotle's ethics. This is clearly untrue: Greek concepts of value are traditionally 'biological'. In this context, too, the eugenic theories of the *Republic* seem less extreme.

10. Protagoras, in *Protagoras* 323 A, says explicitly that every citizen must be capable of attaining this skill.

11. Properly conditioned—and hence indelible—true opinion, that is. At *Rep.* 430 B Plato distinguishes it from true opinion which may come to a man without this system of conditioning.

12. There is no exact equivalent for *thumos*: it denotes the seat of the emotional and passionate elements in man, but may also be the seat of thought. *Kradie*, heart, may be the physical object, or, like *thumos*, the source of various desires and thoughts. (In fact the distinction between the physical and the psychological is invalid here, cp. Böhme, op. cit.)
  For the phenomenon mentioned in the text, cp. *Iliad* i. 188/192. In a passage which begins 'His "heart", *ētor*, was divided over the course to pursue . . .', it turns out to be 'Achilles' and not his *etor* or any other psychological function that must control Achilles' *thumos*. Cp. also *Iliad* xix. 65 f. The attitude is that of 'common sense', here and in Plato.

13. The world-view epitomized by '*soma sēma*', 'the body is the tomb of the *psuche*', must also have its effect. The body is so much less 'real' than the *psuche* that it cannot possibly dominate it, in the last resort.

14. In so far as he understands what is needed, that is. The ordinary man, however, does not know what would lead him to 'true' *eudaimonia*.

15. On this topic, cp. Hackforth, *Moral Evil and Ignorance in Plato's Ethics*, CQ 1946, pp. 118 ff.

16. These passages make it quite clear (and cp. *Laws* 863 c ff.) that these two forms of ignorance are not equivalent to the ignorance of the major

and minor premisses of the Aristotelian practical syllogism. Simple *agnoia* cannot be ignorance of the minor: for the minor premiss of the *practical* syllogism expresses an individual fact, cp. *E.N.* 1147ª, which is not the only thing which can be taught, in opposition to what can be imparted by exhortation and elenchus. Simple *agnoia* must include ignorance of skills, in opposition to holding the wrong moral tenets and general view of life. The two analyses are quite different, answering to the very different emphasis of the Platonic and Aristotelian systems.

17. Secondarily, though Plato, on the basis of his psychology, and of the implications of *kakos*, is able to assert that it is in the individual's 'real' interests to be liquidated, if he is an incurable *kakos*, criminal, *Laws* 862 E 1. The state's interests, however, take first place; as do those of the universe generally, ibid. 903 C.

18. Plato does not see this point; but since, 862 D, he acknowledges that the correct treatment for criminals might be to honour them, if this proved efficacious in correcting their faults, his views of punishment are sufficiently flexible to allow the reader to suppose that he would readily have accepted this consequence too, if it proved necessary to civic *eudaimonia*; as, of course, he should.

Hackforth, op. cit., p. 119, does not go far enough. It is not sufficient that Plato should term *dikaia* such acts as are done *not* under the influence of passion or appetite. He must also devise a system of punishment in accordance with this terminology; and this his basic presuppositions render him quite incapable of doing.

XV

ARISTOTLE: ANALYSIS

A. PROBLEM AND SOLUTION

(i) *A Change of Emphasis*

THE moral theory of Plato is evidently a limit, for it is an extreme deduction from agreed premisses. It leaves only two alternatives: it must either be accepted as it stands, or, if the Platonic conclusions prove repugnant, a fresh starting-point, with at all events a change of emphasis, must be found. Aristotle, it seems clear, found much of Platonic moral theory distasteful; and it was thus urgently necessary for him to find some such change of emphasis.

Yet he must use the group of terms and ideas which centre on *agathos*, *arete*, and *eudaimonia*, for there are no others suitable; and from these, despite the overtones and implications they have been shown to possess, he must succeed in drawing other conclusions than those of Plato. That he does use these terms is clear: the work formed by the *Ethics* and *Politics* is much more explicitly a textbook on *eudaimonia*[a] than either the *Republic* or the *Laws*, though each of these is, and must be, such a textbook.

Aristotle's problem, however, seems not to have been so difficult as this brief summary would suggest. Plato was forced to push the implications of the terms he was using to the limit, for the shadow of Thrasymachus was always near, even if only in Plato's own mind;[1] and as a result, he was forced to link the terms *dikaios* and *kalon* as firmly as he could to *agathos* and *eudaimonia*. Hence, as we have seen, both *dikaios*, which formerly had been, at least potentially, a term which considered intentions rather than results, and *kalon*, a word which had become in some uses transferred to the system of quiet values, took on the colouring of *agathon* and *eudaimonia*, that is to say adopted the 'logic'—which *kalon* over a great deal of its usage already

[a] Cp. Arist. *E.N.* 1095[a]17 ff.

possessed—of words commending success and decrying failure. To resist a Thrasymachus, nothing else would suffice; and for Plato, if the state, as a result of these changes, became more stable and efficient, the solution was a good one.

If, however, for whatever reason, a Greek moralist should have no cause to dread Thrasymachus, the implications of these terms might not be fully drawn out; and it seems clear that, for Aristotle, Thrasymachus and his kind were not even shadows. Plato had to demonstrate that the *kalon* was the beneficial or profitable, *sumpheron*: Aristotle feels able to oppose the *kalon* to the *sumpheron* (or *ōphelimon*), and apparently be quite confident that as a result his pupils will choose what is *kalon*:[a] a suggestion which the 'immoralists' would have treated with contempt.[b] Furthermore, he maintains that a man should avoid equally 'things which are really *aischron* and those which are merely thought to be so',[c] saying 'we should do neither, so as not to feel shame, *aischune*, at all'.[2] Indeed, the situation has completely changed. To diminish its attractions, Aristotle maintains that the *sumpheron* affords less pleasure[3] than the *kalon*,[d] but this—which is merely asserted, not proved—would not have induced a Thrasymachus to pursue the *kalon*, since, as has been shown, such men, when faced with a choice between the *agathon* or *sumpheron* and the pleasant, chose the former.[e] Lastly, having said quite openly that a ruler's *dikaiosune* is beneficial not to himself but to others, *allotrion agathon*[f]— a proposition which the whole *Republic* (to go no further) was designed to disprove—and that hence some reward in the form of honour and rank must be given to him, Aristotle can add quite calmly, 'And those who find such rewards insufficient are the men who make themselves tyrants.'

This is an extraordinary change of attitude; but the reflective, analytical mode of expression of the last quotation betrays at least part of the solution. The ethical dialogues of Plato always have a certain urgency, and seem to be conducted in the full light of Athenian daily life; whereas, despite Aristotle's assurance that the object of ethical inquiry is not

---

[a] *E.N.* 1162ª34 ff., 1168ª10, cp. also 1121ª5, 1131ª28, and *Rhetoric* 1366ᵇ34 ff., none of which would have attracted Thrasymachus.
[b] Cp. Chapter XI, *passim.*   [c] *E.N.* 1128ᵇ23 ff.   [d] *E.N.* 1168ª10.
[e] Cp. pp. 250, 272 f.   [f] *E.N.* 1134ᵇ5 ff.

knowledge but activity,[a] there is a strong flavour of the lecture room about the last quotation. Aristotle is merely analysing the situation, not attempting to find a remedy.

Yet Aristotle is not only concerned to analyse: he wishes also to commend a particular group of standards and a particular way of life. Taking it as demonstrated that, for one reason or another, Aristotle was not forced to extremes in ethics, we may consider the nature and relationships of the values which he does commend.

(ii) Eudaimonia, Dei, Kalon

The *Nicomachean Ethics*, as was said above, is a textbook on *eudaimonia*. That is undeniable;[4] and yet from the second to the ninth book the *aretai* are described and evaluated not in terms of *eudaimonia*, but in terms of *dei*, it is necessary,[b] and of 'the *kalon*'.[c] Aristotle has, of course, no difficulty in relating his use of *arete*, *dei*, and *kalon* to *eudaimonia*. His avowed reason for discussing the *aretai* at all in a work which deals with *eudaimonia* is that *eudaimonia* is[d]

An activity of the *psuche* in accordance with *arete*, and if there are several *aretai*, in accordance with the best and most perfect.

Again, in one of the passages in which he explains the situation which the Greeks found particularly awkward, that a generous man should apparently lose by his generosity, which thereupon becomes 'another man's *agathon*', and against his own interest, Aristotle says[e]

For the generous man is willing to take less than his due. Or is this not so simple as it appears? Perhaps he tries to get more of a different *agathon*, for example reputation or the *kalon tout court*. ugh!

Aristotle's *agathoi*, as will appear, must be men of property, well provided with external, material *agatha*; but evidently for these *agathoi* the *kalon* is, if not *the agathon*, at all events a very important *agathon*, and one at which the man provided with the other *agatha* should aim.[f] *Eudaimonia* being the state in which an adequate number of *agatha* is possessed, the *kalon* is

---

[a] *E.N.* 1095[a]5.
[b] Cp. *E.N.* 1107[a]4, 1121[a]1, [b]12, 1122[b]29.
[c] Cp. *E.N.* 1104[b]31, 1115[b]12, 1136[b]22.
[d] *E.N.* 1098[a]16.   [e] *E.N.* 1136[b]22 ff.   [f] *E.N.* 1115[b]13.

linked, through *agathon*, to *eudaimonia*. And since 'it is necessary'
that these *agathoi* should do what is *kalon*, *dei* too is linked—
at several removes—to *eudaimonia*.[5]

This system of values is thus one system, and employs the
same terms as does that of Plato; and yet it seems a very different
system. Its distinctive flavour derives from the selection of the
kalon as the most prominent *agathon* in the discussion of the
aretai, combined with the fact that its necessary relationship to
eudaimonia need not be stressed. Aristotle finds himself able to
utilize the attraction which the term *kalon* has for his audience
per se; a solution which, as will be seen in Chapter XVI, has
its disadvantages from the point of view of moral responsibility. Let us first, however, consider the immediate advantages which Aristotle is able to draw from this less closely knit
system.

B. ARISTOTLE'S ANALYSIS OF PERSONAL RESPONSIBILITY

(i) *The* Eudemian Ethics

The last chapter showed the contortions into which Plato
was forced in attempting to accommodate his system of values
and of punishment to the demands of a code of law, in the
particular context of personal responsibility.[a] When Aristotle,
on the other hand, engages in similar discussion, all seems
common sense, for the subject-matter is systematically divided,
and the terminology and point of view seem to be in essentials
that with which we are familiar. This is at all events true of the
Nicomachean Ethics; in the *Eudemian Ethics*, it is true of the solution reached, but the problems which Aristotle finds it necessary to solve before arriving at that conclusion are less familiar.
The *Eudemian Ethics*, in fact, here as in other respects,[6] seems to
be an Aristotelian work of earlier date than the *Nicomachean
Ethics*, one which served to clear the ground. Accordingly, it
is convenient to consider first the discussion of the *Eudemian
Ethics*, for this discussion makes clear the nature of the problem
with which Aristotle was faced; and the solution of any problem
is best appreciated when the nature of the problem is fully
understood.

[a] Chapter XIV, pp. 304 ff.

In the second book of the *Eudemian Ethics*, Aristotle faces a problem which is set for him by ordinary language, by the psychology which he inherits, and by his own psychology. Any psychology which divides, or seems by its language to divide, the personality into independent and conflicting functions—intellect, passion, and appetite, or any others—will be faced with Aristotle's difficulties, as soon as its users grow analytical. If one function interferes with or inhibits another, surely the man acts under constraint: how then can he be held responsible for any action performed while in this condition? The Homeric poems were not troubled by such problems, though the remarkably democratic assembly of psychological functions found there should generate them. The poet's society lacked the sophistication to be baffled by the problems;[a] and this remained true of Greek society down to the beginning of the sophistic movement. The fine-drawn arguments on causation which preceded Aristotle,[b] however, made it necessary that he should recognize the problem and imperative that he should solve it.

In the *Eudemian Ethics*, we see Aristotle slowly freeing himself from the bonds of his own and others' presuppositions. There he lists three psychological functions, desire—further subdivided into wish, passion, and appetite—choice, and thought, and maintains that to act voluntarily or involuntarily must be to act in accordance with one or other of these three functions; and he constructs his argument to discover by elimination which function is in fact the relevant one. That is to say, Aristotle does not attempt to treat the problem from first principles, but in terms of his general philosophy and psychology, without inquiring whether these are suited to the solution of the problem, or whether they rather serve merely to aggravate it. Since, however, he is arguing by elimination, he is able to reject as absurd any untoward results. He could begin with any of the functions listed above. In fact, he chooses appetite, and constructs his argument thus:[c]

1. Let us suppose that voluntary action is what is done in accordance with sensual appetite, *epithūmiā*.

This seems true, for:

2. All the involuntary seems to be forced.

---

[a] Cp. Chapter II, p. 16 and Note 7.   [b] Cp. Chapters V and VI.
[c] *E.E.* 1223[a]28 ff.

3. What is forced is painful.

4. What is done and suffered under compulsion is painful.

From this Aristotle deduces

5. So that if an act is painful it is forced upon us, and if it is forced upon us it is painful.

He continues:

6. But all that is done contrary to sensual appetite (which aims at the pleasant) is painful.

7. Therefore all that is done contrary to sensual appetite is forced, therefore involuntary.

8. Again, to act as the incontinent man does, in accordance with appetite against reason, is unjust.

9. But injustice is voluntary (as we know from 'ordinary language', which Aristotle will not abandon).

10. Therefore to act as the incontinent man does, in accordance with appetite against reason, is voluntary.

But on the other hand:

11. What a man does voluntarily, *hekon*, he wishes to do, *bouletai*, and conversely what he *bouletai* he does *hekon*.

12. But what he *bouletai* he does as a result of *boulēsis*, rational desire.

13. And in Aristotle *boulesis* is defined as *boulesis tou agathou*, rational desire of the *agathon*.

14. The incontinent man, by definition, desires but does not pursue the *agathon*.

15. Accordingly, the incontinent man acts against *boulesis* (by 13 and 14).

16. But to act in this manner is to act involuntarily (by 11).

17. Accordingly, the incontinent man acts both voluntarily and involuntarily in respect of the same action (by 10 and 16).

This, as Aristotle very reasonably says, is absurd. We need not discuss the formal validity of the argument here,[7] since it is evident that the presuppositions involved could lead to no satisfactory conclusion. Again relying on these presuppositions, Aristotle generates similar absurdities with regard to the continent man,[a] who acts in accordance with reason against appetite, and, having treated passion, *thumos*, and rational desire, *boulesis*, in a similar manner, rejects the claims of choice,

[a] *E.E.* 1223[b]11 ff.

prohaeresis, on somewhat different grounds.[a] Since this is an argument by elimination, Aristotle is left with the conclusion that voluntary action is 'acting in accordance with thought, *dianoia*, in some sense';[b] but since the whole argument is thoroughly misconceived, eliminating the other absurdities does not make the remaining possibility any clearer: Aristotle is quite unable to specify more closely what he means by 'acting in accordance with *dianoai*', though he returns to the point later.[c]

For he must first settle the problem left for him by Gorgias and Plato. Gorgias had written in such a way as to entail that the plea 'I did X because Y' was valid for any value of Y;[d] and Plato, in his great fear of the passions, had written that they exert force, *biā*, on the agent.[e] In Plato this is merely a dangerous form of words: it has no effects, and can have none, for on Plato's theory of punishment it is in the last resort irrelevant whether these actions—those which comprise the category of 'voluntary harm', *hekousios blabe*—are voluntary or not. The phrase, however, might have effects if used by those who did not hold the Platonic theory as a whole, and Gorgias' position has similar effects. Accordingly, Aristotle had, as a moral philosopher, and as a legal theorist, to rid himself of this situation, in which practically any act might be involuntary. He states the problem thus:[g] In the case of inanimate objects, *bia* is the force exerted on (say) a stone when one throws it into the air;[f] that is to say, it is a force exerted from without. This is true also of animals: we say that they act *biāi*, perforce, when something moves them from without. Accordingly, when we speak of inanimate objects or animals our use of the term 'force' is simple. In the case of animals we have no need of it to describe the clash between reason and desire, for animals live by desire alone; but in the case of men the use of 'force' is more complex, since we say that the continent man drags himself *biāi* from what he desires, while the incontinent man drags himself *biāi* from what his reason tells him to be *agathon*. It is evident that this problem must be settled before Aristotle can discuss the sense of 'acting in accordance with *dianoia*', for it

---

[a] *E.E.* 1223[b]38 ff.
[b] λείπεται ἐν τῷ διανοούμενόν πως πράττειν εἶναι τὸ ἑκούσιον.
[c] *E.E.* 1224[a]7 ff. Later, 1225[b].   [d] Cp. Chapter VI, pp. 125 ff.
[e] Plat. *Laws* 863 B ff.   [f] *E.E.* 1224[a]7 ff.

may be argued on this basis that both to act with *dianoia* against desire and to act with desire against *dianoia* are to act *akon*, under compulsion; and the same difficulty is then generated here too.

To this problem Aristotle offers a threefold solution.[a] In the first place, the problem may be solved simply by insisting that the same criteria be applied in the case of human action as in the case of animals or inanimate objects: that is, 'compulsion' must be interpreted as external constraint.[b] Secondly, when the spring of action is within the man, there can be no constraint, since there is both pleasure and pain in both the continent and the incontinent man: the continent man feels pain now in acting against his appetite, but has the pleasure of hope (of future benefit, since he is choosing the *agathon* rather than the pleasant), while the incontinent man has present pleasure but expectation of pain. Evidently for Aristotle the presence of pleasure is a sufficient, if not a necessary,[9] criterion of the voluntariness of an action. Thirdly, Aristotle produces a point to clarify the first point: he acknowledges that it is not without reason to say that these men[c]

Act under constraint, *biāi*, and that each in a sense acts against his will, *akon*, as a result of appetite and reason; for these functions, being distinct from one another, are thrust out by one another.

This language, however, is only legitimate of the 'parts' of the soul:

The soul as a whole, whether that of the incontinent man or that of the continent man, acts voluntarily, and neither acts under constraint, though one of the 'parts' of them does. . . .

That is to say, we are dealing with whole personalities, not with springs of action in isolation; and human beings have both thoughts and desires. Accordingly, an act which is an expression of either is *our* act and hence voluntary; which entails that all actions are voluntary, save those which are done under external compulsion very strictly interpreted, and those which are done '*not* in accordance with *dianoia*', however this phrase is to be understood.[d] The problem of Gorgias is thus solved, and the dangers of Platonic language eliminated. The

---

[a] *E.E.* 1224ᵃ20 ff.   [b] *E.E.* 1224ᵇ5 ff.   [c] *E.E.* 1224ᵇ21 ff.
[d] Cp. *E.E.* 1225ᵇ.

Nicomachean Ethics can be brusque with such questions, for the discussion of the *Eudemian Ethics* has cleared the ground;[10] but before the version of the *Nicomachean Ethics* is considered, the nature of the problems which Aristotle had to solve should be pointed out. Neither Gorgias nor any other Greek of the period before Aristotle believed in a universal determinism, psychological or other. *Some* acts, all were agreed, were voluntary: the problem was to discover which, or rather to evolve a theory which should justify beliefs already held. Accordingly, Aristotle could not be expected to discuss the (now) 'classic' free will problem, since he knew of no theory of total determinism, at all events none which thus affected ethical thought. He has dissolved the problems which faced him in the *Eudemian Ethics* to his own satisfaction; and one cannot reasonably expect more.

(ii) *The* Nicomachean Ethics

In the *Nicomachean Ethics*, such problems as these are already settled; and the treatment there, as has been said, is in very familiar terms. It seems familiar for another reason: though Aristotle in the *Eudemian Ethics*, both in the arguments quoted above and in a later passage[a] in which he considers in more detail the implications of 'acting in accordance with *dianoia*', attempts to argue directly to criteria for the voluntary, in the *Nicomachean Ethics* he delimits the area of the voluntary by stating the conditions in which an act is to be termed involuntary: a practice which (now) seems much more familiar to us. Here Aristotle at once[b] turns to actions which are *akousia*, and hence outside the categories of praise and blame, and divides them into those which are done under compulsion, *biāi*, and those which are done as the result of ignorance or mistake, *di' agnoian*. Treating first those done *biāi*, he adheres to the doctrine of the *Eudemian Ethics*, stating it even more clearly:[c] before an action may be termed *akousion* on these grounds, it must be one in which the man compelled contributes nothing at all.[11]

Having stated his position thus firmly, Aristotle is able to deal with much greater brevity than in the *Eudemian Ethics* with the position of Gorgias. He attacks the position in two passages,

---

a *E.E.* 1225[b].   b *E.N.* 1109[b]35 ff.
c *E.N.* 1110[a]2 ff. and 1110[b]2.

which treat slightly different aspects of the problem, but which may well be taken together.ᵃ Aristotle has defined action done under compulsion as action whose first cause lies outside the agent;ᵇ and realizes that it is possible to maintain that actions performed to secure things which are pleasant or *kala* are done under compulsion, for such things are outside a man, and exert force to compel him. Helen, with Gorgias for counsel, might have pleaded thus; but Aristotle replies that on such a supposition *all* actions are *akousia*, since the desire for things which are pleasant or *kalon* actuates all men in all their actions; and he can be confident that no theory which produces such a conclusion will be taken seriously. Gorgias had not stated such a conclusion, though his defence of Helen entails it; and there is no reason to suppose that he would have found it palatable. Adding the point that such actions, being pleasant, cannot be done under compulsion, Aristotle concludes that it is absurd to blame the external world rather than oneself for being susceptible to such things, and to claim the credit for noble actions performed for such motives,¹² while laying the blame for shameful ones upon desire for the pleasant. Accordingly, Aristotle reiterates that actions done under compulsion are not simply actions whose first cause lies outside the agent; one must also be able to say that the man compelled contributed nothing at all.

In the second passage Aristotle considers the internal non-rational springs of action, passion, *thumos*, and appetite, *epithumia*. He rejects the suggestion that actions done at the prompting of such drives are *akousia*, since on such an assumption neither animals nor children ever act voluntarily: a thesis which he can be sure will be rejected as absurd by all. Again, to the suggestion that, of actions performed at the instance of passion and desire, we do the noble ones voluntarily, the base ones involuntarily, he replies that since the same cause, *thumos* or *epithumia*, operates in both cases,¹³ the supposition is absurd. Again, one *ought* to be angry at some things and desire other things, and it is nonsense to say of things which we ought to do that they are *akousia*, that we cannot help doing them. (Again Aristotle shows his respect for 'ordinary language'.) Lastly, what difference is there, so far as voluntariness is concerned,

ᵃ *E.N.* 1110ᵇ9 ff., 1111ᵃ24 ff.   ᵇ οὗ ἡ ἀρχὴ ἔξωθεν.

between 'errors' committed in a cold and calculated manner[14] and those committed in a state of passion? One should avoid both classes of action; and Aristotle concludes[a]

It seems that the irrational passions are not less human than reason is. Accordingly, actions which result from *thumos* or *epithumia* are the man's actions too [i.e. as well as those performed in a cold and calculated manner]. It is absurd, then, to suppose that these are involuntary.

In the *Nicomachean Ethics*, then, Aristotle appeals confidently to common sense and ordinary usage, and feels no need to embark upon complicated analyses; for the discussion of the *Eudemian Ethics* has prepared the way for that of the *Nicomachean Ethics*. The result of both passages is to restore, in the field of involuntary actions performed under compulsion, the common sense which, until the speculations of Gorgias, had prevailed since Homer.

This common sense prevails in the discussion of the remaining group of *akousia*, involuntary actions performed as a result of ignorance of some vital fact. Here it suffices to treat only the discussion found in the *Nicomachean Ethics*, since that in the *Eudemian Ethics* differs from it only in small points which are unimportant here, and in being less complex and detailed. In the *Nicomachean Ethics*, Aristotle, after drawing a distinction between the involuntary and the non-voluntary,[b] makes what is for the present purpose the much more important distinction between acting in ignorance and acting as a result of ignorance. 'Acting as a result of ignorance' is acting while not in possession of some vital piece of information—that the gun was loaded, that the man had a weak heart, and so on—whose lack caused the action to have a nature other than was intended. We need spend no time over this (for it has long furnished a valid defence when not overridden by other considerations), except to note that Aristotle is able to analyse the situation in considerable detail.[c] 'Acting in ignorance' is more important here. The term may be applied in two ways, or at two levels. At its simplest, it serves to distinguish the man who is not in possession of some vital fact from the man who is drunk or angry to such an extent as 'not to know what he is doing'. Such a man,

[a] *E.N.* 1111[b]1 ff.   [b] *E.N.* 1110[b]18.   [c] *E.N.* 1111[a]2 ff.

says Aristotle, acts in ignorance, but not as a result of ignorance, but rather as a result of alcohol or anger. Clearly this is a valid distinction, and clearly too one that will prove of use in the courts.

But this distinction is also relevant on a higher level. We have already seen the great importance for Plato of knowledge of the (true) *agathon* in human action: that for Plato lack of such knowledge must be in the last resort involuntary, and that for him any means are justified in producing this knowledge in the citizens of his ideal states. Since Aristotle's world-view is basically the same as Plato's, it might well seem that he too must acknowledge that ignorance of what would be conducive to one's *eudaimonia* must be involuntary. Aristotle presents his analysis of the situation in terms of the practical syllogism. He supposes that a man, in reasoning about an action, proceeds as follows:[a] Actions of the type X are *kala*, or are *agatha*, or are conducive to my *eudaimonia* (these formulations, for Aristotle, of course being synonymous); but this action is an action of the type X: therefore—the man performs the action. Here we have two premisses. The good man performing a good action possesses both, and naturally acts on the result. Clearly if a man were in some sense or other not in possession of the minor —factual—premiss,[b] any error would be involuntary. But what of the man who is not in possession of the major premiss, the man who is constitutionally depraved, and does not know what would be conducive to his *eudaimonia*? This man, the *mochthē-ros*, Plato might first attempt to reform, but would then kill 'in his own interest as well as that of the state', should he prove incurable. No questions of personal responsibility would be involved.[c] Aristotle is unlikely to countenance such an approach; and he now uses the distinction between 'acting in ignorance' and 'acting on account of ignorance' to escape from Plato's position. Of the *mochtheros*, Aristotle says:[d]

Every *mochtheros* is ignorant of what he ought to do and from what he ought to abstain, and as a result of such 'errors' men become unjust and generally *kakoi*.

But such men act in ignorance, not as a result of ignorance;

[a] Cp. *E.N.* 1144ª31 ff.   [b] *E.N.* 1110ᵇ31 ff.
[c] Cp. Chapter XIV, p. 309.   [d] *E.N.* 1110ᵇ28 ff.

*outside categos
d frame-flow*

and it is not ignorance of the major premiss, but ignorance of the minor, which renders an action *akousion*. Accordingly, the *mochtheros* is fully responsible, the different kinds of ignorance are distinguished, and no Platonic contortions are required.

For this is clearly a reply to the 'Socratic paradox';[a] and though the distinction drawn is a valid one, Aristotle is fortunate in feeling himself able to dissolve the difficulty by simple assertion. For though it is easy enough to appreciate the distinction between the two kinds of ignorance, it is less easy to be convinced that, if the situation is treated, as it must be, in terms of knowledge and ignorance, a man should be blamed even for his ignorance of the major premiss. A modern reader might well say that one should at least inquire whether the man's ignorance of the major premiss was his own fault or not;[15] and Plato would certainly have said that since the possession of the moral major premiss was a necessary means to the universally desired end of *eudaimonia*, any ignorance of it must be—in some sense—involuntary. With this, as has been shown, Aristotle could only agree, if the point were firmly put to him, for his values are Plato's. Here too Aristotle is fortunate in not being forced to knit his system so tightly together as Plato.

In fact, individual moral responsibility seems to have won the day: we seem at last to have reached a moral atmosphere with which we are familiar. It seems rather suspicious, however, that victory should be achieved so easily when the problems are so great; and the next chapter will show that in fact these advantages have inevitable concomitant disadvantages. Aristotle's good fortune is not so great as appears at first sight.

NOTES TO CHAPTER XV

1. The immediate political danger represented by Thrasymachus and his kind had long receded when Plato wrote the *Laws*, though (cp. Chapter X, pp. 213 ff.) the political concepts in general use might be little more satisfactory; but Plato's experience of civil upheaval drove him throughout his life to seek the solution which would most certainly prevent its recurrence.

2. Of course, Aristotle's citizens are so placed that they will not have to do what is *aischron socially* for reasons beyond their control. Aristotle, however, says that one should only feel *aidos*, shame, at actions which

---

[a] Above, Chapter XIV, pp. 304 ff.

are both *hekousia* and *phaula*, 'base', *E.N.* 1128ᵇ26; which might seem to exempt such *aischra* anyway. 'Banausic' activities, however, are *aischron* and *phaulon*; and on the definitions of *E.N.* 1109ᵇ30 ff., to have to perform banausic tasks as a result of poverty would be not only *aischron* but also *hekousion*, for the decision to perform the tasks would be taken 'of one's own accord', and such actions are 'more like *hekousia*', 1110ᵃ12. Presumably, therefore, one should still feel shame at having to perform them.

3. The emphasis on pleasure is paralleled by certain passages in the later Plato. Cp. *Laws* 636 D: pleasure and pain are the two fountains with which the lawgiver has chiefly to deal; 631 ff., the duty of the lawgiver is to see that the pleasures and pains of the citizens are 'correct'; 663 A, to say that what is just is pleasant is useful for the lawgiver, 'for no one would be willing to do anything which was not accompanied by more pleasure than pain'. Again, 733 A ff., Plato seems to say that pleasure is 'what we desire—*boulesthai*—by nature', which entails, given the implications of *eudaimonia* and *agathon*, that pleasure is not merely an *agathon* but the *agathon*, in violent contrast to the doctrine of the *Philebus*, where a contrast is drawn throughout between the pleasant and the *agathon*, cp. especially 45 D and 63 D. The above passages, however, are misleading: the *Laws* and the *Philebus* are works of very different types. The *Philebus* is an analytical dialogue, whereas the *Laws* purports to be a practical treatise. In such a treatise Plato can justifiably hold that the average man pursues pleasure and shuns pain, and recommend that the lawgiver should bear this in mind, without implying either that a man ought to pursue pleasure and shun pain as such, or that he is so constituted psychologically that he must do so. (Though *Laws* 733 A ff. still appears to be a dangerous overstatement of Plato's position.) That Plato's position remains that of the *Philebus* and earlier dialogues is shown by *Laws* 667 A ff., 783 A, 792 D, q.v. Despite the passage of Aristotle quoted in the text, Aristotle's position in this matter is fundamentally the same as Plato's, cp. Note 9 below.

4. It must be, cp. *E.N.* 1095ᵃ17 ff.: all men are agreed that the end is *eudaimonia*, but differ on the interpretation of the term.

5. A *definition* of *dei* is hard to come by; but if passages such as *E.N.* 1111ᵃ25 ff. are considered, it is evident that Aristotle would have said that an action *dei*, is necessary, because it is *kalon* (and cp. 1121ᵃ1); and to say that it is *kalon* links it to *eudaimonia*, as is shown in the text. It should be evident how far this 'it is necessary' is removed from the 'Duty' of a deontological ethic.

6. For the priority of the *Eudemian* to the *Nicomachean Ethics*, cp. E. Kapp, *Das Verhältnis der eudemischen zur nicomachischen Ethik*, diss. Freiburg 1912; also Jaeger, *Aristotle*, Chapter IX *passim*.

7. Unless 3 and 4 assert that the painful and the forced are co-extensive (which is by no means self-evident), 3 and 4 do not entail 5. Further, 2–10 depend on 'ordinary language', 11–16 on Aristotelian terminology; and a clash between the two need not have any philosophical significance in itself.

8. On the analysis of compulsory action in the *Nicomachean Ethics*, cp. Hamburger, *Morals and Law*, pp. 19 ff., and the commentators ad loc.

9. Aristotle, like Plato, seems sometimes to say that pleasure is the end of action, though (cp. the discussion of *E.N.* x, and contrast the discussion of *E.N.* vii) his more careful theory distinguishes *eudaimonia* from pleasure. At *E.E.* 1223ᵃ28 ff., analysed in the text on p. 320, he uses the presence of pleasure in a man as a test of the voluntariness of action. Provided its presence remains a sufficient but not a necessary condition, all is well; but the fifth proposition of that analysis might be held to entail—supposing that no actions are neutral from the point of view of pleasure and pain—that it is a necessary condition. This, however, seems not to be Aristotle's considered theory, at all events in the *Nicomachean Ethics*. (The high position given to pleasure in *E.N.* 1172ᵃ21 is a practical device like that of Plato in the *Laws*, cp. Note 3 above.) The other theory, however, seems always to be lurking in Aristotle's ethical writings.

10. The argument of the *Eudemian Ethics* (or one like it) is historically necessary. It would have been impossible either oneself to pass from the position of Gorgias to that of the *Nicomachean Ethics* directly, or to convince anyone else had one done so. Cp. Hamburger, op. cit., p. 21.

11. Though Aristotle admits a category of diminished responsibility, *E.N.* 1110ᵃ7 ff. (At all events, the discussion of responsibility for actions performed under duress leads him into sufficient difficulties and complexities to make it inevitable that, had he been drawing up a code of law, he should have legislated for such a category.) On the other hand, it is doubtful whether the category of the non-voluntary as defined by Aristotle could have much legal significance, though the distinction is of importance for the moralist. (The continual doubt whether Aristotle is writing law or ethics in this passage is very confusing.)

12. Since naturally the *kalon* would normally induce one to perform actions considered to be noble.

13. *Thumos*, anger or passion, could readily prompt a man to noble actions, particularly in the context of traditional Greek values.

14. Aristotle's phrase is τὰ κατὰ λογισμὸν ἁμαρτηθέντα. That this refers to moral errors committed in cold blood is clear. It cannot refer to mistakes of fact; for these, 1110ᵇ33 ff., are *akousia*, and come under the heading of actions performed as a result of ignorance. The phrase refers, in fact, to the man with a vicious *hexis* (cp. Chapter XVI, p. 332).

15. The question becomes important in the discussion of the *akratēs*, the incontinent man, where, *E.N.* 1147ᵃ11 ff., 1147ᵇ, the *akrates* is likened to the man who is asleep, drunk, or mad, and of his recovery, 1147ᵇ6, the words πῶς δὲ λύεται ἡ ἄγνοια, 'how the ignorance, *agnoia*, is removed', are used. Actions committed in sleep or madness can hardly be imputable; and those committed when drunk are so because one could have helped becoming drunk. Particularly in view of his physiological explanations of *akrasiā*, incontinence, or of the type of men who are prone to the condition, *E.N.* 1150ᵇ25 ff., Aristotle should have made it clear whether a man can help being *akrates* and so falling into this

agnoia. The *akrates* certainly does not act as a result of *agnoia*, for his action would then be *akousion*, which Aristotle certainly does not believe. Accordingly, he must 'act in ignorance' in some sense, if Aristotle can use the word *agnoia* of him; but if he cannot help falling into this *agnoia*, to distinguish him as 'acting in ignorance' from the man who acts as a result of ignorance of some vital fact, while schematically satisfying, has little moral relevance. Such *agnoia* would be involuntary in a common-sense, non-Platonic manner; and hence to treat the *akrates*, if his condition is thus analysed, as if he were acting *hekon*, seems more than a little hard.

XVI

ARISTOTLE: GENERAL ETHICS

A. ARISTOTLE AND *ARETE*

(i) Arete *and Intentions*

THE chief impediment in the way of the development of a
satisfactory concept of moral responsibility in Greek has
hitherto been the nature of *arete*. Accordingly, in order to
appreciate the true nature of Aristotle's position, we must consider the manner in which he uses *arete* and related terms.
Here again he has one immediate advantage over Plato, for he
finds it unnecessary to prove that the quiet excellences are
aretai: *sophrosune, dikaiosune,* and similar qualities are evidently
acknowledged to be *aretai* without argument by his audience.
The reason for this, and its effect upon Aristotle's general
theory, will be discussed below. First we must consider certain
problems created by the 'logic' of traditional *arete*.

Arete, from Homer onwards, always commended the correct
reaction, or the production of the correct result, in a given
situation, regardless of the manner in which the result was
produced or the intentions of the agent; and the explicit linking of *eudaimonia* and *arete* merely emphasized this. Aristotle is
aware of this fact; and his attitude to it is clearly important.
His own moral philosophy makes the problem more urgent. He
has described the moral *aretai* as *hexeis*, acquired and stable
habits of personality:[a] the true *agathos* can be relied upon to act
correctly in any situation. But our bodies also have *hexeis*,
stable conditions of health, which are produced or restored by
the art of medicine. We do not need to become doctors in order
to be healthy, or to cure ourselves when we are sick: we merely
call in the doctor when we need him. Why then should a man
wish to become *phronimos*,[b] and so able to make judgements
about what is *kalon, agathon,* and *dikaion*? He will be no more
able to *do* what he judges to be so if he is a *phronimos* than he

---

[a] *E.N.* 1103ª9, 1139ª16.　　　　　　　　　　　[b] *E.N.* 1143ᵇ18 ff.

will be more healthy if he is a doctor. Surely a man could consult a *phronimos* as he consults a doctor, should his *hexis* become or appear less satisfactory than it should be. In this case, *phronesis* has no contribution to make to one's own *eudaimonia* (and to ensure one's own *eudaimonia* is of course the purpose of having a good moral *hexis* in the first place). Further, since wisdom, *sophia*, as defined by Plato and Aristotle, is concerned only with the abstract and immutable, *sophia* can have no relation whatever to a man's becoming *eudaimon*, for all change and 'becoming' lies outside its province.

Such a rejection of the intellectual excellences inevitably affects the question of moral responsibility; for if *phronesis* is of no value, and *hexeis* are sufficient, it suffices that the correct result is produced by these guaranteed reactions, and intentions remain irrelevant. What has already been said[a] renders it unlikely that Aristotle should be content with such a solution; and in fact he sees very clearly the dangers of the apparently attractive parallel between somatic and psychological states which had stood Plato in such good stead in his attacks on the 'immoralists'.[b] If the parallel is pushed to the limit, there seems no reason why, if we do not learn medicine in order to become healthy, we should learn 'ethics-politics' (or whatever term best suits Aristotle's subject) in order to attain to psychological health and excellence, and hence to *eudaimonia*. Plato could accept this conclusion; Aristotle rejects it, on the following grounds: Firstly, *phronesis* and *sophia* are human *aretai*, and therefore *per se* desirable, since their possession must (help to) render a man *agathos*, good of his kind.[1] The only possible refutation of this would be the denial that *phronesis* and *sophia* are *aretai*; and even the most extreme 'immoralist' was far from denying this. Secondly, Aristotle maintains that *sophia* is after all essential to *eudaimonia*. It is not concerned with a man's becoming *eudaimon*: it has the same relation to a man's *eudaimonia* that a man's health, viewed as the correct arrangement and inter-relationship of his bodily functions, has to his being healthy. That is to say, *sophia* is the formal cause of *eudaimonia*, and thus indispensable.

These points relate to theory. The third is more practical. Aristotle maintains that, the goal of human life being what it is,

---

[a] i.e. in Chapter XV.   [b] Cp. e.g. Plat. *Gorg.* 504 A 4 ff., 517 D ff.

moral *arete* in the sense of the possession of a good *hexis* is not enough: *phronesis* is necessary too,[a]

For *arete* ensures that a man has the right goal, while *phronesis* cares for the means of attaining that goal.

The two are interdependent: without *phronesis*, practical wisdom, one will be unable to take the necessary steps to attain one's goal, however clearly it is envisaged by *arete*. Accordingly, for Aristotle, *arete—kūriā arete*, that is, not *phusikē arete*[2]—is a *hexis*, a stable acquired habit of personality, not only *in accordance with* the *orthos logos*,[3] but actually *accompanied by* 'right reason'; and the *orthos logos*, the 'right reason', is *phronesis*. This distinguishes *Aristotle's* 'good citizens' from the lower grades of Plato's *Republic*, who have only a *hexis* in accordance with the *orthos logos*, which is far beyond their comprehension. This passage may be compared with another, from the second book of the *Nicomachean Ethics*.[b] The sophists and the early Plato had been obsessed by the idea of *dikaiosune* as a *techne*, a skill; in which, as I have said, they were encouraged by the traditional connotation of *arete*. Aristotle must naturally consider this point. If there is no distinction between *arete* and *techne*, then to be *dikaios* is merely to do just things: all artists and craftsmen are judged simply by the results they produce, irrespective of their intentions. Aristotle insists on a distinction: the products of a *techne* do indeed 'have their excellence in themselves', but for true *arete* it does not suffice to go through the motions of (say) *dikaiosune*. We must consider the condition of the agent, and there are three requisites: the agent must know what he is doing; he must choose the act, and choose it for its own sake; and thirdly he must perform it as an expression of a settled and unvarying attitude.[4] The contrast with *techne* is in no doubt.

For Aristotle, then, if an act is to be considered an expression of *arete*, it must be done in full understanding of its nature, properly considered and deliberately chosen, as an expression of a settled policy; and this, when taken together with the discussion of the *hekousion* and the *akousion*,[c] seems to indicate that Aristotle is willing and able to judge a man's responsibility for his acts in an 'enlightened' manner. This is true; and the

[a] *E.N.* 1144[a]7 ff.   [b] *E.N.* 1105[a]30 ff.   [c] For which see Chapter XV.

foregoing discussion shows the great advances made by Aristotle not only on the earlier writers considered here, but also on the later ones. The modern reader of the *Nicomachean Ethics* is faced with an ethical system which, in this respect at least, seems very familiar; and, as a result of the loose construction of the work, is able to forget those aspects which seem less familiar. Here, however, it is necessary to discuss these aspects, in so far as they affect the problem of moral responsibility.

(ii) *The Sources*

First, however, the sources from which Aristotle has developed this theory must be briefly considered. In his discussion of responsibility for individual acts he clearly owes nothing to Plato, who, searching for the general universally applicable definition and for the ideal state, gave little thought to the individual act. Aristotle's predecessors here are those sophists who, like (pseudo-)Antiphon and Gorgias, attempted to analyse the idea of causality in respect of human action.[a]

Other sources are more significant, however. Thus far we are concerned merely with legal defence in the courts; and Aristotle's theory of *arete* naturally goes far beyond this. As we have seen, any man who says 'this is *arete*' is saying 'this is the type of man which a state should have if it is to operate efficiently and (for Aristotle) behave with distinction'. Such a statement covers a man's life as a whole, demanding that certain qualities be exhibited throughout; and in this context it is not difficult to discover why Aristotle lays such stress on the individual, *qua agathos*, 'knowing what he is doing'. Basically, *agathos* has always commended—at least in intention—the men most valuable to the state. Philosophical and political thought has given greater prominence to the need for skill and planning in conducting the administration of the city efficiently and successfully; and accordingly it is not surprising to find Aristotle rejecting the suggestion that any of his *agathoi* should be merely properly conditioned automata. *Agathos* and *arete* commend the qualities which the rulers of his state—that is to say, the whole citizen-body—must possess, and must display in government.[5] It is absurd that such men should be merely conditioned: they might have the right *skopos*, the right picture of what a prosperous

[a] Cp. Chapters V and VI.

state should be, but the government of a state, the realization of this picture in practice, requires practical wisdom, *phronesis*. These men *must* 'know what they are doing': they have no philosopher-kings to do their thinking for them. Aristotle is commending to his audience the same skills, with their implications now more fully understood, as those which the sophists offered to their pupils.

Since Aristotle's view of the *arete* of the whole man is founded, like traditional *arete*, on practical necessities, he is able to justify it, not by any reference to ideals, or to idealistic phrases, but on pragmatic grounds. He has no need to oppose Plato's view of *arete* and its distribution in the state by exhortation, any more than Plato established his view by this means. His own polity entails a different kind of men with different qualities, whose abilities will, he believes, ensure the *eudaimonia* of that polity; and he can therefore simply delineate the nature of these qualities, since they are means to—or constituents of—an evidently desirable end.

(iii) *The Co-operative* Aretai *in 'Ordinary Greek'*

This requires some further explanation. Though the above is certainly the justification for Aristotle's standard of *arete*, and determines the form which that standard takes, Aristotle never states explicitly that this is the case. His standard of *arete* naturally suits the form of polity delineated in the *Politics*, but it is not formally deduced from that polity. Rather is it assumed that the standard will be held already by Aristotle's audience— Aristotle continually appeals to 'ordinary language' in ethical matters[6]—and only needs refinement and clarification. He need not prove that anything which he holds to be an *arete* is an *arete*: he can assume that his hearers will agree. Evidently Aristotle is using values already existing in Athenian society, or in some part of that society. Since the polity of the *Politics* does not differ radically from existing Greek states, that such values should prove suitable is not surprising.

As has been said,[a] anything which makes it unnecessary for Aristotle to knit his system together as tightly as did Plato is an advantage for him; and his reliance upon 'ordinary language' undoubtedly confers such an advantage. In Greek values,

[a] Chapter XV, pp. 316 ff.

however, any advantage normally has accompanying disadvantages; and we have seen that the traditional *arete* of 'ordinary Greek' was inimical to the concept of moral responsibility. Aristotle and his predecessors have deepened the idea of *arete*, and Aristotle in particular has analysed responsibility *in isolation*; but the extent to which the traditional disadvantages have been removed has yet to be shown.

We have seen that traditional Greek values and the historical situation of Athens in the later fifth century combined to produce a crisis of values. The manner in which Plato treated this crisis suggests that there exist only the alternatives of 'immoralism' and the Platonic state in one of its forms, and hence only the two uses of *arete, kalon,* and related terms which are associated with these alternatives. Given ruthless thinking, this may be true; but in Chapter IX we discussed the views of certain 'moralizing' writers who were by no means ruthless thinkers; and neither the 'immoralists' nor the death of Socrates, nor yet Platonic thought, succeeded in eliminating them. In these writers the co-operative excellences were enrolled among the *aretai* not by argument but by suasion and persuasive definition, overt or covert; and in the fourth century such men as Xenophon and Isocrates, themselves incapable of tight logical argument, wrote to encourage such usages, and bear witness to their continued existence. The influence of Socrates himself is naturally strong here: Xenophon records that Socrates, in contrast to the physicists,[a]

In the course of his discussions was always inquiring what is *eusebes*, what *asebes*, what *kalon*, what *aischron*, what *dikaion*, what *adikon*, what *sophrosune*, &c. Those who knew this he held to be *kaloi kagathoi*, whereas those who did not could with justice be regarded as no better than slaves.

Here we have an attempt to convince the 'gentlemen' of Athens, the *kaloi kagathoi*, that it was 'ungentlemanly' not to know about the nature of the quieter virtues, and (presumably) act upon them.[7] *Aischron* and *kalon* naturally behave in a similar manner. In Xenophon's *Apology*[b] the following words are attributed to Socrates:

I do not think I should be ashamed because I am dying unjustly.

[a] Xen. *Mem.* i. 1. 16, cp. iv. 2. 22.   [b] Xen. *Apol.* 26.

adikōs; for this is not *aischron* for me, but for those who have condemned me.

It is not Socrates who should be ashamed of his failure in the
courts, but those who have caused his failure, inasmuch as it is
unjust. A passage of Isocrates is even more surprising:[a]

> I am surprised that some men do not think that . . . victories won
> in defiance of justice are more *aischron* . . . than defeats suffered
> without *kakia*, this too though they know that powers which are
> great, but *ponērai*, often prove stronger than 'good' men, *spoudaioi*,
> who choose to fight on behalf of their native land.

Here both *kakia* and *ponerai* evidently decry injustice, not
failure, and *aischron* is explicitly so used. That such standards
should be applied in the courts is new; in war, they are surprising in the extreme. A little later,[b] the old standard and the new
are in debate to discover whether Athens or Sparta has

> Institutions and customs which are most *kala*.

It is claimed that these are

> *Eusebeia*, piety, in relation to the gods, *dikaiosune* in relation to
> men, and *phronesis*, practical wisdom, in relation to other activities.

Judged by these standards, Sparta comes off poorly. The friend
of Sparta attempts to restore his position by saying that he
meant by 'institutions and customs which are most *kala*' the
Spartans' skill in war and their organization to that end. To
this Isocrates retorts that by means of this skill they destroyed
the Greeks, and claims that everyone would admit that such
men are *kakistoi*, and by implication that such institutions are
not 'most *kalon*'.

These writers, then, assert, as did the 'moralizers' of Chapter
IX, that within certain areas *dikaiosune*, not success, should
determine what is *kalon* or *aischron*. The area, for Isocrates, is
Greece: the Greeks should behave justly to one another. His
Panhellenism is nourished and given definition by his hatred of
Persia: the Persians have no rights, only an expectation that
the Greeks will try to damage them in any way possible. In this
field, whatever is beneficial to the Greeks is *kalon*; but so far

---

[a] Isoc. *Panath.* 185.   [b] Ibid. 202 ff.

as the behaviour of Greeks towards other Greeks is concerned, *kalon* here takes a long step in the direction of the 'moral'.

In these writers each of the strongly emotive terms which mark out the Greek field of values is acquiring a 'quiet' moral flavour as the 'quiet' moral terms already in existence are drawn towards the centre of the field and made attractive by being attached—by assertion—to those already in possession. It is this change, noted at the end of the fifth century and carried on despite difficulties by these writers, which is responsible for the change in atmosphere one feels in passing from a—traditional—writer of the fifth century to one of the fourth;[8] and it is evidently this use of *arete* and *kalon* on whose attraction Aristotle is relying in writing the *Ethics* and *Politics*.

Once again the battle may seem to be won. The co-operative excellences have become *aretai*, and hence desirable, without the necessity of adopting the 'logic' of words commending success and decrying failure. As yet, however, only a part of the range of these terms in such fourth-century writers has been considered; and when the whole has been taken into account, it becomes clear that nothing but the 'immoralist' interpretation of the terms, naturally curbed by the admission of the co-operative excellences as *aretai*, has been removed. The *kaloi kagathoi* are still a social class;[9] *arete* still commends courage, and the *agathos* is still, among other things, the man who lavishes his material goods in the state's interest;[a] the practice of retail trade may still be decried as 'ignorance of what is *kalon*',[b] and 'those *technai* which are most *kalon*'—farming and the military art—are still opposed to the banausic skills,[c] despite the stresses of the Peloponnesian War, which had forced many *agathoi* to perform menial tasks through no fault of their own.[10] To do more *kalōs* than another man may still be—quite naturally—to beat him in a race,[d] and in the speech which Isocrates puts into the mouth of Archidamus, it is said that it would be *aischron* if the Spartans, who once were thought worthy to rule the Hellenes, should now, through failure, have to carry out their commands.[e] Isocrates, with his Panhellenism, may wish to render this last use obsolete, by encouraging just

---

[a] Cp. e.g. Xen. *Mem.* iv. 6. 14, and Chapter X, pp. 213 ff.
[b] ἀπειροκαλίαι, Xen. *Cyr.* i. 2. 3.   [c] Xen. *Oec.* 4. 3.
[d] Xen. *Cyr.* i. 4. 4.   [e] Isoc. *Archid.* 94.

co-operation between the Greek states; but clearly if he does not succeed in doing so, this use too remains fully alive.

The other uses are certainly not dead. The Greek city-state has not changed, and the man of wealth and leisure is still urgently needed to perform his political, military, and economic functions. Accordingly, it is inevitable that the qualities commended in the last paragraph should continue to be expected of the 'best citizens', and therefore that these should continue to be commended as such. They have a right to the title, and Aristotle, even if he would, cannot deny it to them. With the other 'moralist' writers, he can insist that the co-operative excellences are now to be considered as *aretai*, and expect that the traditional *aretai* will make room for them; he can assist in fitting the new excellences into the traditional pattern;[11] but he cannot assert even the pre-eminence of such *aretai*, much less that they and they alone, to the exclusion of all other claimants, are to be considered *aretai*. To do so would be to invite a reaction similar to that of the 'immoralists', in which the criteria of an *arete* must be examined, and possibly the whole Platonic pattern repeated. In Plato's rigid law-state it might be possible to assert that *dikaiosune* is the *chief arete*, and have it accepted; but Aristotle, shunning the extremes of the Platonic solution, merely takes his terms of value as he finds them and investigates their implications, and hence the *aretai* discussed in Books II to IX of the *Nicomachean Ethics* take no precedence one over the other.[12]

In these circumstances, failing the Platonic solution, there is only one answer: the *agathos* must have *all* these excellences, moral, intellectual, social, and economic. The moral excellences must be included, but undue emphasis may not be given to them. This is, after all, the solution of the *Laws*: though Plato gives his citizens no opportunity for uncontrolled and lavish 'splendid living', he makes regulations to ensure that all citizens are sufficiently provided with material goods to be able to perform their civic functions to the full.[13] The *agathos* of the *Laws* must be a man of property too. From the point of view of political theory, these provisions may be sound; but when combined with Greek terms of value, they can only confuse the concept of moral responsibility.

(iv) *The Effects in Aristotle*

We may now consider the position of moral responsibility in Aristotle's ethical theory as a whole. This may be seen most clearly in his discussion of *eudaimonia*. In the *Nicomachean Ethics* he says of this, the end of human activity:[a]

It would be widely spread through the community; for it may be attained, through some study and practice, by anyone who is not maimed in respect of *arete*.

The implications of this, which seems 'democratic', only become clear in the *Politics*, where the following remarkable argument occurs:[b]

Besides, the ruling class should be the owners of property, for they are citizens, and the rulers of a state should be in good circumstances; whereas mechanics, or any other class which is not a producer of *arete*, have no share in the state. This follows from our first principle, for *eudaimonia* cannot exist without *arete*, and a city is not to be termed 'happy' in regard to a proportion of its citizens, but in regard to them all.

That is to say: All the citizens in a *eudaimon* state must be *eudaimon*, and *eudaimonia* depends on *arete*; but mechanics are incapable of the life of *arete*: therefore mechanics are not part of the *eudaimon* state which we are delineating. If *arete* must be used to commend a whole leisured way of life, it must evidently be confined to one class of the community. No Greek would be surprised, for *arete* and *eudaimonia* have always been so confined. *Kalon* naturally behaves similarly. As we have seen,[c] Aristotle's *agathos* acts 'for the sake of the *kalon*'. *Kalon*, therefore, commends all the manifestations of all the *aretai* which make up the complete *arete* of the citizen, a way of life to which the remaining inhabitants of Aristotle's state cannot aspire.

It should be evident that there is nothing here either cynical or retrograde. Aristotle, and the 'moralizers' generally, have extended and deepened the traditional usages of *arete*, *kalon*, and *eudaimonia*. As a result of their thought and practice, the intellectual virtues have taken a more prominent place, and those moral relations which were upheld by the gods have

---

[a] *E.N.* 1099^{b}18. [b] Arist. *Pol.* 1329^{a}19 ff. [c] Cp. p. 317.

become moral *aretai*: a change which, if only those capable of full *arete* are considered, forms an unquestionable advance on traditional thought. If Aristotle's citizens regard the quieter virtues as *aretai*, they will pursue them; and since in judging one another they will be judging other men of property and leisure, they will be able to censure any falling short in the quieter virtues by saying that an *agathos*, in showing himself to be unjust, is falling short in *arete*. Since all such possess social advantages and are not inhibited by poverty from taking part in public life, such advantages need not be considered when one *agathos* passes judgement on another.

This is admirable. In the case of the other inhabitants of the city, however, who, being incapable of *arete*, are not citizens, this view raises problems which the traditional view (probably) did not.[a] Traditional belief in the gods was confused and confusing; but in so far as the gods were believed to be moral, it was their function to apply the same sanctions to all men of whatever status; and accordingly, while there was a belief in such gods, it might be hoped that, even if, as a result of other beliefs about the gods, it did not yet clearly exist,[b] a standard for moral actions which should hold throughout the community might be developed. The necessity for this, in view of the externality of Greek judgements of action where *dikaiosune* was not so guaranteed, is evident; and in the ideas of post-mortem punishment, and particularly in the *language* of the myth in Plato's *Gorgias*,[c] the desire for such a standard can be seen.

Aristotle leaves no hope of establishing any standard for the whole community. Artisans can have no share in Aristotelian *arete* as a whole, for its implications make this impossible; and Aristotle's system of morals and responsibility is founded on this *arete*. We are not told by what standard the actions of those who, being incapable of *arete*, are in the city but not of it, are to be judged. From the point of view of politics this is unimportant, for in Aristotle's city such men have no share in politics; and from the point of view of the courts, since, being men, they are 'first causes of action',[d] and it can be established whether they acted voluntarily and deliberately or

---

[a] Cp. Chapter VIII *ad fin.*
[b] Cp. Chapter VII *passim.*
[c] Especially Plat. *Gorg.* 523 c ff.
[d] ἀρχὴ τῶν πράξεων, *E.N.* 1112^b32.

otherwise, no trouble need arise, *provided that nothing prevents the relevant questions from being asked.* But this is the point; *arete*, linked with *eudaimonia*, is still the highest term of value. The artisan has no claim to this; he may have *dikaiosune*, which is *an arete*,[14] or any other of the *aretai* from which his lack of possessions does not debar him; but he cannot have *arete* as a whole, and it is this *arete* which holds the highest position.[15] Accordingly, when any question of morals and responsibility is to be decided between a citizen, who possesses *arete*, and an artisan, who by definition does not, the citizen's possession of *arete* must still confuse any jury which attempts to decide between them, just as surely as the popular conception of *arete* confused the juries of the Athenian courts. True, since *dikaiosune* is now *an arete* or a facet of *arete*, Aristotle's citizen, if unjust, has smudged his *arete*; but a great deal remains, as a claim against others, while the artisan, even if just, never had this *arete* at all. True, Aristotle maintains that anyone who possesses *arete* as a whole possesses all the *aretai*, and hence will ideally be just;[a] but in practice this cannot always be the case. Accordingly, in decisions between persons of different status, the fact that the highest term of value is used to commend non-moral excellences as well as moral ones will prevent, as in the Athenian courts, the asking of relevant questions, or override the answers when the questions are asked, and hence will still, as it has always done, confuse the question of moral responsibility.[16] True, in the circles of the *agathoi*, the problem is solved; but the solution can only be readily applied in Aristotle's state even here, for in an ordinary (democratic) state only a minority of the citizens are *agathoi*, and there exists no clearly defined body in which Aristotle's solution will hold.

This difficulty arises from the fact that in Aristotle and in Greek generally those qualities which at any time are held to be relevant to *arete* are, except by individual (protesting) authors, not co-ordinated or graded, but merely exist side by side. Plato, by explicitly giving prominence to the quieter virtues, tried to solve this problem.[17] Aristotle's less systematic method of approach involves the loss of this advance; and this entails a further blow to moral responsibility, one which relates to Aristotle's view of life as a whole. In the first book of the

[a] *E.N.* 1098[a]15 ff.

Nicomachean Ethics,[a] Aristotle defined *eudaimonia*, the *agathon* of mankind, as

An activity of the *psuche* in accordance with *arete*, and if there are several *aretai*, in accordance with the best and most perfect.

This is dangerous. Plato, despite his conviction that philosophy is the highest human activity and the one most conducive to human *eudaimonia*, is quite convinced that, men being what they are, human life must be a complex of different kinds of activity: the philosophers must go back into the cave, even if Plato is hard put to it to justify their return. Accordingly, we might expect Aristotle to include in his definition of *eudaimonia* the possibility that its nature might be complex, and include several *aretai*.[18] In the *Nicomachean Ethics*, from Book II to Book IX, such a view seems possible, despite the definition of Book I. The practice of the *aretai* so carefully analysed must surely be *eudaimonia*, or essential to it; and yet Book X, reverting strictly to the dangerous definition quoted above, gives a very different answer.

In Book X Aristotle declares that *theōriā*, abstract speculation, is the most perfect *arete*, for the following reasons:[b] The best *arete* must be that of the best part of us; and this must be the part which seems by nature to rule and take thought about things which are *kala* and things which are 'divine'.[19] So far so good: to be concerned with *kala* might well include moral activities. Almost at once, however, Aristotle repeats that this *arete* must be 'theoretic'. It is, he says, only reasonable that *eudaimonia* should consist in 'theorizing', since we perform this activity with the best part of ourselves, and its subject-matter is the best objects.[20] *Theoria*, too, affords the highest and purest pleasures, can be pursued more continuously than any other activity without fatigue or satiation, and is more self-sufficient than the moral life and the life of politics, since for the latter one needs possessions and friends;[21] and further, *theoria* is pursued as an end in itself, whereas the practical and moral *aretai* seem to infringe upon our leisure. Again, the life of philosophy, the life of the *nous*, is more than human,[c] and we should 'play the immortal' as much as possible, and make every

---

[a] *E.N.* 1098ª15 ff.   [b] *E.N.* 1177ª12 ff.   [c] *E.N.* 1177ᵇ26 ff.

effort to live in accordance with the best of the elements in our-selves; and though the intellect is only a small part of us,

It far outstrips all the rest in power and dignity; and further each man would appear to *be* this part of himself, if indeed that part which has authority is better.

This contention, that we *are* our noblest part, our theoretic intelligence, is absurd, and leads to conclusions as absurd, as the supposition that a man is 'really' only desire or only passion. Accepting this fallacy, Aristotle naturally concludes that the *eudaimonia* which results from the practice of the non-theoretic *aretai* is only *eudaimonia* in a secondary sense. Again the results are undesirable, so far as moral responsibility is concerned. Stewart, in a note on another passage which entails this fallacy,[a] says

We must not suppose Aristotle to mean that the good man devotes himself entirely to his 'intellect' strictly so called; that he gives him-self up to the cultivation of his 'scientific faculties'. If he did, his life would be as one-sided in its own way as that of the politician who sacrifices the good of his nature as a whole to his ambition, or as that of the tradesman who sacrifices it to his desire for gain. . . . Reason realizes itself in the discovery of truth *and* in the regulation of the feelings.

Now from our standpoint this is undoubtedly what Aristotle ought to mean, and the attitude which he should adopt to *eudaimonia*; but it is clearly not the attitude which, in Book X, he does adopt. Aristotle has distinguished *theoria* as *eudaimonia* in the primary sense from moral activity which is *eudaimonia* only in a secondary sense. Accordingly, even if as a general rule of life it must be true that the *eudaimon* devotes time to other activities, since it is humanly impossible to spend one's whole life in solving problems in geometry, theology, and astronomy (even if Aristotle's views justify precisely this), yet how are *individual* decisions to do a *particular* moral act to be taken? On Aristotle's principles, it seems impossible to persuade anyone who could now be solving a particular geometrical problem, thereby securing the highest kind of *eudaimonia*, that he should instead perform some moral act, since this would secure him only an inferior kind of *eudaimonia*, and *eudaimonia*

[a] *E.N.* 1166[a]16 ff., and Stewart ad loc.

is universally admitted to be the end of life. A man must put his emotional and impulsive life in order, so that in the ensuing calm he may pursue his theorizing more readily; but once this is accomplished there seems to be no reason why he should prefer any given moral claim—say that of defending his friends' interests, expected even by traditional standards of *arete*—to his desire to philosophize. Once again the alignment of values prevents the hearing of the claim of the quieter (practical) virtues; and this merely emphasizes the difficulties mentioned above, which arise from the fact that *dikaiosune* has no paramount position; for if Aristotle cannot furnish *dikaiosune* with superiority over an activity so different in kind as *theoria*, nor even suggest the terms on which this might be attempted, it is certain that he cannot satisfactorily furnish the quiet moral virtues with superiority over other *aretai* which seem to be activities of the same order.

The superiority of *theoria* depends on mere assertion; but it is evident why Aristotle makes this assertion, and why he expects to have it accepted by his pupils. As was said above,[a] Plato, Aristotle, and the 'immoralists' are all intellectuals before they are anything else. Nothing could be more natural for a philosopher to assert than that the most satisfying life is that of intellectual activity.

Thus far, however, we have merely considered the *Nicomachean Ethics*, an analytic work of loose construction. In the *Politics* the functions of the whole man in the community must be considered; and here it is evident that Aristotle adopts an attitude similar to that which Stewart would have him adopt. In the *Ethics* arete and *eudaimonia* display certain differences of behaviour. It seems natural to say that the *agathos* should possess all the *aretai*, not merely the best;[22] but it seems equally natural to say that a man should always pursue the highest form of *eudaimonia* of which he is capable. Since the *aretai* are only discussed because Aristotle believes that *eudaimonia* is an activity of the *psuche* in accordance with the highest human *arete*, it follows, as I have said, that a man should pursue this *eudaimonia*—*theoria*—to the exclusion of all others, so far as he is able. In the *Politics*, however, Aristotle naturally considers the *aretai* which a man displays in the community rather than his

[a] Cp. p. 292.

individual *eudaimonia*; and here it is evident that his citizens
are expected to lead a full and active civic life. The reason is
not that Aristotle has changed his mind about the nature of
eudaimonia:[a]

> If we are right in our opinion, and *eudaimonia* is taken to be activity
> in accordance with *arete*, the active life will be the best, both for
> cities and for individuals. Not that a life of activity must necessarily
> have relation to others . . . nor should we consider as practical only
> those ideas which are pursued for the sake of practical results, but
> *much more* the thoughts and contemplations which are independent
> and complete in themselves.

Here we have no sharp dichotomy between the political and the
contemplative lives, but it is evident that the latter is to be
preferred. Aristotle's citizens 'must' pursue an active civic life,
not because they will secure their highest *eudaimonia* as individuals thereby, but because their continued existence as a community in competition with other communities demands it.
Once again Aristotle is fortunate in not being opposed by a
Thrasymachus. An 'immoralist' convinced by Aristotle will now
pursue trigonometry rather than tyranny to secure his *eudaimonia*, and will leave administration to others; if convinced that
Aristotle's other *aretai* are *aretai*, he will pursue them when he
has time to spare; but if he has not the time, he will not curtail
his own *eudaimonia* by functioning less 'well' than might otherwise be the case. The ordinary man will accept the necessities
of life in a city-state; but it must be emphasized that Aristotle
has succeeded no better than Plato in demonstrating why a man
capable of philosophizing should at any moment choose rather
to perform any individual moral or political action.

Accordingly, if we insist on logical rigour, Aristotle, in
addition to the traditional problems of Greek values, has this
new obstacle to the asking of the right questions—that is to say,
the right questions for the present purpose. Aristotle, however,
set out to discover the nature of *eudaimonia*, agreed to be the
end of life. *Theoria* seems to him to satisfy the criteria; and it is
the nature of the concept of moral responsibility, as was said in
Chapter I, to be moulded by other beliefs, rather than itself
to mould others, even if these other beliefs have an effect as

[a] Arist. *Pol.* 1325[b]14 ff.

unfortunate as must be the case here. It must be insisted, however, that even if we remove this obstacle by treating *theoria* as merely co-ordinate with the other *aretai*, all the other problems discussed above[a] remain. Aristotle may be able to assert the predominance of *theoria*, for this is qualitatively different from the *aretai* of practical activity; but to assert the predominance of *dikaiosune*, one practical *arete* among many, is impossible, for the reasons already given. The former obstacle may be due to Aristotle's own predilections: the others are inextricably bound up with the nature of Greek values as a whole.

B. GENERAL CONCLUSIONS

Accordingly, Aristotelian moral philosophy, when taken as a whole, fails, like that of Plato, to provide a completely satisfactory answer to the present problem. In so far as, in considering *arete* and *eudaimonia*, these writers are attempting to solve a different problem, this is not surprising. Some apparent carelessnesses result simply from this difference in aim;[23] but in admitting this we may draw general conclusions as to the defects, from the point of view of moral responsibility, which any moral code or moral theory using Greek presuppositions and Greek terminology must necessarily have.

It has been shown that throughout the period under discussion the basic datum of Greek life, and that on which Greek values are based, is the existence of the small unit, family or city-state,[24] passionately devoted, for excellent reasons, to the idea of its own autonomy and independence, rarely large enough to impose its will on all its neighbours, almost never efficient enough to be able to rely on continuing prosperity or an absence of muddle and confusion. Greek values accurately reflect the problem caused by this situation, and commend those who are from time to time most capable of remedying it, or at all events of preventing disaster. This commendation or valuation gives a man high claims against his society, as has been seen: claims which seem quite justified, but which, in the interests of the rest of society, must be checked in some way, if not by a belief in divine punishment in this world or the next,

[a] Pp. 341 ff.

then by an appeal to (enlightened) self-interest, whether by insisting that the quiet virtues maintain one's psychological health, or by claiming that they are *aretai*, and so a necessary— but not sufficient—qualification for the title of *agathos*. It has been shown that, from the point of view of moral responsibility, none[25] of these solutions is satisfactory; but given the presuppositions and basic values of the Greek city-state, it seems inevitable that these should be the only solutions available. To insist on the pre-eminence of the quieter excellences and to assert that these and these alone should be taken into account when matters of morals and responsibility are to be decided requires certain preconditions: there must either be a dread of divine sanctions in the form of a belief that all men are equal in the sight of gods who will punish without fear or favour, or there must—given Greek presuppositions—exist a stable community large enough sufficiently to sustain the myth of equal contribution to a society to ensure that the courts themselves will judge without fear or favour: a condition which, as has been seen, not even democratic and imperial Athens was fortunate enough to enjoy. It is useless to say 'fiat iustitia, ruat coelum' if one fears that the enforcement of strict justice will result, not in something so problematical as the descent of the heavens, but in the loss of the services or goodwill of a valuable citizen who might well turn the scale by his presence or absence at the next crisis; and Greek values faithfully reflect this situation. The claims of individual merit are undeniable: those of responsibility cannot override them.

Unfortunate as these results may be, they seem inevitable, given the values of Greek life and the facts upon which these depend. Between Homer and Aristotle, great advances were made in investigating the implications of the concept of moral responsibility. The idea of cause was explored with great subtlety, and the results were used in the courts, even though these results could not take priority over all other claims; and the importance of the quieter virtues to smooth, successful, and efficient civic organization was realized, and these excellences enrolled among the Greek *aretai*. To do this, however, to say 'this is *arete*', is to say 'this is the type of man which the city needs'; and accordingly it is natural that both Plato and Aristotle, in attempting to solve the primary problem of rendering the quieter virtues respectable, should approach this problem from the point of view of the 'successful living' of the city as a whole, and define the *agathos* in political terms. To Aristotle and the Plato of the *Laws*, the city required proves to be one composed *essentially* (but by no means entirely) of *agathoi politai*, each of whom possesses all the *aretai*, moral, intellectual, social, and economic: a city in which this term of political efficiency commends the quiet moral virtues as manifestations, among others, of this efficiency, or as means to the desired end. In the artificial environment thus created, one *agathos* can judge the moral responsibility of another with no impediment to his using all the gains in sensitivity made since the time of Homer; but outside this charmed circle there is still confusion. All codes of ethics set ideals; but not all entail judgements which can only be passed in an ideal environment.

The attempted solutions which have been discussed in the foregoing pages, however, seem to be not merely the only solutions which are actually found but also the only conceivable ones, given the conditions first of Homeric society, then of the Greek city-state; and to point this out, together with its inevitable effect on the concept of moral responsibility, has been a primary function of this work. The difference *in structure* between the basic system of Greek values and that to which we are accustomed has been indicated, and its importance shown; for, as has been seen, it is the underlying structure of a system of values, and the world-view by which it is moulded and which it in turn helps to mould, that gives the system its individual character. Piecemeal adaptations, analysis of certain aspects of the system to the exclusion of others, may seem to have changed that character; but when exposed to the rigour of logic or the stress of circumstance, accretions vanish and the basic structure is seen to be unchanged. This structure must at all times exercise an effect on every individual judgement of value passed, however closely such a judgement may resemble in form a judgement drawn from a different system, or however widely it may deviate from what a different system may hold to be reasonable; for, as was said in the first chapter, it is upon the world-view as a whole that individual judgements of value depend, and it is by reference to the world-view as a whole that they must be justified. In order that the Greeks of the period discussed should have a concept of moral responsibility precisely similar to our own, it would be necessary for our world-view and the Greek to coincide completely; and in this light that even Aristotle should differ from views to which we are accustomed seems less surprising.

NOTES TO CHAPTER XVI

1. *Arete* naturally has for Aristotle all the implications which it had for earlier writers. Human *eudaimonia* is evidently an activity of the *psuche* in accordance with *arete*, for the *arete* of anything is the condition in which it is functioning most efficiently, and hence its most satisfactory condition, its *eudaimonia*.

2. '*Phusike arete*', natural *arete*, is manifested, *E.N.* 1144ᵇ3, in uncoordinated impulses of generosity, courage, &c., which, without the direction of intelligence, may do harm as readily as they do good. The complete *arete* of Aristotle's citizens differs from this *arete* in two ways: in the first place, it is properly co-ordinated *arete* accompanied by directing intelligence; in the second, it is possessed by men of an assured social and economic position.

3. Since *logos* can mean both 'rule, principle' and 'reasoning', *orthos logos* can mean either 'correct principle' according to which a man who is not to reason for himself is trained, or 'correct reasoning' on the part of a man who is capable of doing this for himself.

4. The last provision seems both unnecessary and dangerous. For the citizens depicted in the foregoing paragraphs *ethismos*—Aristotle's term for the education in morals which his citizens are to receive—need mean no more than moral education in the manner in which it is practised by all societies. This provision encourages the reader to interpret it as conditioning directed to the end of producing automata. It is evident that such is not Aristotle's intention. The motive for its inclusion may be practical and political, cp. following note.

5. The desire that the citizens may not readily change their minds may well derive directly from the desirability that a city's assembly should not hastily and capriciously reverse the decisions it has made; contrast the behaviour of the Athenian assembly, Thuc. iii. 37 ff., and the strictures of Cleon, iii. 37. 4.

6. For a statement of policy, cp. *E.N.* 1145ᵇ2 ff.

7. The *kaloi kagathoi* (i.e. *kaloi* and *agathoi*) are 'gentlemen'. The phrase implies wealth, property, and culture, however interpreted, cp. Ar. *Eq.* 735 ff. It is thus ideally suited to the type of persuasive definition quoted in the text, for it is immediately attractive and essentially vague. Cp. Isoc. *To Demonicus* 13, for the method of persuasion: *kalokagathia* is said to be shown in keeping vows even to one's own disadvantage (another instance of religious sanctions replaced by social ones), in

contrast to performing expensive sacrifices, which prove nothing but one's own prosperity. So to commend any quality is to render it a 'social asset', for it would be the mark of an *andrapodōdēs*, a 'slavish' man, an *anandros*, a *kakos*, not to possess it. Cp. for similar advocacy of an activity (horsemanship) which, though non-moral, is regarded as a (military) necessity, Xen. *Cyr.* iv. 3. 22.

8. The change of standards is illustrated in an interesting manner in *To Philip* 109. Referring to Heracles, Isocrates says that other writers have harped endlessly upon his valour and upon his labours, but that till now no one has drawn attention to his excellences of *psuche*, his *phronesis* and *philotīmiā* and *dikaiosune*. Now *arete* is a word which is indissolubly bound to Heracles. Every writer of earlier date who mentions him uses it to commend his favoured qualities. This is a striking testimony to the non-'moral' flavour of the word in earlier writers, and also to the manner in which (cp. *Panath.* 72) these fourth-century writers are 'cleaning up' the old heroes to suit new standards.

9. Cp. e.g. Xen. *Cyr.* iv. 3. 23, *Hell.* ii. 3. 12, 15, 19, also the 'explanation', *Mem.* ii. 6. 30; and Isoc. *Antid.* 316 ff. Since Aristotle is using 'ordinary Greek', he must be affected.

10. In the latter passage mentioned in the text the judgement is justified on the grounds of military efficiency, inasmuch as the 'banausic' skills impair a man's fighting abilities. The justification is adequate, but there is naturally, as there has been since Homer, also a very strong social flavour; cp. also Plato, *Laws* 918 ff., a very significant passage. The stresses of war clearly affected this standard in some respects, cp. Xen. *Mem.* ii. 7. 4. An anecdote is told of Socrates' advice to one Aristarchus, who had taken his female relatives under his protection during the stasis, and was finding it difficult to support them owing to the complete collapse of credit in Athens at that time. Aristarchus' view was that he could not expect them to work for their living since they had been 'liberally educated', ἐλευθερίως πεπαιδευμέναι. Socrates, however, held that 'if they were going to do anything *aischron*, death would be preferable'; but that work, i.e. baking and weaving, was not *aischron*. From the point of view of the class whose views Xenophon normally represents, such menial tasks—as the anecdote itself shows—would certainly have been regarded as *aischron* before the war. During the war, many must have been forced to behave in this manner; but when the stress disappeared, values naturally returned to normal.

11. He uses such phrases as ἐφ' οἷς δεῖ καὶ οἷς δεῖ ὀργιζόμενος, ἔτι δὲ καὶ ὡς δεῖ καὶ ὅτε δεῖ καὶ ὅσον χρόνον, 'being angry at the things and with the people one should be angry, and also in the manner, at the time, and for the length of time one should be angry', to express this. Though being angry is sometimes an expression of an *arete*, this depends on circumstances: a point which needs making, if the conflicting claims of the different *aretai* are to be harmonized. Cp. *E.N.* 1125^{b}31 ff., &c.

12. In fact Aristotle says that the *megalopsuchos* is the best, 1123^{b}27, but this judgement has no effect on the rest of the discussion, owing to the loose and analytic method of treatment. The *megalopsuchos* of Aristotle is

naturally an illustration of 'ordinary Greek' standards—that such men
exist is evident from the manner in which they are spoken of, cp.
1124ᵃ20—and reminds us once again that *kalon* commends, and *aischron*
decries, visual characteristics as well as standards of behaviour. Thus the
demand that the *megalopsuchos* shall possess certain physical characteristics, the 'slow walk', the 'deep voice', and the 'level utterance', is,
though Aristotle attempts to give reasons for his selection of such
characteristics, 1125ᵃ12 ff., essentially the demand of ordinary language.
To obtain full approval from his fellows, a man must have such characteristics. Demosthenes, *In Pantaenetum* 52, shows the demand clearly. It
is asked what fault anyone will be able to find with Nicobulus; and the
reply is that it has been said that he is a moneylender, and that 'he is
looked on with jealousy and he walks quickly and speaks in a loud voice
and carries a stick'. This man is the reverse of Aristotle's *megalopsuchos*,
and it is evident that what he does is *aischron* and that, since clearly the
case might go against Nicobulus on these grounds, men in general
admire his opposite, the man who possesses the external characteristics
of Aristotle's *megalopsuchos*. (Plato is not innocent of this, cp. *Theaetetus*
175 E, despite 175 B.)

13. *Laws* 741 D–E. Plato would like complete equality of possessions, 744 B,
but regards this as impossible.

14. True, at *E.N.* 1130ᵃ8, Aristotle can say that *dikaiosune* in the general
sense of displaying courage, self-control, quiet civic behaviour, &c., is
'the whole of *arete*'; and at 1129ᵇ29 he quotes Theognis' 'the whole of
arete is summed up in *dikaiosune*' (Theogn. 147 f., cp. p. 78 above).
This, when Aristotle is analysing the sense of *dikaiosune*, can certainly
be *said*, for this is one of the things which can be said *in isolation* about
justice; but it is evident from the rest of the *Ethics* and *Politics* that
Aristotle's views as a whole prevent *dikaiosune* from assuming this
position. It is significant that in the *Eudemian Ethics* Aristotle maintains
that *kalokagathia* is 'perfect *arete*'. *Kalokagathia* is undeniably a term with
the strongest of social implications, cp. p. 339 f.; and Aristotle, using
'ordinary Greek', must be affected.

15. The discussion of *Politics* 1260ᵃ28 ff. merely serves to emphasize this.
There Aristotle discusses the *arete* of the ruler, the free man, the woman,
the child and the slave; the qualities, that is to say, in virtue of which
each of these may be termed *agathos*, good of his kind; and he naturally
insists that each should possess as much of the favoured qualities as will
enable him to perform his function properly. That *arete* may be used of
members of every class of the community does not set a standard which
will hold throughout the community. *Arete* commends all kinds of
excellence: it may be used of anything which may be termed *agathos*;
and there must always be a set of qualities in virtue of which one would
be willing to say that e.g. a slave is a good slave. The *arete* with which we
are concerned, however, that which is relevant in the courts, is a political
term, and commends and denotes the ability to perform certain services to the state, or the actual performance of such services. Of such
arete artisans, slaves, women, and children are incapable; only Aristotle's

citizens can perform these services in his state; hence only they possess this *arete*, and the claims with which it endows its possessor.

16. In *Politics* 1284ᵃ3 ff. Aristotle maintains that a man who far outshines all his fellow citizens in *arete* and political capacity should not be regarded as part of the state; 'for justice will not be done to the better man, if he is reckoned only as the equal of those who are so much worse than he in *arete* and political skill. . . . Hence we see that legislation is concerned only with those who are equal in birth and capacity' (Jowett, slightly adapted). The claims of *arete* cannot be denied. They must confuse any judgement between a man who possesses it and one who does not.

17. *Laws* 922 A. But 660 E shows the difficulty with which this has been accomplished: the poet must say ὡς ὁ μὲν ἀγαθὸς ἀνὴρ σώφρων ὢν καὶ δίκαιος εὐδαίμων ἐστὶ καὶ μακάριος, that the *agathos*, being (or 'if he is') *sophron* and *dikaios*, is *eudaimon* and blessed. The phrasing shows to what extent, even in Plato's latest writings, the connection between *dikaios* and *agathos* is still felt to be synthetic. Cp. Isoc. *Antid.* 67, where Isocrates, in order to be understood, finds it necessary to speak of '*arete* and *dikaiosune*'.

18. Though, as we have seen, even Plato does not adopt such a view in the *Republic*, where the *eudaimonia* of the philosopher-kings would be to philosophize continually. The *Philebus*, however, has implications which might have been expected to attract Aristotle.

19. The latter category, of course, for Aristotle includes the heavenly bodies.

20. For Aristotle, as for Plato, theology, astronomy, mathematics, and pure thought in general are pursuits far nobler than the study of man, for the objects studied are nobler.

21. It is interesting to note the reappearance of the ideal of self-sufficiency, *autarkeia*, as a point urged in favour of philosophy, *E.N.* 1177ᵃ27. In the last resort the *agathos* has always had to be self-reliant and self-sufficient.

22. Cp. the argument for the necessity of *sophia*, p. 333 above.

23. Cp. Chapter XV, Note 15, and Notes 4 and 5 of this chapter. The 'carelessness' of Note 15 (for even if the problem is insoluble in terms of Aristotle's psychology, he ought to have noticed that he had described as *akrasia*, incontinence, a condition which does not coincide with the definition of *akrasia* in *E.N.* 1145ᵇ12) is evidently due to the fact that Aristotle is not *primarily* concerned with the responsibility of the 'acratic' man, but, in view of the opinions of Socrates and Plato, with the possibility of such a man's existence.

24. Or rather, as has been shown for the late fifth and early fourth centuries in particular, the existence of both family and city-state, without coordinating the claims of each to autonomy and independence.

25. Possibly Plato's myths, particularly that of the *Gorgias*, might supply a solution in theory; but it is evident that, given the mental climate in which he was working, such a solution had little chance of general acceptance in practice.

APPENDIX

(See p. 165)

The Scopas-Fragment of Simonides

SINCE my treatment of the Scopas-fragment seems likely to be controversial, it seems desirable to consider here some of the alternative views which have been offered. Most writers argue that Simonides is using *agathos*, *aischron*, &c., in a 'moral' sense: an argument which, if no distinction is drawn between co-operative and competitive values, has little chance of elucidating the meaning of the poem. In *Sappho und Simonides*, pp. 159 ff., Wilamowitz begins by attempting to show that at the time of Pittacus, on whose words Simonides is commenting, *esthlos* could be used in a (i.e. co-operative) 'moral' sense. He cites from Zenobius the paroemiographer an anecdote which relates that Pittacus said χαλεπὸν ἐσθλὸν ἔμμεναι, 'It is hard to be *esthlos*', on laying down his tyranny of his own free will; of which Solon is said to have remarked χαλεπὰ τὰ καλά, 'Actions which are *kalon* are difficult'. If we could rely on this anecdote, we should have to acknowledge that Pittacus and Solon were using *esthlos* and *kalon* in a 'co-operative' sense in the sixth century. (Such a use, as an isolated gesture, is not in itself inconceivable, cp. Theognis, p. 78 above, and Note 29.) Wilamowitz naturally admits (p. 174, op. cit.) that it is undesirable to rest much weight on an anecdote of this kind, which may well—apart from the actual remarks of Pittacus and Solon, which need not be related to each other—derive from the imagination of a much later period, one which misinterprets these remarks as freely as Socrates misinterprets Simonides' poem. Further evidence is needed. To supply it, Wilamowitz quotes Phocylides frag. 14, πόλλ' ἀέκοντα παθεῖν διζήμενον ἔμμεναι ἐσθλόν, 'to suffer many things against one's own inclinations, while striving to be *esthlos*'. Of this line he says: 'Darin liegt, daß es die *kakoi* vielfach besser haben; was sehr wahr ist, aber nur dann, wenn gut und böse sittliche Begriffe sind, von der Geburt und von der Lebensstellung und von dem Glücke unabhängig.' It certainly follows that *esthlos* is here used without reference to noble birth, which it would be pointless to seek to obtain; but it does not follow that Phocylides is commending *co-operative* excellences by his use of *esthlos*. The contexts in which it appears in the authors who quote it are quite irrelevant, for it is used merely as a tag, without reference to its original context. The situation might well be that of *Iliad* xi. 404 ff., where

Odysseus is trying to screw himself up to the point of facing the enemy alone, little as he wants to, no matter what may happen to him; which is precisely 'to suffer many things' in the interest of being *esthlos*, brave. True, the pattern of thought is different in Homer. Odysseus deduces from his possession of *arete* the conclusion that he ought to behave bravely and suffer though he does not want to (cp. Snell, *The Discovery of the Mind*, p. 159); Phocylides urges a man to suffer in order that he may be *esthlos*. This may well indicate a change in modes of thought, but it does not prove that Phocylides is commending quiet moral excellences by his use of the word *esthlos*. (He might, of course, be commending material success, in the manner of Hesiod saying that the gods have set much sweat and toil in the way of the acquisition of *arete*, *W. and D.*, 289.) Accordingly, Wilamowitz is left with the anecdote of Zenobius to support his 'quiet' moral interpretation of Pittacus' 'It is hard to be *esthlos*'; and this is insufficient, since in Homer too it is difficult to be *esthlos*, even for a wealthy warrior-chieftain; for, as we have seen, *arete* requires high standards of courage, and depends on success, not good intentions. Wilamowitz could, indeed, have cited as evidence Theognis 147 f., which also figures as Phocylides frag. 10 (cp. p. 78 above); but in fact all such collateral material must be irrelevant to the present discussion; for if we suppose that Pittacus meant 'It is hard to be *esthlos*' in a co-operative sense, we must also suppose that Simonides has completely misunderstood him; and it is with Simonides' use of *esthlos* that we are concerned here. Such acts as renouncing supreme power, while they may go against the grain, are under the control of one's own will; but Simonides' standard of *arete*, as I have argued in the text, is not under the control of the will in this way. Simonides might have misunderstood Pittacus; but it seems much more likely, to say the least, that the incorrect version should have found its way into Zenobius. Again, he might have misunderstood him wilfully. Of this there can be no conclusive proof or disproof; but the only motive for such a misunderstanding would be to try to crush what would then be Pittacus' new standard of *arete* by means of the attractions of the old. These attractions are indisputable; but in fact Simonides stresses the disadvantages rather than the attractions. It seems most likely, then, that Simonides supposed Pittacus to be using *esthlos* in the traditional sense. Simonides himself is certainly doing so.[a]

[a] In discussing this problem I have adopted the reading—favoured by Wilamowitz—πόλλ' ἀέκοντα παθεῖν as the text of the Phocylides fragment. It appears in this form in *Anecd. Par.* i. 166. In Clement, *Stromateis*, v. 733, the reading is πολλὰ πλανηθῆναι, and in Plutarch, *De Rect. Aud.* 18, πόλλ' ἀπατηθῆναι. In no case is it essential—or, it seems to me, likely—that *esthlos* should be interpreted in terms of quiet moral values.

Certainly the idea of tyrannical power sets a problem of values for the serious thinker. Clearly it is *kalon*, the mark of an *agathos*, to succeed, and who more successful than the tyrant? Yet the *agathoi*, as a class, must disapprove of anyone who attempts to set himself up over them. This ensures a social—and so apparently moral—disapproval of the tyrant; and so in Solon frag. 32 Bergk Solon says that he would have defiled and shamed his reputation, μιάνας καὶ καταισχύνας κλέος, if he had become a tyrant, as he evidently had the power and the opportunity to do. But success is still the most important end, though there is a vested interest in preventing it in this case; and so in the fourth line of the same poem Solon must say οὐδὲν αἰδεῦμαι, 'I am not ashamed of not having taken supreme power, for I think that I have gained more of a victory over men in acting as I have done.' That is to say, he represents his refusal to seize supreme power as a victory, and hence *kalon*; that he is acting against normal standards is shown both by Solon frag. 33 Bergk and by the prevailing standards of the following century. When Herodotus tells the story of Maeandrius, who also wanted to lay down supreme power, he merely says that Maeandrius wished to show himself most just, *dikaiotatos*, iii. 142 : *agathos* and *kakos* only come into the discussion when his erstwhile subjects taunt Maeandrius with being ill born, *kakōs gegonōs*. Only in the sophistic passage, iii. 80 (cp. p. 178), is *aristos* used as Wilamowitz wishes *esthlos* to be used by Pittacus; and this is evidence merely of the violence of the change which then occurred, not of linguistic usage so much earlier.

We may also consider the recent discussion of this poem by L. Woodbury in *TAPA* 84, pp. 135 ff. Here again the conclusions are misleading. Woodbury acknowledges that the early part of the poem is not related to (co-operative) moral values; but when he reaches l. 14, ἐπαίνημι . . . ἑκὼν ὅστις ἔρδῃ μηδὲν αἰσχρόν 'I praise . . . anyone who does nothing *aischron* of his own free will', he maintains that 'we have here for the first time in this poem a purely moral concept'. This is not so. Simonides may have excellent intentions, but Woodbury's gloss (op. cit., Note 64) 'this criterion gives to *aischron* the ethical sense of . . . merited dishonour' is simply untrue. It would only be true if the line meant that only actions performed of one's own free will could be *aischron*; but Simonides immediately adds ἀνάγκᾳ δ' οὐδὲ θεοὶ μάχονται, 'but against necessity even the gods do not fight'. Evidently it is against the necessity of doing some *aischra* that one cannot struggle : the *aischra* which a man performs of necessity are none the less *aischra* for that. Accordingly, it is immediately clear that *aischron* spans a great deal more than the 'ethical'; and indeed it cannot be shown that the 'quietly' ethical plays any part in it. For there is no need to suppose—

and nothing in the poem itself, properly considered, suggests it—that wilfully performed *aischra* include acts of injustice: the distinction, given the poem as a whole (for which see the discussion in the text, pp. 165 ff.), is presumably between cowardice and mistake, the distinction which Hector was unable to draw in Chapter III (p. 47) and which later writers prove equally unable to draw (p. 157 f.), or between the voluntary mean and niggardly behaviour of a rich man, and the same behaviour exhibited involuntarily by a poor man, or by a rich man who has become poor. Given this situation, it is clear that Simonides has in no sense made *aischron* into a purely moral term, or indeed into a term of 'quiet' morals at all. In fact, even within the limits which Simonides has set himself, he can expect no success. He may say that *he* will praise the man who does not voluntarily do anything *aischron*; but since *aischron* is the most powerful term available to denigrate action, it is incredible that a society should not disapprove of a man whose actions can be so characterized, whether they were performed voluntarily or no. Simonides would have had to restrict *aischron* to the field of voluntary action had he wished to use it as a term of 'quiet' morals; but he has not attempted to do this. Accordingly, *aischron* is not such a term here to any greater extent than it was in Homer; and thus l. 21, 'All things are *kala* with which *aischra* are not mingled', which Woodbury regards as a purely moral judgement, cannot be regarded as such. Its sense depends entirely on the sense which can, on other grounds, be assigned to *aischron* and *kalon*; and this cannot be shown to be that of 'quiet' morals.

Since *agathos/arete*, &c., are not used here to commend the cooperative excellences, we are left with the problem of responsibility in the form stated in the text, pp. 165 ff. This problem is masked for Woodbury by his assumption that *arete* is here overtly the *arete* of the Homeric hero, and that (op. cit., p. 154) Simonides was attempting to console Greek aristocrats for their inability to conform to the Achillean standard. He adds (op. cit., p. 162) that the ὑγιὴς ἀνήρ, the 'healthy man', is Simonides' ideal: the man who is not *kakos* nor utterly *apalamnos*, and 'knows city-benefiting justice'. This could only be the case if (accepting the hypothesis that we are concerned with Homeric *arete*—which is essentially true, for *arete* has not changed since Homer) their inability to be perfect Homeric heroes entailed that the Greek aristocrats of the day could not apply *arete*, *agathos*, and *aristos* to themselves. Again, this is not true: after all, socially speaking the Homeric suitors, though indifferent fighters, were the *aristoi* of Ithaca, and we have already seen in Theognis the claims of two classes of people, neither of whom had the exact characteristics of the Homeric hero, to be *agathoi*. Simonides, in fact, points out the difficulties of traditional *arete* and its instability, and the unlikelihood that any man will be perfectly *agathos*, or remain in this condition for very long. He does not say that the terms cannot be applied at all in his society— indeed, ll. 8–9 make it abundantly clear that they can—and no society would have agreed with him if he had said it. Accordingly, the claim that Simonides' ideal is the ὑγιὴς ἀνήρ, the 'healthy man', is for my purposes misleading. It may satisfy Simonides that a man knows 'city-benefiting justice', but if he cannot term such a man *agathos* (and clearly he cannot), and if there are men in the state who can be termed *agathoi* without regard to their justice (and clearly there are), then Simonides' solution to the problem with which I am concerned is clearly no solution at all.[a] Only when a writer can commend the ideal of justice by means of the most powerful terms of value which his society possesses will the claims of moral responsibility be given a fair hearing.

[a] Again, when W. C. Greene, *Moira*, p. 68, says 'Simonides replies with an analysis of the nature of goodness quite in keeping with the spirit of the new Athenian democracy,' the same reservations must be made.

SELECT BIBLIOGRAPHY

J. BÖHME: *Die Seele und das Ich im homerischen Epos*, Leipzig and Berlin, 1929.

C. M. BOWRA: *Tradition and Design in the Iliad*, Oxford, 1930.

G. M. CALHOUN: *The Growth of Criminal Law in Ancient Greece*, Berkeley, 1927.

—— 'Homer's Gods: Prolegomena', *Transactions of the American Philological Association*, vol. lxviii.

—— 'Zeus the Father in Homer', *Transactions of the American Philological Association*, vol. lxvi.

J. CARRIÉRE: 'Nouvelles Remarques sur Théognis', *Revue des Études Grecques*, 1954.

E. R. DODDS: *The Greeks and the Irrational*, Berkeley, 1951.

E. EHNMARK: *The Idea of God in Homer*, Diss. Uppsala, 1935.

J. FERGUSON: *Moral Values in the Ancient World*, London, 1958.

H. FRISCH: *Might and Right in Antiquity*, translated by C. C. Martindale, Copenhagen, 1949.

G. GLOTZ: *Histoire Grecque*, vol. i, Paris, 1925.

—— *La Solidarité de la famille dans le droit criminel de la Grèce*, Paris, 1904.

J. GOULD: *The Development of Plato's Ethics*, Cambridge, 1955.

W. C. GREENE: *Moira*, Harvard, 1944.

D. GRENE: *Man in his Pride*, Chicago, 1950.

G. M. A. GRUBE: in *Studies presented to Gilbert Norwood*, Toronto, 1952.

W. K. C. GUTHRIE: *Orpheus and Greek Religion*, London, 1935.

R. HACKFORTH: 'Moral Evil and Ignorance in Plato's Ethics', *Classical Quarterly*, 1946.

M. HAMBURGER: *Morals and Law; The Growth of Aristotle's Legal Theory*, Yale, 1951.

F. HEINIMANN: *Nomos und Physis*, Basel, 1945.

W. JAEGER: *Aristotle*, translated by R. Robinson, Oxford, 1948.

—— *Paideia*, translated by G. Highet, Oxford, 1944/6.

J. H. KELLS: 'Antiphon and Homicide Law', *Proceedings of the London Classical Society*, vol. i.

G. B. KERFERD: 'The Doctrine of Thrasymachus in Plato's *Republic*', *Durham University Journal*, December, 1947.

A. LANG: *The World of Homer*, London, 1910.

K. LATTE: 'Schuld und Sünde in der griechischen Religion', *Archiv für Religionswissenschaft*, vol. xx.

I. M. LINFORTH: *The Arts of Orpheus*, Berkeley, 1941.

ED. MEYER: *Geschichte des Altertums*, iii (Ed. 2) Stuttgart, 1937.

L. MOULINIER: *Le Pur et l'impur dans la pensée des Grecs*, Paris, 1952.

M. P. NILSSON: *Geschichte der griechischen Religion*, Handbuch der Altertumswissenschaft, v, Munich, 1941/50.

—— *Greek Piety*, translated by H. J. Rose, Oxford, 1951.

—— *Homer and Mycenae*, London, 1933.

R. B. ONIANS: *The Origins of European Thought*, Cambridge, 1951.

B. E. Perry: 'Mental Parataxis', *Transactions of the American Philological Association*, vol. lxviii.

N. M. Pusey: *Alcibiades and τὸ φιλόπολι*, Harvard Studies in Classical Philology, 1940.

J. de Romilly: *Thucydide et l'impérialisme athénien*, Paris, 1947.

L. Ruhl: 'De Mortuorum Iudicio', *R.G.V.V.*, ii. ii, 1903.

Ed. Schwartz: *Ethik der Griechen*, Stuttgart, 1951.

Paul Shorey: 'On the Implicit Ethics and Psychology of Thucydides', *Transactions of the American Philological Association*, vol. xxiv.

T. A. Sinclair: *A History of Greek Political Thought*, London, 1951.

B. Snell: *The Discovery of the Mind*, translated by Rosenmeyer, Oxford, 1953.

G. Thomson: *Aeschylus and Athens*, London, 1941.

U. von Wilamowitz-Moellendorff: *Sappho und Simonides*, Berlin, 1913.

L. Woodbury: 'Simonides on ἀρετή', *Transactions of the American Philological Association*, vol. lxxxiv.

Fondation Hardt: *Entretiens sur l'antiquité classique*, Tome 1, Geneva, 1952.

INDEX LOCORUM

(Reference is to page. Figures in brackets refer to the notes at the end of the chapters. For the aid of the Greekless reader, I have, where this seemed desirable, given more than one form of the title of a work, and added some abbreviations used in the text, where the relation of these to the title is not obvious. Clarity, rather than consistency, is the criterion here.)

GENERAL INDEX

(Reference is to page. Figures in brackets refer to the notes at the end of the chapters.)

Homer, and compulsion, 10 f.; and the gods, 11 ff.; and *moira*, 17 ff.; and *agathos*, 31 ff.; justification of use of *agathos*, &c., 34 ff.; and women's *arete*, 36 f.; and the quiet virtues, 37 f., 40 ff., 46 ff.; and the sanction of society, 48 f.; claim of *agathos* against society, 49 ff.; homicide, 52 ff.; and the chariot race of *Iliad* xxiii, 56; and the values of the fifth and fourth centuries, 238 f.

Homicide, accidental, in Homer, 52 ff.; in Draco's homicide law, 99; incurs 'pollution', 100 f.

Homicide, indemnity for, 94; forbidden by Athenian law, 94, 110 (15).

Homicide, justifiable, in Draco's homicide law, 99 f.; in *Tetralogies*, 103 ff.; in fourth century, 106 f.

Homicide, wilful, in Homer, 52 ff.; in Draco's homicide law, 99.

Homonoia, 211.

Hoplites, values of, 160, 197; loss of basis for claim to be *agathoi*, 215 (6); and possible reply, 235 f.

Hosios, quiet moral usages of, 132 ff.; and the barter-relationship, 134 ff.; and 'pollution', 135 f.; and suppliants 174; effects on moral responsibility, 137 f.; why useless to moralists, 138.

Household, in Homer, 35 f., 37, 41 f., 54 f.; in fifth century, 230 f., 241 (16), 241 (17), 262 f., 264, 314 (8).

Husbandman (in *Electra*), and *arete*, 176 f., 195 ff., 215 (1).

Immoralists, 188, 220, 232 ff., 270 ff., 279 (4); and 'ordinary men', 233 f., 239, 245 f., 248, 282; and new uses of *arete*, &c., 265 f., 269; cannot be refuted by Platonic logic, 278; and 'solution' of *Republic*, 283 ff., 291.

Incest, does not cause 'pollution', 110 (17).

Independence, as mark of *arete*, 34 ff., 53 f., 158, 223, 230 ff., 241 (13), 348, 354 (24); and philosophy, 354 (21).

Intellectual movement, 273, 292, 346.

Intelligence, co-operative behaviour as a mark of, 40.

Intentions, irrelevance of in Homer, 46 ff.; in fifth century, 165 ff.; in certain trials, 209 f.; in Plato, 304 ff.;

and 'pollution', 97 ff., 102 ff.; new sensitivity to, in Sophocles, 114 (28); in Aristotle, 319 ff., 332 ff.

Jealousy, divine, 63 f.

Jonahs, and 'pollution', 96 f.

Judgement, moral, dependent on general beliefs, 4.

Juries, Athenian, swore to observe strict justice, 202; but did not, 201 ff.; not swayed merely by pity, 204 f.; not immoral, 206.

Kakon, not the mark of the *kakos* to do, 42, 172; and *aischron*, 264 ff.; in Plato, 249 ff.; and Crito, 265 f.; and Polus, 266 ff.; and Callicles, 270 ff.; and see *Agathon*.

Kakos, 30 ff.; in Homer, 31 ff.; divine attitude to, 38, 172 f.; irrelevance of intentions, 47; traditional usage in fifth century, 156 ff.; and the fate of Socrates, 259; co-operative usages of, 114 (28), 172 f.; reasons for, 179; in *Apology*, 260 f.; in *Crito*, 265 f.; and see *Agathos*.

Kakotēs, does not mean 'wickedness' in Homer, 57 (9); spurious occurrence of, in Hesiod, 82 (20); in Empedocles, 143, 151 (16).

Kaloi kāgathoi, 227, 236, 253, 254, 337, 339, 351 (7), 353 (14).

Kalon, in Homer not true contrary of *aischron*, 43 f.; does not solve problem, 44 f.; disruptive of civic order, 109 (14); traditional use of, in fifth century, 156 ff., 169 (5), 182, 224; of visible objects, 163; co-operative uses of, 181 ff.; weakness of, 187 f., 250; in *Apology*, 261; in *Crito*, 265; and Polus, 266 ff.; in *Laws*, 312 (5); in Aristotle, 316 ff., 325, 341; in Isocrates, 337 f.

Kant, I., 2 f., 253.

Katharos, in Homer, 60 (23), 87; in homicide contexts, 89, 107, 112 (24); in 'Orphics', 141 ff.

Kidnappers, justifiable homicide to kill, 99 f.

Kings, Homeric, 34 f., 37 f., 235 f.

Kitto, H. D. F., 80 (3).

Knights errant, 169 (2).

Kosmios, 273 f.

158 f.; new values in, 182; but no new use of *arete*, 189 (1).

Pinutos, should be angry at seeing *aischea*, 41; unnecessary for *agathos* to be, in Homer, 37; but most *agathoi* must be, 58 (16); not completely unvalued, 61; and ideal hero, 61.

Plague, and non-moral gods, 62.

Plato, Chapters XIII and XIV *passim*; no label readily fits, 140; criticism of mystery-cults, 146 ff. and Simonides, 196; must justify Socrates, 259; problem of values unchanged in, 259; need not refute unheld positions, 239 f., 273; tricks Thrasymachus in *Republic*, 274 ff., 287 ff.; his ethics the logical result of Greek values, 311 f.

Pleasure, and Callicles, 271 f.; and Plato, 303, 329 (3); and Aristotle, 317, 320 f., 323, 329 (3), 329 (9).

Pleonexiā, 235 f., 255.

Polemarchus, 268 f., 279 (6).

Polītikē technē (*aretē*), 227 f., 236 f., 244 ff., 298, 300.

'Pollution', not incurred by homicide in Homer, 54; sense in which found in Homer, and Hesiod, 86 f., 109 (13), cp. 148 (2); in later writers, 87 ff.; range of examples, 88; not restricted to myth or legend, 89; dangerous, 89 f.; some indelible, 90, 110 (18); does not behave in accordance with categories of morals, 91; origins of belief, 91 ff.; an attempt to solve a psychological problem, 97; creates other problems, 97 ff.; in *Oedipus Tyrannus*, 98 f.; in Athenian homicide law, 99 ff.; sophistic solutions, 102 ff.; in *Tetralogies*, 102 ff.; in *Oedipus at Colonus*, 105 f.; in *Orestes*, 105 f.; in fourth century writers, 106 ff.; does not depend on 'cult of souls', 111 (21); partly an experimental issue, 112 (24); the reason for exile of homicide, 112 (25); but exile and 'pollution' not necessarily related, 87, 96; Euripides' attempt to change usage, 114 (29); effect on *hosios*, &c., 135 ff.; and 'Orphics', 142; and oaths, 216 (11).

Polus, 266 ff.

Polygnotus, 146.

Ponēros, see *Kakos*.

Power-politicians, 188, 193 (23), 220 ff., 234 f.

Practical syllogism, 327.

Proletariat, solidarity of the, 224.

Prosperity, divine reward for quiet virtue, 66, 138 ff., 165.

Protagoras, and *aischros*, 170 (10); and administrative skill, 227; and *dikaiosune*, 237 ff.; and *sophrosune*, 247 f.; and *agatha*, 251; and responsibility, 295, 312 (4).

Psūchē, in Homer, 67; in 'pollution' contexts, 92; in 'Orphic' belief, 141 f.; in Plato, 152 (25), 170 (10); in *Republic*, 285.

Psychological beliefs, effect of, 5, 27 (7); in *Republic*, 285, 312 (1); in Aristotle, 319 ff.

Public opinion, in Homer, 48 f., in Hesiod, 154; in fifth century, 154 ff.; and Socrates, 155; in Plato, 312 (5); in Aristotle, 317.

Punishment, divine, for sins of fathers, 68; in this life, 138 ff.; essential foundation of traditional morals, 164 f., 239; after death, impossible in Homeric Hades, 67, 81 (14); uncoordinated example of, 81 (14); in fifth century, 140 ff., 151 (24), 152 (25); extent of belief doubtful, 151 (23).

Punishment, Platonic theory of, 299 ff., 304 ff.

'Puppet of the gods', 302 f.

Rape, 29 (15).

'Razor's edge', 119, 128 (4).

Responsibility, relatively unimportant in Greek morals, 1; but a fruitful method of approach, 2, 7; affected by other beliefs, 3 ff.; in competitive and co-operative activities, 6 f.; generally unaffected by divine interference, 14, 27 (7), 116 ff.; exceptions to rule, 16; unaffected by divine psychological interference, 16; unaffected by *moira*, 22 ff., 119; exception, 23 f.; in *Septem*, 120 f.; in *Oresteia*, 121 ff., 129 (8), 129 (10); and oracles, 118 ff., 123 ff.; and the sophists, 102 ff., 124 ff.; and 'pollution', 97 ff., 102 ff.; and *hosios*, &c., 137 f.; effect of mystery-cults, 147 f.;